PEACE EDUCATION
IN AMERICA, 1828–1990
Sourcebook for
Education and Research

by
ALINE M. STOMFAY-STITZ

THE SCARECROW PRESS, INC.
METUCHEN, N.J., & LONDON
1993

Frontis: Fannie Fern Andrews (1867–1950), pioneer peace educator and international educator, founder of the American School Peace League before World War I. Her portrait hangs in the Grend Hall of the International Bureau of Education in the Palais de Wilson, Geneva. She is shown in the robe she wore when she received her Doctor of Philosophy degree from Radcliffe College in 1923. (Photograph reproduced by permission of the Schlesinger Library, Radcliffe College, Harvard University, Cambridge, Massachusetts)

British Library Cataloguing-in-Publication data available

Library of Congress Cataloging-in-Publication Data

Stomfay-Stitz, Aline M.
    Peace education in America, 1828–1990 : sourcebook for education and research / by Aline M. Stomfay-Stitz.
        p.   cm.
    Includes bibliographical references and indexes.
    ISBN 0-8108-2595-3 (acid-free paper)
    1. Peace—Study and teaching—United States—History.   2. Peace movements—United States—History.   I. Title.
JX1904.5.S86   1993
327.1'72'07073—dc20   93-993

To My Mother, Irene B. Wegrocki and To the memory of my
father, Adolph Wegrocki, M.D.,
and my father-in-law, John Stomfay-Stitz, Ph.D.

A SPECIAL DEBT OF GRATITUDE IS EXPRESSED TO ALL PEACE EDUCATORS—PAST, PRESENT, AND TO COME. THEIR LIVES ARE, AND HAVE BEEN, THE INSPIRATION FOR THIS BOOK.

> . . . Yet, today I call you to my
> riverside,
> If you will study war no more . . .

Excerpts from "On the Pulse of Morning" delivered by Maya Angelou, noted poet.

Inaugural of President William Jefferson Clinton
January 20, 1993

CONTENTS

FOREWORD

The first ideas and plans for this book grew out of the activities of children and young people, our own three sons, the youngsters I taught in elementary schools, and finally, the students I taught in several colleges, since 1983. Our eldest son, working on a Boy Scout badge, shared his fears about the future of our planet. As he worked on an environmental project, his enthusiasm became contagious and roused me from my apathy. My concern for the future of our own children soon grew to include ever widening circles of other children, to include all children and young people who deserve a safe future and a world at peace.

A few years later, several of my college students formed a campus group to earn money for the hungry. As we ladled out soup at our Students' Peace Network Alternative Lunch or fed the homeless at our community soup kitchen, I recalled other young people who joined groups such as the American School Peace League or signed pledges against America's entry into war during the 1930s.

As American forces went off to the Gulf War in January 1991, I read the letters of children printed in our newspapers and experienced a sense of déjà vu. Many expressed pride in our forces and strong sentiments of patriotism. Others showed concern for the young victims of bombings, the children of Iraq, Israel, and Kuwait. Of greatest frequency, was the deep anxiety for the safety of their loved ones. One child in a Louisiana school wrote:

> I have a dream that Saddum* Hussein will leave Kwuait*. And that there will be peace instead of war.

*Original misspellings retained

President Bush and Hussein will settle their difference
by talking and negotiating. By obtaining peace, the
lives of many young soldiers will be saved. They will
never have war again.

Another question was frequently asked: "Why are there
wars, anyway?" Months later, while going through the
papers of Fannie Fern Andrews, founder of the Peace
League, at Radcliffe College, I read similar echoes from the
past. Adelaide Errington, ten years old, on June 6, 1908
wrote a "Composition on War" that she submitted to the
Peace League essay contest:

> War is a very sad thing. It causes sorrow and death, and
> I think that instead of war, we should have arbitration
> . . . Soldiers get very little food and money, but they are
> very brave to risk their lives for their country. I do think
> arbitration is much fairer.

Almost nine decades separated Adelaide from our own
generation of children. During this time, we have made little
progress in helping them achieve a peaceful world or
understand why wars still persist. In each one of those
decades, I learned from my research, educators asked the
same question over and over again—"Why isn't there
education for peace?" I tried to find some of the answers,
during the course of research that stretched out almost ten
years, in many different parts of the country where I was
teaching. First, I learned that there were strong peace
movements at various times in the past century. Perhaps
education for peace had been a part of these social movements, as a "micromovement," as one researcher phrased it.
Perhaps education for peace had been just one more utopian
effort, a long line of experiments, similar to Fruitlands or
New Harmony, that had been tried or failed.

When I first heard of peace education, I could not believe
that it was virtually unknown to most in the educational
community. My initial inquiry uncovered the publications of
the National Council of Teachers of English (*Educating for*

Peace in 1940) and the Association for Supervision and Curriculum Development (*Education for Peace* in 1973). My search began in educational writings or curriculum materials but soon embraced other disciplines: political science, international relations, philosophy, psychology, sociology, anthropology, geography, women's studies, and the humanities. While the excellent historical research of others on the American peace movements provided the first evidence, I soon adopted a yardstick to measure these efforts. How did these events relate to their role in education? Were these efforts taken into the classroom? Were there textbooks or other curriculum materials?

In searching through educational writings and especially curriculum I began with primary sources that included: records, reports, speeches, lectures, yearbooks, and writings of educators and researchers in each historical period. Representative sources were from the American Association of School Administrators, American Historical Association, Association for Supervision and Curriculum Development, International Peace Research Association, National Education Association, American School Peace League and Citizenship League, and Institute of International Education.

For each decade under study, peace education and curriculum literature were examined, when available. Secondary sources were analyzed in books, journals, and periodicals concerning peace education from the following: Bibliographies on Peace Education or Research, *Dissertation Abstracts International, Education Index, Poole's Guide to Nineteenth Century Periodicals, Readers' Guide to Periodicals, Current Index to Journals in Education, International Index to Periodicals, National Union Catalog,* and the *Swarthmore College Peace Collection Catalogs.* In this way, I hoped that I would find evidence of peace education, all along, as an issue or part of the curriculum in America's past. The examples that confirmed my thesis were representative and many more needed to be discarded because of the manuscript's length. In sum, peace education in America had indeed existed, but powerful forces had subverted the mission of courageous men and women in their efforts. The chronicle was one rich in human understanding and actions and existed as a proud record from history.

This book grew out of a twofold mission. The first goal was to share the hidden strand of history that is peace education in America with those in education, research, and the general community, hopefully parents and others who may at some time also share my concerns. We can all be guilty of dreaming a foolish dream, that alternatives to violence should be considered to replace the procession of wars that stretched from millennium to millennium.

Hopefully, this study and the resources shared, will serve as a sourcebook or reference guide for those in the community as well as the academic area. The pages of the Resource Directory (Appendix) offer proof that groups and organizations are already working toward these praiseworthy goals. In addition, in the 1990s, technology is already being used to form international cooperative learning groups of young people, as in the Global Peace Awareness project, linked together by satellite or computer modems, sharing and communicating as pioneers in telecommunications for peace and cultural understanding.

The second goal was especially directed to the children of America. They deserve to know of the thoughts and deeds of the children of other generations and their dreams for a world of peace. Through the dusty pages of education yearbooks, minutes of organizations, buried among the statistics and reports, were the writings, poetry, and even prayers of children.

As I searched the files at the Library of Congress and National Archives for photographs, I saw the faces of children as they labored in America's mines and mills. It was only in 1920 that social justice was achieved with government restriction on child labor, and only after social reformers had worked for several decades to bring about change. Yet, in the 90s, child labor has once more become widespread in some American businesses and in off-shore industries.

The eager faces of children at the turn of the century can be seen in the book's photographs as they presented peace petitions. In recent years, I have seen children engaged in activities for peace, drawing their own posters or bearing balloons with peace slogans. These children, past and present, convinced me more than ever, that the seeds for a peaceful world needed to be planted in young hearts, nourished with love and concern, and encouraged to grow.

Perhaps, this study will also awaken parents to the need to teach skills to resolve conflicts within the family, as an antidote to the overpowering inroads that violence has made, especially in television and video games. Conflict resolution skills are still not considered a part of the American mainstream, nor even taught in most classrooms. Psychologists are concerned that young children have become desensitized to violence. The next step for parents would be to become active and critical participants in government at all levels, by questioning, questing for truthful disclosure of official policies, becoming advocates where their children's future lives are affected. Similar work has been carried on for decades by advocates in the various early childhood and educational organizations.

An emerging ecological ethic shown by American children and young people is a positive, growing force in America's schools. In some cases, children have become activists and successfully used the boycott of products to draw attention to environmental issues. At the same time, parents and teachers can make the connection here with concern for the environment and the need for a peaceful, stable world. As witnessed by the Gulf War, the critical causes of the conflict still exist, such as nuclear weaponry, unstable nations, and a damaged ecology. In past history, through human action, there have been positive changes to political and economic institutions. In the area of persistent warfare, we have overlooked that within the human dimension, the means exist to bring about change.

The lessons learned from the past and the importance of

being educated about global issues has remained on the periphery of American social and community life. There have been some signs of hope. For example, the John D. and Catherine T. MacArthur Foundation, in an example of unprecedented community education, offer videotapes on various peace and environmental issues to American public libraries, through an outright grant or at a reduced price. Librarians, in communities where I've inquired, report that parents are taking these free tapes home and viewing them with their families. Hopefully, they are also talking to them about the personal responsibilities needed in order to sustain a peaceful world.

Those in education entrusted with the nurturance of a new generation can especially identify with the thoughts of an unknown delegate to a peace conference in the early years of the century. Yella Hertzka wrote:

> Those who plant splendid growing trees
> Can seldom expect to rest beneath their shade.

Teachers or parents never really know the extent of their influence on young lives. Yet, each and every one of us who touches the lives of the young, can be a seed-sower or tree-planter for peace—by work, deed, or example. This new era of the nineties may be our second and last chance to make a difference. Perhaps, one day, all of the world's children can look back and thank us. As the first years of post-Cold War history unfold, growing numbers in education, the social sciences, and humanities, sincerely believe that changes in attitudes and beliefs, through education and action, can make a peaceful world possible for all of the world's children. This is their rightful heritage from the past.

Aline M. Stomfay-Stitz, Ed. D.
Christopher Newport University
Newport News, Virginia
July 4, 1992

ACKNOWLEDGMENTS

The research for a hidden strand of America's intellectual history—peace education for almost two hundred years—was possible only with the assistance of many—family, colleagues, and friends. First, my family continued to encourage and support me during my college teaching, as I guarded precious hours for writing, along with teaching, and the usual scholarly activities. My mother, Irene B. Wegrocki, provided a model of patience and perseverance during this period as well as throughout my life. Her example of helping others, based on deep spiritual roots, has been an inspiration; my husband, Emery Stomfay-Stitz, spent long hours re-reading and proof-reading—again, and again, supporting me and urging me to continue through to attain my goal; my children, Peter, John, and Robert, offered admiration and helpful comments; my sister, Elizabeth (Betsy) and her family, Walter and Ellen Kardy, offered invaluable assistance. They never failed to come to my rescue at critical times. Betsy Kardy was very helpful in gathering resources from the Washington, DC, area, while Ellen, a librarian in the shadow of Capitol Hill, brought books and print resources to my attention, that I would have missed. My loving Stomfay-Stitz family, Yolande, Alexa, and John and our beloved family friends, George and the late Frances Bradner, have all been a cherished part of our lives during this period. My treasured family cast an ever-present circle of love and pride that sustained me through periods of doubt and self-criticism.

Colleagues at Northern Illinois University, DeKalb, IL, showed a sustained interest in my project. To each one I express my thanks for their faith: Rodney Borstad, for ten years of encouragement; Raymond Fox, Dorothy Seaberg, and Pamela Farris; and at Nicholls State University, Thibodaux, Louisiana, Helon Harwell, Philip Bergeron, Jr. and James Barr. Sharon Goad, Director and Fran Middleton at the Ellender Library at Nicholls were valuable colleagues who facilitated the loan of many essential books and periodicals. In the past year, Virginia Purtle, Dean of the College of Social Science and Professional Studies and Lora Friedman, former Department Chair, and Linda Morgan, Chair, Department of Education, Christopher Newport University, arranged released time for completing the final manuscript revisions. Catherine Doyle, Access Services, and the entire staff at Smith Library were outstanding, promptly fulfilling all last-minute requests.

I owe a special debt of gratitude to librarians—the unsung, unrecognized champions of the academic world. They truly made this book possible. The staffs at several libraries helped me in earlier stages of the research: the Swarthmore College Peace Collection, University of Wisconsin Library and Wisconsin Historical Society Library in Madison, University of South Florida Library in Tampa, Florida Southern College Library in Lakeland, the Swen Parson Library and Archives at Northern Illinois University, Rockford College Library and Archives (James Michna and Joan Surrey), and the Swem Library at the College of William and Mary in Williamsburg.

My search for photographs was aided by Wendy E. Chmielewski, Curator at the Swarthmore College Peace Collection and Marie-Helene Gold at the Schlesinger Library at Radcliffe College, who were responsible for the searches that uncovered many historic photographs. Wendy Thomas helped me locate critical papers in the Fannie Fern Andrews Collection at the Schlesinger Library, as I worked my way through boxes and folders. The quest for photographs was aided by several in the Washington, DC area: Cheryl Nelson, Gelman Library, George Washington University; Dale Connelly, Still Picture Division, National Archives; and the helpful staff at the Prints and Photographs Division, Library of Congress.

My requests for materials and literature from a wide variety of peace-related groups and especially, religious organizations were answered promptly. To all involved in peace and justice ventures, my gratitude is boundless. The Resource Directory (Appendix) was aided by their responses. My colleagues in COPRED (Consortium for Peace Research Education and Development) provided me also with materials and access to their activities. The pages of our COPRED journal and newsletters were critical to my research. I am proud to be a member of this organization. I am indebted to James Gould for sharing his resources on women peacemakers. Ake Bjerstedt, School of Education, Malmo, Sweden, from the Peace Education Commission, International Peace Research Association, has been a valued colleague in providing me access to the work of others in peace education throughout the world.

Many Florida friends have shared my vision in the years that I worked there and inspired me to complete the project: Jean and Paul Puchstein, Kathy and Jim Riley, Ann Kremer, Gia Dennis, Jim and Val Willard, Sara Thrash, and Carol Larson. Fran Schmidt, co-founder of the Abrams Peace Education Foundation in Miami and one of the earliest authors of conflict resolution curriculum guides for the classroom, was a special inspiration. Fran generously shared her expertise and curriculum materials with me. The encouragement of Fran and Ralph Schmidt is gratefully acknowledged.

Finally, I wish to thank Neil Katz, Syracuse University and David List, who read an earlier draft of the manuscript. Their comments and suggestions were helpful and provided a new direction.

All of these family members, colleagues, and friends have my lasting gratitude for helping to make this book a reality.

1. STRANDS OF HIDDEN HISTORY

INTRODUCTION

Peace education in America is a strand of America's intellectual past that has been a hidden history, a tenuous chronicle held together by human efforts not always clearly documented. The noted historian, Daniel J. Boorstin, Librarian of Congress Emeritus, has warned of the problems encountered:

> The historian-creator refuses to be defeated by the biases of survival . . . torn between . . . efforts to create anew what . . . was really there and the urgently shifting demands of the living audience.[1]

Peace educators for more than two centuries dreamed of a world without war or violence. Peace education in the forthcoming chapters will be depicted with additional goals for political and economic justice as a touchstone for the perfection of our society. Peace education is dynamic and changing. In the early decades, a goal for peace education was the prevention of America's entry into World War I, a mission that certainly failed. Peace educators turned their attention to educating for a society where nonviolence would replace war and conflict.

Efforts of peace educators, however, were seriously frustrated by charges of Communist affiliation and lack of patriotism. Personal vilification, guilt by association, and character assassination were the experiences of peace educators in past decades.

At various times, peace education was also opposed by the

1

private sector, primarily business-management organizations that considered such reforms as child labor legislation, Social Security, and workplace safety regulations as a threat to profitability. Peace educators were also involved in social reform as a goal for economic justice for the working class. Peace education advocates were also a prime target for special interest groups, such as the munitions industry in the 1920s and the defense industry in the 1960s, 1970s, and 1980s.

Peace education was also linked to efforts in the 1920s for woman suffrage as a strategy to share political power. Even after receiving the right to vote, women still did not achieve substantive power to change the status quo in the political arena. Recent trends in peace education and feminist writings underscored that serious consideration be given to this issue in the future. The writings and voices of peace educators in the past largely went unheeded and ignored. Only in recent years has peace education received respect as a serious goal for study and inclusion in the curriculum.

HISTORICAL IMAGES

Images of the child as peacemaker have sifted through our group consciousness in recent years though evanescent as the fireflies of midsummer. Children have been involved in peace activism with their families, throughout the 1980s, stitching their own designs into the Peace Quilt or embroidering muslin squares to encircle the Pentagon with the Peace Ribbon. Soviet and American children were integrated into numerous cultural exchange groups. Together the young leaders of tomorrow scaled Caucasian mountain crests or explored the Mississippi aboard a riverboat. As the decade of the nineties unfolds, future plans for increased post-Soviet-American cross-cultural exchanges have been promoted as education for peace in action.

The historic first meeting in the Vatican of the head of the

Roman Catholic Church and the last leader of the Soviet Union provided a leitmotiv in the unfolding epic of transformation. The cordial conversations bore witness to the change of attitude and behavior that could inaugurate a future millennium of peace. The establishment of diplomatic ties between the Vatican and the former Soviet Union also carried the promise of long-awaited freedom of religion for millions of Soviet citizens after decades of adversity, imprisonment, and even death in the cause of faith. The revelation by Gorbachev that he was baptized a Christian as a child, provided an additional proof of the miraculous power of a person's freedom of conscience, the spiritual roots that have remain unconquered even under extreme persecution.

Images of children and youth involved in peace activism evoked for many teachers the memories of Maria Montessori, a pioneer peace educator.[2] Education was the cornerstone of peace, she believed: the child is endowed with messianic powers and capable of regenerating the human race and society. Educators and humanitarians for almost two hundred years shared a dream: through education, peace and justice would be possible in American society.

Past efforts of peace educators in the schools have remained obscure, known only to a few peace researchers or persistent historians. However, as far back as the early 1800s, peace educators planted the seeds of an awareness that a potential existed for a peaceful world.

Peace education has been described as multifaceted and cross-disciplinary with a myriad of dimensions, including peace and social justice, economic well-being, political participation, nonviolence, conflict resolution, and concern for the environment. Prominent educators and humanitarians—Jane Addams, Fannie Fern Andrews, John Dewey, Horace Mann, Lucia Ames Mead and her husband, Edwin Mead—along with teachers, writers, organizations, and young people, have joined together to present a historical rationale for peace education.

From 1828 until the present, there have been numerous

examples of teachers and children inspired to take action in
the cause of peace as an illustration that they can make a
difference in history. Historians have pointed out that
slavery, deeply entrenched in American society, was out-
lawed as an institution because of human action. The
message is clearly one of hope: through empowerment and
transformation, children and teachers can effect changes in
values and attitudes.

Following the Napoleonic Wars in 1815, fifty different
peace societies were founded. Their official journals, *The
American Advocate of Peace, The Calumet,* and *The Harbinger of Peace,* preached a message that children could be
educated as disciples of peace. Young people were invited to
join the societies. Separate groups for women were founded
in New England in the 1820s.

George C. Beckwith, a minister and peace agent, was
briefly secretary of the American Peace Society in addition
to editing the Society's journal, *The Advocate of Peace.* One
of his publications, *The Peace Manual,* urged teachers to
preach the evils of war and "train up everywhere a generation of peace-makers."[3] In the decades before the Civil War,
Beckwith along with many other factions of peace activists
became opponents of slavery.[4]

Horace Mann, founder of the American common schools,
wrote and lectured that education could be the instrument
for insuring that society would be freed from the ever-present
state of war. Moral and ethical values, especially found in
education, were the goals Mann deemed essential for the
perfection of human society. He was especially vocal in
warning of the dangers of militarism in American society.
The growing violence—the mobs, riots, burnings and lynchings—were dangers that called for preventive measures
through education, Mann wrote.

Thin threads of peace education revealed an early awareness in America that a more peaceful society was possible.
From the turn of the century, an early peace movement took
shape with several International Peace Congresses held.[5] In

relation to peace education in America, the events were especially auspicious. A Boston school teacher, Fannie Fern Andrews, began her campaign for peace education in America's schools at the Stockholm Peace Conference in 1910. She envisioned an umbrella organization, the American School Peace League, with a dream of involving a half million school teachers and their children, from kindergarten to the college campus.

Andrews believed that "through the schools and the educational public of America, the interests of international peace and justice would become a reality."[6] At the same time, she believed, the youth of America could be reared in the ideals of good citizenship and international understanding. These components of peace education unfolded, in an evolutionary manner, with emphasis on various aspects at different times, throughout the period under study.

From 1912 through 1916, the League became organized, promoted and published textbooks, held oratory and essay contests, and inaugurated May 18 as Peace Day in the schools.

The efforts of Fannie Fern Andrews also included plans for an International Bureau of Education that would serve as a central clearing house for research, an international library, and the publication of an education journal. Andrews' accomplishments were noteworthy in a society that had not yet given women the right to vote.

John Dewey, one of the most prominent educators in American educational history, included a blueprint for the abolition of war through his involvement in the Outlawry of War campaign. Dewey connected his vision of an ideal school in a democracy with the values of peace. A believer in pacifism, he wrote extensively on the growing militarism in America's schools and colleges.[7]

Threads of a global perspective emerged in the period between the wars, expressed as world citizenship in the 1920s and in the 1930s as international friendship and goodwill. Peace educators who advocated such policies were often in conflict with the expressed government policies of isolationism which ended only with Hitler's aggressive expansion of power and America's entrance into World War II.

Peace educators envisioned a new generation as members of a world community in a family of nations, especially after the establishment of the United Nations in 1945. The charter drawn up at the San Francisco conference proclaimed the "faith in fundamental human rights . . . and in the equal rights of men and women." These strands of a global perspective have been frequent themes during the past decades. The emphasis on human and equal rights without consideration for gender have given a current urgency to include such themes in peace education.

The realities of post-World War II produced treaty settlements that helped to establish permanent dictatorships in Eastern Europe. The growing rift between the United States and the former Soviet Union became permanently embedded into a Cold War policy that lasted until the incredible world events of 1989–1990 signalled the disintegration of the Iron Curtain and dismantling of the Berlin Wall. However, for the greater part of this period, a policy of cautious détente and the fear of nuclear war characterized the era.

With the development of the atomic bomb in 1945, several generations forfeited the security of a life lived out as a child, parent, and grandparent. Down to our present day, the nuclear arms race overshadowed humanity with the ominous threat of planetary annihilation. Hopes for lessened super-power tensions became a reality only in the shadow of the nineties.

The violence of student protests and citizen activism during the Vietnam War produced growing interest in nonviolence and conflict resolution as strategies for change. These became central threads in peace education.

Peace education in the Nuclear Age of the 1970s and 1980s added a new dimension, a world order perspective as demonstrated by the establishment of the World Law Fund, which later became the World Policy Institute and the World Order Models Project.[8]

During this period, leading educational organizations joined also in activities for peace education. The Association for Supervision and Curriculum Development (ASCD) issued a yearbook, *Education for Peace,* a landmark volume that viewed society as dependent on a global set of networks with peace education as a major force. The National Education Association (NEA) joined a growing list of educational organizations that advocated a new way of thinking as well as a call for leaders and an advocacy of peace education. Executive Director, Terry Herndon stated: "The methods of peace are superior to the methods of war, and in this nuclear age, may be basic to the survival of civilization."[9] Other leading educational organizations established Peace Education special interest groups.

PSYCHOLOGICAL FACTORS

Children living under Nuclear Age stress have been the subjects of major research since the 1960s.[10] The children studied revealed their awareness of nuclear warfare and weaponry. The research also revealed that the emotions expressed by the children were fear, horror, and grief after separation or loss of loved ones. In some cases, there was apathy or a sense of "psychic numbing."[11] The limited number of children involved in the sample was a variable that needed to be considered.

Research in the 1980s with college age young people centered on the significant area of attitude changes, described as "strategies of the general population toward nuclear war . . . in relation to health, welfare and survival." College students revealed they were more likely and willing to become involved in antinuclear advocacy and activism after receiving course information about the nuclear arms race.[12]

Research on the political socialization of children added a new dimension. After the Vietnam conflict a group of children studied revealed a general acceptance of the necessity of war. These attitudes reflected the opinions of adults within their sphere of influence, parents as well as teachers.[13] As final changes are being made in this manuscript, extensive research has been launched after the Gulf War of 1991, documenting the stress and fear that deeply affected large groups of children. In many American schools, teams of counselors and psychologists were called in to alleviate the emotional trauma. The journal, *Young Children,* of the National Association for the Education of Young Children, featured a poster, Teach Peace, on the cover of their March, 1991 issue and included an editorial and article on assisting teachers and caregivers with children's concerns about the War. Childhood experiences, from the 1960s through to the 1990s, as well as the emotions and attitudes generated, were revealed as a major source of the values and beliefs held by children.

As violence has become widespread in the post-Cold War world psychologists have included children of war, the victims of violent political upheavals and nationalist uprisings, as a focus for research. The work of James Garbarino, President of the Erikson Institute for Advanced Study in Child Development, has documented the impact of international violence on young victims in his book, *No Place To Be a Child: Growing Up in a War Zone,* based on travels to Cambodia, Mozambique, Nicaragua, and the Middle East.[14] Special sections for the enhancement of research and activism for peace were started in the 1990s by The American Association of Sociology and the American Psychological Association (Division of Peace Psychology) (to be discussed in a later chapter) with a publication, *Journal of Peace Psychology* planned.[15] Other organizations in psychology had similar goals, such as the National Psychologists for Social Responsibility, International Society for Research on Aggression, Society for the Study of Social Issues (APA), and the International Association of Applied Psychology, with an emphasis on conflict resolution and the psychology of peacemaking.

Psychologists and sociologists have stressed that exposure to violence and acquiescence to war can serve as a desensitization process which could prepare children to accept experiences based on aggressive actions against others. Moreover, the classic research of Albert Bandura produced convincing evidence that aggression and violence viewed by children produced an overwhelming urge to repeat similar acts against others.[16]

Acceptance of violence as a way of life and as a major method of solving conflicts became more apparent with a nationwide increase in murder, accidental gun accidents, and gun assaults (many drug-related) involving children and young people especially in the eighties and nineties. Increased rates of child abuse, neglect, and victimization raised serious questions about the cycle of violence institutionalized in American society.[17]

PEACE EDUCATION AS A SIGNIFICANT CURRICULUM STRAND

Events in the 1980s have confirmed that America as a nation-state has been affected by events in far corners of the globe. The clouds of radiation from Chernobyl, the machinations of OPEC oil cartels, increasing trade deficits, the deindustrialization of leading American industries with resulting unemployment, the off-shore operations of multinational corporations—all offer credibility to the fact that global events cause repercussions in American society. The interdependence of our world community and the role of America in the international sphere demand a new way of thinking, especially a multicultural, global perspective that teaches respect for the differences of others.

Demographers have predicted for the remainder of the

century substantial shifts in the racial and ethnic composition of our future population. The heavy influx of Hispanic and Asian groups, along with illegal immigration, points to a significant effect on American communities.[18] One prediction is for a combined group of minorities to replace the current white majority. A new phase of an ever-changing society is predicted—a multicultural one to replace the traditional Anglo-American majority that has been predominant in the past.

One of the major trends in peace education since the 1980s is an increasing attention to the development of conflict resolution or peacemaking skills, one of the original components of peace education. The pioneer groundwork of Theodore Lentz, Gene Sharp, Barbara Stanford, and Susan Carpenter centered on the peaceful, creative resolution of conflicts. New ground has been broken in relating this aspect of intergroup and interpersonal conflict to the realities of a diverse American populace.[19]

Predictions of change mandate a greater need to teach our children and young people, explicitly and overtly, an understanding, tolerance, and acceptance of the differences of others. Skills for better communication and to resolve conflicts appear to be a necessity and no longer considered an option in the curriculum.

As this century enters its waning years, numerous educational materials have been produced to further an understanding of Nuclear War Education or some variant of Peace Education or Global Education, in American schools. Some efforts met with controversy and difficulty. For example, administrators and educators faced charges of bias and propaganda in their use of the social studies materials that largely comprised the Nuclear War curriculum. Public school systems, such as Dade County (Florida); Milwaukee; Brookline (Massachusetts); Portland (Oregon) and San Francisco have led the way with inclusion of nuclear arms, conflict resolution, and peace-related issues in their curriculums.

Educators of the past century kept alive the idea that education for peace was possible for our children. Those colleagues from the past century taught many of the same skills in the classroom that are presently being taught. They gave instruction in Palmer penmanship, parsed sentences and wore out Noah Webster's spellers while preparing for spelling bees. At different times in the past though, the value of peace as a needed component for the education of humanity was taught through a wide variety of community service projects or through the teaching of history and literature. Various journals, textbooks, and curriculum guides developed since 1828 prove that some classroom teachers of America cherished the hope that peace was a value to be taught.

Thus, a historical and psychological rationale for peace education exists, having been nurtured throughout the nineteenth and twentieth centuries by peace educators and organizations who shared the vision of a world without war for American children. Their ideas were implemented by a pragmatic blueprint for education. They recognized the power of the written and spoken word. Their writings were a legacy of faith in the human spirit and a new hope for humanity.

These efforts of peace educators in the national sphere deserve a place in the chronicle of America's intellectual history. Educators of previous generations were involved in peace and justice education and activism, not for a few decades, but for almost two centuries. Their efforts and contributions are worthy of our attention and our study.

Notes

1. Daniel J. Boorstin, *Hidden History: Exploring Our Secret Past* (New York: Harper & Row, 1987), 23.
2. Maria Montessori, *Education for Peace* (Chicago: Henry Regnery, 1972).

3. George C. Beckwith, *Peace Manual or War and Its Remedies* (Boston: American Peace Society, 1847), 247.

4. Beckwith, 247.

5. John Whiteclay Chambers II, ed. *The Eagle and the Dove: The American Peace Movement and United States Foreign Policy, 1900–1922* (New York: Garland Publishing, Inc., 1976).

6. The American School Peace League, *Yearbook, 1913–1914* (Boston: The American School Peace League, 1913), 90.

7. Charles F. Howlett, *Troubled Philosopher: John Dewey and the Struggle for World Peace* (Port Washington, NY: Kennikat Press, 1977).

8. Richard A. Falk, *Explorations at the Edge of Time: The Prospects for World Order* (Philadelphia: Temple University Press, 1992).

9. Terry Herndon, "A Teacher Speaks of Peace," *Phi Delta Kappan* 64 (April 1983): 530.

10. John E. Mack, "Psychosocial Effect of the Nuclear Arms Race," *Bulletin of the Atomic Scientists* 37 (1981): 18–23; and John Mack and Sybille Escalona, "Children and the Threat of Nuclear War" in *Behavioral Science and Human Survival,* edited by M. Schwebel (Palo Alto: Science and Behavior Books, 1965).

11. Robert J. Lifton, "Beyond Psychic Numbing: A Call to Awareness," *American Journal of Orthopsychiatry* 52(1982): 619–629.

12. Karen J. Winkler, "Sociologists, Psychologists Urge Study of Questions Concerning Nuclear War," *Chronicle of Higher Education* 31 (11 September 1985): 7, 12.

13. Howard Tolley, Jr. *Children and War: Political Socialization to International Conflict* (New York: Teachers College Press, 1973). See also Robert Coles, *The Political Life of Children* (Boston: Atlantic Monthly Press, 1986) and *The Moral Life of Children* (Boston: Atlantic Monthly Press, 1986).

14. Lana Hostetler, "From Our President. Scuds, Sorties, and Yellow Ribbons: The Costs of War for Children." *Young Children* 46(3) (March 1991):2; and Fred Rogers and Hedda B. Sharapan, "Helping Parents, Teachers, and Caregivers Deal with Children's Concern about War." *Young Children* 46(3) (March 1991): 12–13. See also James Garbarino, Kathleen Kostelny, and Nancy Dubrow. *No Place To Be a*

Child: Growing Up in a War Zone (New York: Lexington Books, 1991).

15. *Division 48 Newsletter:* The Division of Peace Psychology 1 (2) (April 1991): 5.

16. Albert Bandura and R. H. Walters, *Social Learning and Personality Development* (New York: Holt, Rinehart and Winston, 1963).

17. Cathy Widom, "The Cycle of Violence," *Science* 244 (April 1989): 160–165.

18. Fox Butterfield, "Why Asians Are Going to the Head of the Class." *New York Times Education Life Supplement,* 3 August 1986, XII:18.

19. Susan L. Carpenter, *A Repertoire of Peacemaking Skills.* Fairfax, VA: Consortium for Peace Research Education Development, George Mason University, 1974; Theodore F Lentz, *Towards a Science of Peace: Turning Point in Human Destiny* (New York: Bookman Associates, Inc., 1955); Gene Sharp, *The Politics of Nonviolent Action* (Boston: Porter Sargent, 1973); and Barbara Stanford, *Peacemaking: A Guide To Conflict Resolution for Individuals, Groups and Nations* (New York: Bantam Books, 1976).

2.   ORIGINS OF PEACE EDUCATION, 1828–1900

SEEDS OF PEACE EDUCATION

During this era stirrings for peace and recognition of the role of education were part of a broader agenda for reform, primarily in New England, with Boston and Concord as the intellectual hub. Writers in the early peace society journals recognized that education could be a vehicle for change and reform. They realized, however, that fervent aspirations were insufficient and that practical actions would have to play a prominent role in reforming society. Leading figures in contemporary affairs aroused the social conscience of citizens. Women's rights, prison reform, temperance, and the antislavery movement had their genesis in the early decades of the 1800s. In subsequent years, women's groups in particular, learned valuable lessons from these early years of activism. The first writings on peace education reflected some of the philosophical foundations that developed during the same period.

Ralph Waldo Emerson and Henry Thoreau, among others, launched a "great adventure in liberalism" that placed an emphasis on the mind rather than on the world of commerce.[1] In the early nineteenth century, community leaders, most often the minister and lawyer, became advocates for issues that could improve society. Men and women joined in experiments with utopian colonies, such as Brook Farm and Fruitlands in the 1840s.

Threads of idealism and pragmatism developed during this period and surfaced in peace education throughout the nineteenth century. Idealism, in the sense of a striving for human perfection, and pragmatism, which emphasized practical affairs and consequences rather than theories and postulations, were woven into the lives of both Emerson and Thoreau. Both writers bequeathed a legacy of intellectual arguments in the form of essays between 1840 and 1860. Transcendentalism, as conceived by Emerson, acted as a stimulus for the individual mind.

Emerson believed that intuition, an instinctive knowledge, was more reliable than society's standards or government's laws. His essay, "Self-Reliance," stressed that the individual conscience was essential to perfect human society. Yet Emerson was also a practical Yankee who recognized that other forces—pragmatic considerations as well as intuition—motivated human action.[2]

Thoreau expanded on the theme of the primacy of the individual conscience with one of the earliest examples of civil disobedience. To protest the Mexican War, which he considered unjust, he refused to pay a poll tax. As a result, he spent one night in the Concord village jail.

Emerson, a Unitarian minister, taught for a short while before launching a career on the lecture circuit to supplement his writing. Thoreau was also a teacher and with his brother John founded a school in Concord where corporal punishment was banned and nature study dominated the curriculum. After his brother's death, however, Thoreau's venture as an educator ended. Forced to earn a living, he then became a tradesman and crafted wooden pencils. His writings such as *My House by Walden Pond,* were early evidence of a simple lifestyle imbued with stewardship for the natural world.

These literary figures, in turn, influenced Margaret Fuller, a woman whose writings added a dynamic voice for women's rights in the 1840s and 1850s. Fuller edited *The Dial,* a short-lived, Concord-based literary magazine. In its pages she argued for the legal protection of women and recognition of their "magnetic or electric influence" as a moral force in society. Fuller was one of the earliest writers to recognize the inherent nature of women to oppose war.[3]

Fuller also believed that intuition was a spiritual force that endowed women with special talents for nursing and teaching. However, pragmatism also entered her thinking. This was reflected in her proposal that teachers be examined before being allowed to teach in the newly-formed common schools. Reasoning that the common schools needed 60,000 teachers, her plan called for a centrally located normal school with two outstanding teachers to qualify women before entering the classroom.[4]

Idealism and pragmatism thus emerged as twin influences on the spiritual side of human nature. The importance of forming an individual conscience on moral issues, a heritage from the Concord philosophers, created a foundation for the early years of peace education. Moreover, at this time the peace societies of Massachusetts and the utopian visionaries, along with Horace Mann's reports on education and the antislavery writings of William Lloyd Garrison's *The Liberator*, shared center stage. All of these developments and tendencies enveloped mid-nineteenth century New England with an aura of humanistic thought and action, and helped to sow the seeds of peace education there and elsewhere.

PEACE SOCIETY JOURNALS

The earliest writings on peace education in America date to the early decades of the nineteenth century. The early peace societies were the source of these writings. The indigenous American organizations assumed a distinctive role and heralded the possibility of universal peace. The American Peace Society was founded in Boston in 1828, and by 1850 fifty distinct American peace societies were in existence.[5]

In the writings of the official peace society journals, *The American Advocate of Peace, The Harbinger of Peace, The Advocate,* and *The Calumet,* two interrelated themes emerged. First, was the importance of Christianity and the teaching of the Gospel as a way to form a public conscience in favor of peace. Second, was the role assigned to education in accomplishing these goals. The perfection of both the individual and society were dictums for education.

Education and the printed word were considered of prime importance from the formative days of the peace societies. The importance of pamphlets, tracts, and essays disseminated in "favour of Peace" were reported to have produced a "great and visible change in the public mind."[6]

Using a method that was popular in the pre-Revolution days, one of the early peace pioneers, Elihu Burritt, adopted the broadside format to spread the cause of peace. He distributed simple sheets of paper, known as "Olive Leaves for the Press," to two hundred newspapers. In this way he reached perhaps two million Americans. Burritt also published the first newspaper in America that disseminated information devoted exclusively to the principles of peace and freedom.[7]

A largely self-educated individual, Burritt gained recognition as a peace leader in the 1840s. He wielded influence as the editor of *The Advocate of Peace,* the official journal of the American Peace Society. From 1844–1851 he edited *The Christian Citizen.* It featured a special children's section through which Burritt hoped to ". . . mold the minds of youth to oppose war." He used graphic illustrations to further his ideas. For example, the children's section used mathematics problems which required children to use "war casualties and blood loss to find the answers."[8]

SPREADING PEACE

The principles of peace spread also by a designated advocate—the peace agent—who was especially chosen for the role. The primary responsibility of this office centered around "correcting public opinion on the subject of war."[9]

The peace agent undertook direct action: the actual selling of the issue of peace. Usually he was a minister who travelled throughout an assigned territory. On his travels, he would sell inexpensive pamphlets, tracts, or leaflets on peace issues, especially ones stressing the horror and destruction of war.

Aggressive recruitment and conversion to the principles of peace characterized the methods of the peace agents. Young people in schools and theological seminaries, among others, were prime targets of their recruitment drives. For instance, Reverend Asa Mead of Brunswick, Maine, travelled throughout New Jersey and western New York for three months on a recruiting campaign. He formed six new peace societies, including one at the Bangor Theological Seminary.[10] Reverend George C. Beckwith, minister and peace agent, wrote to the Secretary of the American Peace Society relating details of possibly the first student peace society in America at Middlebury College (Vermont) in 1836. He reported that approximately 150 students had formed the Peace Society of Middlebury College, an auxiliary to the American Peace Society ". . . to illustrate the inconsistency of war with Christianity."[11]

Elsewhere in New England similar recruitment efforts occurred. In 1835, for example, The Bowdoin Street Young Men's Peace Society was established in Boston in the hope that "this noble example will be followed by young men of many of our churches . . . with the distribution of books . . . and exposés of the evils and sins of war."[12]

Thus, Christian education came to the forefront as the main process for achieving a peaceful society. The twin roles of school and church were considered of paramount importance, with the teacher and clergy united in a common cause. The power of the Gospel message rang out according to the peace agent as one of the "revealed objects of the messiah's mission" and only by this influence would the "predicted peace of the world be effected."[13]

Significantly, too, the periodicals of the early peace movement, especially *The Calumet,* a journal of the American Peace Society, elaborated on the correlation between education and justification of peace as necessary for democracy.[14]

Illustration and enforcement of the role of education became the duties of the minister. The hope was that this role for education as a way to promote peace would be extended to the "seminaries of learning from the Infant school up to the University."[15] Beckwith, Secretary of the American Peace Society (1837–1870), outlined the important roles of the minister and the teacher:

> The moral suasion of the gospel, the power of Christian truth and love must be applied . . . Still more, if possible do we expect from teachers. Their influence is universal: they are scattering everywhere the seeds of character . . . every common and Sabbath school . . . ought to be a nursery of peace.[16]

The editor of *The Advocate of Peace* and author of three publications, Beckwith expounded on peace issues in the 1840s.[17]

The early peace pioneers like Beckwith believed that when children were educated in the Christian discipline as disciples of peace and educational institutions were united in the cause, a peaceful society could exist.

Through their journal articles from 1828 to the 1840s the peace societies continued to stress that education for peace would bring about the beneficial progress of society. A representative opinion, written in a peace society journal, expressed the idea that improvements had already been made in "the science of education . . . to extend the benefits of Christian instruction to every land, to every class of people."[18] This reference was perhaps a recognition of the efforts of Massachusetts to achieve a state-supported common-school system for the younger generation.

ROLE OF WOMAN AS MOTHER AND TEACHER

An expanded role for females as teachers—both within the family and in the schools—was stressed by the peace journals and other educators in the 1830s and 1840s. Women were extolled as a source of intellectual power and patriotism and deemed capable of "promoting a higher tone of moral sentiment" throughout the world:

> The mother who educates her son for a useful life . . . or she who sows the seeds of knowledge in some rustic mind performs a deed of patriotism.[19]

The American Peace Society considered mothers and teachers as the "primary molders of character":

> Are you a mother? You can train your children to a love of peace and a deep habitual abhorrence of war. Are you a teacher in a Sabbath or any other school? You can impress your views of peace upon the minds of your pupils and insure your spirit into their hearts.[20]

Several examples of the separate efforts of women's peace societies illustrated their zeal for the cause. A pamphlet titled, "On the Duty of Females to Promote the Cause of Peace" stated that the influence of the "female sex on the destinies of the world is fully as great as that of the male sex, though it is not so obvious."[21]

Two separate female peace societies existed at this time, perhaps others. The Philadelphia Peace Society stated in their constitution preamble that "by associating their energies, women may do much to change public opinion by forming themselves into a society." Women were also exhorted to exert pressure at home "with their father, husband, brothers and sons."[22] The members of the Essex County Olive Branch, banded together because women in that community showed a "distaste for military parade and glory." They wished to use their influence to further the cause of peace. A reservation expressed by the women of the

Essex County Olive Branch stated that "We have limited moral and pecuniary means . . . and expected but little of (our) efforts."[23]

Reports of these separate female societies often revealed an additional area of focus. Equal rights for women was a subject that appeared in writings in the early 1800s and throughout the nineteenth century. As a student in 1881, Jane Addams wrote impassioned essays as editor of the Rockford Seminary student magazine on the inequalities of legal protection. Toward the end of the century leading European feminists, such as the Countess of Aberdeen and Baroness Bertha von Süttner, reported on the progress American women had made since the formation of the National Council of Women in 1881. The first president of the Council was also the president of the Women's Christian Temperance Union.[24] The nineteenth century, therefore was characterized by a missionary zeal that united women in their efforts for social and political reform.

The early stirrings of the separate peace societies for women can be considered the genesis of a strand of the women's rights movement that came into prominence in the next century. The dreams of women for an equal voice in American society began in New England and other centers of culture along the eastern coast. Women who joined groups for peace sponsored by the Society of Friends may have influenced women's peace groups throughout the century. Undoubtedly yearnings for peace and the hope of improving society were carried along by women as they moved westward with their families toward the new frontier.

In popular literature and journals the duty of a woman as the child's first teacher and the shaper of ethical character appeared often as a theme. Through education and the development of the moral character in the individual, the peace societies believed that a perfection of society would result.

The sins of society were looked upon as merely a flaw that could be corrected. A salvation call for education as a panacea needed to transform the character of the child echoed from the writings of peace societies. Education could be the savior of society and capable of transforming it so that humanity might live together in harmony. The role of woman—first mother, first teacher—imprinted an indelible stamp in the annals of the peace societies.

HORACE MANN

A hope that was frequently articulated was that education would be the instrument for insuring that society would be free of war. This common belief forged a link with one of the founders of America's common school system, Horace Mann.

Mann's early education was in Calvinism with Puritan roots embedded in a theocratic, God-centered society. While a young man, however, Mann parted paths with Calvinism and became a Unitarian, due in part to his belief that the early Puritan education of the child within the family was often barbaric. He believed, instead, that education by the state (and specifically, the state of Massachusetts) based on natural law and ethics would be a better course of action. This would also be an improvement over the early education in the family as was practiced in the Massachusetts Bay Colony of previous generations.

Mann formulated a blueprint for state-supported education that had as its major goal a Christian education based on natural laws as essential moral education for the child. This goal was also shared by early peace educators who wrote in the peace society journals.

The emphasis on character formation for citizenship shaped education in the nineteenth century. The common school was viewed as the agency that could improve the character of the individual and at the same time remedy the ills of society. Like his contemporaries the peace journal writers, Mann trusted that education could bring about a new, peaceful society.

A deeply religious man, Mann also showed vision and insight into human nature. His lectures indicate that he believed war and violence were ills of society that could be changed by a moral conscience and deliberate action. Many of his sentiments concerning conflict in society were similar in tone to the admonitions of the peace society.

> And what was the first school established by Congress?
> . . . It was the Military Academy at West Point. It is the Normal School of War . . . The object of the common Normal School is to teach teachers how to teach: so the object of the Academy is to teach killers how to kill.[25]

Through education, Mann asserted, a new generation could be "educated to that strength of intellect which shall dispel the insane illusions of martial glory."[26] Only with the elimination of war from human society would the sentiments of universal brotherhood be possible.[27]

As Secretary of Education for the state of Massachusetts, Mann used his lectures and annual reports to promote the common school system. He viewed education as a preventive measure against the growing violence of American society in his day. He believed that "the mobs, the riots, the burnings, the lynchings" in his society were because of "vicious or defective education" of children.[28] Without education, law and order in society and the protection of private property, would be at the mercy of violent individuals who could take the law into their own hands. But with a free, universal education and the moral uplifting of conscience, he thought violence would be quelled. He wrote: "We want godlike men who can tame the madness of the times . . . and say 'Peace, be still!' "[29]

Mann recognized the deep roots of violence in American society as flaws that called for deliberate improvement. His remedy was education as the primary agent of change that could create a new society freed from domestic violence and the horrors of war:

> What can save us, and our children after us, from eternal, implacable, universal war, but . . . a generation of men (and women) who were educated from childhood to seek for truth and to revere justice.[30]

Mann also raised his voice to oppose the vast sums of money spent on war and military procurement while the common schools had to beg for leftover crumbs. He reported that Massachusetts had paid a militia bounty of $30,000 to soldiers for three or four training sessions, while such a sum could have "sustained the sinking hearts of those females who keep school for a dollar a week or for nine pence a day." Such monetary appropriations for the "moral renovation of society through a universal education of the people" deserved better treatment, he believed.[31] This early recognition of the welfare of the individual in relation to the needs of government echoed throughout American history, up to the present day. Questions about the role of military expenditures versus human needs presented a perpetual dilemma for American society.

Mann raised a vigorous voice against war and violence as national policy, showing that education was considered less important than military matters. The founder of the common school movement dreamed, as did the architects of the peace societies, that education was the major instrument by which society could be changed and perfected. Education could be the vehicle for shaping a more perfect, peaceable nation, one worthy of the hopes and dreams of the founding fathers.

EARLY AWARENESS OF PEACE EDUCATION

By the late nineteenth century moral education for citizenship was the primary purpose of education and judged as equally important as academic education by the early authors of peace education. This was reflected in the educational and social science literature as well as in textbooks written in this era.

The common school system in these decades experienced an overwhelming tide of immigration from Europe while at the same time some regions lost population due to the movement westward. These were demographic pressures presenting unique problems.

The curriculum field as an independent area of study was still in an embryonic stage. References were made to the "course of study" or to "the programme" and each appears to have been used interchangeably with the term curriculum.

With the founding of the Herbart Society in 1895 the influence of both Johann Friedrich Herbart and Charles Darwin cast the mold for curriculum at the turn of the century. Emphasis was on the ethical function of studies in line with Herbart's belief that the public school was an adequate agency for the development of moral character.[32]

Herbart viewed moral development as the primary aim of education with perfection of the individual character as the major goal. The concept of "apperception" was central to his theory. Herbart considered thinking as the perception of new ideas with assistance from past experiences. He conceived the term "apperceptive mass" to explain his theory that a group of ideas helped the student to assimilate new information from the senses of a previous experience. This cluster of ideas would help the learner when receiving new sensory data.[33] For example, ideas should be correlated with history and literature, and presented as mutually interdependent. These, in turn, could be used as techniques for shaping the social and moral attitudes of children.

The Herbart Society published an annual *Yearbook* to further expand the philosophy of its principal advocate. Education was conceived as a revelation of the moral order of the world with a system of ethics growing out of the "very heart of the studies themselves" for the purpose of uplifting humanity. Literature, history, and geography were regarded as the most plausible subjects to study to fulfill this ethical duty of education. The prime object would be to train the child as a citizen by revealing "his place and office in the moral order of the world."[34]

Charles DeGarmo, Lida and Charles A. McMurry, and C. C. Van Liew contributed to the *First Yearbook* in 1895. Several years later in 1898, John Dewey and Nicholas Murray Butler, President of Columbia University for many years, joined the original contributors on the Executive Committee. While Dewey was not a chapter contributor to the *Fourth Yearbook* there were liberal sprinklings of his "Ethical Principles" in several chapters. Dewey's theories were expressed as concern for the social functions in education. He described subject matter as a "circle of thought . . . the side that fits the child to live as one of many and not as one for itself . . . a true place in the social order."[35]

Dewey reasoned that the existing social structure was complex and impossible for the child to perceive but various "phases of historical development may be selected" which would give the child the "essential constituents, as through a telescope."[36] To teach the concept of religious toleration, for example, the teacher would move from the general idea in society as a whole to the specific focus on Roger Williams (Rhode Island colony) and his times, with the enlarged notion applied to the present social life."[37]

The *Fourth Yearbook* also stressed that the subject-matter focus should be on the ethical value of history teaching which affords "insight into what makes up the structure" of society.[38] Emphasis on the ethical value of history was placed by Charles A. McMurry, a protégé of Herbart. McMurry published a number of pedagogical treatises for use by teachers while he taught at the Northern Illinois Normal School in DeKalb (later Northern Illinois University) from 1899 to 1915.[39]

Through the influence of McMurry the emphasis on the ethical value of history teaching persisted for several decades after the turn of the century. McMurry's major textbook contribution was published originally while he was still at the University of Chicago. The book went through several printings. The first edition stressed using history and literature to "strengthen moral character." Reference was made to the treatment of war in history. But McMurry stated that an emphasis on "the bloody and destructive work of war" should not be given prominence in history books.[40]

By the 1911 edition, however, the moral character of history teaching was replaced with the "aim of history" being to "socialize a child" by helping him or her to understand better the "interests of the social classes which they represent." This change could be considered as a mirror of the goals set forth in the *Fourth Yearbook* and a reflection of Dewey's influence.[41]

TEXTBOOKS REVEAL THIN THREADS OF PEACE EDUCATION

McMurry also wrote textbooks, primarily a collection of pioneer stories for history classes.[42] He believed that a study of pioneer life provided a "series of object lessons in character and morals" for the purpose of exerting a direct moral influence on the formation of character. Included in his collection was a story about Abraham Lincoln as a peacemaker, relating an incident in his life that occurred while he was a clerk in a New Salem country store. Other stories offered concrete evidence of humans faced with conflict in daily experiences which called for an ethical decision "furnishing concrete materials upon which moral judgments are developed."[43]

Henry B. Carrington produced a textbook that stressed the social values and citizenship training of the *First* and *Fourth Yearbooks* written in the spirit of McMurry's ideals. The moral function of history from the *First Yearbook* was joined with the social function theory of the *Fourth Yearbook*.[44]

Charles Sumner, for example, wrote an essay that was popular with peace societies and educators, "The True Grandeur of Nations." This became a classic and was included frequently in the bibliographies of peace educators in subsequent decades:

> Let the grandeur of man be discerned, not in bloody victories . . . but in the blessings which he has secured . . . in the triumph of justice . . . in the establishment of perpetual peace.[45]

The ideal citizen was the person who believed that "all men were brothers," wrote John Haberton.[46] Former President Benjamin Harrison, in a graduation address, agreed that "a just and perfect society will not be established . . . throughout the world" until the Golden Rule becomes the law of life.[47]

With the skillful inclusion of selections from history and literature, Carrington documented the nineteenth century goals of education and the formation of moral character. The process of education was considered idealistic and pragmatic, with both domestic and international peace as the praiseworthy result.

A history textbook was written by Mary Murray and presented the student with facts on American wars "communicated in such a manner as to strengthen a love of peace."[48] Written during a period when slavery was providing the wedge between regional factions and within the peace societies, Murray took a stand firmly in opposition to the evils of slavery "religiously, morally and politically."[49]

Murray's textbook reflected her society's contemporary attitudes. As the slavery issue grew into a major divisive force in American society, peace journals reflected a humanistic attitude that condemned slavery and evoked sympathy for the victims. A common theme was echoed repeatedly: "All slavery originates in and is perpetuated by violence."[50]

Since the early 1800s the journals of the peace societies revealed the soul-searching that the slavery issue evoked.

The growing awareness of the evils of slavery, particularly its biblical justification as an institution, aroused deep emotions in growing segments of society. Activism in the abolitionist movement and the Underground Railroad tested the consciences of those in the peace societies.[51] The primacy of the individual conscience, as delineated by Thoreau, may have played a role in many decisions and perspectives regarding the Civil War.

Murray's history text was written five years before the Civil War broke out. Her insight revealed an awareness that moral character and courage were essential: "The nation that is now blessed with peace . . . carries within her bosom a branch which may yet kindle a flame."[52]

John Fiske wrote a history textbook that added a new facet to an awareness for peace education. Fiske believed that history needed "to bring out with fresh emphasis the pacific implication of federalism." Those involved in the War were not prosecuted.[53] Reconciliation and humane feelings toward those involved in the war motivated many in the postwar years. He also stressed the economic implications of war and specifically the effects of protective tariffs and industrial competition. The remedy to industrial or military strife, he believed, was a council or parliament with some principles of international law as a definite sanction. He concluded his text with the "picture of a world viewed with cheerful homesteads, blessed with a sabbath of perpetual peace."[54]

CONTEMPORARY LITERATURE: LEGACY OF DARWIN

As the century drew to a close and the year of 1900 approached, a historic moment for peace occurred in Europe at The Hague in Holland. An international peace conference was called by the Tsar of Russia with Germany, England, France, Japan, and the United States among the nations represented. There was a buoyant hope that the standing armies of Europe would be reduced and the growing, bellicose rumbles would be stilled.

The principal purpose of the meeting was to try a new method, arbitration, to effect a reduction of armaments and limitation of military expenditures. In fact, for the first time in history, an agreement was reached to use arbitration to settle international disputes. A second agreement was reached in 1907, but by that time many of the signatories were already inching toward war. Indeed, the seeds for World War I had already been planted when the nineteenth century drew to a close.

For a period of five years (1895–1899) the Hague Peace Conference inspired a prodigious outpouring of literature on peace, the causes and effects of war, and possible solutions, including education for peace. In one bibliography approximately 186 books, journals, pamphlets, and reports were listed by the author to support the primary thesis.[55] Included in the bibliography were most of the classics of the early peace movement—books by Beckwith and early peace society leaders, such as William Ladd, Noah Worcester, Josiah Quincy, William Ellery Channing, and Samuel May; the journals of the peace societies; and the proceedings of the peace conventions, conferences, and congresses of the 1800s.

An examination of several articles revealed a distinct awareness that education for peace had the potential of enlightening a new generation. A common theme was that education as a system could bring before youth a true sense of the moral and economic abominations of war.[56]

The theories of Charles Darwin appeared to be influential. The Darwinian theories of evolution, natural selection, and survival of the fittest were rationalized.[57] Harry Vrooman recognized that educational institutions were already teaching the rights and duties of citizenship. They were also the natural vehicles to teach the dignity of civilization and the destructiveness of war. War had been an inheritance of our race by mere habit as a survival of the most militant tribes. Civilization should evolve naturally into a humane society where all could live in harmony. Vrooman declared that by the turn of the century society would witness "the steady progress of the race toward humanity. . . . (as) members of the family of nations."[58]

Criticism of the growing involvement of the military in the schools appeared to be based on the Darwinian theory that militarism was a step backward for society: militarism was equated with barbarism, a mark of the Dark Ages while the nineteenth century was symbolized by progress and civilization. Militarism was conceived as a constriction and strangulation of freedom. Peace on the other hand, was viewed as the keystone of intellectual freedom and essential for the education of civilized men and women.[59]

Public opinion was identified as a major force in the prevention of war. The moral forces of shared ideas in the community could single out the shame of war and promote the ideal of the "Brotherhood of man."[60]

AFTERTHOUGHTS

The nineteenth century forerunners of peace education recognized the dual roles of church and school and linked teacher and clergy as vital to the spread of peace. Dependence on the messages of peace and Christian dogma at times reflected the theocracy of the Massachusetts Bay Colony of previous centuries. By the end of the century, however there were signs that the exclusivity of Christianity as a concomitant for reform had ended. Women's groups appeared to learn lessons from actions in other reform areas. For example, the National Council of Women in their efforts for women's rights stressed an interfaith effort and openly revealed their inclusion of several Judeo-Christian denominations in the Council's work. The imprimatur of Christianity, however, left a permanent mark on the peace society writings as they revealed an early awareness of peace education.

Peace education in the early years of the 1800s also reflected the contemporary philosophical and literary mainstream of the Boston-Concord literati with idealism and pragmatism as modus operandi. In the early 1900s, theories and aspirations would be wedded to practical plans for action, such as the writings of curriculum guides and textbooks by the American School Peace League.

Peace education and woman suffrage became interwoven themes in the early twentieth century with hopes for an equal role for women in the determination of social and political events. The Woman's Peace Party in 1915 grew out of frustration when women realized that diplomacy failed to prevent war. Peace education was viewed by educators as a plan for also improving the skills of women by enlarging their sphere of influence in the political arena. An example was the network of influential decision-makers, male and female, put together by Fannie Fern Andrews from 1914 to 1916 in forming the American School Peace League. Even after women received the right to vote, throughout the twentieth century, aspirations for true power have dominated each decade of American society.

The primacy of conscience and the rights of the individual in relationship to government raised ethical questions. The civil disobedience of Thoreau has been reflected a thousand-fold as citizens faced unjust or unpopular laws. From the men and women engaged in the Underground Railroad to the Sanctuary movement of the 1980s (shelter of Central American political exiles) citizens searched for answers that begged obedience to a higher law.

As the exhortations of Horace Mann in the 1840s showed, citizens have faced an ongoing dilemma about human needs versus military spending. Mann first raised the issue of the economic survival of underpaid teachers and educational needs versus military spending. The ethical issue has been sloganized as "Guns or Butter" and has persisted for almost two centuries. Furthermore, the exorbitant costs of the arms race on the economies of the superpowers, with resulting lowered standards of living for large groups of the citizenry has perhaps been a cogent factor in ending the Cold War era. Human needs should take priority over weapons that soon became obsolete, peace advocates argued. The debate about "Guns or Butter" continued throughout the 1980s and into the 1990s.

Throughout the 1800s peace education gathered its forces and seemed, perhaps on the threshold of becoming an educational movement. There was an embryonic awareness instead that a more perfect, peaceable society was possible. By the late 1800s the building blocks moved into place: educating the child in ethics first, then by increments, educating individuals for citizenship. As the twentieth century began, peace education in America may have been perceived as a guiding light to illuminate the conscience of humanity.

Notes

1. Vernon L. Parrington, *Main Currents in American Thought: An Interpretation of American Literature from the Beginnings to 1920, Vol. Three: 1860–1920: Beginnings of Critical Realism in America* (New York: Harcourt, Brace and Company, 1958), 31.
2. Background sources on Transcendentalism, women's rights and other social reform movements of the early century were: Lawrence Buell, *Literary Transcendentalism: Style and Vision in the American Renaissance* (Ithaca, NY: Cornell University Press, 1973); Margaret Fuller (Countess Ossoli), *Woman in the Nineteenth Century and Kindred Papers Relating to the Sphere, Condition, and Duties of Woman* (Boston: John P. Jewett Company, 1888); Van Wyck Brooks, *Literature in New England: The Flowering of New England, 1815–1865* (Garden City, NY: Garden City Publishing Co., Inc., 1944); and Austin Warren, *The New England Conscience* (Ann Arbor, MI: University of Michigan Press, 1966).
3. Margaret Fuller, *Woman in the Nineteenth Century* (Boston: John P. Jewett Company, 1888), 221.

4. Fuller, 222.
5. Ruhl J. Bartlett, *The League To Enforce Peace* (Chapel Hill: University of North Carolina, 1944), 4.
6. *The Harbinger of Peace* 1 (January 1829), New York: The American Peace Society, micro-opaque (New York: Clearwater Publishing, 1978), 149.
7. Elihu Burritt, "Letter to George Bancroft, 'An Early Document in the Peace Movement, 21 April 1849,' " In letters to *The Outlook* by M. D. De Wolfe Howe in *The Outlook* (21 September 1907): 134–136.
8. Harold Josephson, ed., *Biographical Dictionary of Modern Peace Leaders* (Westport, CT: Greenwood Press, 1983), 126.
9. *Harbinger* 2 (June 1829): 32–33.
10. *The Calumet* (September–October 1831), 46–47. New York: The American Peace Society, micro-opaque (New York: Clearwater Publishing, 1978), 46–47.
11. *The Advocate of Peace* 1 (December 1836), Hartford, CT: The Connecticut Peace Society, micro-opaque (New York: Clearwater Publishing, 1978), 149.
12. *The Calumet* 2 (April 1835), New York: The American Peace Society, micro-opaque (New York: Clearwater Publishing, 1978), 199.
13. *Harbinger* 1 (January 1829): 253–254.
14. Reading of the peace society journals showed that peace was considered as a preventive measure against war by enlightened citizens.
15. *Advocate of Peace* 1 (June 1829), 253.
16. George C. Beckwith, *Peace Manual or War and Its Remedies* (Boston: The American Peace Society, 1847), 245.
17. Josephson, *Biographical Dictionary of Modern Peace Leaders*, 63–64.
18. *Harbinger* 1 (January 1829): 253–254.
19. "Elm," "Christianity and Patriotism," *Southern Literary Messenger* 8 (September 1842): 600–606.
20. Beckwith, 245.
21. *The American Advocate of Peace* 1 (March 1836), Hartford, CT: The Connecticut Peace Society, micro-opaque (New York: Clearwater Publishing, 1978), 379.
22. *The American Advocate of Peace* 1 (June 1836), Hartford, CT:

The Connecticut Peace Society, micro-opaque (New York: Clearwater Publishing, 1978), 44.

23. *Advocate* 1 (March 1836): 379.
24. Countess of Aberdeen, "The Coming Triennial Meeting of the Council of Women of the United States at Washington," *The Arena,* 23 (February 1895): 340.
25. Horace Mann, *Lectures on Education* (Boston: Ide Dutton, 1855), 241.
26. Mann, *Lectures,* 242.
27. Mann, *Lectures,* 13.
28. Mann, *Lectures,* 53.
29. Mann, *Lectures,* 53.
30. Mann, *Lectures,* 253.
31. Mann, *Lectures,* 253.
32. National Herbart Society, *First Yearbook,* (Denver Meeting, 1895), ed. Charles A. McMurry (Chicago: University of Chicago Press, 1907), 10.
33. S. Alexander Rippa, *Education in a Free Society* (New York: Longman, 1980), 186.
34. *First Yearbook,* 11.
35. M. G. Brumbaugh, "Method of the Social Function of History," in National Herbart Society for the Scientific Study of Teaching, *Fourth Yearbook,* (Washington Meeting, 1898), ed. Charles A. McMurry (Chicago: University of Chicago Press, 1989), 31.
36. Frank G. Blair, "Social Function of History," in *Fourth Yearbook,* 44.
37. Blair, *Fourth Yearbook,* 39.
38. Blair, *Fourth Yearbook,* 44.
39. An extensive collection of primary source materials on Charles A. McMurry can be found in the Archives at Northern Illinois University, DeKalb, Illinois, including correspondence, course notebooks, and textbook manuscripts.
40. Charles A. McMurry, *Special Method for History and Literature in the Common Schools* (Bloomington, IL: Public School Publishing, 1893), 93.
41. McMurry, *Special Method,* 1911 edition, 9.
42. Charles A. McMurry, *Pioneer History Stories* (Winona, MN: Jones Kroeger, 1891), 7–10.

43. McMurry, *Pioneer History Stories*, 7–10.
44. Henry B. Carrington, ed. *Beacon Lights of Patriotism or Incentives to Virtue and Good Citizenship. In Prose and Verse with Notes, Dedicated to American Youth* (New York: Silver & Burdett, 1894).
45. Charles Sumner, "The True Grandeur of Nations," in Carrington, *Beacon Lights*, 137.
46. John Haberton, "The Ideal Citizen," in Carrington, *Beacon Lights*, 148.
47. Benjamin Harrison, "The Critical Conditions of Labor," in Carrington, *Beacon Lights*, 268–272.
48. Mary Murray, *History of the United States of America. Written in Accordance with the Principles of Peace* (Boston: Benjamin B. Mussey Co., 1852), Preface, n.p.
49. Murray, 439.
50. *The Harbinger of Peace* 2 (March 1830), New York: American Peace Society, micro-opaque (New York: Clearwater Publishing, 1978), 129.
51. Several peace society journals carried accounts of the horrors of slavery as well as war. See Dorothy Sterling in *Ahead of Her Time: Abby Kelley and the Politics of Antislavery*. New York: W.W. Norton, 1991.
52. Murray, 439.
53. John Fiske, *American Political Ideas Viewed from the Standpoint of Universal History* (New York: Harper Brothers, 1885), 99–100.
54. Fiske, 150.
55. "Bibliography on Peace and War" in Harry C. Vrooman, "The Abolition of War: A Symposium," *The Arena* 23 (February 1895): 138–144.
56. H. Pereira Mendes, "The Solution of War," *North American Review* 161 (August 1895): 161–169: and N. S. Shaler, "The Last Gift of the Century," *North American Review* 161 (December 1895): 674–684.
57. Frederic Passy, "The Advance of the Peace Movement Throughout the World," *Review of Reviews* 17 (February 1898): 183–188; Bertha von Süttner, "Universal Peace—From a Woman's Standpoint." *North American Review* 169 (July 1899): 50–61; Franklin Smith, "Peace as a Factor in Social and Political Reform," *Popular Science Monthly* 53 (June 1898):

240–255; and Thomas E. Will, "The Abolition of War," *The Arena* 23 (February 1895): 127–137.
58. Thomas E. Will, 127.
59. Harry C. Vrooman, "The Ethics of Peace," *The Arena* 23 (February 1895): 118–144.
60. H. Pereira Mendes, 168.

3. EDUCATION FOR WORLD CITIZENSHIP, 1901–1930

SEEDS OF OPPOSITION

Red-baiting as a subtle method to silence the opposition of peace advocates first appeared during this period. Organizations involved with peace issues, such as the Women's International League for Peace and Freedom (which is still active) and individuals, such as John Dewey, criticized the further entrenchment of militarism and especially the military training of youth in the public schools. During and immediately after World War I, peace advocates were linked with pro-German, "Pacifist-Socialist" alliances and accused of disloyalty.

Charges of un-Americanism appeared to alter the course of action for women's organizations engaged in peace or social reform, including the Women's International League for Peace and Freedom and the American School Peace League. The latter, for example, appeared under a thinly-disguised new name, the American School Citizenship League. Moreover, a textbook written for that group confirmed its change of focus to a group promoting citizenship courses in history and having few remnants of the original peace education goals.

As America entered the 1900s, peace education gained additional advocates. Lucia Ames Mead and her husband, Edwin Mead, along with Fannie Fern Andrews, devoted their entire adult lives to writing, lecturing, and inspiring others to join a formidable network for a noble mission, peace education, and international education.

The Meads wrote extensively in books, journals, and peace society publications of their dream for an enhanced citizenship. This would be one that transcended the nation-state to encompass the world. Edwin Mead held an enviable position of power as the director of the World Peace Foundation. In her writing, Lucia Mead also provided a bridge between the New England tradition of Transcendentalism and education for world citizenship.

This era also marked the inclusion of a new concept, as delineated by Lucia Ames and Edwin Mead: the promotion of international or world law as a worthy goal for peace education. While Andrews can be considered as an educational generalist in promoting peace-oriented classroom activities and curriculum guides, the Meads concentrated their attention on the possibilities of world law to end warfare. Americans could be worthy, patriotic citizens, but the progress and civilization of the new century demanded an additional role, that of world citizenship with the machinery for international justice, they reasoned.

Fannie Fern Andrews, founder of the American School Peace League in the years before World War I, dreamed of an organization for all of America's teachers and school children. She promoted May 18 as Peace Day, a holiday that was celebrated annually for a decade. She travelled and lectured extensively abroad and organized her European colleagues for a conference to establish the group with a library and journal for world citizenship and friendship.

The life of Jane Addams provided an embodiment of the world citizen of the new century. In her speeches and writings, as well as her accomplishments as a humanitarian, her idealistic dreams meshed with practical plans for social and political reform. Her commitment to nonviolence and pacifism dominated her activism as she lived out her philosophy. She punctuated her life with deeds that would uplift humanity and prove that human reason could bring about significant change. Her concern for the economic causes of war added a new dimension to peace education as a hunger for economic and social justice. This strand of peace education still remains as an unfinished agenda for American society.

The involvement of both peace educators and suffragists in separate female organizations added a significant leitmotiv during the early decades of the century. They recognized the value of networks and common goals. Yet they still relied to some extent on male decision makers as shown by the early committees of the American School Peace League, which were augmented by scores of prominent male educators and administrators under the benevolent auspices of the National Education Association. Success with formation of the Woman's Peace Party in 1915 and achievement of the franchise in 1920 showed that unified efforts to advance women's rights required long years of planning and hard work.

AMERICAN SCHOOL PEACE LEAGUE

The year of 1909 was a turning point for peace education with two events of significance. The first was a select gathering of educators, clergy, and philanthropists who convened at Lake Mohonk in New York State. The Conference had been inaugurated in 1895 and continued for 22 years. The Lake Mohonk group chose the president of Columbia University, Nicholas Murray Butler, as presiding officer. The group appointed a Committee of Ten to consider the advisability of a National Council of Peace and Arbitration.[1]

Butler lectured and wrote extensively on a viewpoint held in common with other intellectuals in the pre-World War I period. Butler and his colleagues believed that the Darwinian process of evolution would result in the eventual disappearance of war. He reasoned that through education and a system of world law, a machinery for the peaceful resolution of conflict would become a reality.[2] The focus on international law was an emphasis that emerged in the closing years of the nineteenth century as the subject of many journal articles.

The Conference leadership included the presidents of several prestigious colleges and universities: Johns Hopkins, Cornell, Michigan, and California. These men urged the Conference to "encourage acceptance of the subject of international arbitration at colleges and universities" including the sponsorship of essay prizes on this subject.[3]

Prior to the Lake Mohonk Conference, Edwin Ginn, founder of the textbook publishing firm, Ginn and Company, announced plans for an International School of Peace to serve as the "nucleus of a great endowment and a clearing house for receiving and disbursing contributions."[4] In 1909 the World Peace Foundation was established with Edwin Mead as managing director with the financial backing of Ginn. Educational programs took place and a series of pamphlets on peace issues published. The trustees and directors of the World Peace Foundation met first at the Lake Mohonk Conference. Lucia Ames Mead, in 1897, had been invited to deliver an address titled "The Education and Influencing of Public Opinion." It was a prophetic moment because she would spend the next decades of her life engaged in education for peace, as an instructor and lecturer.

Ginn also provided financial support to other groups such as the American School Peace League.[5] Ginn did not actually publish any of the curriculum guides that were written by committees of the American School Peace League, and its successor organization, the American School Citizenship League. Earlier in 1902, though, Ginn established an International Library in Boston which published and distributed at cost peace literature to schools or other interested parties.[6]

The second event of importance took place in May of 1909 in Chicago, the Second National Peace Congress. These meetings served to test the political waters for Fannie Fern Andrews, a Boston school teacher, who played a central role as a peace educator and pioneer in international education.[7]

Andrews served as a member of the Committee on Educational Institutions. She also shared the meeting rostrum at the Peace Congress with Jane Addams, founder of Hull House and Samuel Gompers, founder of the American Federation of Labor.

Andrews completed her training at the Salem Normal School two years after Jane Addams completed her studies at the Rockford Female Seminary. She augmented this training with a Bachelor's degree from Radcliffe in 1902 and then at mid-life returned to graduate school, earning a Master's degree in 1920. She continued her graduate study and earned a doctorate in 1923 at the age of fifty-six.[8]

From the contacts she made at the Congress Andrews formed a network of colleagues sympathetic to the cause of peace education. She united the educational forces from leading peace groups into an umbrella organization, the American School Peace League. The League was formed in 1908 as the result of activities of educators who attended the First National Peace Congress in New York in 1907.

The term network has been described as a web of interests and attitudes that include common goals of many individuals. As envisioned by Andrews, the Peace League was conceived as a network to be buttressed by key decision makers representing different interests. Its membership included school superintendents, government officials, directors of key organizations, college presidents, and even the President of the United States at one point. These provided forceful elements united in a calculated course for peace education.

Andrews unfolded her blueprint at the Second National Peace Congress in 1909. The contacts she made assisted her in various ways in forming the League. A fellow Bostonian, Rose Dabney Forbes (Mrs. J. Malcolm Forbes) worked on the Finance Committee. She proved to be a valuable contact because Forbes later made substantial contributions to the Peace League during its early years. Colleagues on the Educational Committee were future League officers and committee members. They included Lorenzo D. Harvey,

President of the National Education Association that year, who was also a pioneer in vocational-technical education from the Stout Institute, Wisconsin; and Lucia Ames Mead, a Director of the American Peace Society and also a Boston-area school teacher.

Others served on the Committee on Resolutions, such as David Starr Jordan, President of Stanford University, pioneer biologist who served as the President of the National Education Association (NEA) during the early years of the League and an influential mentor for Andrews. On the Program Committee were Jane Addams and the presidents of America's leading women's colleges: Agnes Irwin of Radcliffe, M. Carey Thomas of Bryn Mawr, Mary Wooley of Mount Holyoke, and Caroline Hazard of Wellesley.[9]

Andrews outlined her plans for the newly organized American School Peace League to the assembled Peace Congress delegates:

> The League aims to acquaint all the teachers of this country . . . the 500,000 teachers with all these forces that are working for world peace . . . to induce educational gatherings, associations, to take some part of their program for the subject of . . . peace.[10]

At a Saturday morning teachers' meeting Andrews addressed those who were her prime target, America's educators. Her speech related specifically to her expectations for America's teachers:

> The American School Peace League aims to acquaint the educational public of America, in order that the teachers may be influenced to emphasize the broad humanitarian principles of right and justice which transcend all national boundaries . . . We hope that every teacher in the country will join the League. There are no dues.[11]

As the teachers left the meeting Andrews presented each one with a *Manual of the Peace League* and a brief bibliography.

Appropriately, Andrews chose May 18 as the central focus for the promotion of Peace League activities. On that date in 1899 the First Peace Congress was held at The Hague in Holland. For the first time in history an attempt was made to use arbitration to settle international disputes and a permanent tribunal was established toward that end. Organized as Peace Day, May 18 was celebrated annually in schools in various parts of America during post-World War I days. Later, however, the holiday underwent a metamorphosis and became Goodwill Day, which was observed until the 1930s.

Renaming Peace Day may have been a wise move because of the controversies that surfaced during the Red Scare of 1919–1920 when pacifists were linked with socialists and pro-German elements and branded as unpatriotic. America's entry into World War I also affected the expansion of peace education. Undoubtedly, these events caused the League to change its policy and concentrate on citizenship and goodwill instead of peace education.

The League organized with a governing council and provided representation through branches in several states. League officers provided speakers for educational meetings and conventions. Aware of the need to further disseminate information, the League also made materials for Peace Day observation available to the schools. It donated additional printed literature to libraries. If requested, the League also assisted with the organization of student branches.[12]

Andrews planned the annual meetings of the American School Peace League to coincide with those of the NEA. From 1912 to 1916 the League had the approval of the NEA, which passed several resolutions each year praising its activities. One of these resolutions was specifically printed in a bulletin titled *Peace Day,* which was commissioned by the United States Bureau of Education and disseminated throughout the country.[13]

The NEA also invited other school-related groups to meet in tandem with its annual conferences. The Garden Association of America, Educational Press, American Home Economics, Religious Education Association, and National Committee on Agricultural Education were school-related organizations that met in 1913 under the auspices of the NEA.[14]

The NEA provided a bridge between educators of the nineteenth and the new century. As far back as 1847 Horace Mann had called for a "national organization of teachers" that would "enlighten the guiding forces of the mind . . . (and) generate the impulsive forces of the heart."[15] The NEA was an advocate for child welfare, engaged in developing an awareness for child safety and protection.

In the years before America entered World War I, the NEA and its president, David Starr Jordan, gave outstanding support to the Peace League. A "Peace Letter" from Andrews was included in the NEA *Bulletin* at its annual meeting in 1914 even though it contained a controversial position on the peace issue:

> The request, made at the beginning of the school year by certain superintendents, that there should be no discussion of this subject in the classroom (the War) is apparently in line with President Wilson's policy. . . . But today, when the significance of this world object-lesson comes more and more into light . . . it is hoped that . . . the teachers . . . should take the matter under serious consideration.[16]

Andrews designed her organization for peace education as a campaign to involve all segments of the educational spectrum from the youngest child in kindergarten to peace clubs on the college campus. She urged teachers and students to unite in a common cause, "to build up a new people whose country is the world, where countrymen are all mankind."[17]

Andrews' plan also envisioned a curriculum and textbook for peace education including a course of study for history and citizenship for use in the elementary schools.

Education for peace received credibility as a seriously conceived curriculum through the work commissioned by the

Children presenting petitions for world peace before World War I to William Jennings Bryan (1860–1925). He was the Secretary of State in Woodrow Wilson's administration, but resigned in 1915. (Photograph from Historical Pictures Services, Chicago.)

American School Peace League. During this era, education for peace also gained the aura of respectability, due to its sanctioning by prominent citizens, such as Butler, Jordan, and Ginn.

LUCIA AMES AND EDWIN MEAD

Lucia Ames and Edwin Mead devoted their entire adult lives to the cause of peace. Their writings, lectures, and public addresses reflected an advocacy of peace education on an international scale. Lucia Ames was considered one of the most prominent women in the peace movement in the early decades of the new century.

Lucia Ames Mead was educated in public and private schools in Chicago, where her father had moved from New Hampshire following her mother's death. She received training as a music teacher and gave piano lessons in the Boston area. A strong influence on her life, while a young adult, was William Torrey Harris, a leading philosopher and educational leader. He served as the United States Commissioner of Education at the turn of the century. Lucia Ames attended lectures given by Harris at the Concord Summer School of Philosophy. She became a gifted lecturer in her own right and by 1886 was offering courses in "Nineteenth Century Thought." At the close of the century she became actively involved in the woman suffrage movement. She married Edwin Mead, then editor of the *New England Magazine* while in her forties. Lucia Mead was a prolific writer who wrote a children's book, a novel, and several works on peace issues. Her major work on peace education was dedicated to Rose Dabney Forbes, Chair of the Finance Committee for the Peace League, who proved to be a generous benefactor.[18]

Lucia Mead recognized the importance of the economic causes of war described as a "lack of elementary knowledge of international economics."[19] She believed that financial

Lucia Ames Mead (1856–1936), shown above, worked independently as well as with her husband, Edwin Doak Mead (1849–1937), for peace education and advocacy in the early decades of the nineteenth century. (Courtesy of Lucia Ames and Edwin D. Mead Papers, Swarthmore College Peace Collection, Swarthmore, Pennsylvania.)

and economic considerations were often crucial factors that precipitated a declaration of war. She stated that, "It would be well for American children to learn this year's annual budget and that we are spending nearly four-fifths of it on something connected with war, past, present, or future."[20] Her concern for the far-reaching effects of military spending were similar to Horace Mann's views of the previous century. As you recall, (from Chapter 2) Mann first posed the ethical dilemma of military expenditures versus human needs.

The basic theme in Lucia Mead's writing was that peace and justice were attainable through a permanent court of international justice. She carefully developed this theme and quoted historical examples from varied sources, such as the Bible and Shakespeare. In addition she paid tribute to Emerson with his definition of a new patriotism—"the delight which springs from contributing . . . to the benefit of humanity."[21]

With dedication to an international court of law, she believed, America would develop a broadened spirit of internationalism. She wrote that "Love of humanity no more weakens love of country, than love of one's family . . . The child must be taught that he is first of all a human being, a citizen of the world, a child of God."[22]

Lucia Mead also stressed that the work of the American School Citizenship League (successor to the Peace League) should include the "study of world organization and all that contributes to international good-will."[23] The celebration of Peace Day, May 18 was renamed Goodwill Day, in recognition of the opening of the first Hague Conference.[24]

Her husband, Edwin Mead, was an avid reformer in the Boston area. As editor of the *New England Magazine,* he campaigned for social justice, woman suffrage, municipal socialism, and other liberal issues. He believed, as did his wife, that international law would further the cause of justice and peace.[25]

A major and recurring theme that Edwin Mead put forth was the direct relationship between peace and social justice and the teaching of morals and ethics in education. In an early article he stated:

> Children must be taught that there are not two kinds of morality, one for nations and one for the individual; they must be inspired with a feeling of brotherly love toward all peoples, without distinction of race, color or religion.[26]

He further expanded this theme with the idea that "righteousness and justice" should be the basis of life with children taught that "love of country cannot stand opposed to love of humanity."[27]

Edwin Mead extolled those who gave service to humanity as heroes of peace. The spark of inspiration for this writing was the steel industrialist Andrew Carnegie's announcement that he was establishing a commission and funding it with $5 million for pensions to be awarded to heroes of peace, especially to those who had shown their courage and devotion by saving lives. Mead believed that the awards were a recognition of the fact that "the esteem and glorification of the soldier had been out of all proportion to the honor paid the heroes of other fields than the battlefield," and that nonmilitary service often revealed a greater risk and higher courage for a "nobler and more useful end" than war.[28] Carnegie's commission for peace heroes provided a touch of irony because post-World War I hearings revealed that Carnegie and other industrialists garnered excessive profits from the building of ships and weaponry. The Carnegie Hero Fund Commission, of course, continues to exist and still makes annual awards to those Americans who save lives.

As a prominent lecturer, Mead spoke often to young people in the Boston area and expanded his favorite topic, the "Heroes of Peace" to include Horace Mann and "His Work for Better Schools, Mary Lyon and her College for Girls and Dorothea Dix and Her Errands of Mercy."[29] Mead also lectured in favor of a "new teaching of history," which would support education for character formation and social service rather than "power and show."[30] He believed that a new theme was needed in human history.

Lucia Mead expressed a similar sentiment when she stated that true patriotism was shown with "the quiet satisfaction of saving fellow men from accident and death; saving forests and water power . . . creating beauty, happiness and health for multitudes."[31] She helped Jane Addams organize the Woman's Peace Party and wrote several other publications.[32] Her attitude reflected a foreshadowing of an ecological ethic. Edwin and Lucia Mead were pioneers who sowed the seeds of world citizenship and peace education.

JANE ADDAMS: PEACE AND BREAD

While Jane Addams, founder of Hull House, has been considered primarily a social worker and activist in the international peace movement, her efforts toward the promotion of peace education have received recognition only in recent decades.

"Peace and Bread" was the slogan that was central to the life of Addams. It articulated her philosophy that poverty and deprivation were the primary causes of war. She recognized that economic and social justice, symbolized by the earning of daily bread were essential components for peace. Born in Cedarville, Illinois in 1860 Addams had a Quaker father who believed in equal rights for women.[33]

"Peace and Bread" as a slogan originated perhaps as the phrase "bread-givers" and was used first by Addams while a student editor at the Rockford Female Seminary. The Seminary was founded in 1844 by a group of ministers and women teachers from upper New York State and later became Rockford College (still in existence).

The first college class at the Seminary entered in 1855 with a plan of study that was "both a classical and scientific course of four years each" with several departments in mathematics, natural science, history, English literature, ancient and modern languages and mental and moral philosophy.[34]

Addams was editor of the *Rockford Seminary Magazine* in 1881 and also president of the senior class. She wrote several articles which revealed her formative ideas on social justice. Practical Christianity and the formation of "holy character" were considered the lodestones of education and echoed some of the same sentiments as the writers of the early peace society journals.

Addams reflected the influence of her teachers as well as guest lecturers who visited the Rockford campus, such as Bronson Alcott, founder of the utopian colony Fruitlands in Concord and John Heyl Vincent, cofounder of the Chautauqua movement.[35]

Idealism interwoven with pragmatism were evident in the early writings of Addams. While a student of twenty-one she wrote:

> We have planned to be 'bread-givers' throughout our lives, believing that in labor alone is happiness and that the only true and honorable life is one filled with good works and honest toil . . . We will strive to idealize our labor and thus happily fulfill woman's noblest mission.[36]

Addams gave wide coverage in the student magazine to the issue of woman suffrage and reported on a bill that was introduced into the Wisconsin legislature that would permit women to vote in general elections:

> That maiden women of property are compelled to submit to taxation without representation is a fact that has long been seething in the blood of the granddaughters of Revolutionary heroes . . . Questions concerning the greater wrong of slavery so long kept this in the background.[37]

As editor of the student magazine, Addams also observed that many former students travelled to the far corners of the

Jane Addams, founder of Hull House, carried on a lifetime of service to humanity, through education and advocacy, as well as by promoting world peace. (She was the first President of the Woman's Peace Party. Photograph 4-G-4-1 from National Archives.)

globe as teachers and missionaries. This exposure to an early version of world citizenship may have affected her as a youthful student. The "Personals" columns contained news from "Burmah, Micronesia, Honolulu, Turkey, India and Japan." Also, former students reported that they were "engaged in teaching the Freedmen," the former black slaves at the close of the Civil War.[38]

When the first principal of the Rockford Seminary, Anna P. Sill, passed away in 1889 Addams wrote a memorial in praise of her mission to "train the young women of a new country for Christian usefulness . . . We are bound to perpetuate this primate spiritual purpose," she wrote.[39] The twin virtues of idealism and pragmatism were admired in others by Addams and may have been her early motivation as a "bread-giver."

The seeds of education for world citizenship may have been planted while Addams was a student. The brotherhood of man was extolled above national loyalties:

> The unity of humanity is a great thought. The brotherhood of man is greater . . . for the first time made possible as the hope of ages.[40]

As editor of the *Rockford Seminary Magazine* Addams also included a selection on the "Heroism of the 19th Century" and expressed the desire that Americans show their love of country with broader views:

> We are of the common family when we find each other in distress . . . and hasten to the rescue . . . Man's mind is diverted from warfare . . . The ravages of war with all its untold horrors and glories yield to true development in science and religion. We, living in this 19th century, are witnesses, to this wondrous change.[41]

Considered as a citizen of the world by her generation, her ideals—Christian morality and concern for humanity—were similar to those the early peace societies nourished. Her ideals also echoed the nineteenth-century lectures of Horace Mann.

After founding Hull House in 1889 at the age of 29, Addams spent her life working and teaching in order to improve the lives of tenement dwellers in the Chicago slums. A college student reported that she spent her summer vacation as a volunteer at Hull House. A typical activity was teaching neighborhood residents how to make children's clothing from discarded woolen overcoats.

Her classmate from the Rockford Female Seminary, Julia Lathrop joined her in forming at Hull House, the Plato Club for the discussion of philosophy. An occasional leader of the group was John Dewey then a young professor at the new University of Chicago. The club was composed primarily of elderly men who enjoyed the pursuit of philosophical readings.[42]

One of the most influential women of her era, Addams showed deep concern for the plight of children during World War I. She joined Quaker groups to distribute food in Europe in 1919. Her concern as a "bread-giver" was shown by her address given in London in 1921 as President of the Women's International League for Peace and Freedom:

> I have just come from Vienna . . . I found people from every nation in Europe . . . who are trying to keep alive the children in that desolate city . . . I believe there is a great moral challenge that could quench the lust of war . . . (with) plans for feeding millions with whom you are associated in a family.[43]

Leo Tolstoy may have influenced Jane Addams, especially with his writings on nonviolence. His pacifist philosophy bolstered the ideals of Addams who advocated nonviolent means as agents for change in pursuit of peace and world citizenship. Addams even visited Tolstoy in Russia. The author of *War and Peace* lived the simple life of a peasant on his estate. Addams wrote:

> We believe that we are not obliged to choose between
> violence and passive acceptance of unjust conditions for
> ourselves and others; (We) believe, on the contrary,
> that courage, determination, moral power, generous
> indignation, active good will, can achieve their end
> without violence.[44]

Addams especially taught that education for world citizenship could serve as a vehicle for peaceful change, "Education
is a leading out . . . another testimony of the human race, to
faith in itself and God that through all its changes" life could
finally be perfected.[45]

From her Midwestern roots Addams' perspectives grew to
encompass world citizenship as a new kind of internationalism. She described this type of international citizenship as
"cosmic patriotism," a force with the power "to move masses
of men out of their narrow national considerations . . . into
new reaches of human effort and affection."[46]

Addams adhered firmly to her Quaker pacifist views on
nonviolence and opposition to all wars, in spite of the
perceived just causes for World War I. Her reputation as a
most revered American degenerated because of her strong
stand on war. Near the end of her life she was attacked for
her unyielding stand against U.S. entry into World War I.
She became a victim of character assassination in a right
wing, anticommunist campaign that touched the lives of
many peace educators. Undoubtedly these events hampered
her ability to garner support for peace issues.

JOHN DEWEY

John Dewey envisioned the school as an agent for change
and as the instrument capable of perfecting society. This
theme was developed with infinite variation in his books—
*My Pedagogic Creed, School and Society, Democracy and
Education, Human Nature and Conduct,* and *The Child and
the Curriculum.*

Limited attention, however, has been paid to Dewey's concern for the causes of war—economic, social, and political—nor to his support of education for world citizenship. Dewey was in agreement with American participation in World War I. However, his postwar lectures and writings revealed a complete reversal as he evolved into a firm pacifist. His involvement in the Outlawry of War Crusade has been fully documented in recent years with a scholarly study by Charles F. Howlett.[47]

Dewey believed that there was a legal alternative to international diplomacy that deserved to be tried. He joined Salmon O. Levinson, a lawyer and others in a crusade that advocated methods to delegalize war as a method of settling disputes. He believed that the establishment of an international code of law with a court of justice would also be a necessary step to settle disputes by means other than war.

Dewey believed that educational change should proceed in a peaceful, cooperative manner. He wrote:

> The final significance of what is taking place in Russia is not . . . to be grasped in political or economic terms, but is found in change . . . as an educational transformation . . . a new type of education . . . peacefully and gradually (producing) the required transformation in other institutions.[48]

When he visited Russia, after the Bolshevik Revolution, Dewey wrote, "Only in a society based upon the cooperative principle can the ideals of educational reformers be adequately carried into operation."[49]

Dewey championed the dignity of labor in which idealism and pragmatism were joined. Participation in productive work, he said, was the chief stimulus and guide to self-educative activity for pupils and "provides the most direct road to connecting the school with social life."[50]

To accomplish the goal of educating young people for world citizenship. Dewey believed that teaching of history and geography should be reformed. Such reform, he said,

was needed "for cultivating a socialized intelligence consti-
tutes its moral significance."[51] Dewey was convinced that
change must come about in the environment of society:

> We may desire abolition of war, industrial justice,
> greater opportunity for all. But no amount of preaching
> good will or the golden rule . . . will accomplish the
> results . . . There must be change in the arrangements
> and institutions. We must work on the environment,
> not merely on the hearts of men.[52]

Dewey opposed the entrance of the military into the
schools. At the close of World War I the National Defense
Act was passed (1920) marking the first time in history that
military personnel were permitted to hold training classes in
the schools. Dewey's opposition stemmed from the establishment of the Reserve Officers' Training Corps (ROTC) on
college campuses and the use of tax money for the summer
training camps for youth. Instead, Dewey advocated a
universal training for social service, not for militarism, a type
of Civilian Service Corps that several administrations have
also supported. In fact, Dewey can be credited with one of
the earliest plans for volunteer youth community service, an
idea that has persisted throughout the twentieth century.
Dewey's visionary idea was achieved with passage of the
National and Community Service Act of 1990. This Act will
establish community service programs on a part-time basis
for young adults, working through schools or other community agencies.

Dewey's views were unpopular, especially his admiration
for Bolshevik ideology. Yet, his visit to the Soviet Union
obviously influenced his views. Dewey dreamed of a child-
centered classroom where the child could experience democracy in action with firsthand involvement. He also envisioned
educating children in an environment characterized by
cooperation.

PEACE EDUCATION AND WOMAN SUFFRAGE

During this period, peace education and woman suffrage were often interwoven themes. Many of the same women, such as Andrews, Lucia Mead, and Addams, were actively involved in peace education and suffrage and moved in concentric circles with different groups. Women of privilege and leisure joined them, along with professional women in the fields of education, law, and social welfare.

As early as the 1909 National Convention of the Woman Suffrage Association, Lucia Ames Mead had a report read which commented on the fact that "all of the women who took part" in the Second National Peace Congress "were suffragists."[53]

The year of 1915 was a decisive one for the pioneers of peace education. At the annual meeting of the American School Peace League in Oakland, California, Andrews stated that only through education would a final peace and political reform be possible when the war ended. She expressed her fear that "civilization is hanging in the balance" with education also "at the crossroads."[54]

In numerous writings and addresses at this time, an embryonic political awareness was in evidence. On January 10, 1915, in Washington, DC, representatives from "all the leading women's organizations and movements assembled to consider measures for promoting and formulating peace sentiments in this country and throughout the world." The Woman's Peace Party was formally organized with Addams as the first president.

A new era of political activism was inaugurated. Peace education gained an additional forum. Political activism meshed with education for peace. Education had been recognized as a valid and plausible method for bringing about change in institutional structures. This had been evident in the early decades of the peace society, as expressed by journal writers.

Throughout the century, ethereal dreams for peace became formalized first as theories and then after 1900, as practical plans for political activism. The early strivings for peace shown by the women of the Essex County Olive Branch, for example, came to fruition in the bid for power behind the Woman's Peace Party. The women founders dared to dream of a share in the decisionmaking process. They deemed that they also belonged at the diplomatic tables along with the appointed statesmen. The first dictums of the peace society journals proclaimed that woman was the nurturer of humankind, the first teacher with an instinctive sense for peace and harmony. Political activism to bring about a peaceful world became the next step in the evolution of women. They recognized that the path to further progress was through official government circles and the political power structure. Their agenda was set: first, gain the right to vote and then, with political power, secure a world of peace.

The keynote address at the January, 1915 meeting of the Woman's Peace Party was given by Carrie Chapman Catt from New York who provided the rationale for the unprecedented movement of women into political activism:

> The women of this country were lulled into inattention . . . by reading the many books put forth by great pacifists . . . But when the great war came, and the women . . . waited for the pacifists to move and they heard nothing from them, they decided all too late to get together themselves and to try to do something at this eleventh hour.[55]

The preamble and platform adopted at that historical conference gave a prominent place to peace education and the role of women. Women were considered nurturers and guardians of human life, present and future:

> We demand that women be given a share in deciding between war and peace in all the courts of high debate, within the home, the school, the church, the industrial order and the state.[56]

The platform of the Woman's Peace Party declared as its intent the enlistment of all American women in arousing the nations to "respect the sacredness of human life and to abolish war." The following measures were adopted:

(1) The immediate calling of a convention of neutral nations in the interest of early peace.
(2) Limitation of armaments and the nationalization of their manufacture.
(3) Organized opposition to militarism in our own country.
(4) Education of youth in the ideals of peace . . .
(6) The further humanizing of governments by the extension of the franchise to women . . .
(8) Action toward the gradual organization of the world to substitute Law for War . . .
(10) Removal of the economic causes of war.[57]

Several measures had been actively promoted since the turn of the century. For example, measure 8 closely resembled the major work by Lucia Ames Mead. [58] Measure 3 was debated in books and articles for many years.[59] Measure 10 was attributable directly to the influence of Addams.[60] The major components of peace education were present in this document: peace, social justice, human rights, economic well-being, and political participation for all.

The franchise for women became a central issue along with peace. By 1913, for example twelve states had granted women the right to vote on matters within the state borders, but it was not until 1920, of course, that the ratification of the nineteenth amendment gave women nationwide the right to vote.

The Woman's Peace Party made rapid progress. In April, 1915 it met at The Hague and those participating passed a resolution calling for an international conference of women to present practical proposals for a postwar peace settlement. The decision was made to hold the conference at the same

time and place as the official governmental peace conference. This strategy was similar to that of the American
School Peace League which met in tandem with the NEA's
annual meetings from 1913–1917.

The leaders of the victorious allies met at the Paris Peace
Conference to begin reshaping the postwar world. However,
the original plans of the Woman's Peace Party to meet at the
same time and place as the Paris Conference fell through and
they met in Zurich instead. By coincidence their meeting
took place on the same day on which the terms of the peace
treaty were published.

There were 147 delegates at the Zurich Conference and
they included women well known in all branches of political,
literary, educational, and social life, according to one
participant.

The resolutions which they passed bore a striking resemblance to the Fourteen Points formulated by President
Wilson. Not surprising, however, since Addams had met
previously with the President to discuss the platform of the
Woman's Peace Party. She elicited President Wilson's
comment that it was "the best formulation I have so far
seen."[61]

One of the proposals of the Woman's Peace Party called
for an International Council for Education for the purpose of
promoting the idea of "a world organization, international
ethics and citizenship." The rationale set forth was:

> The International Congress for Permanent Peace seeks
> to accomplish a basis for a new human civilization . . .
> We must begin with the education of the peoples.[62]

Specific recommendations were:

> The development of an international spirit . . . The
> young should be made familiar with the evolution of
> peoples and with the lives of the great men of all times
> . . . Instruction in civics should develop a world
> consciousness and give an introduction to the duties of
> world citizenship.

The primary role of woman as nurturer was given prominence: "Higher schools for women should train the woman
as a world-citizen for her responsible task as mother of
humanity."[63]

Several name changes occurred as the Woman's Peace
Party took on international overtones. After its founding
meeting in Washington, the Party next met at The Hague
and called itself the "Women's International Congress."[64]
Four years later in Zurich, the Party called itself the
"Congress of the Women's International League for Peace
and Freedom," the name it still goes by today (minus the
term "Congress").

The proposals of the Woman's Peace Party for the peace
settlement were one of many that were offered, officially and
unofficially, by a broad spectrum of organizations during the
period from 1914 to 1916.[65]

PEACE EDUCATORS ACQUIRED A PACIFIST-SOCIALIST LABEL

The war years were characterized by a growing pattern of
suspicion and animosity toward the foreign-born. After
decades of open acceptance of the immigrant, restrictive
policies were adopted. Labor unrest increased as the result of
several major strikes. The inauguration of the Communist
Party of America in 1919 did little to allay tensions. During
the so-called "Red Scare," the anarchist and the radical
reformers, including several peace educators, were labelled
and categorized as communists and socialists.

Suspicion and claims of unpatriotism have clouded the
accomplishments of peace educators throughout the twentieth century, up to the present. Especially misunderstood
were their efforts to alleviate poverty or attack the social or
economic causes of war as a necessary first step toward social
and economic justice. Many of the reforms advocated by
peace educators were enacted in subsequent years, such as

Social Security and child-labor legislation. The strands of social and economic justice have become contemporary objectives in peace education.

The roots of mistrust and charges of unpatriotism need to be examined in greater detail. The reasons for these allegations may be that (1) large numbers of German immigrants at the turn of the century also joined the American Socialist Party; (2) official government prosecution began with the Socialists, many of whom were also pacifists. Any who opposed the war for religious or ideological reasons were labelled together with the socialists and prosecuted under wartime legislation; and (3) women, endowed with newly acquired political power after enfranchisement in 1920, may have represented a growing challenge to the status quo of business-corporate interests represented in the government.

Judging by the results the attempts to silence and discredit peace groups, especially women, were successful. For example, as we have heard previously, the American School Peace League changed its name to the American School Citizenship League and attempts were made to veil the origins of its peace education textbooks. In fact, the masking of peace origins extended as far as the honorary degree citation from Radcliffe for Fannie Fern Andrews, founder of the League. Her accomplishments in international education were stressed, with only one reference to her work in peace education.

THE AMERICAN SOCIALIST PARTY AND ANTI-GERMAN SENTIMENT

The American Socialist Party arrived on the political scene in the early years of the century with large numbers of German immigrants in its ranks, so much so that the Socialist Party was often associated with German ancestry. The Party captured mayoral elections in cities such as Milwaukee,

Wisconsin, a primarily German city as well as Schenectady, New York, Reading, Pennsylvania, and Bridgeport, Connecticut. Municipal socialism in American political life has been documented but often ignored in history texts. In 1912, for example, the Socialist Party claimed 1,200 public officers with 79 mayors in 24 states.[66]

With the entrance of America into World War I, a documented campaign of hatred against the Germans was instigated. The German soldier was depicted as an inhuman barbarian who was guilty of committing unspeakable atrocities against the civilian population being conquered. Posters in the early days of the War pictured graphic details of "the Hun" with bayonet poised to slaughter Belgian babies according to one widely-circulated legend.[67]

Military training designed to motivate recruits to consider the enemy as subhuman has been a familiar tactic, repeated in World War II against the Japanese and in the Vietnam War against the "gooks." Obedience to authority persisted also as an important factor in transforming a new recruit into a soldier prepared to kill a fellow human.[68] Civilian propaganda was directed against anyone of German origin. Family histories recorded attempts during World War I to anglicize the names of children as disguise for their original, German baptismal names.

The Socialist Party was particularly strong among German immigrants in Milwaukee. In the municipal campaign of 1912, for example, their platform called for "an honest municipal government." Calling for the reelection of its candidates, the Party claimed that it had given the city "the best administration it ever had; its work has challenged the attention and interest of the nation."[69]

The interests and needs of the worker were espoused by the American Socialist Party in an age of reform. Its rallying cry for workers' rights was centered on the fight against control by trusts of the basic necessities of life, such as bread, ice, gas, and coal. A small number of capitalists were able to fix the price of most commodities, according to Socialist writers.[70]

The Milwaukee Socialist Party, for example, called for public ownership of utilities and the "complete overthrow of modern plutocracy."[71] Milwaukee's business practices were investigated and subsequently regulated by the federal government during Wilson's term of office. Thus, there may be some basis for the Socialist claims against trusts.

Socialist writers of the period continued to uphold the thesis that economic conditions were the principal causes of war. Violence—domestic, industrial, and international—was viewed as a working class struggle with the worker pitted against the capitalist.

George R. Kirkpatrick was the Socialist Party candidate for the vice presidency in the campaign of 1916. He made a strong case for the study of the economic roots of war and quoted both Addams and David Starr Jordan. Kirkpatrick, along with other officials of the Socialist Party, were sentenced to twenty years in Fort Leavenworth for "conspiracy to obstruct the draft."

The rights of the laboring class in relation to the rise of the corporation in the late nineteenth and early twentieth centuries have been explored in depth by major historians. One interpretation has been that during this era:

> The climate of opinion . . . was hostile to organized labor . . . There developed . . . a double standard of social morality for labor and capital . . . read in the history of labor organization and in the record of social legislation.[72]

Education in America has also been criticized for reinforcing cultural biases and exploiting some groups at the expense of others.[73] An additional thesis has been proposed that the public school system, the traditional path for upward mobility, was organized along racial, social, ethnic, and class lines, becoming a vehicle for the maintenance of the status quo, while the peace advocates became identified with dissenters who were challenging the established order. These threads of dissent were documented in the annals of social reform.[74]

These threads may also have entangled the efforts of peace educators during this period as they attempted to expose the causes of war and especially the economic underpinnings that hindered the cause of peace. Their genuine concern for economic and social justice presented a moral cause worthy of concerted efforts through several decades.

The vilification of peace educators during this period became a stark reality. Despite her stature as a woman of high ideals and an international reputation, Addams, Andrews, the Meads and others were still considered by their detractors to be part of the "Pacifist-Socialist movement." The toll in physical and mental health can only be read between the lines. In the case of Edwin Mead, for example, his biography recorded a severe nervous breakdown in 1915 that left him incapacitated for almost a decade.[75]

LUSK COMMISSION IINVESTIGATIONS

The activities and organizations of peace educators were scrutinized as the result of the Lusk Commission investigations in New York State.[76] The activities and organizations of peace educators were targets. The reports filled five volumes. The mission allegedly examined "Socialism and labor" in 16 different countries as well as American "Revolutionary Industrial Unionism." R. W. Finch, formerly associated with the Bureau of Investigation in the U.S. Justice Department claimed credit as the investigator in charge. Although the Commission was formally established in 1920, given the prodigious output its work undoubtedly began several years earlier.

The reports reflected an anti-German and anti-socialist stance. For example, discussion of the presence of pacifists on the Ford Peace Ship (1915) identified 30 individuals who had German-sounding names and were active in peace, "pro-German or international movements" or who were organized "against preparedness."[77]

The official New York State legislative body was empowered to investigate and document activities. The primary
thesis expressed was that socialism was being aided "in
educated circles through Pacifist, Religious, Collegiate societies."[78] Based on innuendo and guilt by association, the Lusk
Commission justified their activities on the basis of "American patriotism." It marked the first time that anti-socialist or
anticommunist campaigns were used against peace educators
during the 1920s. The pattern of suspicion was set for
subsequent decades.

The activities of the Woman's Peace Party, discussed
previously, were assessed by the Commission as a part of the
"Pacifist-Socialist movement." A meeting was revealed
where "six of the twenty-one delegates to a peace conference
were represented as being Socialist."[79]

The early history of the group, which later became the
Women's International League for Peace and Freedom,
became a target for anti-socialist accusations from right wing
groups in the name of "Patriotism." This record has been
documented with a publication of feminist history.[80]

Andrews, Edwin and Lucia Mead, Addams, and Jordan
were among the peace educators investigated by the Lusk
Commission. In Andrews' case, she was listed as being
invited to attend a meeting because "there must be some
trained pacifists behind the scenes."[81]

The Lusk Report described Lucia Mead as "a very ardent
internationalist" who asked to have "copies of the platform
of the Woman's Peace Party sent to "the foreign members of
the Berne Bureau."[82] Mead was also head of the Massachusetts Woman's Suffrage Association and considered a "cen-
trist" and more to the right than other factions of women
pacifists. Crystal Eastman was identified as forming the left
wing of the women's peace movement.[83]

Despite the publicity and criticism generated by the Lusk
Report, an analysis of personal letters written by Lucia Mead
to Secretary of War John Weeks a few years after their
publication, emphasized her continued concern for educa-

tion and opposition to the National Defense Act of 1920, which brought military training into the schools. She spoke of the more formidable problems of illiteracy and deaths through homicide and industrial accidents. The improvement of social conditions should be a focus for the government rather than surveillance of groups, she wrote to Weeks, referring to actions begun under the aegis of the War Department. Weeks replied that a system of national defense was needed for groups that advance "absurd political beliefs."[84]

Edwin Mead also came under the Lusk Commission's scrutiny for supposed pro-German sentiments, as indicated in the following letter:

> Mr. Edwin D. Mead, whose sympathetic attitude toward the German point of view is of course well known to you writes me that he will be here on Wednesday.[85]

Such questionable patriotism was thoroughly discussed in an entire chapter (VIII) as "Development of American League to Limit Armaments." The justification was that the "German propagandists" stimulated pacifist sentiment in America to bring about a "peace favorable to Germany."[86]

Addams was a particularly vulnerable target, but received greater scrutiny in a subsequent study undertaken 14 years later. The Lusk Commission Report was presented then as "indisputable documentary evidence of the Red movement up to the year 1920."[87] Her half-hearted support of the War contributed to her unpopularity. Addams herself furnished a cogent reason why many perhaps feared the latent political power of American women as they pondered their position in the 1920s:

> The most prophetic event in our War period was the quiet, world wide enfranchisement of uncounted millions of women in countries (abroad) . . . (it) creates a new world feeling among women, a new world power of

unknown strength. It can mark the beginning of a new world peace if we work hard enough for just world politics.[88]

Educational organizations and institutions of higher learning received special attention in the Lusk Commission Report. "Academic and Scholastic Socialist Activities" were discussed:

> It is not easy to know how deeply Socialism has penetrated the college and university, how much of the teaching of economics and sociology is purely scientific and how much is the tinge of propaganda.[89]

A particular object of criticism was the Civil Liberties Bureau founded in 1920, the successor to the American Union Against Militarism. The aims of the Bureau were "the maintenance in war times of the rights of free speech, free press, peaceful assembly, liberty of conscience and freedom from unlawful search and seizure," that is, guarantees from the Constitution.

The Lusk Commission described the Bureau and its adherents, including Addams and Jordan (whose names were on the organization's letterhead) as "very popular with the drove of slackers, pro-Germans, Socialists . . . who grasp at any chance to pose as conscientious objectors."[90] The linkages of peace advocacy with the enemies, Germany and Socialism, were forged and cast a shadow on the efforts of other peace educators well into the future.

THE NATIONAL SECURITY LEAGUE

During the same period, a second investigatory group, The National Security League, emerged to reinforce the American decision to enter World War I. It was organized in 1917 only a few months before America's actual entry into the War. This "Congress of Constructive Patriotism" could be described as being made up of predominantly military-industrial-business interests.[91]

The group's statement of principles called for universal military training, "Patriotism Through Education," augmented military and naval forces, and "an American campaign for national defense." Examination of the membership of this organization revealed veterans' associations from past wars which were identified as "patriotic societies." Business-industrial interests were represented by the National Association of Manufacturers, Boards of Trade, and Chambers of Commerce in several states.[92]

Individual names on the extensive listing of subcommittees and delegates revealed armament manufacturers, such as Colt and Remington. Wall Street interests included magnates of industry, such as Vanderbilt, Whitney, and Astor and financiers, such as Loeb, Schiff, Guggenheim, and Lewisohn. This appeared to be one of the first of many attempts throughout the twentieth century to justify the interests of business-industry and sanction wartime profit-making under the guise of "patriotism." Years after the War—in the 1930s—an investigation confirmed that excessive profits were garnered by a select few and shaped into an early, loosely-formed prototype of the military-industrial complex.

THE LUSK COMMISSION REPORT INSPIRED FURTHER ANTICOMMUNIST CAMPAIGNS

The Lusk Commission Report was reincarnated in 1934 by Elizabeth Dilling, a "super-expert-patriot" with the mission of preserving "America, Christianity, the American Constitution and American liberty."[93] Dilling's exposés can be considered the most far-reaching, right-wing attack on peace educators or activists.

Educational groups were also scrutinized in the interests of "Constructive Patriotism." The Progressive Education Asso-

ciation was described as a "competitor of the radical National
Education Association, a radical left-wing teachers' group."
Progressive educators—Dewey, Rugg, Kilpatrick, and
Washburne—were termed radicals.

The activities of Addams received particular scrutiny for
the dual sins of pacifism and radicalism:

> Greatly beloved because of her kindly intentions
> toward the poor Jane Addams has been able to do more
> probably than any other living woman . . . to popularize
> pacifism and to introduce radicalism into college,
> settlements and respectable circles.[94]

Addams' membership in many "suspicious" organizations
was cited as proof of her pacifism and socialism:

> A member of the socialistic National Consumer League
> . . . contributing editor of the *New Republic,* an
> advocate of revolutionary socialism, on the National
> Save Our Schools Committee . . . director of the
> National Association for the Advancement of Colored
> People, World Court Committee, Foreign Policy Asso-
> ciation and the American Association for Old Age
> Security.[95]

These social reform groups were painted with the same
brush of radicalism and socialism. Throughout the wartime
years socialism was a central issue and few reform efforts
escaped exposure by so-called "patriotic investigators."[96]

Several peace educators did protest "Red Scare" tactics in
a book that attempted to expose the source of the propaganda directed against them.[97] Lucia Ames Mead, for
example, endorsed the book by Norman Hapgood. The
major thesis was that the red-baiting stemmed from a
"Spider Web Chart" which was prepared by Lucia R.
Maxwell, librarian of the Chemical Warfare Service in the
War Department. Links between organizations and women
leaders were shown by the "Web" to justify charges of an
international conspiracy.[98]

The "Socialist-Pacifist Movement" was described by Maxwell as being a "fundamental and integral part of International Socialism." Listed were groups such as the General Federation of Women's Clubs and the National League of Women Voters.[99] The major aim of pacifists was described as being to "disarm the United States so that the Bolsheviks can take it."[100]

Hapgood described the so-called "Professional Patriots" as conservative businessmen who opposed child labor laws, industrial welfare, or any progessive measures that they deemed to be un-American. Peace education, however, would be suspect for decades into the future. Charges of conspiracy could be used effectively to hamper the progress of peace education. The entanglement of "The Spider Web" undoubtedly succeeded. Anti-German and anti-pacifist became woven together so that anyone who was allied in any way with "peace" was condemned as being disloyal to America.

CURRICULUM FOR WORLD CITIZENSHIP

During this period the aims of the Cardinal Principles of Secondary Education (1918) exerted a major influence on curriculum development and peace education.

Although education for morals and ethics still played a role in education at this time, the influence of life experiences on the student was deemed most crucial. In fact, curriculum was described as "the experiences in which pupils are expected to engage in while in school and the general sequence . . . as a reflection of life purposes, adapting conduct to the needs of life."[101] However, a new component was added which was described as a "world-wide" interest.[102] In addition, one of the essential needs for students was deemed "proper training for citizenship."[103] These themes set the stage for education, especially peace education. The themes were also reflected in several textbooks developed by the American School Peace (and Citizenship) Leagues.

One concept proposed at this time was "the idea of a Humanized education." It held that the "primary business of education" was to "make the student at home in the modern world and to enable him to work with the dominant forces of his time."[104] A common core of knowledge, generally recognized as the humanities was regarded as "those common elements of knowledge and training which should become the social inheritance of all pupils."[105]

The teaching of history was a subject area that was re-introduced as "historical civics . . . a perspective for present civics projects."[106] The major instructional strategy of the civics program was the "project method" described as a course of study which is "more significant in the lives of students."[107] For example, descriptions of 285 projects were included in a published collection considered representative of the work undertaken in numerous school systems. The Civics Club, for example, was a common extracurricular activity designed to develop a spirit of mutual helpfulness and efficiency in self-government.

The student was first introduced to projects in the school and local community and then his/her interest expanded to include the world. For example, a Louisville school gave an assembly program on "famines" as the result of "intensive studies in geography, resources and existing conditions in . . . war-torn Europe." The class was divided into committees to "present bread, meat, butter, and sugar conditions of the world and to stress world needs and show that nations should come to the rescue."[108]

The project method focus in civics sometimes helped the efforts of peace educators. For example, as a result of one project the children in Kalamazoo, Michigan heard a lecture by Jane Addams "on the suffering of the children in the war-countries of Europe." This further "stimulated a letter-writing campaign to their congressmen and a fund-raising project to send funds to President Herbert Hoover" for the suffering and starving people in Europe."[109]

During the twenties, citizenship education in the schools had progressed from rote memorization of historical facts to pupil participation in school and community. Activities included world citizenship and friendship for other nations. Harold and Earl Rugg were typical of progressive school reformers who encouraged the direct involvement of pupils by participating in democracy with first-hand activities.[110] Earl Rugg, in particular, credited the "War-issues courses" with eliciting inquiries into the values of citizenship and patriotism.

Progressive educators during this period were beginning to recognize the importance of economics and world trade. One educator recognized the key role of "historical geography" and showed an early awareness of geopolitics:

> In my classes in history I have endeavored to collect all the war maps possible . . . The student can see why Belgium is the battleground.[111]

Toward the end of the twenties, the aims of the Cardinal Principles of 1918 had come to fruition, with the active participation of students in extracurricular projects for direct training in citizenship. In secondary schools, the civics and industrial clubs trained students "for the business world and other future contacts."[112] One chart illustrated the activities of a Chicago "Clean-up and Paint-Up Project." Student action included "alley lots cleaned, outbuildings painted, rats killed, woodwork varnished and fences painted."[113]

CURRICULUM GUIDES FOR PEACE EDUCATION

Several guides for peace education were major accomplishments during this period. Two were published by the American School Peace League, one in 1914: *A Course in*

Citizenship and *Course with Type Studies, Books 1, 2, 3, and
4. (An American Citizenship Course in United States History)*
published in 1921 by the League's successor, the American
School Citizenship League. In addition, a student textbook
from 1928 incorporated the aims of peace education and
citizenship education.

The American School Peace League implemented its
blueprint for peace education with a planned curriculum,
which reflected directly the major goals of contemporary
curriculum developers. A curriculum guide was the direct
result of committee efforts, groups of classroom teachers
working together. The guide illustrated the objectives of
peace education, especially as they related to the formation
of good citizens.[114]

Idealism and pragmatism were evident in the Cabot-
Andrews curriculum guide of 1914. The aim was "to devise a
practical working outline for teachers, designed to aid their
efforts in giving children an ideal of human brotherhood."[115]
The wish was also expressed that the guide would offer
"ethical instruction that would pass into ethical action with
opportunities both for action and training in grasping the
principles of right-doing."[116] The idealistic dream of teaching
children a praiseworthy goal, love of humanity through
peace education, was wedded to pragmatic instruction in
civics and ethics.

A carefully planned sequence of instruction was designed,
beginning with grade one through grade four, with children
taught about noted heroes and national holidays. The goals
for a future generation were emphasized as the attainment of
a "co-operative spirit . . . and individual power, physical,
intellectual or moral."

The History Committee reported in League *Proceedings*
that "highly socialized men or women were demanded in a
Christianized democracy like ours."[117] These sentiments of
idealism, combined with a pragmatic spirit were similar to
those expressed by Mann in an earlier generation:

Our nation cannot afford to have ignorant, prejudiced
or corrupt citizens . . . Every child in our nation belongs
in the teacher's care. If she can instill and inflame in him
love and loyalty to his ties, she will have rescued and
redeemed the nation.[118]

The sequential development for the teaching of peace and
goodwill appeared in the Cabot-Andrews guide in the units
for grades seven and eight. Here, the ideals of membership
and citizenship in the "World Family" were key concepts.
During March, the "Growth of Law as an Agency for
Promoting Good-Will" was taught. The keynote for the unit
was written by David Starr Jordan, a major force in
Andrews' network and President of the NEA in the early
days of the League. His selection stated: "Peace is the
permanence of law. Under Peace, the affairs of nations as
well as the affairs of individual men will be settled by
judges."[119]

The chapter objective in "World Family" brought the
pupils into direct relationship to the goodwill movement by
urging them to do what they can to help "in the broader
sphere of world relations."[120] The authors had carefully
planned to advance the student through membership in a
family, school, town, state, nation, and then the world in
order to outline the obligations that such world citizenship
entailed: "These obligations make up the sum total of
citizenship. . . Before one is an American, he (and she) is a
human being."[121]

The Cabot-Andrews guide had suggestions for study that
included the published works of peace education network
contacts. Books by Jordan, Addams, Andrews, the Meads,
as well as the *Yearbooks* of the American School Peace
League were all suggested in a special section labeled:
"Special Reading for the Teacher."

Just as Andrews gathered her colleagues together to
develop peace education activities she also used them as a
soundingboard for pretesting the curriculum outline. She

sent copies of the course of study to "nearly a hundred superintendents of schools, presidents of colleges and of normal schools and professors of education throughout the United States."[122]

The League roster, for example, listed hundreds of key decisionmakers. These comprised a communications and distribution system already in existence. This network of educators, formed originally at the time of the Second National Peace Congress in 1909 further expanded from 1911 to 1916 in the course of activities at the Peace League and the NEA's annual meetings. Andrews reported that the reception of the course outline survey was "almost uniformly favorable" and consequently many talks were being given as a result, at educational meetings in America and in Europe.[123] It was at these meetings that she proposed her plan for an International Bureau for Education, with headquarters preferably in The Hague.

The years after World War I ended, marked a new path for the American School Peace League, which was renamed the American School Citizenship League. In the Preface to *Book 1* of the *Course with Type Studies,* the background of the curriculum guide authorship was explained. The History Committee of the Peace League completed most of the writing, which commenced in 1913 in Philadelphia, at the time of the meeting of the NEA. The Committee included: Philander P. Claxton, United States Commissioner of Education, who had authorized publication and distribution of the *Peace Day Bulletin.* Others on the committee included: Charles E. Chadsey, Dean of the College of Education at the University of Illinois; James Van Sickle, Superintendent of Schools, Springfield, Massachusetts; and John Hall, Dean of the School of Education at the University of Nevada. Andrews reserved for herself the final editing responsibility.

The four books in the *Type Studies* published for the American School Citizenship League in 1921 were in sharp contrast to the Cabot-Andrews peace education text of 1914. There were limited discussions of teaching the causes of war and little identification with peace education or the original organization.[124] Citizenship education became the central focus and provided a direct link to peace education through the parent organization, the original American School Peace League. In reaction perhaps to the adverse publicity from the Lusk Commission charges of the prior year (1920), all references to peace education activities were omitted from the *Type Studies*. The low profile of the American School Citizenship League was apparent throughout the text. Citizenship education had replaced peace education. The evolution of the course involved eight years of curriculum development, writing, and editing. The history texts produced were described as "An American Citizenship Course in United States History." The vigorous attacks of the Lusk Commission and the National Security League, as well as the legitimization of World War I, may have been the overwhelming circumstances. It was apparent that the original purpose of the curriculum guides as peace education had been changed.

ADVENTURES IN CITIZENSHIP: LITERATURE FOR CHARACTER

In 1928, a textbook appeared with goals similar to those of the American School Peace League. Grace Hull Stewart, an English instructor and C. C. Hanna, Head of the English department at Lakewood (Ohio) High School were the authors. *Adventures in Citizenship: Literature for Character* included world citizenship as a major aim in order to "promote the spirit of good will among nations."[125]

Recognition was given to the Cardinal Principles, with organization of the book designed to reflect "vocational competence, worthy home membership, leisure activities and good health."

In general, the aim of the curriculum guide was to teach citizenship through literature with a "program of literary

value plus constructive activity which will create good
citizens now." Exercises for the development of American
patriotism emphasized world citizenship, exalting courage,
honesty, and good character. The student met first, "Heroes
of America" and then "World Heroes." The adventures
which accompanied the text subdivisions played an "important part in the formation of habits, attitudes and points of
view that will impel young people to be civically and morally
desirable persons."[126]

The portrayal of these "Heroes" reflected the goals of
early peace educators. The emphasis was on heroes whose
ethical conduct and social service were of help to humanity.
Scientists and inventors dominated the list. But for the first
time a new type of hero emerged, "The public-spirited
businessman who enters the public-service field for the sake
of public service."[127]

In the section, "Part V. Adventures in the Making of a
Citizen," peace education and a global perspective were
championed by Newton D. Baker, former Secretary of War
in Woodrow Wilson's Cabinet. He had become an "ardent
peace exponent" due to his wartime experiences. His "Peace
Message to Young Americans" declared that "the common
interest of all people in peace is greater than any possible
self-interest which part of the people can gratify through
war."[128] He challenged America's young people to organize
"the forces of good will and conciliation" for the friendly
amicable "machinery that would keep peace."[129]

The Stewart-Hanna text proposed a variety of projects,
topics, and class activities to support peace education. For
example, a study of peace societies and their histories was
suggested, along with the observance of May 18 as Goodwill
Day.

Students read about youth organizations, such as the
Fellowship of Youth for Peace, World Brotherhood of Boys,
and International Post Box (Girl Scouts). Recognition was
also given to projects that involved geography and economics
and showed students that the "total cost of one week of

World War I could have been spent for the greater good of the community."[130] This was a theme included in the writing of Lucia Ames Mead.

The importance of moral and ethical values received prominence. In a pioneering effort at values clarification, "Problems for Consideration," the student faced moral dilemmas that called "for the courage and honesty of a good citizen in their solution."

The Stewart-Hanna textbook thus emphasized the ideals of world citizenship as well as traditional moral values that had persisted from the nineteenth century—threads from the early peace society journals that had been expressed also by Mann, Andrews, Addams, and the Meads.

WRITINGS ON WORLD CITIZENSHIP

A valuable link between peace education and citizenship education came into view. William G. Carr devoted his entire book, *Education for World-Citizenship* to various aspects of "World Citizenship and the Schools" as related to various parts of the curriculum. He recognized the revitalized, reorganized field of social studies and the "value of socialized extra-curricular activities" in teaching children "why and how to co-operate." He believed, as did many educators writing during this era, that "the social studies must be the heart of the curriculum."[131] He cited increased legislative enactments requiring instruction in civics and history with emphasis on the "social aspects of education." He summed up that the major goal of education should be "pleasant association and effective co-operation."[132]

Carr linked citizenship education and peace education, as being unbreakable bonds necessary in an age of "increasing interdependence of nations."[133] Cooperation, he stated, must be the process by which education for world citizenship could be accomplished because "the very existence of the race of men may depend upon our ability to learn the lessons of co-operative world citizenship." In a stern warning, he said:

> If these lessons go unheeded the entire fabric of civilization cannot long endure . . . We must choose instead between co-operating or risking the destruction of everything which makes co-operation worthwhile.[134]

Carr praised American schools as playing an important role in toppling the barriers of distrust and hatred for foreign countries. He stressed that through organizations students benefited the most in learning about world citizenship.[135] He especially singled out the American School Citizenship League as a good example.[136]

SCIENTIFIC RESEARCH STUDY FOR WORLD FRIENDSHIP

During this era, the scientific research study was advocated as the appropriate method for formulating a course of study for world friendship and understanding. Henry Lester Smith and Sherman Gideon Crayton of Indiana University authored a definitive study.[137]

The results of a questionnaire sent to 450 educators concerning a program for world friendship revealed that "integration of subject matter throughout the curriculum . . . with material that could be concrete and distinctly objective" would be the most efficient method.[138] Smith and Crayton believed that the curriculum should give the child "the truth concerning other peoples . . . while permitting him to formulate his own attitudes of mind."[139]

Smith, Dean of the School of Education at Indiana University, also addressed the Atlanta meeting of the NEA in 1929 and outlined many of the major results of the survey:

> We realize that if the individuals who compose a nation are to realize this training for world friendship and

understanding, they must receive such training before
they reach maturity and . . . through the medium of the
public schools.[140]

Recognition was given to the concept of peace as a
desirable individual trait: "If peace, harmony and understanding exist within the child's family, he will have the
necessary background for an understanding of the desirabil-
ity of such a relationship with the Family of Nations."[141]

A common theme expressed frequently by educators
writing during this era was that the organization of the
League of Nations should be the standard bearer for world
citizenship.[142] Peace education and world citizenship in this
period reflected the latent power of a growing force for
international understanding.

FANNIE FERN ANDREWS AND INTERNATIONAL EDUCATION

The efforts of Andrews as a pioneer in international
education deserved wider recognition. Along with the first
stirrings for peace education, the parallel goal of international education emerged. Andrews played a central role in
these endeavors. She forged common bonds with educators
in other nations. As an outgrowth of her American School
Peace League activities, she travelled extensively throughout
Western Europe and Great Britain. Her plans for an
international council on education were approved as early as
1910 at the time of the Eighteenth Peace Conference held in
Stockholm. Andrews' plans included an international library, a translation division, and an educational journal, all
designed to function as a clearinghouse for international
education. Her dreams failed at first, but eventually were
achieved years later.

Andrews was in frequent contact with ministries of
education and became convinced that their official approval

was necessary before infusion of peace education in the curriculum, national or international, would be possible. In 1911, President William Howard Taft named her as special Collaborator in the United States Office of Education. During her meetings with educational leaders and government officials in America and abroad, she had received their unofficial support.

She visited The Hague frequently, the site of the international tribunal for arbitration, and so, approached the government of the Netherlands as a logical host for her organizing conference to set up the bureau for international education.[143] In 1912 she visited several ministries of education and discerned that the majority of European countries were interested and would be represented at the conference. However, within months after the invitations were issued only two had accepted, France and Switzerland. In fact, even the United States declined an invitation because of congressional passage of the Deficiency Act in 1914. The Act required the express permission of Congress before the government could allow official representation at any international congress.

Postponement of the conference was inevitable until 1914. Then in January of that year the Netherlands once again issued invitations. Since Europe was then on the eve of World War I, interest in the conference was limited and the response discouraging. Andrews' proposals were considered the best approach to an international bureau of education. However, it was not until 1929 that the International Bureau of Education was finally established in Geneva. It later was absorbed as an affiliate of the United Nations Educational, Scientific, and Cultural Organization (UNESCO). The Center's present library contains 100,000 books, periodicals, journals, and documents on education throughout the world; a microfiche collection from international conferences on education; and several computerized data bases from UNESCO and other organizations including the American-based ERIC Clearinghouse on Higher Education.[144]

Andrews received her doctoral degree in international relations from Radcliffe in 1923. Her doctoral dissertation was on the legal aspects of the mandatory system, one of the earliest examinations of the growing problems of the Arabs, Jews, and Christians in Palestine under the British Mandate. Her book on this subject, *The Holy Land Under Mandate,* reflected on the issues of Zionism and the independence of a Palestinian state and was based on extensive travels she made to that region.[145]

Her citation for an honorary degree from Radcliffe read:

> Dr. Andrews is extraordinarily well equipped for the multifarious tasks she undertakes as a representative of her country abroad and as an official at home . . . She has the background of natural gifts, breadth of scholarship, extensive travels, and contact with great minds and outstanding personalities.[146]

It is especially Andrews' early conception of the vital role of citizenship education in a democracy that is worthy of recognition. Guidelines from the National Council for the Social Studies (NCSS) emphasized that preparation of students as "citizen actors" in a democracy should constitute the central role of the social studies teacher.[147] Andrews first conceived that preparation for citizenship played a vital role in the curriculum. America's educators and researchers can be justly proud of Fannie Fern Andrews as a true pioneer of peace and international education.

AFTERTHOUGHTS

The chronicle of peace education in this era reveals two distinguishing elements. The first is the heritage of ethics and a moral education for America's youth as a logical goal for education. The second is that education for world citizenship, a legacy of this period, can be viewed as an antecedent of our contemporary global education. Evidence of these elements and their links appeared especially in the writings of those who authored the curriculum of this era.

The school textbooks and writings of peace educators of this period underscored the emergence of a new mindset. This mindset embodied the concept that world citizenship, when blended with character education, could be translated into activism. This activism was manifested to some degree in the schools in this era. For example, children engaged in community service projects and participated in Civics Clubs as common extracurricular ventures.

The nineteenth-century penchant for character education took on new meaning as an ethical base for the transmission of the culture and mores of society. Peace educators, such as the Meads, reshaped this emphasis on morality to encompass world law with a mechanism for achieving international justice.

As an outgrowth of reforms initiated by Progressive educators, economics, world trade, and an embryonic geopolitics appeared to seep into the curriculum, especially in social studies. The attention of children was also directed to the lives of children in other lands and, in some cases, American youth reached out to foreign children as pen pals in a gesture of friendship.

Finally, according to one writer, in this era citizenship education and peace education became linked as unbreakable bonds needed for a world of interdependent nations. Indeed, world citizenship was presented as the rightful inheritance of America's youth.

The concept of an American as a world citizen showed a logical progression. Connections were made between education for citizenship, first at home, and then incrementally by rationalizing the need for education for world citizenship. Global education has been described mistakenly as a child of the post-World War II era or even the 1960s. Yet, the roots of a global perspective undergirded the idea of world citizenship advocated by many peace educators of this era. Historic parallels between this era and America in the 1990s now seem more logical as events on the world scene change with ever greater rapidity and highlight the interdependency of nations.

Notes

Sources for historical background of this period were: Daniel J. Boorstin, *The Americans: The Democratic Experience* (New York: Random House, 1973), and *A History of the United States* (Lexington, MA: Ginn & Co., 1983); Alistair Cooke, *Alistair Cooke's America* (New York: Alfred A. Knopf, 1973); Sidney Lens, *Radicalism in America* (New York: Thomas Y. Crowell, 1969); *Marvels of 1924,* ed. Francis J. Reynolds (New York: International Magazine Co., 1925).

Sources for background in education for this period were: Theodore Brameld, *Patterns of Educational Philosophy* (New York: World Book Company, 1960); Frederick G. Bonser, *The Elementary School Curriculum* (New York: Macmillan, 1921); Raymond E. Callahan, *An Introduction to Education in American Society* (New York: Alfred A. Knopf, 1961); Lawrence A. Cremin, *The Transformation of the School: Progressivism in American Education, 1876–1957* (New York: Alfred A. Knopf, 1961); *American Education: The Metropolitan Experience, 1876–1980* (New York: Harper Row, 1988); and Carlton Washburne, *What Is Progressive Education?* (New York: The John Day Company, 1952).

Sources for the history of the American peace movement were : John Whiteclay Chambers II, ed. *The Eagle and the Dove: The American Peace Movement and U.S. Foreign Policy, 1900–1922* (New York: Garland Publishing, Inc., 1976); Charles Chatfield, ed. *Peace Movements in America* (New York: Schocken Books, 1973); Charles DeBenedetti, *The Peace Reform in American History* (Bloomington, IN: Indiana University Press, 1980); C. Roland Marchand, *The American Peace Movement and Social Reform, 1898–1918* (Princeton:

Princeton University Press, 1972); and D. S. Patterson, *Toward a Warless World: The Travail of the American Peace Movement, 1887–1914* (Bloomington, IN: Indiana University Press, 1980).

1. Lake Mohonk Conference on International Arbitration, Reports 1909, ed. Lawrence M. Haughton, micro-opaque (New York: Clearwater Publishing, 1976), 185.
2. David S. Patterson, "Nicholas Murray Butler," *Biographical Dictionary of Internationalists,* ed. Warren F. Kuehl (Westport, CT: Greenwood Press, 1983), 495–496.
3. C. Roland Marchand, *The American Peace Movement and Social Reform, 1898–1918* (Princeton: Princeton University Press, 1972), 100–101.
4. Darryl Revoldt, "Edwin Ginn," *Biographical Dictionary of Internationalists,* 295.
5. Revoldt, "Edwin Ginn," 295.
6. Patterson, *Toward a Warless World,* 134.
7. Second National Peace Congress, *Proceedings,* ed. Charles E. Beals, (Boston: American Peace Society, 1909), 454–455.
8. Clinton F. Fink, "Fannie Fern Andrews," *Biographical Dictionary of Internationalists,* 19–20.
9. Second National Peace Congress, *Proceedings,* 455–456.
10. *Proceedings,* 46–47.
11. *Proceedings,* 49–50, and *American School Citizenship League: An Eleven Year Survey of the Activities of the American School Peace League from 1908 to 1919* (Boston, 1919), 11.
12. The American School Peace League, *Yearbook, 1913–1914* (Boston: The American School Peace League, 1913), 90.
13. United States Bureau of Education, *Peace Day Bulletin* (Washington, DC: United States Bureau of Education, 1912), 8.
14. National Education Association (Department of Superintendence), *Bulletin,* Cincinnati Meeting, 24–26 February 1915 (Washington, DC: National Education Association, 1915), 24.
15. Edward T. Fairchild, President's Address, National Education Association *Bulletin,* September 1913 (Washington, DC: National Education Association, 1913), 7.
16. NEA *Bulletin,* February 1915, 24.
17. Fannie Fern Andrews, "The Relation of Teachers to the Peace

Movement," *Education* 28 (January 1908): 289. Other publications by Andrews were: *The Freedom of the Seas: The Immunity of Private Property at Sea in Time of War* (The Hague: M. Nijhoff, 1917); *The Holy Land Under Mandate* (Boston: Houghton Mifflin, 1931) and *Memory Pages of My Life* (Boston: Talisman Press, 1948). Her Master's thesis from Radcliffe College in 1923 was "The Mandatory System After the World War." Magazine and journal articles included: "Charms of Kidney Pond," *New England Magazine* 38 (April 1908): 222–228; "Parents' Associations and the Public Schools," *Charities* 17 (November 24, 1906): 335–343; "Course of Study in Good-Will," *Religious Education* 6 (February 3, 1912): 570–573; and "Relation of Teachers To International Peace," *Journal of Education* 68 (December 17, 1908).
Note: The personal papers of Fannie Fern Andrews are in Schlesinger Library at Radcliffe College in Cambridge. They include 91 volumes and 163 boxes of folders, pamphlets, brochures and correspondence, including some of the prize-winning essays of children submitted during the years that the Peace League held annual essay contests.

18. Lucia Ames Mead, *Law or War* (Garden City, NY: Doubleday, Doran & Co., 1928), viii. Rose Forbes (Mrs. J. Malcolm) was the author of *The Peace Movement and Some Misconceptions,* n.p., n.d. In John Lofland, et al. *Peace Movement Organizations and Activists in the U.S.: An Analytic Bibliography* (Binghamton, NY: Haworth Press, 1991), 52. See also the excellent, carefully-researched biography, *Lucia Ames Mead (1856–1936) and the American Peace Movement* by John Craig (Lewiston, NY: Edwin Mellen Press, 1990). The papers of Lucia and Edwin Mead are in the Swarthmore College Library Peace Collection.
19. Lucia Mead, 24.
20. Lucia Mead, 26.
21. Lucia Mead, 31.
22. Lucia Mead, 30–31.
23. Lucia Mead, 30–31.
24. Lucia Mead, 30.
25. Darryl Revoldt, "Edwin D. Mead," *Biographical Dictionary of Internationalists,* 494.

26. Edwin Mead, "The Teaching of Peace," *The Outlook* 83 (16 June 1906): 355–357.
27. Edwin Mead, 356.
28. Edwin Mead, "Heroes of Peace," *The Outlook* (14 November 1908): 577–582.
29. Edwin Mead, "Heroes," 577–582.
30. Edwin Mead, "Heroes," 577–582.
31. Lucia Mead, *Law or War,* 30.
32. Darryl Revoldt, "Lucia True Ames Mead," *Biographical Dictionary of Internationalists,* 495–496. Other publications by Lucia Mead included: *Great Thoughts for Little Thinkers* (New York: G. P. Putnam's Sons, 1889); *To Whom Much Is Given* (New York: T. Y. Crowell & Co., 1899). *Memoirs of a Millionaire* (Boston: Houghton Mifflin, 1889); *Milton's England,* Boston: L. C. Page & Co., 1903); *Primer of the Peace Movement* (Boston: American Peace Society, 1904); *Patriotism and the New Internationalism* (Boston: Ginn & Co., 1906); *Swords or Plowshares* (New York: G. P. Putnam's Sons, 1912); and *Law or War* (New York: Doubleday, Doran and Co., 1928). Other articles by Lucia Mead were: "How Schools Should Instill Patriotism," *Journal of Education* 80 (July 9, 1914); "Practical Suggestions for Peace Day," *Journal of Education* (May 7, 1914), and others too numerous to mention. She was also a frequent writer of letters to editors and overlooked few opportunities to write or speak about peace issues.
33. Catherine W. McCulloch, compiler, "Illinois Friends of Woman Suffrage," notebook, n.d. (Evanston, IL: Woman's Library, Northwestern University, 1943), in the Archives, Rockford College, Rockford, IL, 19. McCulloch, a lawyer, was a classmate of Jane Addams. She served as legal advisor and vice president of the National Woman's Suffrage Association.
    Note: A collection of primary source materials, including student publications of the Rockford Female Seminary as well as memorabilia of Jane Addams are also in the Archives at Rockford College. Other reflections on Jane Addams' formative student years appeared in Lucy F. Townsend, *The Best Helpers of One Another: Anna Peck Sill and the Struggle for*

Woman's Education (Chicago: Educational Studies Press, 1988).

34. *Rockford Seminary Magazine,* 1 (January 1873): 5.
35. *Rockford Seminary Magazine,* 8 (April 1880): 264.
36. *Magazine,* 8 (April 1880): 110.
37. *Magazine,* 8 (April 1880): 110.
38. *Magazine,* 1 (July 1873): 32, 39.
39. Jane Addams, *Memorials to Anna P. Sill, 1840–1889* (Rockford, IL: Daily Register Electric Print, 1889), 72.
40. *Magazine,* 9 (December 1881): 204–205.
41. *Magazine,* 9 (December 1881): 264.
42. Jane Addams, *My Friend, Julia Lathrop* (New York: Macmillan, 1935), 50–51.
43. Jane Addams, "Disarmament and Life," *Jane Addams on Peace, War and International Understanding,* ed. Allen F. Davis. (New York: Garland Press 1976), 177.
44. Jane Addams, *Peace and Bread in Time of War* (New York: Macmillan, 1917), 50.
45. *Rockford Seminary Magazine,* 9 (November 1881): 34.
46. Jane Addams, *Newer Ideals of Peace* (New York: Macmillan, 1906), 237.
47. Charles F. Howlett, *Troubled Philosopher: John Dewey and the Struggle for World Peace* (Port Washington, NY: Kinnekat Press, 1977) and Harriet H. Alonso, *The Women's Peace Union and the Outlawry of War, 1921–1942* (Knoxville, TN: University of Tennessee Press, 1989). Alonso identified the twenties as a most encouraging decade for peace activists who were engaged in lobbying, but still suspect because peace was considered a "subversive" activity. (Preface, xv). An Appendix of Interwar Peace Organizations identified several engaged in peace education, including many high school peace clubs in the New York City area.
48. John Dewey, *Impressions of Soviet Russia and the Revolutionary World* (New York: New Republic, 1929), 64.
49. John Dewey, *Impressions,* 86.
50. John Dewey, *Impressions,* 90.
51. John Dewey, *Impressions,* 96.
52. John Dewey, *Human Nature and Conduct* (New York: Henry Holt Co., 1922), 29. See also William Paringer, *John Dewey*

92 Peace Education in America

and the Paradox of Liberal Reform (Albany, NY: State University of New York Press, 1990).

53. The History of Woman Suffrage, Vol. V., ed. Ida Husted Harper. (n.p.: National American Woman Suffrage Association, 1922) 253.
54. Fannie Fern Andrews, "The American School Peace League and the European War," Proceedings, The American School Peace League, 1914–1915 (Boston: The American School Peace League, 1915), 9–10.
55. Woman's Peace Party, Addresses at the Organizing Conference, January 10, 1915 (Chicago: Woman's Peace Party, 1915), 260. See also Catherine Foster, Woman For All Seasons: The Story of the Women's International League for Peace and Freedom. (Athens, GA: University of Georgia Press, 1989) and Robert Booth Fowler, Carrie Catt: Feminist Politician (Boston: Northeastern University Press, 1986).
56. Woman's Peace Party, Addresses, xx.
57. Addresses, 261.
58. Lucia Ames Mead, Law or War.
59. Katherine Devereaux Blake, "Peace Heroes," The Kindergarten-Primary Magazine 24 (March 1912): 179; Bertha Johnston, "To Exercise the Heroic Impulses: A Substitute for Military Drill," The Kindergarten-Primary Magazine 24 (April 1912); David Starr Jordan, "Our Blighted Race," Journal of Education 82 (9 September 1915): 213; W. D. Parkinson, "Public School and Military Drill," Journal of Education 82 (November 1915): 451–453.
60. Jane Addams, Newer Ideals of Peace, 234.
61. "Towards Peace and Freedom," Report on the Zurich Congress of the Women's International League for Peace and Freedom (1919), reprint, John Whiteclay Chambers II, ed. The Eagle and the Dove, 460–461. Biographies of Woodrow Wilson include: Jan Nordholt, Woodrow Wilson: A Life for World Peace (Berkeley: University of California Press, 1991) and August Heckscher, Woodrow Wilson (New York: Charles Scribner's Sons, 1991).
62. Report, 461.
63. Report, 461.
64. Report, 461.
65. David Starr Jordan, Ways To Lasting Peace (Indianapolis:

Bobbs-Merrill, 1916) and *Towards an Enduring Peace: Symposium of Peace Proposals and Programs, 1914–1916* (New York: American Association for International Conciliation, 1916).

66. Bruce M. Stave, *Socialism and the Cities* (Port Washington, NY: Kennikat Press, 1975), 10–66.
67. Sam Keen, *Faces of the Enemy: Reflections of the Hostile Imagination* (New York: Harper Row, 1986); Jacques Ellul, *Propaganda* (New York: Vintage Books, 1973); and Robert Jay Lifton, *Home from the War* (New York: Simon and Schuster, 1973).
68. Stanley Milgram, *Obedience to Authority: An Experimental View* (New York: Harper Row, 1974).
69. Social-Democratic Party, *Milwaukee Municipal Campaign Book, 1912* (Milwaukee, WI County Central Committee of the Social-Democratic Party, 1912), 12.
70. *Milwaukee Municipal Campaign Book,* 14.
71. *Campaign Book,* 14–15.
72. Samuel Eliot Morison and Henry Steele Commager, *Vol. 2, The Growth of the American Republic* (New York: Oxford University Press, 1950), 153. Pioneers of American labor unionism in many ways shared a fate similar to that of peace advocates. In the early struggles for labor organization, the government's use of troops during the 1919 steel strike was justified on the grounds of "violent agitation by so-called Bolsheviki and radicals," discussed in Alan Dawley, *Struggles for Justice: Social Responsibility and the Liberal State* (Cambridge, MA: Belknap Press of Harvard University Press, 1991), 243–250. A second treatise by Robert K. Murray, "Communism and the Great Steel Strike of 1919," *Mississippi Valley Historical Review* 38 (1951): 445–466 concluded that "the decline which organized labor experienced during the twenties stemmed . . . from the alleged connection between communism and the steel strike of 1919."
73. *Harvard Encyclopedia of American Ethnic Groups,* ed. Stephen Thernstrom (Cambridge, MA: Harvard University Press, 1980), 303.
74. Carl Kaestle, The Evolution of an Urban System: New York City, 1750–1890, diss., Harvard University, 1970; Michael Katz, *Class, Bureaucracy and Schools: The Illusion of Educational*

Change in America (New York: Praeger, 1971); and David B. Tyack, *The One Best System: A History of American Urban Education* (Cambridge, MA: Harvard University Press, 1974).

75. Revoldt, "Edwin D. Mead," *Biographical Dictionary*, 494.
76. *Revolutionary Radicalism: Its History, Purpose and Tactics with an Exposition and Discussion of the Steps Being Taken and Required to Curb It Being the Report of the Joint Legislative Committee (of New York State) Investigating Seditious Activities* (Albany, NY: J. B. Lyon, 1920). Also known as the Lusk Commission Report.
77. *Revolutionary Radicalism*, 988.
78. *Revolutionary Radicalism*, viii.
79. *Radicalism*, 977.
80. Nancy Cott, *Decades of Discontent: The Women's Movement, 1920–1940* (Westport, CT: Greenwood Press, 1983) and *The Grounding of American Feminism* (New Haven: Yale University Press, 1987). A conclusion reached was that anti-socialist and later anticommunist charges were used as a weapon by those in economic and political power whenever women's organizations took action for peace and social justice causes.
81. *Radicalism*, 977.
82. *Radicalism*, 978.
83. Nancy Cott, *Decades of Discontent*, 201.
84. Cott, 210.
85. *Radicalism*, 977.
86. *Radicalism*, 1077.
87. Elizabeth Dilling, *The Red Network: A "Who's Who" and Handbook of Radicalism for Patriots* (Kenilworth, IL: Published by the author, 1934), Dedication, n.p.
88. Jane Addams, *My Friend, Julia Lathrop* (New York: Macmillan, 1935), 209.
89. *Radicalism*, 1112.
90. *Radicalism*, 1078.
91. National Security League, *Proceedings of the Congress of Constructive Patriotism* (Washington, DC: National Security League, 1917).
92. National Security League, 3.
93. Dilling, Dedication, n.p.
94. Dilling, 51.
95. Dilling, 259.

96. James Weinstein, *Ambiguous Legacy: The Left in American Politics* (New York: New Viewpoints, 1975), 21.

97. Norman Hapgood, *Professional Patriots: An Exposure of the Personalities, Methods and Objectives Involved in the Organized Effort to Exploit Patriotic Impulses in These United States During and After the Late War* (New York: Albert and Charles Boni, 1927).

98. Hapgood, 102–103.

99. Hapgood, 102–103.

100. Hapgood, 102–103.

101. Frederick G. Bonser, *The Elementary School Curriculum* (New York: Macmillan, 1921), 1.

102. National Society for the Scientific Study of Education, *The First Yearbook,* including "Some Principles in the Teaching of History," ed. Lucy Salmon (Chicago: University of Chicago Press, 1902), 59.

103. National Society for the Study of Education, *The Twentieth Yearbook of the National Society for the Study of Education: Part I. Second Report of the Society's Committee on New Materials of Instruction* (Bloomington, IL: Public School Publishing Company, 1921), 116.

104. Glenn Frank, "The Approaching Renaissance of Western Civilization," The Third Lecturers' Conference on Public Opinion and World Peace (Washington, DC: The International Lyceum and Chautauqua Association, 1922), 261–264.

105. *Twentieth Yearbook,* 116.

106. *Twentieth Yearbook,* 117.

107. *Twentieth Yearbook,* 117–119.

108. *Twentieth Yearbook,* 147–148.

109. *Twenty-Second Yearbook,* 148–149.

110. Harold O. Rugg, "Do the Social Studies Prepare Pupils Adequately for Life Activities?" National Society for the Study of Education. *The Social Studies in the Elementary and Secondary School, Part II. Twenty-Second Yearbook.* Cleveland Meeting, 27 February 1923 (Bloomington, IL: Public School Publishing Company, 1923), 1–28.

111. E. V. Latham, "The Use of Current Events in the Study of Historical Geography," *Proceedings of the High School Conference,* University of Illinois (Urbana, IL: University of Illinois, 1914), 326–327.

112. National Society for the Study of Education, *The Twenty-Fifth Yearbook: Part II. Extra-Curricular Activities* (Bloomington, IL: Public School Publishing Company, 1926), 98–99.
113. *Twenty-Fifth Yearbook,* 99.
114. Ella Lyman Cabot, Fannie Fern Andrews, and others, *A Course in Citizenship and Patriotism* (Boston: Houghton Mifflin, 1914), Preface, n.p.
115. Cabot, Andrews, Preface, n.p.
116. American School Peace League, *Yearbook, 1913–1914,* 73.
117. *Yearbook,* 73.
118. Cabot, Andrews, xxii.
119. Cabot, Andrews, 359.
120. Cabot, Andrews, 374.
121. Cabot, Andrews, 374.
122. Cabot, Andrews, vi.
123. Cabot, Andrews, vi.
124. *Course with Type Studies, Books 1, 2, 3, and 4. (An American Citizenship Course in United States History)* (New York: Charles Scribner's Sons, 1921. Published for the American School Citizenship League).
125. Grace Hull Stewart and C. C. Hanna, *Adventures in Citizenship: Literature for Character* (Boston: Ginn and Company, 1928).
126. Stewart and Hanna, xx.
127. Stewart and Hanna, xx.
128. Stewart and Hanna, 343.
129. Stewart and Hanna, 349.
130. Stewart and Hanna, 349.
131. William G. Carr, *Education for World-Citizenship* (Stanford, CA: Stanford University Press, 1928).
132. Carr, 4.
133. Carr, 5.
134. Carr, 5.
135. Carr, 5.
136. Carr, 23.
137. Henry L. Smith and Sherman G. Crayton, *Tentative Program for Teaching World Friendship and Understanding in Teacher Training Institutions and in Public Schools for Children Who Range from Six to Fourteen Years of Age* (Bloomington, IN: Indiana University, Bureau of Cooperative Research, 1929).

138. Smith and Crayton, 26.

139. Smith and Crayton, 26.

140. Henry L. Smith, "Education for World Friendship and Understanding–Abstract," *Proceedings,* Atlanta Meeting, 8 June–4 July 1929 (Washington, DC: National Education Association, 1929), 231–237.

141. Smith and Crayton, 29.

142. William R. Lingo, "World Peace through Education with Text of Plan," *Educational Review* 70 (October 1925): 128–133 and Boutelle E. Lowe, *International Education for Peace* (Brooklyn, NY: F. Weidner Publishing Co., 1929).

143. David G. Scanlon, "Pioneers of International Education, 1817–1914," *Teachers College Record* 62 (January 1959): 219.

144. "Center in Geneva Builds an Unusual Library on Higher Education but Funds Are Limited," *Chronicle of Higher Education* 35 (25 January 1989), A38.

145. Fannie Fern Andrews, The Mandatory System After the World War. Master's thesis. Radcliffe College, 1923 and *Holy Land under Mandate.* (Boston: Houghton Mifflin, 1913).

146. Citation upon admittance to the Associates of Phi Beta Kappa in 1942. Biographical sketch. p. 10. Papers of Fannie Fern Andrews. Schlesinger Library, Radcliffe College.

147. National Council for the Social Studies. "Revision of the NCSS Social Studies Curriculum Guidelines." *Social Education* 43 (April 1979): 261–278 and "Social Studies for Early Childhood and Elementary School Children Preparing for the 21st Century: A Report from NCSS Task Force on Early Childhood/Elementary Social Studies." *Social Education* 53 (January 1989): 14–23.

4.   EDUCATION FOR INTERNATIONAL FRIENDSHIP AND GOODWILL, 1931–1941

INTRODUCTION

The early years of the thirties were auspicious ones but one event in particular had far-reaching implications for humanity.[1] Leo Szilard, an Hungarian-born physicist, recorded in his memoirs that he received his first inspiration, while out walking on a London street, for the chain reaction that would enable the design of the world's first atomic bomb. He confided:

> As the light changed to green and I crossed the street . . . it . . . occurred to me that if we could find an element which is split by neutrons and would emit two neutrons . . . if assembled in . . . large mass (it) could sustain a nuclear chain reaction.[2]

Science and technology cast a long shadow into the future and influenced forthcoming political events throughout civilization. The power of the atom with its unknown consequences for humanity would overshadow each subsequent decade, including the present.

In 1933 President Franklin Delano Roosevelt presided over the Montevideo Conference and ushered in a new Pan American policy for the United States. He proclaimed that he would dedicate America "to the policy of the good neighbor." Despite his benevolent intentions growing numbers of Americans had become suspicious of America's participation in World War I. Isolationism became a political

98

reality and coexisted alongside the good neighbor policy. Isolationism and internationalism, conceived as a thrust for world citizenship, were twin influences during the thirties. These provided an impetus to intellectual and political debates in diplomatic as well as educational circles.

In 1933 Adolf Hitler came to power with a campaign built around the slogan "Work, Freedom and Bread," the rallying cry for his National Socialist Party. He received a mandate from the electorate when 13 million Germans voted him into office.[3]

A master of propaganda, Hitler was portrayed to the German people as a leader especially attentive to youth. Photographs taken of him in this decade often showed him surrounded by admiring groups of uniformed boys or girls.[4] His plans included selective breeding to produce a superior strain of human, for his so-called master race. At the same time, he was planning for the extermination of groups which he deemed as inferior and undesirable, a plan that would be implemented during the war years of the 1940s. (The extent of the resultant holocaust and decimation of Germans and other conquered peoples unfortunate enough to be Jews, gypsies, mentally retarded, or handicapped was realized fully only in post-World War II years.) By 1934, Hitler assembled a private army of 445,000. He gained support from Germans with a program that promised solutions for unemployment and inflation.[5]

By the late 1930s Hitler had launched an offensive into the Saar, the Rhineland, and Austria that would ultimately engulf a major portion of the globe in a massive world war. Such moves in Germany reaffirmed for many people that militarism, as a German national trait, was an ingrained force from past history. In 1932 in Japan a militarist regime also came into power and joined Germany as an Axis ally.

A renewed interest in internationalism and a reinforcement of aspirations for a global perspective strengthened education for peace between the two world wars. As in the past, ideas were shaped by forces in American society and by international events. General themes were formulated by educators with concepts that have continued from this era, 1931–1941, until the present day.

During this era the central tenets of peace education were:

(1) *The interdependence of the nations of the world and a knowledge base in geography and history as a reflection of the importance of world trade.* Educators devised curriculum units for public and religious-based programs that included an embryonic global perspective.

(2) *World citizenship—a precept carried over from the previous decade—was recommended as an adjunct to citizenship education for newly enfranchised women.* The American School Citizenship League in particular continued to write and disseminate its four textbooks for citizenship education and added units in each for world citizenship. These goals had been promoted by Fannie Fern Andrews since 1974 and by Lucia and Edwin Mead from as far back as the 1920s.

(3) *"The brotherhood of man"—expressed as international friendship and good will for humanity.* This was considered more than a slogan by the peace educators of the nineteenth century. A research study undertaken in the 1930s provided added confirmation that this concept was on a solid, curricular base. Progressive educators viewed this area as the logical evolution and destiny for American education.

(4) *Examination of the role of education in a democracy, especially the inclusion of character education helped to expand sentiment favoring an ethical, value-based education.* Moral education was often translated into character development and became a focus of several educational yearbooks.

These themes were often intermingled. For example, a leading woman suffragist, Carrie Chapman Catt, first advocated citizenship education for women in their first years of enfranchisement and then turned next to the promotion of peace education with international friendship.

These themes and voices reverberated throughout the 1930s until the call to war in 1941 once more beckoned the American people with idealistic and praiseworthy motives. World War II ended efforts for peace education. But at the same time there was a reawakening as to the need to devise ways to end civilization's deadly grip on war. Until the outbreak of the global conflict, peace educators envisioned a new generation as members of a world community in a family of nations. These goals were reflected in the curriculum as education for international friendship and goodwill.

EVOLUTION OF A GLOBAL PERSPECTIVE: WOMAN SUFFRAGE AND CITIZENSHIP EDUCATION

Carrie Chapman Catt, a prominent woman suffragist who had led women to a successful enactment of the right to vote in 1920, was actively involved in efforts for world peace during the thirties. Fifteen years earlier, in 1915, she had assisted Jane Addams in the founding of the Woman's Peace Party. Then in 1925, she convened the first of several Conferences on the Cause and Cure of War, which became annual events until America's entry into World War II.

At the First Conference, Catt addressed the 450 delegates who represented 5 million women members of nine sponsoring organizations. She reminded them of their struggles in the suffrage movement: "Agitation for a cause is excellent; education is better; but organization is the only assurance of final triumph . . . in a self-governing nation."[6]

She believed that education for the informed exercise of citizenship was paramount. A second objective, however, was to reach out beyond America's borders in international friendship and goodwill. On several occasions, Catt also noted that women had only a rudimentary knowledge of "parliamentary procedure" and deemed their civic education as a first step. Others had taken up this same cause. The League of Women Voters was founded in 1920 to help educate women in their first year of citizenship, although two prototype groups and programs were formed in an earlier decade, including a political science course for women. The League, of course, has continued until the present day to inform women of the issues involved in making intelligent decisions at the voting booth.[7]

Catt outlined the role that peace education should play in the life of the child. In 1925, at the Conference on the Cause and Cure of War, she stated that:

> The child should be equipped to perform his part in a social structure which has a world basis. The home, the library, the school and the church should be effective means to this end. With this as the first aim of education, a special care must be taken in the teaching of . . . history, geography and language . . . as textbooks are interpreters of the world as a whole.[8]

A major objective of Catt's advocacy at these Conferences was the enactment of the Kellogg-Briand Pact of 1928. The Pact was conceived jointly by President Calvin Coolidge's Secretary of State, Frank Kellogg, and the French premier, Aristide Briand, who believed that a pact between America and France might prevent conflicts like World War I.[9]

International organizations and American peace groups, such as the American School Citizenship League and the Outlawry of War Crusade (Chapter 3), supported such action well into the thirties. The Pact was signed by most nations, condemned war, and included provisions to settle disputes peacefully, but it had few actual enforcement sanctions. Moreover, within a few weeks of its signing, it was reported that the United States Congress had "appropriated $245 million to build new warships." The accomplishment of creating the Kellogg-Briand Pact was one result of the efforts of thousands in a full-fledged peace movement.

Little popular support was shown for the noble principles

of the Pact even though for generations people had dreamed of the formal, legal elimination of war.[10] For decades, statesmen and scholars would postulate on what would have happened if the Pact had been upheld and adequate safeguards for enforcement also put into place.

Another object of Catt's advocacy was the World Court which was set up at The Hague at the close of the nineteenth century and was long considered the solution for international disputes. In 1930 Catt "led delegates up Capitol Hill" as an activity at the fifth Conference on the Cause and Cure of War. The delegates presented petitions for Senate ratification of the World Court protocol. They had planned to urge President Herbert Hoover to offer evidence of the "sincere purpose of our government to uphold its commitments made through the Paris Pact."[11] However, the protocol had never been formally ratified by the United States. In 1935 President Franklin D. Roosevelt attempted to follow through on demands that the United States join the League of Nation's Court. Isolationism was at its peak however, and Roosevelt's proposal was defeated.[12]

WAR AS A PROFITABLE VENTURE: THE NYE COMMITTEE HEARINGS (1935)

The Nye Committee hearings in 1935 brought the munitions industry under public scrutiny. Excessive profits that were garnered in partnership with government interests and Wall Street bankers confirmed that war was profitable for a fortunate few. Gerald P. Nye, United States Senator from North Dakota and Committee chair, made a plea to educators to give "an equal place for peace" in the school curriculum. Some day, he reasoned, the question will be asked of educators: "Why was such education so long overlooked or ignored?"[13]

Educators in increasing numbers responded to Nye's entreaty with an outpouring of journal articles, books, research studies, and curriculum materials on peace education. In the decade from 1930 to 1940 there were over 100 citations of journal articles.[14]

The Nye hearings evoked visions of the National Security League, which included arms merchants and prominent Wall Street business interests. A few months before America's entry into World War I (1917), the league began to cloak its activities with patriotic slogans under the guise of preparedness. It then pushed strongly for increased military expenditures, with telling success, both during and after the war. But Nye reiterated what has become a much-repeated argument about the cost of security, noting that America had increased its defense budget 197 percent since 1913. He quoted Nicholas Murray Butler, then President of the Carnegie Endowment for World Peace, who calculated that money spent on World War I could have given "a thousand dollars salary to (each and every one of) 125,000 nurses and school teachers," an argument similar to that voiced by Horace Mann in the prior century.[15]

In addition, the role of propaganda or "the selling of the war" to the American people was exposed as the product of an efficient publicist. George Creel, the head of the Committee on Public Information during World War I, revealed in 1920 that the War "was a plain publicity proposition, a vast enterprise in salesmanship, the world's greatest adventure in advertising."[16]

THE GREAT DEPRESSION

An economic event in October, 1929, the advent of the Great Depression, portended a long period of adversity as a large portion of the nation coped with a precarious daily struggle for survival. The global economy was choked with huge war debts. Unemployment plagued the working classes in America and aboard. Questionable credit practices and unethical and speculative dealings on Wall Street had precipitated the financial crash, a tragedy that changed the course of American economic, social, and political history for decades. Though impacted by these circumstances, peace education moved forward on several fronts.

Peace Education with a Global Perspective

Two landmark Depression-era studies forged a direct link between peace education in the thirties and the global education curriculum of later decades, the 1970s and 1980s. The interdependence of nations and "the brotherhood of man" were themes that were expressed repeatedly in a Yearbook, *Character Education.* In 1932, the Yearbook's central theme was that, "The citizen of the future must be a citizen of the world."[17]

The Yearbook was published under the auspices of the NEA and included George S. Counts, professor of education at Columbia University, and a leading proponent of Progressive education.[18] Counts wrote a book in 1932, *Dare the School Build a New Social Order?* that moved past the usual advocacy for the child-centered school to a new viewpoint that the school could function as an agent for change in a new society.

Before America's youth could become world citizens, a critical examination of the concepts of patriotism and nationalism was needed. The role of patriotism was a special area of interest. This sentiment must be widened to embrace "other races and peoples" so that various sects can "somehow learn to live together in peace." This was necessary because "Interdependence . . . is the rule of life." These were the primary themes discussed in the Yearbook.

Nationalism was considered another "provincialized" attitude which the Yearbook considered worthy of study because war is "the chief defender of national security . . . causes, battles, victors, conquest . . . the oldest story of the classroom." However, as the Yearbook noted, the Nye

Commission had pointed out that insufficient attention had been paid to the fact that war was a "possible destroyer of civilization" and the curriculum had not included its "real role of suffering and devastation."[19]

Finally, a plea was issued for "Constructive Citizenship" as a vital aid for character education. A new attitude needed to be cultivated:

> Can we not be free to teach that the aim of our character training in citizenship is 'Our Country when she is right and our pledge to help make her right when she is wrong'?[20]

An aura of scientific research developed with the introduction of a Good Citizenship Test that supposedly would measure significant knowledge, such as "promoting peace among nations" with a " + .70 correlation with intelligence and a + .36 correlation with socio-economic status."[21] The Neumann Test of International Attitudes claimed to measure student perceptions of "national, international, imperial and militaristic problems."[22] A similar study by Smith and Crayton in 1929 (Chapter 3, pages 82–83) perhaps piqued interest in providing a research base for the serious study of attitudes and values.

Study of the attitudes needed for world citizenship and international friendship emerged in related areas. In his report of the Commission on Social Studies, also in 1932, Charles Beard, the noted historian, stated that "American society operates on a world stage" and the "rights and obligations of the United States in the family of nations . . . come clearly within the circle of thought which must be covered by social studies." Beard believed that the development of attitudes needed for world citizenship must be implicit in all instruction, but most specifically in social studies.[23]

Education for peace through international understanding was the theme developed in a study in 1937. Paul Monroe,

Director of the International Institute and professor of education at Teachers College, Columbia University, wrote of the "Disarmament of the Mind" as a condition for international understanding. He recognized the importance of new forms of communication, films and radio, as instruments for educating the general public through adult education as well as children in the public schools.[24] He believed that public school education of the younger generation should contain materials concerned with the social, economic, political, and cultural problems "not only of our own people . . . but various other peoples" as a necessary ingredient for international understanding.[25]

Professor of education, I. L. Kandel also from Teachers College stated:

> Development of international understanding is the concern of every subject in every grade of the school and . . . can only grow out of a proper teaching of nationalism.[26]

The nationalism that Kandel envisioned, though, was similar in concept to that expressed by Counts in the Yearbook, *Character Education*. It was a nationalism that would stress the interdependence of the world's people and their "common efforts as the normal trend of civilization." This kind of nationalism, Kandel believed, would furnish "a basis of common human understanding . . . and interlocking interests among nations."[27]

Role of Education in a Democracy

In 1935 the concern expressed by Counts for the use of education as an agent for social change appeared in a new guise in a Yearbook of the NEA's Department of Superintendence, titled *Social Change and Education*.[28] William G. Carr, author of *Education for World Citizenship*, a book on peace education (Chapter 3) was named as a "source of inspiration and factual data."[29] Reference was made to the revolutionary changes—social and economic—that were a way of life as Roosevelt launched various New Deal programs in an attempt to bring about reform and recovery to America. A basic reconstruction of society through education was called for with a warning that America was far from the classless, democratic society it needed to be. According to the NEA Yearbook such reform was mandated because "an actual oligarchy of wealth" appeared to be the reality of American society.[30]

An elementary plea for social justice emerged with this Yearbook. Discussion included "human rights and the shared control of social affairs . . . for all" because "laissez faire capitalism and social democracy are incompatible." Education was extolled as an important part of "the national process." In another treatise by Jesse H. Newlon reference was made to the fact that "the school was an indispensable instrument . . . for new social concepts" in Russia, Italy, and Germany with their "revolutionary regimes."[31]

Newlon pointed out that "powerful forces and subtle influences operate to control government and education . . . and the United States is no exception."[32] He mentioned explicitly the different pressure or power groups that exerted influences such as the Daughters of the American Revolution, the Socialist Party, the American Legion and the American Peace Society" as "advocates of public education . . . for different social ends."[33]

CURRICULUM FOR INTERNATIONAL FRIENDSHIP AND GOODWILL, 1931–1941

Growing awareness that education for peace deserved a place in the postwar curriculum motivated educators from both public and nonpublic schools to create innovative ways to teach for international friendship and goodwill. Religious groups and others promoted these causes in seminars, in textbooks, through peace projects, and by various other means.

Religious Groups

Major religious groups produced representative studies and guides for peace education. The emphasis on nonviolence in Quaker (Society of Friends) education was established early, during the days of William Penn's Pennsylvania colony. Quaker education also included a curriculum of "practical subjects" and coeducation as well as complete equality in the education of all races and classes.[34]

Quaker sponsorship of Institutes of International Relations and International Work Camps was initiated in 1934. International seminars were designed to "promote international understanding by bringing together for a period of study . . . students from different countries."

The emphasis on international goodwill as a major concept in Quaker schools became evident in a study of textbooks:

> The schools of this religious sect endeavor to emphasize the international idea especially in geography. In history, no peace propaganda is obvious . . . but an effort is made to find heroes who save other people's lives rather than those heroes which take them.[35]

Quaker education put into practice a peace education curriculum with an international perspective. It has remained as a viable model for the classroom up to the present. Cooperation, the instillment of nonviolence, and conflict resolution have been installed in Quaker classrooms as basic attitudes for behavior and remain as exemplary models of peace education.

In addition to the Society of Friends, contributions to peace education appeared from programs developed by other church organizations. In the thirties, a book of activities for children in Protestant Sunday schools by Annie Sills Brooks encouraged world friendship.[36] A curriculum was designed for a junior vacation school of ten days. During this time each child wrote an essay on peace. Activity projects included making and sending gifts to people of other races and countries. For example, American children were encouraged to send dolls to children in Mexico and Japan. The curriculum was similar to one designed by the American School Peace League. A prayer written for the daily program by a "Mary Jane" provided one of the few insights into the thoughts of children involved in a peace education project:

> O, dear heavenly Father, help us to keep peace, love and kindness in our hearts. We thank thee for our Bible school and parents . . . Some children think that just because they are white that you love them better, but we know that you love them all just as good as you love us. Amen.[37]

Two books from 1930 and 1937 contained peace education activities for the use of Jewish youth and adult groups. The major purpose of the *Jewish Peace Book* was to foster in children the "will to peace." Participation in the International Goodwill Day on May 18 was recommended.[38] Jewish children listened to peace stories, especially those concerning peace heroes. Salmon Levinson of the Outlawry of War peace crusade was cited as one who made a significant contribution to world peace.[39] Peace devotions for Jewish celebrations, based on Genesis and Isaiah were outlined. Friendship with foreign countries was encouraged as well as study abroad or joining peace societies.

Jewish themes for peace education were based on Talmudic literature[40] with the role of the Jewish teacher stressed:

> Throughout the ages, the Jewish teachers have sought to teach peace . . . One would have to quote the whole chapter on peace from the Talmud to recall what paramountcy has been attributed to peace by the masters of Judaism.[41]

Abraham Cronbach, author of the *Jewish Peace Book,* described an unusual event that was celebrated as part of World Goodwill Day, May 18, 1931. He described it as the first occasion when the "youth of all nations pledged each other by telephone their goodwill and expressed their common purpose to put an end to the war system."[42] He reported that:

> Telephone connections were made, from nation to nation and finally, from hemisphere to hemisphere until all continents had been linked together as they have never been united before . . . London and Washington were the focal points at which calls were received throughout the day.[43]

International friendship and goodwill linked young people together for peace symbolically, around the world. The Jewish peace education writings were significant at a time when Jewish persecution was beginning in Nazi Germany and anti-Semitism was detected in other areas. The Jewish Peace Fellowship is still in existence, actively involved with the design of peace education materials and formation of action groups.

International Friendship in a Textbook

Young Americans in 1934 were introduced to a textbook that integrated geography, history, and spiritual values, within the framework of peace education.[44] The text, *The Story of Nations* by Lester B. Rogers, Fay Adams, and Walker Brown, encouraged a "clear understanding and a real appreciation of the peoples of other nations in this modern close-together world." The goals were expressed as:

> The peace of the world is in the hands of the youth of America; in the hands of the youth of all nations . . . For thousands of years war has been the curse of mankind . . . Families have learned to live together in peace . . .

> Why cannot nations learn to live in harmony? . . .
> World friendship seems the best way to solve the
> problem.[45]

The final chapter opened with the story of the statue,
Christ of the Andes, a common theme in textbooks of the
early twenties that included a peace education emphasis. The
story was told to illustrate the fact that arbitration of national
conflicts, in this case between Chile and Argentina, had
become a reality. The will of the people in both countries
motivated their bishops to seek peace. To cement their
resolve, the cannons guarding the borders were melted down
and cast into a statue of Christ. This memorial to peace was
then placed on a slope in the Andes between the two
countries. The chapter developed the theme that the youth
of every land needed to show a "willingness to cooperate
with others in achieving the greatest good for mankind."[46]
The theme was one used frequently by educators:

> We must have a new patriotism, an international as well
> as a national patriotism . . . Peace and Good Will must
> become the new patriotism of mankind . . . World
> friendship is the hope of mankind.[47]

International Friendship with a Global Perspective

As war clouds darkened Europe, the National Council of
Teachers of English published a volume, *Educating for Peace*
that included twelve curriculum units suitable for peace
education.[48] The positive approach stressed using the theme,
"Building Good Will Among Peoples." The international
character of peace efforts included "creating channels of
direct or indirect contact for the free exchange of ideas in
many fields in order to develop a kind of world-wide entente
cordiale."[49]

The theme for this volume, "International Relations in the
Curriculum," stated:

An understanding of our interdependence, both as
individuals in a community and as nations in a world
community, is a theme that should run through every
year, from kindergarten through high school and
college.[50]

The objectives reflected a global perspective that was
expressed as an "interdependence of peoples in science, art,
and literature as well as in social, political, and economic
living." Patriotism was equated with internationalism as
being complementary and not contradictory to good citizenship.[51]

The curriculum units included: World Peace, Modern
International Problems, Life in Japan or China, and Fascism
and Nationalism. This latter unit was designed for secondary
schools by James A. Michener, noted author. At that time,
he was director of social studies at Colorado State College of
Education.[52]

The unit on World Peace, for example, included activities,
such as: "Investigate the profits made by the leading
munitions makers of our country in the past World War
(and) . . . dramatize a mock disarmament conference."[53]
Michener's unit on Fascism and National Socialism suggested
the following activities: "Construct a bar graph showing the
growth of the Nazi Party between 1923 and 1933 . . . Imagine
that you are a young German boy whose father was
unemployed . . . now he is a brownshirt trooper."[54]

Several units in secondary education were treated as a
"problem" or issues course which could include: "A study of
the causes of war, the part played by propaganda in
fomenting these, attempts at peaceful adjustments . . .
literature as the means of interpreting these conflicting
interests."[55]

Educating for Peace broke new ground in peace education.
A practical treatise that was written by classroom teachers
for use in schools, it was a worthy successor to the
teacher-produced textbooks designed by the American

School Peace League and its successor organization, the American School Citizenship League. Committees of teachers designed, wrote, and field-tested the units before they were used in the classroom.

Recognition was given to the importance of the interdependence of individuals and nations in a world community, the necessity for cooperation, and the economic requirements of nations as underlying causes that influenced peace. Educators offered a philosophy of hope in a time of pessimism. Their long-range, futuristic viewpoint under the shadow of war was not generally held at that time.

A history textbook, *National Governments and International Relations* written by Frank Magruder shortly after the attack on Pearl Harbor also included an optimistic outlook on the potential for peace education.[56] Magruder had written history textbooks since the 1920s. Several basic tenets of peace education were expressed in the Foreword: "The greatest world problem is to learn to live together happily with peace and justice . . . We can have an economic world community."[57]

International friendship and good will were proposed in the Magruder text as one method to prevent wars. Young students were urged to "develop an International Mind . . . with four loyalties: to family, to country, to God, and humanity."[58]

Several themes from peace education textbooks in the past were repeated in the Magruder textbook: the treatment of war in school histories; the inclusion of stories of peace heroes who gave their lives for social justice; and the story of the Christ of the Andes statue.[59]

An actual unit on peace that was taught to an American Problems class for high school seniors was published in 1939.[60] Carl Winter, a classroom teacher in Sacramento, California, designed his own unit when unable to find materials available. Among his resources were the Headline Books designed by the Foreign Policy Association. Major objectives were: to study Nationalism, armaments and the armament makers, as well as to discuss the Court of International Justice, the Kellogg-Briand Pact, and the international work of humanitarian organizations, such as the Red Cross and the Salvation Army.[61]

International Friendship and Citizenship Education

The dream of education for a world community, a family of nations, would be expressed quite forcefully by peace educators writing in the post-World War II years of this century (see Chapter 5). Hopes for the future characterized the postwar era in spite of the shadow of atomic destruction.

Much ground work for these fervent hopes was laid in the 1930s. Tentative stirrings of a global perspective emanated from the writings of Depression-era peace educators. The interdependence of nations and peace as a cherished value for individual and communal welfare appeared repeatedly as themes. Character and citizenship education were linked together by progressive educators, peace organizations, and others and expanded to include the whole community.

Throughout the thirties several organizations began programs designed to influence public opinion for the elimination of war, to further the aims of the League, or to advance the cause of the Kellogg-Briand Pact. Education was considered the best way to form a moral foundation and support in order to persuade the citizenry to think and act reasonably in favor of peace.[62] Slowly, the realization grew that public opinion represented not only a chance for collective action, but also a form of sanction that could be imposed. This belief was reinforced with recognition that "peace will not come until the public mind is trained to think in terms of peace."[63]

Community Peace Education projects were proposed by the National Council for the Prevention of War.[64] The cultivation of intelligent public opinion was regarded as essential with marathon roundtables, lectures, debates, pageants, plays, and literature as activities. Other programs included World Peaceways, a mass education project that promoted a peace program with advertisements, weekly radio broadcasts, and a special monthly bulletin.[65]

Spiritual values continued to provide the foundation for American society as they had in previous centuries. Peace educators emphasized the need for "world brotherhood." The Church Peace Union organized a course of ten sessions known as the Junior League of Nations. Children were encouraged to develop new attitudes for "international good will, world-mindedness, a knowledge of the life and ways of other peoples and attitudes of friendliness toward them."[66]

At the same time parents and teachers were urged to make conscious efforts to resist compulsory military training in the schools which was first promoted as a form of physical education. The peace educators who wrote during this period believed that the offering of financial aid and other "outright grants" was unfair to other students. The school system was becoming overly militarized, according to the peace educator. A Massachusetts report (1929) was cited in dictating that in that one state alone 15,000 boys between twelve and nineteen were taking military training.[67]

Educators during this period were visionaries, expressing a philosophy of hope and optimism. They addressed issues that would be of vital importance to American society in the future. Opposition to the military presence in the schools was begun in the 1800s by Horace Mann and others and it continued through the early years of the nineteenth century. Opposition was especially vigorous in the 1920s when John Dewey and other Progressive educators reacted to the National Defense Act (1920), which firmly established the military presence in schools.

By the thirties, military training in schools was fought openly on the grounds that it was inimical to Progressive education. Peace advocates argued that such training blocked "creative thinking" and stressed instead conformity and submission to authority. Such arguments echoed far into the future, with concern raised about the problem of obedience to authority, a syndrome studied by researchers seeking answers to military behavior in time of war.

American School Citizenship League

During the Depression era the American School Peace League operated under its new name, the American School Citizenship League, and emphasized citizenship education.[68] The guidance of the NEA was still a sustainable, benevolent presence.[69] Essay contests, the observance of Good-Will Day, exchange of professorships continued, along with the use of the textbooks that were developed in earlier years (Chapter 3). The Citizenship League promoted the teaching of history as a way to enhance "international good will" with its belief that "international friendship" could be further enhanced through the teaching of geography and literature.[70]

ACCUSATIONS OF SOCIALIST/COMMUNIST AFFILIATIONS CONTINUED INTO THE THIRTIES

Fears of socialism and communism in the thirties began in the 1920s with government raids of socialist groups. In each subsequent decade, up to the present, came charges that peace proponents had forged Red-tinged educational alliances which were foreign to democratic institutions.

Historians debated the primary reasons for the suspicion and overt opposition to peace-related issues and groups which existed in the thirties. These could be delineated as:

1. Fear that those who opposed military training in the schools would instill antimilitary attitudes among American youth;
2. Concern about the espousal of communist philosophy as advocated by some progressive educators, especially

at the influential Teachers College of Columbia University. (This advocacy, incidentally, was later repudiated by many of the Progressive educators.);

3. Suspicion in the public mind that internationalism or the striving for world citizenship or world government was similar to the goals espoused at early Socialist Internationals of 1921 and 1936;

4. Reaction against many of the social and political changes set into motion by Roosevelt's New Deal legislation. Scapegoating and blaming socialist groups and their suspected fellow travelers for Roosevelt's program, and raising fears that other revolutionary changes were forthcoming, some believed might forestall further New Deal reforms;

5. Concern about the growing membership of American youth in Socialist and Communist Party groups. These groups were especially evident in high schools and colleges, and due to their expanding youth membership, became a strong movement in the thirties.

Various groups and techniques were used to engender suspicion of peace advocates. Ever since passage of the National Defense Act (1920)—which paved the way for military training in the schools—peace-oriented groups that opposed such practices were branded as being unpatriotic and un-American. For example, the American Defense Society, active in both the twenties and the thirties stated that:

> Pacifist propaganda . . . is intended to create a spirit of disloyalty by forming . . . groups . . . who pledge not to fight for their country.[71]

In addition, the Society further propagated the belief that pacifist activity would render the nation "defenseless" so that the "Reds according to their own statements would take advantage of our weakness to incite insurrection and revolution."

On the other hand, Progressive educators based their opposition to military training on pedagogical grounds. They opposed it primarily for the reason that imaginative problem solving, based on productive work in the classroom, would be replaced by an authoritarian, rote training mode of instruction. Such instruction, they believed, was one certainly not in harmony with the stated goals for progressive reform. In addition, military training under the guise of physical education was considered a mask for the inculcation of violence, force, and militarism in the curriculum, an issue opposed as far back as the nineteenth century (Chapter 2).

The thirties became an era in which the "Social Reconstructionists," such as John Dewey, William Heard Kilpatrick, John Childs, Theodore Brameld, and George Counts formulated their precepts that pointed the way to reform of American education and society. Detailed study of *Social Frontier,* their journal, first published in 1934 at Teachers College of Columbia University, showed biases that were antibusiness, anticapitalist, and critical of the traditional American "rugged individualism." Instead, the journal revealed an advocacy for socialism and a "collectivist social order."[72]

By 1937, however, changes in their thinking had occurred. This was particularly evident when George Counts renounced his editorship of the *Social Frontier* and joined an anticommunist group at the college. In addition, he later would become involved in a fight to rid a New York City teachers' union of communist infiltration, an effort that finally succeeded in 1941.[73] Even John Dewey, who expressed open admiration for the progressive educational reforms instigated by Russian schools after the Bolshevik Revolution, recanted his views in the 1930s.[74]

The publication of Elizabeth Dilling's book, *Red Network: A 'Who's Who' and Handbook of Radicalism for Patriots* (1934) included the labeling of Progressive educators (and several peace educators) as part of a "socialist-pacifist" plot. Her charges were based in part on the study of the thousand-page *Lusk Report* from the 1920s, and on the view that a so-called "Spider's Web" of subversive organizations and groups were involved in peace activities (Chapter 3, pages 67–73).

As early as the 1900s, Internationalism was proclaimed as a noble ideal for America's younger generation. The term continued in a logical evolution into the 1920s and 1930s as synonymous with international cooperation for the common good. The origin of the term was garnished with an aura of "divine aspiration after a more complete realization of justice and brotherhood." Internationalism was also envisioned as a "World State" with "international justice and friendship." In this sense then it was considered an ideal that would appeal to the youth of America as one that was praiseworthy and "more glorious than . . . conquest or political domination."[75]

The general public may have had a different understanding of the term "International," however. It may have been associated in the popular mind with the meaning given it by the federation of early socialist organizations in the latter half of the nineteenth and early part of the twentieth centuries. For example, Karl Marx and Friedrich Engels founded the First International in 1864, with the Third formed in Vienna in 1921, and a Fourth in 1936 by Leon Trotsky in opposition to Stalinist communism. In the public mind, the linguistic origins and distinctions between "Internationalism" and "International" perhaps became blurred and unclear.

America in the thirties was truly at a crossroads in history. New Deal attempts to ameliorate devastating economic conditions were controversial. Family histories as well as official documents and writings of the era indicate that millions of citizens, shaken by The Great Depression, no longer put faith in the government or the traditional way of life they had known, especially the free enterprise system. Evidence of the backlash against capitalism can be read in the fact that members of the Socialist party governed the city of Bridgeport, Connecticut from 1933 to 1957.[76] Truly,

America lived through turbulent times, perhaps as unsettling as those of the Industrial Revolution in a previous century.

Reading between the lines of press and magazine articles, an aura of fear was detected with an imminent sense of foreboding that society would experience a revolution, as the nation was undergoing deep-seated and fundamental changes. In education, the effect of the economic collapse was certain and widespread, with 770 schools closed and no provisions made for 175,000 children.[77] Such changes would affect the activities of peace educators in subsequent decades, especially as they became more convinced that social or economic justice was a necessary adjunct to peace education.

In the final analysis, writers in the thirties expressed grave concern for America's youth, especially those in large cities with "foreign populations." The enticement of the Young People's Socialist League and Young Workers' Communist League of America in the twenties and into the thirties posed an ideological threat for education and American tradition. One writer quoted directly from the Handbook of the Young People's Socialist League in order to expose their activities such as debates, talks, and studies on socialism. Meetings of those groups included reports on the "history of the labor movement and of the Socialist movement."[78]

Of greatest interest were suggestions for improving the efficiency of their "Socialist campaign" for youth. Children were urged to hold meetings during class recesses and after school in order "to discuss the problems of the school." Children were also expected to distribute leaflets and circulars including "small and striking stickers with slogans . . . containing material in support of the struggle." Other activities suggested were a "boycott of some teachers . . . school strikes . . . and singing revolutionary songs."[79] Disruptive activities such as these would probably arouse the ire of any principal or teacher. A natural consequence of these activities was the fear that impressionable youth would be lured into "the Socialist struggle."

On the college campus, several Communist-affiliated organizations engaged in a similar skirmish for student members. In 1930 about one in every four persons between the ages of 15 and 24 was unemployed, a statistic that certainly helped to foment discontent and questioning attitudes in young people. It was inevitable that some of these discontented youth would gravitate toward Socialist and Communist groups. Indeed, the growth in membership of Socialist and Communist groups and in pacific student groups at this time has been documented.[80]

Historians recorded that a full-fledged antiwar student movement became a reality in the thirties. A poll conducted by the Intercollegiate Disarmament Council indicated that 92 percent or 24,000 students wanted a worldwide reduction of armaments.[81] Reports indicated that a strain of sympathy toward peace issues existed even though in the minority. Peace scholars, in retrospect have posed the following questions about this development: Where did these attitudes toward peace originate? Did these attitudes come from home, school or church? Did these young people participate in early school activities, such as the American School Peace League? The answers are unknown. However, there is the supposition that many high school students in the late twenties and early thirties were a part of school and campus-based peace education groups. For example, in the New York City area in 1934, alone, ten groups identified with "peace education" or "anti-war" were recorded.[82]

Reports contained news of antiwar strikes that may have involved 500,000 in 1937 and the signing of the Oxford Pledge by thousands of students across America who refused to support the government in any war.[83] These strong pacifist currents could perhaps be attributed in some small measure to the teaching and activities of pro-peace groups of previous decades. Perhaps the pacifist attitudes of these students were nurtured at an earlier time while they were still in elementary and secondary schools. There was only faint proof of this, however, and if true, this was only one small sign of success when measured against the years of failure and indifference to peace education.

AFTERTHOUGHTS

On the negative side, during this decade a rationale was developed for the suspicion that peace educators were unpatriotic and un-American. This rationale was given sanction by official agencies, such as the Lusk Commission (New York State) and U.S. War Department, and influenced attitudes toward peace educators for several decades. The red-baiting that occurred, with accusations that peace educators were part of a "Pacifist-Socialist" conspiracy, evolved obviously first from strong anti-German and then later anti-Bolshevik (later anti-Soviet) sentiments. These attitudes toward peace groups have existed to one degree or another from the 1920s to the 1980s. In the 1980s, of course, peace activists especially—and even the authors of peace education curriculum guides—were branded in a similar manner by right-wing critics.

A tragic mistake and misunderstanding occurred because peace educators and social reformers were branded unfairly and had no recourse to clear the record of the half-truths and innuendoes levied against them. Forgotten amid the swirl of red-baiting were some of the positive things they had tried to accomplish. Indeed, most of the social reforms supported by peace educators—as necessary changes to bring about social justice—later became law during the New Deal days such as child labor, social security, and maternal welfare legislation. These reforms were enacted even though they were originally opposed by business interests, such as the National Association of Manufacturers. Social justice remained a worthy goal for peace educators despite the recurrent risks of being called unpatriotic.

As a result of accusations over the course of several decades, peace education has been literally barred from the literature of American education. A body of knowledge and writings, rich in human understanding, became more recondite and further removed from the mainstream, perhaps known only to a few pacifist organizations. Yet, peace educators, such as Fannie Fern Andrews and her American School Peace League before World War I, enjoyed the official collaboration of the NEA. Furthermore, the official government Bureau of Education even circulated the League's *Peace Bulletin* throughout the country.

The peace educator moved from the position of honored colleague to that of banned recalcitrant in a matter of two decades. After the thirties, the American School Citizenship League (renamed because of charges of unpatriotism), ceased to produce textbooks. Observance of Peace Day and later Goodwill Day became a memory. The effect on the personal life of the founder, Fannie Fern Andrews, can be discerned from examination of her papers at the Schlesinger Library (Radcliffe College). While correspondence concerning the Peace League and later the Citizenship League is in evidence, including the prize-winning essays written by children during the years of the annual contests, scant mention was given in later years to her founding activity. A citation accorded her by the Phi Beta Kappa Society at Harvard, called attention to her work in international education. The Citizenship League is the only organization mentioned.[84]

The decades of the twenties and thirties carried a sad message. Red-baiting seriously affected the status of peace education, impeding the efforts of its proponents. As a result, peace education never became a major strand of American educational or intellectual history, philosophy or pedagogy, in spite of the courageous and outspoken efforts of educators and humanitarians in the public schools and higher education. Yet, peace education echoed also in America's churches, synagogues, Sunday schools, and other houses of worship—even classrooms throughout the forties—but the message of peace was ignored. Each decade showed evidence of church groups involved in peace education from the youngest child in Sunday School to adults in group discussion programs.

The few examples of courage in each decade need to be reevaluated and even retooled for future use. The National Council for Teachers of English, for example, in 1940 exhibited courage in promoting their resource book, *Educating for Peace*. The units designed by classroom teachers for the use of their students still appear to be timely and appropriate. *Educating for Peace* offered a rare backward glance into a rationale for peace education at a time in American history when the opportunity for ending war may have existed. A few years after its publication, the United Nations was chartered, but like peace education has remained largely ignored or maligned. It is only in the late eighties and early 1990s that peace educators and political scientists have rallied to proclaim that it may be the only existing institution with the potential to end worldwide poverty and deprivation for most of the world's children and also provide a vehicle for international justice.

Notes

1. Sources for historical background in this period were: Frederick Lewis Allen, *Yesterday: The Nineteen-Thirties in America* (New York: Harper Brothers, 1940); Daniel J. Boorstin, *The Americans: The Democratic Experience* (New York: Random House, 1973); George F. Kennan, *Russia, the Atom and the West* (New York: Harper Brothers, 1957); Wilfrid Knapp, *A History of War and Peace, 1939–1965* (New York: Oxford University Press, 1967); and Basil Rauch, *Roosevelt: From Munich to Pearl Harbor* (New York: Creative Age Press, 1950).

   Sources for background in education for this period were: James B. Conant, *The American High School Today: A First Report to Interested Citizens* (New York: McGraw-Hill, 1959); Lawrence A. Cremin, *The Transformation of the School* (New

York: Alfred A. Knopf, 1961); John Dewey, *Problems of Men* (Westport, CT: Greenwood Press, 1946); Edward A. Krug, *Salient Dates in American Education, 1635–1964* (New York: Harper & Row, 1966); David B. Tyack, *The One Best System: A History of Urban Education* (Cambridge, MA: Harvard University Press, 1974); Ralph W. Tyler, *Basic Principles of Curriculum and Instruction* (Chicago: University of Chicago Press, 1949); and Paul Woodring, *A Fourth of a Nation* (New York: McGraw-Hill, 1957).

2. Richard Rhodes, *The Making of the Atomic Bomb* (New York: Simon and Schuster, 1986), 29.

3. David Irving, *Göring: A Biography* (New York: William Morrow and Company, Inc., 1989), 104.

4. *Deutschland Erwacht (Germany Awakened)* (Siemenstadt, Germany: Bilderdienst Altona-Bienfeld, 1933), 58,139. This volume contains photographs of the early years of Hitler's National Socialist Democratic Party (NKSD), depicting the human-interest side of the Nazi leaders.

5. Irving, 139.

6. Jacqueline Van Voris, *Carrie Chapman Catt: A Public Life* (New York: The Feminist Press at the City University of New York, 1987), 198–199.

7. Van Voris, 154–155.

8. Bessie L. Pierce, *Citizens' Organizations and the Civic Training of Youth: Report on the Commission on the Social Studies, Part III* (New York: Charles Scribner's Sons, 1933), 90. Quotation from the *Findings of the Conference on the Cause and Cure of War* (Washington, DC: January 18–24, 1925).

9. Sources for discussion of the peace movement during the 1930s are: Charles Chatfield, ed. *Peace Movements in America* (New York: Schocken Books, 1973); and Charles DeBenedetti, *The Peace Reform in American History* (Bloomington, IN: Indiana University Press, 1980).

10. Walter LaFeber, *The American Age: United States Foreign Policy at Home and Abroad Since 1750* (New York: W. W. Norton Company, 1989), 329.

11. Van Voris, 211. For a discussion of the issues surrounding the defeat of legislation for the World Court, noted as a "triumph of American isolationism" see Michael Dunne, *The United*

States and the World Court, 1920–1935 (New York: St. Martin's Press, 1988).
12. LaFeber, 364.
13. Gerald P. Nye, "Educating for War or Peace," *Progressive Education* (May 1935): 314.
14. Compilation from *Education Index* and *International Index*.
15. Nye, 310.
16. George Creel, *How We Advertised America* (New York: Harper Brothers, 1920), 4. Cited in Van Voris, 141.
17. Department of Superintendence of the National Education Association, *The Tenth Yearbook: Character Education* (Washington, DC: National Education Association, 1932), 13.
18. *Character Education,* 13. An additional source quoted in the Yearbook was by another Commission member, Goodwin Watson, "Does World-Mindedness Depend upon Good-Will or Information? Upon Character or Intelligence?", *Religious Education* 21 (1926): 188–194.
19. *Character Education,* 184–185.
20. *Character Education,* 283.
21. *Character Education,* 352.
22. *Character Education,* 360.
23. *Report of the Commission on Social Studies, Part I* (New York: Charles Scribner's Sons, 1932), 48.
24. National Society for the Study of Education, *The Thirty-Sixth Yearbook, Part II: International Understanding through the Public School Curriculum* (Bloomington, IL: Public School Publishing Company, 1937, 14–15.
25. NSSE Yearbook, *International Understanding,* 14–15.
26. *International Understanding,* 39.
27. *International Understanding,* 41.
28. National Education Association (Department of Superintendence), *Social Change and Education. Thirteenth Yearbook* (Washington, DC: 1935).
29. *Social Change and Education,* 6.
30. *Social Change and Education,* 132.
31. *Social Change and Education,* 140.
32. *Social Change and Education,* 140.
33. *Social Change and Education,* 146–147.
34. Howard H. Brinton, *Quaker Education* (Wallingford, PA: Pendle Hill, 1949).

35. Bessie L. Pierce, *Civic Attitudes in American School Textbooks* (Chicago: The University of Chicago Press, 1930), 251.
36. Annie Sills Brooks, *Adventuring in Peace and Goodwill* (Boston: Pilgrim Press, 1930).
37. Brooks, 91.
38. Abraham Cronbach, *The Jewish Peace Book for Home and School* (Cincinnati: Department of Synagogue and School Extensions of the Union of American Hebrew Congregations, 1932), Preface, ix.
39. *Jewish Peace Book,* 69.
40. Abraham Cronbach, *Quest for Peace* (Cincinnati: Sinai Press, 1937), 160.
41. *Quest for Peace,* 160.
42. *Quest for Peace,* 124.
43. *Quest for Peace,* 124–126.
44. Lester B. Rogers, Fay Adams, and Walker Brown, *The Story of Nations* (New York: Henry Holt and Company, 1934).
45. Rogers, Adams, and Brown, 52.
46. *Story of Nations,* 67.
47. *Story of Nations,* 68.
48. Ida J. Jacobs and John J. DeBoer, coeditors, *Educating for Peace: A Report of the Committee on International Relations of the National Council of Teachers of English* (New York: D. Appleton-Century Company, 1940).
49. *Educating for Peace,* 73.
50. *Educating for Peace,* 143.
51. *Educating for Peace,* 144.
52. *Educating for Peace,* 195–196.
53. *Educating for Peace,* 161.
54. *Educating for Peace,* 196.
55. *Educating for Peace,* 145.
56. Frank Abbott Magruder, *National Governments and International Relations* (New York: Allyn and Bacon, 1943).
57. *National Governments,* viii.
58. *National Governments,* 575.
59. *National Governments,* 573.
60. Carl Winter, "A Unit on Peace," *Social Education* 3 (January 1939): 33–36.
61. Winter, 36.

62. Clyde Eagleton, *Analysis of the Problem of War* (New York: Ronald Press Company, 1937), 51.
63. Arthur Watkins, *America Stands for Pacific Means: A Book for Boys and Girls on the Principles and Practice of Social Cooperation* (Washington, DC.: National Capitol Press, 1937) 55.
64. Guy Talbott, *Essential Conditions of Peace* (Gardene, CA: Institute Press, 1938).
65. Talbott, 59, 63.
66. Annie Sills Brooks, *Adventuring in Peace and Goodwill* (Boston: Pilgrim Press, 1930).
67. Elizabeth M. Lobingier and John L. Lobingier, *Educating for Peace* (Boston: Pilgrim Press, 1930), 126.
68. Pierce, *Citizens' Organizations and the Civic Training of Youth*, 82.
69. Pierce, 83.
70. Pierce, 83.
71. "Some Facts about the 'Red' Movement and What It Means to America, Taken from the 1924 Textbook of the Citizenship Training Course, Citizens Military Training Camps, 1924", reprint by American Defense Society (a pamphlet). Quoted in Bessie Pierce, *Citizens' Organizations, 91*.
72. Diane Ravitch, *The Troubled Crusade: American Education, 1945–1980* (New York: Basic Books, Inc., 1983), 82–89.
73. Ravitch, 89.
74. John Dewey, *Impressions of Soviet Russia and the Revolutionary World* (New York: New Republic, 1929).
75. W. T. Stead, "Internationalism as an Ideal for the Youth of America," *The Chautauquan*, LIV (May 1909): 333–337. Reprint in John Whiteclay Chambers II, ed. *The Eagle and the Dove* (New York: Garland Publishing, 1976), 148–151.
76. Bruce M. Stave, ed. *Socialism and the Cities* (Port Washington, NY: Kennikat Press, 1975), 157. An analysis of the origin and development of the American Communist Party was explored in *American Communism* by James Oneal and G. A. Werner (New York: E. P. Dutton & Co., Inc., 1947).
77. S. Alexander Rippa, *Education in a Free Society, An American History*, 4th ed. (New York: Longman, 1980), 282.
78. Pierce, *Citizens' Organizations*, 220–221.

79. Pierce, 221.
80. Patti McGill Peterson, "Student Organizations and the Anti-War Movement in America, 1900–1960" in Charles Chatfield, ed. *Peace Movements in America* (New York: Schocken Books, 1973), 122–123.
81. Peterson, 123. See also Eileen Eagan, *Class, Culture, and the Classroom: The Student Peace Movement of the 1930s.* (Philadelphia, PA: Temple University Press, 1981).
82. Harriet Alonso, *Women's Peace Union and Outlawry of War, 1921–1942,* (Knoxville, TN, University of Tennessee Press, 1989) Appendix, 184.
83. Peterson, 125.
84. The papers of Fannie Fern Andrews, Schlesinger Library, Radcliffe College. The citation given to Dr. Andrews when she was admitted to membership in the Phi Beta Kappa Associates, April 17, 1942 stated: "She organized the American School Citizenship League," p. 10. A short biography included in the Index (notebook) describes the "correspondence relating to the organization by Dr. Andrews in 1908 of the American School Citizenship League, the first organized attempt to introduce the teaching of the international aspects of education into the schools of the United States. Dr. Andrews was the first educator to undertake such an ambitious project," p. 1.

5.   ATOMIC AGE TO SPACE AGE, 1942–1960

DREAMS AND REALITIES OF A NEW ERA

The dream of America as a world power became a reality during this era, especially after World War II. Educators envisioned a new generation as members of a world community. But before these dreams could become a reality there would need to be fundamental changes in American education.[1]

One proposal concerned the education of the people so that they could become politically mature and able to discern problems and pose solutions. For the younger generation, socialization in the acceptable, positive attitudes for peace would need to be undertaken. Such idealistic dreams were translated into education for peace in the early years of the forties. All of the pent-up dreams that remained unexpressed as the war raged appeared in several writings of peace educators. However, by the close of the period little evidence of peace education existed.

During this period, the importance of public opinion became a new area of study for peace education. The process, which had begun with simple "Olive Leaves for the Press" distributed by Elihu Burritt in the nineteenth century, by the 1940s had grown to encompass the power of advertising and the media. The science of propaganda and power to manipulate public opinion made an impact on educators who realized the minds of ordinary people could be influenced in a positive manner for peace education.

Life-long learning, especially for political and civic responsibilities, gained a place on the educational agenda.

The Japanese attack on American naval forces at Pearl
Harbor in 1941 forced America's entrance into the War. In
Europe and later in Asia, American military and naval forces
fought alongside allies in bloody but victorious engagements.
Monte Cassino, Bastogne, Iwo Jima, and Guadalcanal
became living history for the American people and not just
names on a map. American industry mobilized quickly to
supply the troops that headed into battle in remote corners of
the globe. American armed forces rallied once more as they
did in World War I convinced of their mission to bring
freedom, liberty, and democracy to nations enslaved by
dictators.

A letter written by a young American killed during World
War I could epitomize the praiseworthy convictions of both
generations. Kenneth MacLeish wrote to his family before
his death:

> If I find it necessary to make the supreme sacrifice
> always remember this. I am so firmly convinced that the
> ideals which I am going to fight for are right and
> splendid ideals that I am happy to be able to give so
> much for them.[2]

Up to this point, peace education recorded only a few,
inspiring examples of limited success if judged by the impact
made on American education. This impact was manifested in
promising dreams and accomplishments, such as the work of
the American School Peace League in the early years of the
century, which was carried on by the American School
Citizenship League. Their publication of several textbooks
for citizenship education in the twenties and creation of May
18 as Peace Day could be included as tangible evidence of
peace education in action. World War II, however, brought
a cruel end to further plans and programs. At the same time,
there was also a realization that war itself as an institution
and instrument for settlement of disputes was a consummate

failure. Plans and hopes for the international settlement of conflicts lingered as bitter memories. The international courts of justice and League of Nations had also failed to provide civilized humans with a way to settle their differences nonviolently.

BIRTH OF THE ATOMIC AGE: IMPACT OF HIROSHIMA

One landmark event—the civilian bombing and destruction of the city of Hiroshima—changed forever the thoughts and actions of civilized people. The Atomic Age arose from the ashes of Japanese cities and exerted powerful pressures in the 45 years that followed. They were crucial ones for peace education.

On August 6, 1945, the first atomic bomb was dropped by an American plane on Hiroshima. The decision to use the bomb against the Japanese to hasten the end of the war and save Allied lives was made by President Harry Truman, who succeeded Franklin D. Roosevelt after his death. Final victory for the Allies was declared on August 14, 1945, ending America's participation in a second world war within a generation.

Echoes of Hiroshima resounded throughout this era, 1942 through to 1960. Beginning in 1941 the government had set up an Advisory Committee on Uranium to proceed with the preliminary developments necessary to harness the chain reaction for the world's first atomic bomb. The decision to proceed with the bomb's manufacture was made when the United States entered the war. The supersecret Manhattan Project, established with J. Robert Oppenheimer as its head, consisted of three primary laboratories, which still exist and are used for nuclear testing.

An Italian physicist and Nazi refugee, Enrico Fermi, led a team to produce the first atomic chain reaction in 1942. By 1945 the first successful test occurred in New Mexico, named "Trinity."

The bombing of Hiroshima unleashed unprecedented death and destruction on innocent human targets. A few days later a second bomb was dropped on Nagasaki. The Atomic Age was born out of the horror of destroyed cities and loss of lives. The further development of the thermonuclear bomb, including the hydrogen bomb, increased the destructive power exponentially, culminating in a destructive capacity that is now one thousand times that of the original atomic bombs.

One survivor of Hiroshima described her experiences:

> I saw many people running naked, all of their skin was peeled off, as if they had rags on their bodies. I didn't understand why they were naked. Later, I learned that suddenly everything blew away.[3]

With the advent of the Atomic Age, several new factors affected the traditional viewpoint of war as fought in past centuries:

1. the use and control of atomic and later nuclear weaponry became a moral issue debated throughout subsequent decades and especially a consciousness-raising concern and mission for the major religious bodies of the world;
2. the traditional theory of the "just war" and other historical justifications from the past were considered irrelevant in the face of nuclear weaponry. Humanity now had the power to bring about the end of the world and all civilization as a final act if a nuclear weapon were ever used again;
3. traditional warfare and armaments could become obsolete as long as the ultimate weapon existed for total planetary destruction; and,
4. the controlling instruments of power, nuclear weapons, were now in the hands of a new entity, the President and advisory agencies of scientists and military experts

formed into a conglomerate that was influenced by special interest groups of defense contractors. This unified group that was legitimized by the government came to be known as the military-industrial complex.

In the early years of the forties, however, these advances in science and technology—and especially the potential use of atomic energy for good or evil—provided educators with a challenge: to reassess education in light of the new Atomic Age. Scientists expressed the idea of the "mastery of the forces of nature" as far back as 1932.[4] On the other hand, humanity was deemed capable of destruction as a race unless new ways of education and cooperation were devised.[5]

Albert Einstein, whose theory of relativity was a key concept in developing the nuclear chain reaction, spoke out for peace education. As early as 1934 in an address to the Progressive Education Association, he had expressed his opposition to military training and questioned the "necessity for inculcating in youth a military spirit."[6] His statement had an added touch of irony. He did not realize at that time the important role education for peace would play during the Atomic Age and up to the present as a result of his scientific contribution to nuclear weaponry.

PEACE EDUCATION IN THE HANDS OF THE PEOPLE

In the final years of the war writers expressed their desires for a new world order in the postwar era. The people of America experienced hardships of various kinds. The personal loss of human lives constituted the ultimate sacrifice for families and added another dimension to the issue of patriotism and loyalty to country. Gold stars on small blue banners appeared in windows throughout the war years to signify the loss of a family member—a husband, son, daughter, sister or brother. America's schoolchildren had learned for generations that the highest, most noble form of patriotism took place on the battlefield. The pages of their history books glorified warriors of the past—Richard the Lion-Hearted, Lord Horatio Nelson, General Ulysses S. Grant, or General Robert E. Lee.

The two world wars had brought personal loss to America's families. The overwhelming horror of Nazi brutality as the forces of evil were unleashed on the world seemed to justify all hardship and sacrifice. After victory the thoughts of educators turned to ways to build a better world for the future.

Several books in the early forties articulated these dreams:

> We, the people, are the same in every country (with) . . . the same desires . . . loves . . . (we) ask but a little happiness for a little while on this earth.[7]

A future for the next generation of children motivated expressions of deep-seated emotions:

> We leave these children a world in which there is no order, a world into which we . . . hardly dare bring children.[8]

Alexander Meikeljohn, a former president of Amherst College, decried the killing of civilian populations by "bullets or bombs or starvation" because the "peoples of the earth are not, like spiders and flies . . . irrevocably doomed."[9]

Robert Havighurst, pioneer psychologist and educator, believed that peace would be a problem until "the great majority of our people understand what peace means."[10] Until then, there would be scant hopes for a lasting peace, he charged. Peace education had been a failure in the past because it did not go far enough nor proceed boldly enough. Furthermore, it had not "led people to see what sacrifices were necessary for establishing peace" nor had it made people willing to pay the costs of peace. The peace education taught in the twenties and thirties was lamented by Havighurst who claimed that it had been viewed as "though it was stupid at best and treasonable at worst." He considered it a tragedy that peace education was "too often lumped together with subversive activities."[11]

Havighurst confirmed that the labeling of peace educators and social reformers in previous decades had taken a serious toll. His comments confirmed that the accusations against those who taught peace education created a doubt of loyalty in the minds of most people. These misconceptions emerged from the Lusk Commission hearings and the Dilling book in the thirties. Pacifists were imprisoned during the war years along with conscientious objectors, such as Jehovah's Witnesses. Indeed, the mere allegation or suspicion of unpatriotism or disloyalty if levied against a pacifist was a serious charge that could result in a prison sentence.

Education for the average American citizen was considered as a necessary ingredient for lasting peace. Mark May was a psychologist who wrote in a publication of the Institute of Human Relations at Yale University that he hoped the forces of education could persuade "people to try as an experiment some plan of international relations that could prevent future wars." As a necessary part of this new education, an effective "education for citizenship" would be required as training for parents, teachers, and friends before the next step—constructive, peaceable attitudes for the socialization of the child—could take place.[12]

Education for citizenship was first proposed for America's children and young people during the 1920s and 1930s. A form of political science or citizenship education had been undertaken by groups, such as the League for Women Voters, in the years after women received the right to vote (in 1920). Then, in the early 1940s the concept gained momentum as a means to "produce political maturity in a people."[13]

Mortimer Adler, while a professor at the University of Chicago, rationalized that citizenship education for large groups of the populace could become a "public education for peace." He justified this stand with the argument that only the adult "who knows how to think can really judge . . . the serious problems which confront responsible men and women." He argued that by the nineteenth century "there was no general public discussion of the problems of peace."[14] A continuous, life-long learning of the political and social responsibilities for citizenship emerged as a serious proposal. Education for peace was considered as the "prime instrumentality for effecting the mental, moral, and cultural changes prerequisite to peace."[15] This could be translated into the need for critical thinking skills, analysis, synthesis, and problem-solving skills necessary for survival in an Atomic Age.

Adler, as a prominent educator and a persistent critic of American education for the past forty years, advocated a classic, academic education, one that would crystallize the powers of critical thinking. History, social science, moral, and political philosophy were the major areas of study, he believed.[16] In light of past hearings and investigations of the role played by propaganda in past wars, educators continued to advocate the importance of critical-thinking skills as vital for education from the forties up to the present. Problem-solving and critical-thinking skills are included as basic components for peace education programs by curriculum designers in the eighties and early nineties.

SOCIALIZATION OF THE CHILD

The process of the child's socialization became an important area of interest that has continued to occupy the attention of sociologists and psychologists for the past five decades. Mark May wrote in the forties that the child's socialization was a vital area of education because the habits, attitudes, and loyalties really reflected the "customs, ideals, beliefs and laws of the group" and society. These were essential for education in the sense of social conditioning. The positive attitudes of tolerance, good will, and a new type of intercultural education would be "favorable to the maintenance of peace between groups."[17]

With increasing frequency, educators and psychologists appealed for a world where wisdom and clear thinking would once again reign. It was only in such a society that children could be conceived, nurtured, and guided to maturity. As the war drew to a close, thoughtful dialogue moved into a new mode, one that was future-oriented and included an overwhelming desire to reject the past, especially war. Educators and others appeared in print describing their images about the potentiality of peace education—if only it could ever succeed.

PEACE EDUCATION AND POSTWAR EDUCATIONAL REFORM IN THE SHADOW OF THE COLD WAR

For a few short years after the war ended the hopes of peace-loving people were strengthened by the establishment in 1945 of the United Nations with a charter drawn up at the San Francisco Conference. The historic document proclaimed the "faith in fundamental human rights . . . and in the equal rights of men and women." While similar in some respects to the League of Nations, the Security Council had one important difference which was the right of the five great powers (United States, Great Britain, the Soviet Union, France, and China) to exercise a veto on any question. The charter also permitted the use of force for peacekeeping. United Nations forces have been called to aid various nations throughout the past 45 years.

During the mid-forties as victory appeared to be imminent, statements appeared that equated the new peace with a golden age or as a "Second World Renaissance." The new period characterized an era of "world leadership . . . side by side with Russia, certainly one of the two great states of the postwar world."[18] Once victory was achieved educators turned their attention to a postwar examination of the goals and purposes of education. Other critics joined with Mortimer Adler in a flood of books with provocative titles such as *Quakery in the Public Schools, Educational Wastelands* and *Why Johnny Can't Read.* Renewed criticism of the public school system opened the field of discussion.

Several choices played an important role in the unfolding discussion about the purpose of education: first, a classic education was proposed as one that would teach children to "think straight . . . and widen their horizons." This was the approach advocated primarily by Adler and his adherents. A second choice involved a major curricular change known as "life adjustment education," an approach recommended by a commission which had studied vocational education in 1945. This new educational program was designed to serve the needs of a majority of youth. These members of the younger generation were those not committed to either a college preparatory program or a vocational career. Life adjustment education stressed the importance of "creative achievement as well as adjustment to existing conditions." Life adjustment education inaugurated a period of experimental programs that persisted for many years with an emphasis on personal-social problems and educational solutions.

In the forties, Ralph Tyler produced his classic theory of the four fundamental areas for curriculum development: the purposes, experiences provided, organization of those experiences, and evaluation.[19] His was a major contribution to curriculum development and would influence the design of programs in peace education, as well as other fields of education in future decades. Many of the best-conceived peace education programs in the seventies and eighties were based on Tyler's model for curriculum design.

Within a few years after victory, a growing rift between the two allies developed. A "cold war" had been declared as the Soviet Union established permanent dictatorships in the Eastern European areas that had been liberated by advancing Russian troops during World War II. This had been done with the consent of the Allies at the Yalta Conference. Soon Albania, Bulgaria, Poland, Hungary, Romania, Czechoslovakia, and Yugoslavia became satellite nations under the hammer and sickle. A state of undeclared war existed until the Malta Summit (1989) when President George Bush and Mikhail Gorbachev declared that the arms race and Cold War had ended. This announcement was buttressed by an "official" announcement to this effect on February 1, 1992 that coincided with the visit to the U.S. of Gorbachev's successor, Boris Yeltsin, first democratically-elected President of the newly independent Republic of Russia. However, the ideological conflicts of the Cold War era caused serious disruption in the evolution of peace education until the mid-1970s (this will be discussed in more detail in Chapter 7).

EDUCATION AS AN INSTRUMENT OF NATIONAL POLICY

The moral dilemma of freedom versus the government's role in education in the name of national security was first outlined for educators by the Educational Policies Commission in 1949. The Commission underscored the problem of education in light of increasing Cold War tensions. The report stated that "we must maintain our part in the Cold War." The Commission continued:

> If the schools develop programs that contribute to the nation's needs in this time of crisis, and if they can convince the public that these contributions are useful, then education can command the support it will deserve as an instrument of national policy.[20]

Support for the Cold War was a critical turning point for American education. Education "as an instrument of national policy" was interpreted by one educator, Louis Jaffe, to mean an end to the major objective of postwar education, teaching for peace and international understanding. Jaffe declared that the Commission report was in error and could be considered as a perversion of basic American educational policy and purpose.[21]

The NEA's American Association of School Administrators included many activities in a Yearbook, *Schools for a New World* that reflected on the problems of education. Robert Havighurst included his area of interest, critical thinking, a skill especially needed by students in the postwar era in order to interpret data and identify points of view or bias. Such thought processes would be needed for the new generation that faced a new reality—technology—with the atomic bomb making "one world the theater of all political, social, and economic progress."[22] In 1945, this prophetic view was not widespread. Havighurst did not specifically call for a form of what is now known as Nuclear War Education, but the goals were similar. For example, he and many other educators believed that our younger generation deserved to know of the realities of life lived out with nuclear weapons. Not until the late 1970s, however, did teaching about nuclear weapons become an issue widely espoused as a topic in the curriculum. As a result, Nuclear War Education became a part of the public school curriculum in several states, to be discussed in a subsequent chapter. However, Betty Reardon, a pioneer peace educator whose work has spanned several decades, noted sadly that not one curriculum in physics was submitted for inclusion in a national survey of peace education programs conducted in 1988.

The second major reality of the postwar era was also explored—conflicting ideologies. Education faced two distinct, competing spheres of influence: the ideology of freedom-loving Western democracies and the social philosophy and totalitarian controls of the Soviet Union. History in subsequent decades recorded the reactions to events on the world stage, all in light of these two leading ideologies and as unmistakable influences on the next generation. For this reason the major role of the school would need to be to teach "allegiance to the basic ideals of democracy."[23] Education as an instrument for national policy would need to be the *modus operandi* because of the political realities of the Cold War.

SPIRITUAL VALUES IN THE FORTIES

The Cardinal Principles of 1918 (Chapter 3, page 73) had included a major principle in its treatise which was education for ethics and morals. Educators in the forties also showed concern for the teaching of spiritual values. They considered it to be an instrument to establish a "creative society of brotherhood, peace, and security." The following in particular were considered of merit in a democratic community:

> Cooperation, self-denial, tenacity, self-sacrifice, courage, kindness, generosity, sense of duty, loyalty, justice, freedom, sensitivity to beauty, creative thought and sharing a common cause.[24]

Education for ethics and morals appeared as a noble legacy from the founding days of the common schools. Horace Mann had legitimized the goals of education as complementary to ethical behavior when based on Judaic-Christian doctrines. Christianity emerged often as an unofficial but reigning religion in the schools of the nineteenth century. However, the spiritual values and principles of ethical behavior advocated in the forties appeared only to encompass the Golden Rule.

During the 1940s an awareness of social justice, often interpreted as the concept of "the brotherhood of man," also emerged as a major focus for some educators: this theme appeared with greater frequency in discussions of spiritual values. A typical goal of the educator was translated as:

> The insights, aspirations, and possibilities that are uniquely human . . . attained by good living in the nature world. Ideals of justice and cooperation, love of beauty, intellectual curiosity—such values and appreciations develop in human living.[25]

Specific activities were planned in several schools to encourage the formation of spiritual values. One such program also exhibited an early form of the global perspective, based on multicultural education. The school day was devoted to "Good Neighbors of the Western Hemisphere." Each class represented a different nation of the world and made an intensive study. On May Day each class carried the flag of its nation in a procession around the school grounds. A program included music and folk dances of the different nations. Another activity was an all-school Olympics that was carried out after study of the history of the games and their purpose. Celebration of Brotherhood Week stressed the ideals and "recognition of the worthy contributions by various racial, national, and religious groups."[26] International friendship, spiritual values, and social justice all received reinforcement in a few school programs.

In the months before the war ended, the NEA's American Association of School Administrators published a Yearbook, *Morale for a Free World, America and Not America Only.* Education for morale could produce "a better way of life for humanity" and was needed especially for the postwar years of transition.[27]

Social studies was the content area deemed of greatest interest because the teacher could develop "informed and purposeful citizenship" by "building the emotional drives of loyalty to democracy."[28] In 1944, teachers urged their students to take part in "war duties" as an "apprenticeship in citizenship." Teachers were also called on to participate in the "widest possible range of opinion-forming public services."[29]

CURRICULUM FOR THE ATOMIC AGE IN THE FORTIES

Growing awareness that education for peace deserved a place in the postwar curriculum motivated educators from both public and nonpublic schools to create innovative ways to teach in the new "One World" of the forties.

A research study appeared as part of a curriculum for peace education. A survey of Alabama teachers in the 1947–1948 school year involved a total of 365 teachers in 29 school systems and six colleges.[30] Descriptions of the actual curriculum used in peace education offered an unusual opportunity to assess what was actually taught. Educational activities included a study of the United Nations, international correspondence, units on world culture, and the "development of character through understanding, good will, and the interdependence of all peoples." Most of these components (except for the United Nations) had been included in peace education programs in the twenties and thirties. The reference to character showed the influence of the NEA Yearbooks, *Character Development* and perhaps, *Spiritual Values,* from 1944 and 1947. On the college level one course covered the "teaching of peace and the program of the United Nations."[31]

Religious groups produced representative studies and guides for peace education. Tentative interest emerged in the forties from the Quakers (Society of Friends). The emphasis on nonviolence characterized Quaker education, a force from the original colonies in Pennsylvania in the eighteenth century and especially the development of strains of pacifism and nonresistance.[32] The Quaker principles would become components of peace education and activities in later years. In 1941, a Peace Commission of the Friends World Committee for Consultation included the economist and pioneer peace researcher, Kenneth Boulding. The Commission published a *Peace Study Outline.*[33] A new examination of the social order included study of the "close connection between the roots of war and the social order of society" with recognition of economic causes, such as "access to markets . . . and essential raw materials." Tentative strains of social and economic justice came to the forefront in this study.[34]

In addition to the Society of Friends, other churches and organizations made contributions to peace education through curriculums and programs. These were designed for adult education discussion and study groups perhaps in recognition of the importance of educating the general public about the problems and issues of peace.

PEACE EDUCATION FOR THE FIFTIES UNDER A DIFFERENT GUISE

By the close of the forties, several events shocked Americans into the realization that the Cold War could continue for some time into the future. Communist forces had conquered China and the Soviets exploded their first atomic bomb. The Truman Doctrine had been inaugurated to effect a containment of communism. Almost any country and people resisting attempted communist aggression were rewarded with military and economic support, a policy that has been extended into the 1980s. Under the Marshall Plan $12 billion were given to help rebuild European economies and hopefully to prevent the spread of communism. The Cold War, of course, persisted throughout the past 45 years controlled by a policy of containment, a cautious détente, and finally, persistent fear of nuclear war. By 1992, substantial changes had been made in relations with former Cold War enemies and destruction of nuclear weapons on a limited scale began.

By the beginning of the 1950s, the Cold War had escalated into a serious one in a sensitive part of the globe, Korea. This region had been divided at the 38th parallel into zones of occupation at the close of the war, with the Soviet Union in the north and the United States in the south. The United States called on the United Nations for aid after communist forces invaded United States-occupied territory in South Korea in 1951. Once more, American armed forces took up arms on foreign soil until a cease-fire was declared by General Mark Clark in 1953.

Throughout the decade, a diminished output of peace education was apparent. The fervent writings of the early forties expressed as personal pleas for peace education appeared only on rare occasions. The historic background for this period included concern for purging America's schools and faculty of Communist Party affiliation. Accusations and half-truths as to the involvement of America's educational community in a conspiracy seemed to be taken seriously. Since the publication of the Dilling book (1934) joining so-called "peace front" organizations or any group with the peace label constituted a hazard.

PEACE EDUCATION AND SPUTNIK

In 1957, the Soviet Union launched Sputnik and succeeded in being the first to place a man-made object into orbit around the globe. Sputnik had far-reaching consequences for American society, especially for education. Throughout the sixties, programs would be developed during an era that called for innovation and improvement. The race in outer space continued with the United States launching Explorer I and the Russians Sputnik II and III.

American education once more came under scrutiny as had occurred in the postwar years of the forties. The lack of technological and scientific expertise was blamed on inadequate preparation in America's schools. Innovative curriculum projects were launched as a response and these continued on into the sixties.

More formal measures were taken by the American government which responded to Sputnik with the National Defense Education Act of 1958. Perceiving that the "security of the Nation" required a fuller development of the technical skills of its young, federal programs were initiated in the fields of science, mathematics, engineering, and modern foreign languages. Federal aid for education though controversial became a significant feature in American schools. For reasons of national security, education under the National Defense Education Act reflected national policy and spelled out explicitly the aim of the bill: "The defense of this Nation depends upon the mastery of modern techniques developed from complex scientific principles."

Civilian research and development departments of aviation industry contractors, such as Lockheed, Fairchild, and McDonnell Douglas, cooperated with the Department of Defense in the development of space vehicles. This alliance continued for the past three decades in creating a military-industrial complex that has become a decisive factor in American defense policy. Of greatest concern, though, was the fact that government officials came into power, especially in the Cabinet of Ronald Reagan, after employment with leading defense contractors. Conflict of interest charges became commonplace over the course of several decades with the issues still unresolved in the nineties.

ENTRANCE OF CONFLICT RESOLUTION

Theodore Lentz founded the Lentz Peace Research Laboratory in 1945, considered the oldest continuously operating peace research center. He studied group behavior and reported that the "processes of group activity and development" had future implications.[35] He attempted to study the "successes and . . . failures of groups all the way from a cosmopolitan club (involved in international friendship in colleges) to the Security Council of the United Nations." Recognized as a pioneer in conflict management, Lentz reasoned that the problems of world peace were related to the dynamics involved in resolving conflicts peacefully. He stated:

> The problem of world peace includes the problem of utilizing differences, minimizing conflicts and harmonizing purposes of the members of any group which functions . . . for world peace.[36]

Conflict resolution gained momentum in subsequent decades and finally became a permanent component of peace education in the seventies and eighties with numerous programs designed for America's classrooms.

PEACE EDUCATION UNDER THE GUISE OF INTERNATIONAL ACTIVITIES

Several examples of an emergent version of global education and world order education appeared in this decade. An early planetary perspective, concerned about the physical and ecological safety of the earth, and then, a global perspective, with a central focus on the interrelationship of nations, found expression in the fifties.

There was renewed interest in the development of a world community. George Counts, a leading Progressive educator, along with Leonard S. Kenworthy, Samuel Everett, and Christian O. Arndt believed that peace, freedom, and a free world were possible through education.[37]

The realities of the Cold War and an increased arms build-up should have made educators even more fearful of the potential for atomic destruction. Yet, in increasing numbers during the fifties educators continued to offer a philosophy of hope and an intrinsic belief in the success of their efforts through education.

The concept of transformation was a common theme. Leonard Kenworthy expressed this idea as essential to an international program with dreams of creating "a world community."[38] However, he warned that "nothing short of transformation of our education systems" was likely to produce the kind of results needed to build a world society. Transformation became a major component of peace education programs in the more recent decades, often characterized as a need for changes in attitudes that called for a new mindset.

Kenworthy's vision of transformation served as primary motivation for development of the concept of world order education and global education in the seventies and eighties (to be discussed in Chapters 7 and 8). The idea that the world could be changed first by the individual and then spread to the other segments of society began as far back as the days of the first peace societies. The Darwinian theory of evolution and the natural progress of civilization carried on the idea into the twentieth century, expressed as a new millennium of peace and change.

Students in the fifties engaged in a wide variety of school activities to promote international friendship. A publication of The John Dewey Society included descriptions of programs, projects, and activities, many directly related to peace education. A description of a peace crusade begun by a fourth grade class at McKinley School in Youngstown, Ohio, included peace education and international friendship. They adopted a prayer:

> Our dear Heavenly Father, we pray for peace for children and families all over the world. Help us to live the Golden Rule—so there will be no more war.[39]

Their aim was to "write to one child in America . . . and to one child abroad." Other grades joined in the crusade by publishing a school newspaper, "World Peace Crusaders."

Teaching World Affairs in American Schools may have had a misleading title. The goals and objectives of peace education were apparent in many of the activities described. For example, the public school system of Minneapolis, Minnesota demonstrated support for the aims of the United Nations with a peace education project that involved sixth-graders from 75 elementary schools. A Commission of International Understanding and World Peace supported the goals of the United Nations and included the following committees: (1) Utilizing Students of Other Lands in School Activities; (2) International Correspondence; and (3) United Nations Recognition Days.[40] Folk dances were demonstrated, students shared a meal with foreign college students and panel discussions were held on the purposes of the

United Nations—all designed to further "international understanding."[41]

Thirty years later, the Minnesota-Saint Paul area has become a hub for several innovative programs in peace education, including an annual Peace Child Festival with child-oriented action projects. An active program of exchanges with Soviet and post-Soviet schools engaged a large number of classrooms, as well as an exchange of drawings, paintings, tape cassettes, letters, and photographs. Perhaps these children had parents who received their early socialization in peace education through activities in the fifties that were disguised as international friendship and cooperation.

Junior Year Abroad programs increased in popularity with the programs of 14 colleges joined together to provide international experiences for college students. Peace studies, a new academic program, began on the college campus. Manchester College in North Manchester, Indiana, founded by one of the historic "peace churches," the Church of the Brethren, established a program (1948) in their liberal arts college that offered an opportunity for students to work actively on the war-peace problem as well as in volunteer community or church service.

William Kilpatrick, one of the architects of Progressive Education, advocated projects and activities to replace pure subject matter acquisition as the major goal of education. Writing in the Foreword to *Teaching World Affairs in American Schools,* Kilpatrick believed that the world was now one society and a "proper understanding and appreciation of world affairs" was essential.[42]

A philosophy of hope, among images of nuclear destruction, was expressed often in the writings of educators in the Atomic Age. The full implications of a potential world holocaust did not dim their dreams for a peaceful world. Educators still carried out their fundamental task of educating a future generation but in a world that required transformation and a new dialectic of thought and action.

Religious groups continued to produce representative

studies and guides for peace education, as they had done in previous decades. The Presbyterian Church in 1951 published a course outline for adult group discussions. Included were background readings, study questions, and suggestions for action. In a study of the relations between the United States and the Soviet Union, a question was posed: "Should we open bilateral negotiations with Russia on present points of friction? . . . Be ready to negotiate." Round table or panel discussions, role playing, world order workshops, training conferences, and community action projects engaged the active participation of those involved.[43]

INTERNATIONAL FRIENDSHIP AND A PLANETARY PERSPECTIVE

The curriculum for peace educators in the fifties expressed goals that included not only a global view but an expanded outlook, a planetary perspective. In a study that stressed international experiences for children, Leonard Kenworthy developed a cogent theme for peace:

> If . . . the decision of mankind is . . . to move toward a better world community established in peace, justice, and freedom, then the schools will have a tremendous role to play.[44]

Kenworthy based his optimistic viewpoint on historic precedent. Education would again be called upon to accomplish a near-impossible feat as it did when it undertook to educate a generation of new immigrants in the nineteenth century. Education's role involved a "mobilization for peace" in order to prepare children for life in "the world community" and one that required a new education for the twentieth and twenty-first centuries. This education needed "a planetary perspective . . . a cockpit view of the entire world," he believed.[45]

The visionary goals Kenworthy outlined included a synthesis of spiritual values and an international outlook:

> Learn about the earth as the home of man . . . the interdependence of the peoples of the world . . . the long struggle . . . to replace conflict with cooperation.[46]

Kenworthy's curriculum suggested several projects designed to develop international friendship and included sending crêpe paper dolls to French children, undertaken by a school in Philadelphia; the inclusion of the story of the Christ of the Andes statue; and a reading of the lives of Gandhi, Schweitzer, and Einstein. Kenworthy's ideal curriculum also incorporated the goals of the NEA Yearbook, *Spiritual Values* as well as *Teaching for International Understanding* from the thirties.

INTERNATIONAL FRIENDSHIP AND CITIZENSHIP EDUCATION

As the decade of the fifties drew to a close, peace education and citizenship education linked together once more as they had been in previous decades. A textbook, *Teaching the Social Studies: A Guide To Better Citizenship* by Ernest W. Tiegs and Fay Adams, included several concepts deemed necessary for "developing desirable human relations among nations."[47] They suggested that children acquire "insights, understandings, and attitudes in behalf of international peace." The curriculum included activities with an international theme, involving the International Red Cross, the International Boy Scouts, the International Postal Union, and UNESCO.[48]

A "Chart for Citizenship Education in the Elementary Schools" mirrored a global perspective for peace. It was developed by the Bureau of Elementary Curriculum Development of the New York State Education Department and included major concepts basic to an understanding of human relationships. These were: interdependence, adaptation and conservation, cooperation, democracy, and progress. One concept, however, included the adoption of a defensive posture:

> The undemocratic systems of other peoples are a threat to our security . . . We must practice democracy and defend it everywhere in order to maintain and strengthen it.[49]

This strong statement reflected the concern of the times, that an ideological battle was being waged and demanded the vigilance of all.

Peace educators writing in the postwar years in this era expressed often their dreams of education for a world community. There were definite signs of a global as well as a planetary (ecological) perspective which appeared in the writings of peace educators. The curriculum expressed the importance of the interdependence of nations and of peace as values for individual and communal welfare. Character education and citizenship education were linked together as important components in the life of the child as the future American citizen.

ANTICOMMUNIST INVESTIGATIONS: FORTIES AND FIFTIES

A number of investigations unleashed an era of anticommunist activities that flourished throughout the forties and continued through the fifties. These all had a negative effect on the evolution of peace education.

Many researchers believe that a definitive history of anticommunism as a dominant American policy has not yet been written.[50] Scores of historians, scholars, and peace researchers have faced an ideological morass of conflicting theories throughout the Cold War.[51] A thorough discussion of anticommunism covering several decades would not be within the scope of this study, which is primarily an examination of the curriculums and educational writings in peace education. However, several determinants that affected peace education can be stated:

1. A confusion existed that created conflicting information about peace organizations and activities because these were deliberate, defined missions for Communist Party propaganda and organizations, such as the World Peace Congress. For example, the House Un-American Activities Committees in 1960 and 1963 produced a "Selective Chronology of the World Communist Movement" published in several volumes for the years from 1918–1957.[52] The World Peace Congress in Stockholm in 1950 was discussed. The conclusion reached was that the Congress was "used as a sounding board for Communist propaganda . . . to launch the boldest . . . maneuver of the whole Communist peace movement— the world-wide circulation of 'peace' petitions." The reported mission of the House Un-American Activities Committee's publication was to bring home "the seriousness of the communist danger."[53]

2. The association of Communist "peace groups" was a documented activity for Soviet espionage agencies. Association with a peace group, therefore, carried the hazard of prosecution with prison or deportation under the Smith Act (later declared unconstitutional), which made it a federal crime to advocate the overthrow of the government by force and violence.

Hence, the undercurrent of distrust that first emerged with Elizabeth Dilling's book (1934) that listed those involved in the "Pacifist-Socialist conspiracy" continued to cloud any activities that contained the words "peace" or "pacifist."

Possible prosecution could be a serious deterrent to any peace education publication whose writings could be analyzed solely on ideological grounds.

These two determinants also continued to influence peace education or activities in the succeeding decades of the sixties and seventies.

Anticommunist hearings had a predecessor in the Special Committee to Investigate Communist Activities in 1931.[54] The format of House Committee hearings continued into the forties and crystallized in 1948 with testimony from Elizabeth Bentley, a former Communist member, that heightened an awareness of the presence of Communists or former Communists in high government posts.[55] Bentley reported that her activities as a courier involved collecting documents from several groups of Communists in various government agencies. She supplied the Federal Bureau of Investigation with the names of those with Communist affiliation which resulted in the conviction of 11 Communist Party leaders in 1949.[56]

However, the most infamous event involved Alger Hiss, a government official who was a participant in several postwar diplomatic meetings—Yalta, San Francisco, and Dumbarton Oaks. The name of Hiss became synonymous with Communist deceit and their penetration into sensitive areas of governmental internal and foreign affairs. Hiss played a major role in the resulting espionage trial in 1949 where he was accused by Whittaker Chambers, a former Communist Party member and editor of *Time* magazine, of being a spy who turned over sensitive classified documents to Soviet agents.[57] Hiss served a prison term as a result. The political career of Richard M. Nixon also emerged from his appearance at the Hiss trial as a young Republican Congressman from California.

Unfortunately, Hiss was also the president of the Carnegie Endowment for International Peace during the postwar years and this association also tarnished the name of legitimate peace advocates.[58] Since its founding by Andrew Carnegie in the twenties, the organization had been engaged in a wide variety of peace activities.

Anticommunist investigations brought back memories of the Red Scare of the twenties when there were genuine fears that the Bolsheviks were an impending threat to national security. In 1938 the first of many House Un-American Activities Committees came into existence.[59] These committees actively performed investigatory services and published volumes of testimony to document Soviet penetration into sensitive areas of government, education, labor, and cultural organizations throughout the forties and into the fifties.[60]

Historians and scholars concluded generally that Communism posed a "direct challenge to the free enterprise system in the United States."[61] There was no mistaking that the original Marxist dialectics promulgated frequently by Soviet leaders, such as Stalin, Malenkov, and Krushchev, all advocated the overthrow of capitalism. The capitalist state, therefore, was the official enemy and target of the Soviets during Cold War days.

Anticommunism, as a result, became the official policy of the U.S. government and this persisted with varying degrees of intensity until 1989–1990. With the astonishing events in Eastern Europe and the new mindset of those in the former Soviet Union, including the Russian President, Boris Yeltsin, these past doctrines were declared as remnants from discredited Stalinism.

On the other hand, scholars and researchers also pointed out that reliance on the dominant policy of anticommunism veiled other threats equally as serious, issues that have since proved to be detrimental to national policy. For example, the growth of the economies of Japan and West Germany have continued relatively unimpaired and unhampered by trade or other economic constraints with resultant harm and negative effects on some segments of American technological, industrial or economic interests.

In addition to the political ideologies, anticommunism was

targeted as the mission for redemption of the Russian people
and a goal for numerous religious groups who decried the
godlessness of the communist states as particularly offensive
to a nation like America, created with an aura of divine
sanction. For decades Americans retreated to a cover of
isolationism in pre-World War I days. The pursuit of
anticommunism may have invoked similar goals of protecting America from the perils posed by attack from far
shores—first, from Bolsheviks and later from Russian Communists.

The era of McCarthyism, named for Republican Senator
Joseph McCarthy of Wisconsin, became synonymous with
the fifties as a period of suspicion and confusion.[62] The
period has been well documented with a comprehensive
appraisal of the fear and hysteria generated until McCarthy's
death in 1957.

Throughout the 1950s, universities were particularly vulnerable to attacks on the loyalty of specific tenured professors. Due to such attacks some professors at the University of
California and University of Washington were discharged.
However, the investigations of 1952 and 1953 on subversive
activities in education were concentrated especially on the
schools and municipally funded colleges of New York City.
Diane Ravitch, a noted educational historian, underscored
the fact that large numbers of teachers were expelled from
their classrooms between 1950 and 1959 based on information from "informers and defectors." As a result, 200
resigned under investigation and an additional 200 who
refused to answer questions were summarily dismissed.[63]
Schools and institutions reflected public consensus and
sympathy for anticommunist activities. The principles of
academic freedom and civil liberty took a back seat when
weighed against the threat that subversive views were being
taught to children and young people.

For those in education, the realization surfaced that they
were especially vulnerable to attack because they could
influence young minds and advocate a specific ideology. An

era of loyalty oaths and an ouster of "disloyal teachers"
began in the late forties and was most active in the fifties.
Thirty-three states had legislation permitting dismissal of
those who refused to sign loyalty oaths. This consisted of a
pledge to support the state and federal constitutions and to
promise (in some states) that the teacher was not a member
of the Communist party, nor would teach or advocate the
forcible overthrow of the government.

AFTERTHOUGHTS

Underlying themes during this period included the implications for atomic power and the realities of the Cold War.
Education was deemed by many as an instrument of national
policy. At the same time a rationale for federal aid to
education completed a cycle that started with the National
Defense Act of 1920, followed up by the National Defense
Education Act of 1958.

The relationships between the public schools of America
and the federal government were shaped and codified during
this crucial postwar period. The military training of the
young, strongly opposed as a method to militarize a generation at an early developmental stage, produced some
opposition. The use of school facilities for intensive training,
to prepare for future service in the armed forces created even
closer ties with the military. By the eighties these joint
ventures of the military with the public schools would receive
persistent criticism. For example, minority youth most often
succumbed to military enticements of grants, free tuition,
and other financial assistance. For some it represented the
only way out of poverty. These issues emerged with a
vengeance during the Gulf War in 1991, as male and female
recipients of ROTC tuition subsidies found themselves thrust
into battlefield positions.

Spiritual values continued to provide the foundation for
American society as they had in previous centuries. The

contributions of religious groups toward the unfolding of peace education revealed an emphasis on nonviolence, a legacy from the Quakers. Other church groups developed programs for adult education. In the postwar years, religious bodies helped to form peace groups here and abroad. Pax Christi, an international Catholic peace organization, for example, founded groups in France and Germany to open dialogue and to initiate healing and reconciliation between former enemies.

World War II cast a shadow forward over several later decades. An entire generation experienced the war and would influence social and political actions through to the eighties and nineties. Former veterans in some states, for example, form a powerful voting bloc and exert influence through groups, such as the American Legion and the Veterans of Foreign Wars. In politics, the rise of right-wing factions with strong support of "peace-through-strength" defense policies impacted events throughout the eighties.

As the era opened, an outpouring of writings by peace educators expressed the desire for a lasting peace. The failure of peace efforts in previous decades once more emphasized that war was also a failure. There must be alternative ways to solve geopolitical disputes. The need for education arose to include a broader segment of the general populace with an early realization that life-long learning—especially in the responsibilities for citizenship—could be a powerful influence on public opinion.

Recognition of the socialization process as a vital early childhood influence found expression, as in a previous decade. The child needed to acquire positive attitudes, habits, and values that would lead to new ways of thinking about peace. Psychologists and educators also discussed the implications for critical-thinking and problem-solving skills. After all, these were needed to discern bias and propaganda as well as the motives behind political actions.

However, the impact of the Cold War marked by ideological conflicts between communism and capitalism proved to be an overwhelming influence. America appeared at times to be gripped with paranoia as the years of McCarthyism raged against any who were unfortunate enough to be accused of communist leanings. By the close of the period, limited examples of peace education existed. The few peace-oriented curriculum projects or writings that surfaced were carefully repackaged to promote international friendship so as to escape detection and accusation that they were the products of alleged subversive activity.

Notes

1. Sources for history of education during this period were: James B. Conant, *The American High School Today: A First Report to Interested Citizens* (New York: McGraw-Hill, 1959); Lawrence A. Cremin, *The Transformation of the School* (New York: Alfred A. Knopf, 1961); John Dewey, *Problems of Men* (Westport, Connecticut: Greenwood Press, 1946); Diane Ravitch, *The Troubled Crusade: American Education, 1945– 1980* (New York: Basic Books, 1983); S. Alexander Rippa, *Education in a Free Society, An American History* (New York: Longman, 1980); and David B. Tyack, *The One Best System: A History of Urban Education* (Cambridge MA: Harvard University Press, 1974).
2. Letter of Kenneth MacLeish, brother of Archibald MacLeish, poet and former Librarian of Congress. Private printing (1919). In the Archives, Rockford College, Rockford, IL.
3. "Words of Fire," *Los Angeles Catholic Worker,* Hiroshima Survivor Interview" (*Catholic Agitator*) (August 1983): 1–2.
4. NEA., Department of Superintendence, *The Tenth Yearbook: Character Education* (Washington, DC: NEA, 1932), 15.
5. *Character Education,* 15.
6. Albert Einstein, "Education and World Peace: A Message to the Progressive Education Association," *Progressive Education* II (December 1934): 440.
7. Elizabeth Jordan, *War's End: In Times of War, Prepare for Peace* (Greensburg, PA: King-Murphy, 1940), 14–15.

8. Jordan, 14–15.
9. Alexander Meiklejohn, *Education between Two Worlds* (New York: Harper and Brothers, 1942), 244.
10. Robert J. Havighurst, "The Educational Problem," in George B. DeHuszar, ed. *New Perspectives on Peace* (Chicago: University of Chicago Press, 1944), 162.
11. Havighurst, 167.
12. Mark May, *A Social Psychology of War and Peace* (New Haven: Yale University Press, 1943), 21.
13. Mortimer Adler, *How To Think About War and Peace* (New York: Simon and Schuster, 1944), 240.
14. Adler, 271.
15. Adler, 293.
16. Adler, 272.
17. May, 20.
18. Arthur A. Ellerd, Jr. "Winning the Peace: The Second World Renaissance," *School and Society* 61 (January 6, 1945), 3.
19. Ralph W. Tyler, *Basic Principles of Curriculum and Instruction* (Chicago: University of Chicago Press, 1949).
20. Educational Policies Commission. *American Education and International Tensions* (Washington, DC: NEA, 1949), 30.
21. Louis Jaffe, " 'American Education and International Tensions (1949)'," *Harvard Educational Review* 20 (Winter 1950): 1–10.
22. American Association of School Administrators, *The Twenty-Fifth Yearbook: Schools for a New World* (Washington, DC: NEA, 1947), 6.
23. *American Education and International Tensions,* 30.
24. National Elementary Principal, *The Twenty-Sixth Yearbook: Spiritual Values in the Elementary Schools* (Washington, DC: NEA, 1947), 14.
25. *Spiritual Values,* 14.
26. *Spiritual Values,* 49.
27. American Association of School Administrators, *The Twenty-Second Yearbook: Morale for a Free World: America and Not America Only* (Washington, DC: NEA, 1944), 222.
28. *Morale for a Free World,* 220.
29. *Morale for a Free World,* 220.
30. Eoline Wallace Moore, "Are We Educating for Peace?," *School and Society* 70 (December 24, 1949): 425–426.

31. Moore, 426.
32. Peter Brock, "The Peace Testimony in 'A Garden Enclosed.' " *Quaker History* (Autumn 1965): 72–74.
33. Peace Commission of the Friends World Committee for Consultation, *Peace Study Outline: Problems of Applied Pacifism* (Philadelphia: Peace Commission of the Friends World Committee for Consultation, 1941).
34. Peace Commission, 69–70.
35. Theodore F. Lentz, *Towards a Science of Peace, Turning Point in Human Destiny* (New York: Bookman Associates, Inc., 1955), 145. See also Kurt Lewin, *Resolving Social Conflicts, Selected Papers on Group Dynamics.* (New York: Harper & Row, 1948) Part II & Part III.
36. Lentz, 145.
37. Commission on Small Books of the John Dewey Society, *Teaching World Affairs in American Schools: A Case Book* (New York: Harper & Brothers, 1956).
38. Leonard Kenworthy, *Introducing Children to the World in the Elementary and Junior High Schools* (New York: Harper & Brothers, 1956), 8–9.
39. John Dewey Society, *Teaching World Affairs in American Schools,* 139.
40. *Teaching World Affairs,* 207.
41. *Teaching World Affairs,* 174–176.
42. *Teaching World Affairs, x.*
43. Paul N. Poling, *Let Us Live: For God and the Nations* (Philadelphia: Presbyterian Church in the United States Board of Christian Education, 1951), 42.
44. Kenworthy, 8–9.
45. Kenworthy, 6–7.
46. Kenworthy, 10–11.
47. Ernest W. Tiegs and Ray Adams, *Teaching the Social Studies: A Guide to Better Citizenship* (New York: Ginn & Company, 1959), 199.
48. Tiegs and Adams, 203.
49. Tiegs and Adams, 210–211.
50. Richard Flacks, *Making History: The Radical Tradition in American Life* (New York: Columbia University Press, 1988), 293. See also John Lewis Gaddis, *The Long Peace: Inquiries into the History of the Cold War* (New York: Oxford

University Press, 1987) and Fred Inglis, *The Cruel Peace: Everyday Life in the Cold War* (New York: Basic Books, 1991), Part I—Waging Cold War and Part II—The Balance of Terror. From the Communist viewpoint, see Eduard Shevardnadze, *The Future Belongs to Freedom,* (New York: The Free Press, (Macmillan) 1991).

51. A series on the studies of Communist influence, titled *Communism in American Life* with Clinton Rossiter as General Editor was published by Harcourt, Brace and World, in the late fifties and early sixties and served as a comprehensive basis for a political and philosophical examination of the major issues. These volumes were: Theodore Draper, *The Roots of American Communism* (1957); Robert W. Iversen, *The Communists and the Schools* (1959); David A. Shannon, *The Decline of American Communism* (1959); Theodore Draper, *American Communism and Soviet Russia* (1960); Ralph Lord Roy, *Communism and the Churches* (1960); Clinton Rossiter, *Marxism: The View from America* (1960); and, Frank S. Meyer, *The Moulding of Communists* (1961).

52. U.S. Congress. House. Committee on Un-American Activities. *World Communist Movement: Selective Chronology, 1918–1957),* published in three volumes, prepared by the Legislative Reference Service of the Library of Congress. Vol. II: 1946–1950, 425.

53. *World Communist Movement,* 425.

54. U.S. Congress. Special Committee to Investigate Communist Activities in the United States, *Investigation of Communist Propaganda.* Report No. 2290, 71st Cong., 3rd sess., January 17, 1931.

55. George Carpozi, Jr., *Red Spies in Washington* (New York: Trident Press, 1968), 226–227.

56. George Carpozi, 227.

57. Whittaker Chambers. *Witness* (New York: Random House, 1952), 708–709.

58. Hiss's affiliation with the Carnegie Endowment for International Peace was confirmed by Charles Bohlen in his book, *Witness to History: 1929–1969* (New York: W. W. Norton & Co., 1973), 251n. Chapter 18, "Defeat of Joseph McCarthy," offered a detailed portrayal of the methods McCarthy used

during the hearings for Bohlen's confirmation as Ambassador to the Soviet Union, 309–336.

59. U.S. Congress. House. *Investigation of Un-American Activities in the United States. Hearings. Vol. 7*, 76th Cong. 1st sess. 1939.

60. Several of these investigations were published as:
U.S. Congress. House. *Communist Activities among Aliens and National Groups, Hearings,* Part I, 81st Congr. 1st sess., 1950;

———. *Organized Communism in the United States. House Report No. 625*, 83rd Cong., 2nd sess., August 19, 1953;

———. *Communist Activities among Professional Groups in the Los Angeles Area, Hearings, Part I,* 82nd Cong., 2nd sess., 1952;

———. *Colonization of America's Basic Industries by the Communist Party of the U.S.A.,* 83rd Cong., 2nd sess., September 3, 1954; and,

———. *The Communist Conspiracy: Strategy and Tactics of World Communism: Part I, Communism Outside the United States, Section E; The Comintern and the CPUSA (Communist Party of the United States of America). House Report No. 2244,* 84th Cong., 2nd sess., May 29, 1956.

61. Richard J. Barnet. *Roots of War* (New York: Atheneum, 1972), 263.

62. A comprehensive discussion of the effects of McCarthyism and the resulting loyalty investigations that affected American education was undertaken by Diane Ravitch in her volume, *Troubled Crusade: American Education, 1945–1980.* Chapter 3, "Loyalty Investigations," contained extensive documentation. See Notes on Sources, pp. 360–363. Richard M. Fried, *Nightmare in Red: The McCarthy Era in Perspective* (New York: Oxford University Press, 1990) explored the antecedents of McCarthyism. Red-baiting was employed against peace activists, the majority of whom were female in previous decades, and as "a weapon in disputes between management and labor," devised as a "useful union-busting device in several 1948 strikes," (p. 86)

63. Ravitch, 102.

6. PEACE EDUCATION IN A NUCLEAR AGE, 1961–1970

INTRODUCTION

Peace education during this decade reacted to critical events in American society: dissent and unrest, the Vietnam War and antiwar movement, and the civil rights movement.[1] Children and young people played an active role in the civil rights struggle during this decade. In the South they attended Freedom Schools, marched along with their parents, were jailed, and even died during the struggle to gain rights they were guaranteed under the Constitution.

As the fifties drew to a close the excesses of McCarthyism evoked demands for conformity. The so-called "witch hunts" and widespread political inquisition that occurred certainly convinced many that only adherence to political orthodoxy would be permissible. Those who still wished to promote dreams of "peace" could expect to be labeled as Communist Party sympathizers. Peace-oriented individuals who were also pragmatists recognized that ideological causes needed to wait for a more opportune moment. For these reasons, the complete turnabout that occurred in the sixties appeared remarkable in retrospect. However, not many education curriculum projects could be identified and there were only a few examples of writings of educators, primarily in the area of international or religious education.[2]

In the sixties a definite turning point in peace education could be discerned. Up to this point peace education had been advocated as a way to prevent or eliminate war, a goal that failed as witnessed by the procession of wars since the turn of the century. With the advent of nuclear weaponry peace educators, though few in number, turned instead to a future-oriented conception–the dream of a world without war with an added goal of social justice.

Though an impossible dream, an ideal that could be reached only against insurmountable odds, peace educators believed that education could be a touchstone for the perfection of society. Positive goals were expressed in this decade as ones that matched the needs and dreams of society for a peaceful world. In growing numbers peace educators also became involved in direct action. The dilemma of scholarship/research versus activism piqued the conscience of many involved in peace issues and continued to pose a fundamental dilemma to all who needed to make such choices.

Peace education unfolded with major components that grew to include a global perspective, nonviolence, conflict resolution, and world order values as basic building blocks. Peace education could serve as a vital linchpin in crafting a peaceful future.

DEFINITIONS

Four major strands of peace education appeared during this decade: (1) nonviolence, (2) global education, (3) world order education, and (4) conflict resolution. Though appearing in embryonic form, each component was developed by pioneer educators during the sixties, such as Lee Anderson, James Becker, Kenneth Boulding, Leonard Kenworthy, and Betty Reardon. All expanded and refined their original definitions in the subsequent decades of the seventies and eighties.

The first strand, nonviolence, evolved slowly from several meanings that were debated and conceptualized by peace researchers throughout the past three decades. One of the generally accepted connotations was derived from Gandhi's principle of "ahimsa" as taken from the Sanskrit word for "nonviolence or noninjury."[3] According to Gandhi's original concept the absence of violence also included the positive in which the person became transformed so that the desire to harm could not arise. Gandhi considered this a latent force in all humans. Martin Luther King Jr. and other primarily religious leaders added the component of spiritual love or "agape" as a response to their aggressors. As related to peace education, however, the precept of nonviolence developed into a major component in curriculum development. Positive peace and the embryonic concept of transformation that permeated the peace education curriculum in the eighties may have been derived originally from this definition.

The second strand, global education, involved efforts to bring about changes in the content, methods, and social context of education in order to prepare students for citizenship in a global age. One component included developing a global perspective as a frame of reference or new mindset. In this way it was possible to view the world as a set of economic, environmental, social, and political systems with concern for international cooperation for the common good.[4] However, in the sixties Leonard Kenworthy, a pioneer educator in global education and international education, first wrote about world affairs education, an early version of global education. He expressed the need to bring an international perspective into the classroom so that children could learn about people in other parts of the globe.[5]

The third strand, world order education, arose in the seventies primarily from the fields of political science and law, but was first delineated in the sixties by Grenville Clark, Richard A. Falk, Saul H. Mendlovitz, Betty Reardon, and Louis B. Sohn. World order education encompassed strategies of transition from the present international system to a model of world order with major goals such as (1) prevention of war, including disarmament, arms control, and peacekeeping; (2) economic welfare; and (3) social justice, including human and social rights.[6]

The fourth strand, conflict resolution, drew from several sources in the behavioral sciences in a deliberately conceived attempt to provide skills and strategies that would mediate conflict between individuals, social groups, or nations and provide alternatives to force and violence. Certainly the widespread dissent and civil disobedience that characterized the sixties provided a classic lesson in the necessity of learning the basic tools to settle differences.[7] Conflict resolution expanded considerably later in the seventies with contributions from the interdisciplinary fields of psychology, political science, sociology, law, history, social welfare, communications, anthropology, education, and international relations. Later, distinctions arose between interpersonal, intergroup, and international conflict resolution (to be discussed in Chapters 7, 9 & 10 in more depth.)

These strands made it possible at last to flesh out a more complete definition of peace education. Peace education could finally be defined as a planned program with key concepts of positive peace among individuals, groups, nations, and the global environment, including the values of social justice, nonviolence, economic well-being, ecological balance, and participation in decision-making by using the process of conflict resolution.[8]

PEACE EDUCATION IN THE SIXTIES: INFLUENCED BY THE STRUGGLE FOR SOCIAL AND POLITICAL JUSTICE

The evolution of peace education resulted directly from the political and social dissent of the sixties. The civil rights and antiwar movements, the march on Montgomery, race riots, sit-ins, boycotts, and campus disorders were domestic events which contributed to an era of unprecedented agitation that deeply affected American society.

During this decade the antiwar movement increased in intensity. Originally conceived as support for the anticommunist government in South Vietnam, American involvement continued until 1973 when troops were withdrawn. This ended an undeclared war that was fought without hope of victory. The Vietnam war years had unmistakable implications for American society. Thousands became disillusioned with their government's militaristic policy, cynical of official efforts to contain the war, and critical of government secrecy that was revealed by publication of the Pentagon Papers in 1971.

The sixth decade of the century also witnessed the invasion of Cuba, the Bay of Pigs debacle, and the Cuban missile crisis which brought the nation to the brink of nuclear war. Violence also left deep scars on the American psyche with the assassination of young president, John F. Kennedy, as well as his brother, Robert, and the civil rights leader, Martin Luther King Jr.

The Nuclear Age witnessed the development of powerful bombs, missiles, and warheads. A test ban was proposed in 1963 which led to underground testing for a short period. The Cold War also continued with a growing rift between the superpowers. The American policy of containment with nuclear deterrence dominated political and military issues. For all of these reasons, peace education was closely examined by many involved in the civil rights and antiwar movements of the sixties.

The Civil Rights Movement

The civil rights struggles in this decade produced a stream of lasting visual images from television, newspapers, and magazines: the faces of Northern white middle class students, male and female, joined together with marching blacks and led at various times by leaders such as William Sloane Coffin, Martin Luther King Jr., or James Farmer.

The complicated, interwoven themes of civil rights and antiwar protest have been the subject of volumes written in recent decades from the standpoints of military strategy, foreign affairs, political science, psychology, sociology, and peace research.

For those in the peace movement the civil rights struggle appeared as a way to bring about political change and to secure social justice for oppressed Southern blacks, rights guaranteed by the Constitution but subverted by local, racist policies. For the first time in their lives many Americans recognized the bitter truth and reality of life lived out by large segments of fellow Americans. The American system had become a giant contradiction between the stated ideals of democracy and the reality of practices on the local community level. A political, moral, and human rights crusade motivated the actions of thousands of Americans (many still students) on behalf of poor, disenfranchised blacks in regions of the South.[9] The Montgomery Bus Boycott that began in 1955, the Greensboro lunch counter sit-ins, events in Birmingham in the sixties—all added values and goals to the agenda of many courageous Americans during this decade.

Peace education in action in pursuit of social justice best described the efforts of children involved in the Birmingham civil rights action. In 1989, Taylor Branch, the noted Pulitzer Prize-winner, examined primary sources and described the poignant young players in a tense drama:

> George Wall, a rough-looking police captain, confronted a group of thirty-eight elementary school children and did his best to cajole or intimidate them into leaving the lines, but they all said they knew what they were doing. Asked her age as she climbed into a paddy wagon, a tiny girl called out that she was six.[10]

Before the day was over 75 children had been crammed into Birmingham's jail cells. American television screens carried scenes of black children attacked by dogs, drenched with water hoses, and then marched off to jail. The national publicity underscored the recalcitrance of the city's white leaders as sympathy turned toward the black youngsters. Branch recorded that "these shifts of emotion" were the "essence of historic movement; to have caused them raised the sweet thrill of legend."[11] Indeed, four black girls even paid with their lives, as victims of the racist bombing of the Sixteenth Street Baptist Church where they were attending services. Certainly the black children of Birmingham who were involved in nonviolent civil disobedience along with their parents faced perils that would have made even adults blanch with fear.

In the summer of 1964 the Freedom Schools were established in Mississippi and taught by large numbers of students from Northern colleges and universities. From the viewpoint of curriculum development, it appeared revolutionary, starting with the premise that "students can and should make their own curriculum."[12] The theory behind the Freedom Schools also included basic elements of Progressive education because it recognized that the child's interests were the starting point and core for building a curriculum unit. In this case the interests of the students were their basic human rights and need for survival.

This prototype of participatory learning, of course, stemmed from the philosophy of Dewey that called upon students to learn through the experiences of living in a classroom where democracy was the keynote. The black children, young people, and their teachers all jointly participated in decision making and development of the school's curriculum. The black students contributed directly to the curriculum through their work in the Freedom School Convention. The Convention became a model of the steps needed to put together a political platform and served as an example of democracy in action. It was a forum in which students could ask questions and openly discuss issues involving housing, public accommodations, employment, and education. Platforms from different schools were combined and the results presented at a plenary session. Groups from nearby schools gathered over a weekend for a Freedom School Convention, a workshop that included direct instruction from black leaders in the movement, creative drama, and music.[13]

The curriculum was built around the political platform created by the students. Their firsthand involvement conveyed the respect that leaders and teachers had for their ability. Peace education in later decades would include participation in decision making as a basic component, a right accorded to each human in a community. White teachers and their black students in Mississippi during the summer of 1964 provided a classic example of the group dynamics of a peace education workshop as experienced in later decades. The experiences of activists in the Freedom Schools may have cemented the concern for human rights and especially respect for the dignity of the human person as a core value in peace education.

Several white teachers in the Freedom School project penned letters back home to their families that revealed their emotions of anger, sorrow, empathy, and fear as they tried to make a difference in the young lives affected by the Mississippi plantation system.

In addition to the Freedom School Convention format, local classes were taught in community schools. A typical classroom session involved teaching a class on nonviolence as well as a "Core Curriculum, which is Negro History and the History and Philosophy of the Movement." A teacher named "Pam" wrote from Holly Springs, Mississippi and described her experiences:

> We . . . talked about what it means to be a Southern white who wants to stand up but who is alone, rejected by other whites and not fully accepted by the Negroes . . . under-educated and starved for knowledge. They know they have been cheated and they want . . . everything that we can give them.[14]

Students were equally as affected by their experiences. One teacher wrote of her class in poetry writing in Biloxi when a twelve year old handed in the following poem:

What Is Wrong?

What is wrong with me everywhere I go?
No one seems to look at me.
Sometimes I cry.

I walk through woods and sit on a stone.
I look at the stars and I sometimes wish.

Probably if my wish ever comes true,
Everyone will look at me.

The teacher revealed that the child then broke down crying in her sister's arms. The teacher believed that the experiences at the Freedom School "had given this girl the opportunity of meeting someone she felt she could express her problems to."[15]

For those involved in the Freedom School projects in the summer of 1964 their duties were carried out while still grieving over the deaths of three young Freedom Riders, Andrew Goodman, Michael Schwerner, and James Chaney, a black civil rights worker. A young teacher named Martha described her feelings at a memorial service held on August 9, 1964 in Mileston:

Much of the audience and I were also crying. . . . How
the Negro people are able to accept all the abuses . . .
and then turn around and say they want to love us . . .
is beyond me.[16]

A young generation of college students experienced first-hand the magnetism of emotions involved while working in a peace and social justice project. Each day they faced the task of balancing their idealistic dreams with the stark reality of deprivation and violence. Through these experiences, though, a new generation learned to hold fast to their dreams for a better future where "youth has organized to fight hatred and ignorance."[17]

A lasting impression may have been made in the transformation and conversion experiences of those involved in Freedom Summer. Doug McAdam, University of Arizona (1989), assessed the consequences of 212 participants in the Freedom Summer project, which he identified as "high-risk activism." As a result, the author demonstrated a "strong effect of participation on the subsequent lives of the volunteers" who remained "more politically active throughout the sixties . . . and remain so today." A significant statistic was the finding that a concentration of former activists were engaged in teaching or other "helping professions," with consequently lower incomes. McAdam concluded that their summer experiences highlighted "the potential for personal transformation embodied in intense and sustained social action mediated through integration into organizational and personal networks."[18] McAdam's research could certainly be extrapolated to those groups of educators and students who have embarked on similar ventures, such as high visibility environmental projects, grassroots efforts to aid fellow humans, or peace education cultural exchanges to build common bonds with others.

The government responded to the efforts of whites and blacks with the Civil Rights Act of 1964, Voting Rights Act of 1965, and the Civil Rights Bill of 1966. Yet, even government decree did not succeed in eliminating racism from the American way of life. Racism in subsequent decades has returned to varying sectors of American society with increased evidence of racial incidents, especially on the college campus.[19] The smoldering fires of the Los Angeles riot summer of 1992 bear witness to the deeply entrenched attitudes that demand transformation through education.

Peace educators since the sixties recognized the continuing need to bring about changes in the attitudes and values of the

young by trying to remove age-old prejudices and righting
the wrongs of intolerance and bigotry. Peace and social
justice have been reframed and reinterpreted with a fresh
fervor. America's classrooms at present, as they did at the
turn of the century, now contain a new, multicultural
generation speaking many different languages. All are
Americans who need to learn to live together in peace. The
components of nonviolence and the skills of conflict resolution have come to the forefront, joined together with human
rights. All have advanced to become centrifugal motivators
as a result of changing demographics. After several decades
the same mission and agenda remain to be addressed once
more by a new generation. Human rights has continued to be
an item that moved to the top of the agenda for many peace
educators as America moved into the new decade of the
nineties.

The Vietnam Antiwar Movement

American involvement in Vietnam resulted in numerous
antiwar protests, produced campus radicals, and new waves of
dissent. A full-scale antiwar movement developed in the sixties
and the seventies which may have helped end the war in
1973.[20] The rise of peace education as an area of study, along
with the idea that peace research was a worthy undertaking,
grew out of the issues and violence of the sixties.

The war continued during the sixties with increased groups
of Americans sent into battle. Legal issues centered on the
fact that the war was escalated without the consent of
Congress and was actually illegal.[21] Antiwar alliances were
difficult to discern because many protest groups supported a
nonexclusion policy that allowed any group (including
communists) to participate in the movement.

Nonviolence became a major force in peace education and
received growing attention. The confrontation of students on
college campuses, especially at Berkeley in 1964 and student

strikes, vandalism, and riots in high schools were uncommon events in American education. At various times dating back to colonial days, America's younger generation had become involved in dissent sporadically, usually with little effect. The violence of the 1960s and 1970s and police action taken to counter it, however, led many to the quest for the peaceful resolution of conflict.

Peace educators involved in an early design of peace studies courses in colleges and universities in the late sixties turned to the philosophy of Mahatma Gandhi and Leo Tolstoy, whose works were usually included in course syllabi. The nonviolent tactics of civil rights workers and antiwar protesters provided a contemporary model for study because the boycott, sit-in, and nonviolent confrontations were examples from Gandhi's campaigns.

In the closing years of the sixties an education project at Southern Illinois University celebrated the centennial of Gandhi's birth. Gandhian nonviolent philosophy was presented as an offering of hope "to the war weary world . . . (with) serious consideration by our generation which has the power to annihilate the human race."[22]

The philosophy of Gandhi also offered insights into the education of children as a plausible instructional method that had been previously overlooked. Gandhi believed that nonviolence should be the central value as a foundation for education. Gandhi's educational work also involved the application of Dewey's principles of active involvement. For example, he believed that children should be taught native crafts and skills in addition to the principles of nonviolence.[23]

Peace educators made serious efforts in later decades to include nonviolence in their curriculums, which may have reflected a legacy from Quaker education as well as Gandhian philosophy and pedagogy. Respect for the uniqueness of the individual found expression in the work of the Committee on Nonviolence and Children in the seventies and especially the numerous conflict resolution and school mediation programs in the eighties.

Violence posed a formidable problem for the peace educator. The natural occurrence of violence in American history has been recognized. Violence has been viewed first as a fundamental and grim characteristic of the American past.[24] Violence occupied a legitimate position as the legacy of an American frontier mentality that was condoned by some and condemned by others.[25] The violence of jungle warfare and the senseless destruction of Vietnamese villages and civilians raised questions concerning the role of violence as an inherent trait in the American character. The Vietnam War years brought these violence-related issues to the surface.

Demonstrations continued as a greater conglomeration of groups joined together, especially after formation of the National Mobilization Committee to End the War in Vietnam under the leadership of David Dellinger. A mass demonstration occurred, a March on the Pentagon from October 21–22, 1967 with an estimated 50,000 marchers. Pacifists and militant leftists were reported to have clashed concerning different philosophies and strategies for action.[26]

As a footnote to history, the Freedom of Information Act in 1981 declassified Central Intelligence Agency documents concerning the affiliations of antiwar movement groups and individuals. The final analysis of the inquiry ordered by President Lyndon Johnson, who succeeded John F. Kennedy, revealed that there was "no significant evidence that would prove Communist control or direction of the US peace movement or leaders."[27]

THREADS OF A GLOBAL PERSPECTIVE: SUPPORT FOR THE UNITED NATIONS AND WORLD LAW AND ORDER

Concern for international control took two paths with support for the United Nations and the organization of an institution for world law and order, as central to the evolution of peace education. The challenge of shaping the

U.N. into an effective instrument for a worldwide community of nations appeared often in the literature of educators during this period. The absence of international law—anarchy—had been the basis for the spread of war and violence was one hypothesis proposed. The role of the U.N., even though flawed and imperfect, could be expanded to provide a forum for dialogue. Conciliation, negotiation, and arbitration would be the processes that augured well for bringing about a final world peace.

Reliance on the United Nations as a keystone for peace education was reflected in its support by the National Education Association. The NEA established a Committee on International Relations in the sixties. Leonard Kenworthy, at that time a professor of education at Brooklyn College, served on this committee, which also had an official observer to the U.N.[28] The NEA, in effect, served as an official link between America's teachers and the United Nations. This collaboration was apparent throughout the sixties.

The NEA, as it had done in the past, advanced the cause of international education and was instrumental in the formation of an organization, the World Confederation of Organizations of the Teaching Profession (WCOTP).[29] This had been a goal proposed as far back as 1911 by Fannie Fern Andrews when she initiated a plan for a world center in education sponsored by the United States government and the Netherlands.

Teaching for international understanding, a major theme in the thirties, experienced a rebirth in the sixties. The NEA worked for peace through many international organizations and especially the United Nations Commission for UNESCO and UNICEF.[30]

The United Nations designated the year of 1965 as the "International Co-Operation Year: Peace and Progress Through Co-Operation" and a resolution was adopted by the General Assembly.[31] The role of UNESCO received publicity concerning its efforts to increase the number and quality

of schools and also to "eliminate adult illiteracy."[32] The
U.N. outlined forthcoming efforts for global education,
which would include programs in Africa, Latin America,
Asia, and the Middle East.[33]

Educators could empathize with causes that involved food
and education for millions of children. This became a
humanitarian mission of the United Nations. The goal of the
U.N. was an optimistic one that echoed the hope of
generations that they could reverse the pattern of misery and
poverty for a large portion of the world's children. In 1959, a
proclamation in the form of the Declaration of the Rights of
the Child was unanimously approved by the General Assembly in a model edict for all nations of the world:

> Special protection for the child . . . his (and her) right to
> a name and a nationality, to grow and develop in
> health, to enjoy adequate nutrition and other condi-
> tions of social security . . . to receive education, love
> and understanding . . . protected from neglect, cruelty
> and exploitation . . . brought up in a spirit of
> understanding, tolerance, and friendship among peo-
> ples.[34]

The Declaration was implemented by the establishment of
the Children's Fund known as UNICEF, which was intended
to mobilize resources, food, clothing, and medicine for
children in developing countries. Because of the advocacy of
the Committee on International Relations, America's children in the sixties showed concern and empathy towards
those in other lands who lacked basic needs.[35] Many children
were involved in projects and the collection of funds for
UNICEF.

The second facet of support for the United Nations took
the form of exploring alternative machinery for world law
and order. The challenge of shaping the U.N. into an
effective instrument for a worldwide community of nations
appeared frequently in the literature of educators. Political
scientists and educators were concerned with the absence of

international law. The World Law Fund was established in 1961 and began the design of curriculum materials for secondary and postsecondary education. The Transnational Academic Program of the Institute for World Order was a successor of the World Law Fund.[36]

Two professors, Saul H. Mendlovitz, professor of international law at Rutgers University, and Richard V. Falk, professor of international law and practice at Princeton University, developed a framework and a model for world order education primarily for political science courses. This prototype expanded into a four-volume study that was published under the sponsorship of the World Law Fund.[37] Hopefully, higher education could be provided with a new viewpoint or orientation to "international affairs around the world order approach" with recognition that the whole area was complex and diverse enough to require curriculum development at several levels.[38]

The prototype known as the World Order Models Project, was originally designed to bring about political and economic changes, "strategies of transition from the present international system to the projected model of world order."[39] Several goals were projected: (1) prevention of war through disarmament and arms control, peacekeeping, and pacific settlement of disputes; (2) worldwide economic welfare by means of world economic development, technological and scientific revolutions, and attention to environmental problems; and (3) worldwide social justice by securing and protecting human and social rights. These could be translated into peace, economic, and social justice.[40]

The potential for reform in the United Nations found expression in the model for a limited world government with a revision in the United Nations Charter. This was proposed by Grenville Clark and Louis B. Sohn.[41] Throughout the sixties, Mendlovitz, Falk, and Betty Reardon, Director of the Peace Education Program at Teachers College, Columbia University, were the principal supporters of the world order model and wrote frequently on this subject in academic publications.[42] However, Reardon who directed the secondary education program at the Institute in 1963 and participated in the World Order Models Project reported that she later became "a severe critic of what seemed to me its biases."[43]

LIVING WITH ATOMIC POWER

The implications for atomic power were underlying factors of life. The specter of nuclear annihilation replaced the positive presence of atomic power from the previous decade. The atomic bomb or fall-out shelter became a part of American education with many school systems planning for the eventuality of an atomic war.[44]

Government officials targeted school policy-makers in overt attempts to gain acceptance for atomic energy, nuclear weaponry, and similar issues of national security policy. Throughout the sixties, educational organizations provided a forum for individuals prominent in the national security sector to articulate federal policy either in print through education journals or as keynote speakers at annual conventions. Henry Cabot Lodge, Christian Herter, General Lauris Norstad, Dean Rusk, and General William Westmoreland, who occupied various government or military positions in the sixties all addressed educational associations in attempts to influence the academic community.[45]

PEACE EDUCATION CURRICULUM IN THE SIXTIES

By the mid-sixties student activism was at a peak. Against the backdrop of the Cold War and nuclear issues, there were new fears of Soviet infiltration into the peace movement and concerns about the resultant tightening of internal security. Peace education has never been a strong force or presence in American education nor a viable movement. Peace education in the sixties may have been submerged and visible only at brief moments or perhaps merged with world affairs or citizenship education—a reflection of prevailing trends. The principles of peace education were often cloaked in semantics with educators obviously frightened by the prospect of being criticized for involvement with communist propaganda missions—also identified as peace education or peace activism. A more favorable environment was needed if peace education was to flourish.

Tentative threads of peace education could be traced in textbooks and curriculum projects in this period. An awareness of a global perspective was evident as well as a renewed effort to examine the role of social studies in the curriculum.

One viewpoint advanced the concept that law and order and the responsibilities for citizenship should receive greater attention. Citizenship education became the subject of a Task Force on Students and Social Change set up by the Department of Health, Education, and Welfare. It could provide grants for innovative programs in citizenship education.[46]

Criticism was made of the current social studies programs in schools as having changed little despite cataclysmic events in contemporary society. One innovative project sought to counter such criticisms, a program designed by the Lincoln Filene Center for Citizenship and Public Affairs at Tufts University in 1965.[47] The Center published a report setting forth goals for citizenship education which were familiar ones to the curriculum developers of the World Order Models Project, including the development of informed citizens who appreciated the contributions of all cultures and recognized "the interdependence of all peoples."[48]

According to the Center's report, the first goal of citizenship education was to present the student with knowledge "about society, past and present."[49] The report proposed that the study of anthropology, sociology, and psychology be included in citizenship education along with the more traditional study of history, geography, economics, and

political science. It said that world affairs, study of ideologies, and cultural diversity should be prominent features of
the curriculum. Funding for the citizenship education curriculum, it said could come from the Danforth Foundation, the
American Heritage Foundation, and the National Council
for the Social Studies.

Two educators who had written frequently on international understanding and world affairs education, contributed to the Center's published report. James Becker, at that
time director of the Foreign Relations Project of the North
Central Association was cited for his experience in world
affairs education.[50] Leonard Kenworthy was cited as having
"pioneered in this dimension of education."[51]

Evidence of the after-effects of anticommunist activities in
the fifties and sixties were shown in a discussion about
teaching controversial issues. The opinion was advanced that
legislative directives to school systems "to incorporate
anti-Communism courses in their curricula is hardly a sound
approach to a scholarly . . . examination of the contemporary
war for the minds of men." John S. Gibson, who authored
the Center's project report, "New Frontiers in the Social
Studies," reported that even though many school systems
included units on ideologies, most states "wisely decided
against mandating the teaching about Communism."[52]

However, one textbook for secondary education titled
Ideology and World Affairs by Franklin Patterson received a
recommendation because the focus was on many ideologies
and not solely upon communism. Democracy, right-wing
totalitarianism, and authoritarianism presented the student
with a deeper understanding of the threats confronting "the
forces of freedom in world affairs."[53] After the vigorous
anticommunist investigations of the fifties that continued
into the sixties, it was not surprising that educators questioned the wisdom of teaching ideologies. In the hands of a
less experienced teacher the danger existed that bias and
propaganda would be taught. Instead, a balanced and critical
analysis of ideologies could open young minds to attitudes

and values involved in questioning the issues. Concern for bias and presentation of viewpoints became a recurrent debate in peace education literature.

World affairs education in the sixties provided evidence of a bond with peace education. A pilot action-research study in social studies, a landmark curricular approach known as the Glens Falls Project involved an entire school system in the city of Glens Falls in upstate New York that covered all grade levels and subjects.[54] Funding support came from several organizations: The NEA, *Time* magazine, the *New York Times,* the Helen D. Reid Educational Foundation, and the Carnegie Endowment for International Peace.

The Association for Supervision and Curriculum Development (ASCD) mailed a complimentary copy of the study report accompanied by a recommendation for the project as one of the most significant in education and international understanding.[55] The ASCD further believed in the project goal to develop a better understanding of other peoples and other lands, similar to the Filene Center project.[56]

The Glens Falls project served to focus on the emerging concepts of global education and citizenship education. Peace education played a minor role. However examination of the project report showed some minor commonalities with peace education. There was discussion of "the failures of today's violent world" which could be blamed on the failure of education. The solution could be "perhaps the path to eventual world peace . . . (by) building a stable world order."[57] Further discussion emphasized the realities of the Cold War with the constant threat of a nuclear holocaust.[58]

The report concluded with the "need to understand and appreciate the common humanity of (peoples) everywhere."[59] These goals were expressed by peace educators in the past and reflected initial interest in world order values. At the same time, the objectives were also shaped to enforce federal policy with the development of "intellectually competent, morally responsible citizens."[60]

The introduction to the curriculum project expressed

hopes for a stable world order, peace, and cooperation. By the final committee report, however, goals for citizenship and patriotism were substituted, perhaps with recognition that the tenor of the times called for downplaying of "peace projects." A minor reason for this may have been that the project cosponsor was the Carnegie Endowment for International Peace.[61] Alger Hiss, President of the Carnegie Endowment, was convicted of espionage for the Soviets in 1953, ten years earlier. His association with the Endowment, a cosponsor of the project, may have been a sensitive issue to those involved in the Glens Falls program.

AFTERTHOUGHTS

The limited number of peace education materials, curriculum guides or even scholarly writing during this period proved a mystery. Federal funding for educational reform and assistance from private sources, especially foundations and organizations increased considerably. As a result of Sputnik in 1957 innovative curriculum projects and proposals went into effect. The Elementary and Secondary Education Act (Title I) and the Higher Education Act of 1965 were examples of legislation that encouraged research programs in science, mathematics, reading, English, history, and social studies. The few social studies projects that included some elements of peace education were rare examples.

Educators were especially vocal in the sixties with criticism that the structure of the schools was inappropriate for America's children and more suited to training for business and industry. Calls for reform grew in intensity throughout the decade. Forty treatises on the curriculum were published during this era, including the classic research of Jerome Bruner, Robert Gagne, Bruce Joyce, and Mario Fantini, among others.

Almost daily events confirmed the fact that the younger generation, especially high schools and young people in the colleges and universities were engaged in dissent and reform movements, which often escalated into violence. College students especially demanded greater choice in determining their curriculum. They insisted on relevance as an essential right in planning their education.

For the youth involved in a baptism of fire for social justice, involvement with the civil rights and antiwar protests may have changed their personal lives and deeply affected their future decisions. Many peace advocates in the seventies reported that they gained credibility because of their civil rights and antiwar activism, especially involvement with others from different races and ethnic groups. For others, involvement with peace activism changed the course of their lives. Scholars still believe America in the eighties and early nineties has changed because of the political attitudes acquired by young people in the sixties, with many now in leadership positions, including President Bill Clinton.

As was the case in the fifties, few in education were aware that peace education in the past provided historic lessons in alternatives to violence. Peace education appeared to be in a gestation period, preparing a fertile environment for the birth of significant groups in the early seventies, such as the Consortium on Peace Research Education and Development (COPRED) as a branch of the International Peace Research Association and especially the Peace Education Network. The conception of development education and human rights education as unfolded first in Europe and then tentatively explored in America, took place also in the closing years of this decade. The seeds for future research and action had been planted. Americans who engaged in civil rights and antiwar activities became living testaments to the crucial need to develop a new mindset concerning continual violence.

Pioneer peace educators, such as Leonard Kenworthy and Betty Reardon, bravely began to shape peace education by providing several important strands of global and world order education. The era witnessed also the first work of peace researchers such as Peter Brock, who explored the past with his study, *Pacifism in the United States: From the Colonial Era to the First World War* (1968), while Charles De Benedetti, whose major works would appear in later decades began his promising academic career with a doctoral dissertation on the peace movements of the 1920s (The Origins of the Modern American Peace Movement, 1915–1929 (1969)). Detailed accounts of peace leaders from earlier decades also came into print and provided role models from history, including James T. Shotwell and Senator William E. Borah and his role in the Outlawry of War campaign (from the 1920s).[62]

For the reasons outlined previously, the scarcity of books and journal articles on peace education suggest that the excesses of McCarthyism in the 1950s and concern for orthodoxy on controversial issues led to suppression of nearly anything containing the word "peace." Allegations and the seeming documented use of peace groups and projects by the Communist Party for propaganda purposes sowed confusion and misunderstanding in the public mind. Memories of Alger Hiss' association with the Carnegie Endowment for International Peace may have lingered in the public memory. As a consequence, early global education, world order, and projects that came under the peace education umbrella were renamed and repackaged as world affairs or international education.

Confirmation of this issue of misunderstanding as an issue for peace education, was underscored by pioneer peace researcher, Kenneth Boulding:

> When . . . a group of us started the Center for Research on Conflict Resolution at the University of Michigan in 1956, we conceived it as a center for peace research, but we deliberately avoided the use of the word "peace" in the title because of the misunderstandings which might arise.[63]

The shining hours of the decade belonged to the children and young people involved in the civil rights actions in the

South. The younger generation may have inspired and empowered their counterparts in later decades, especially the youth who created personal forms of peacemaking, especially in the eighties. The lessons from Birmingham and the backroads of Mississippi and especially the personal stories of human heroism, however, were largely omitted from the pages of America's history and social studies textbooks.

The sixties demonstrated that the younger generation could be inspired to take action and even, if necessary, sacrifice their lives for human rights. Their actions were examples of empowerment that can be transformed into reality and carried out in the process of daily living. As peace education evolved in later decades, the basic human rights of a citizen in a democracy underscored personal empowerment and direct participation. This strand of peace education was carried on with exceptional valor by unknown black students and their white teachers from the North.

Notes

1. Background sources for this chapter were: Charles E. Bohlen, *Witness to History: 1929–1969* (New York: W. W. Norton & Company, Inc., 1973); David Bouchier, *Radical Citizenship: The New American Activism* (New York: Schocken Books, 1987); George Carpozi Jr., *Red Spies in Washington* (New York: Trident Press, 1968); The *Communism in American Life* series, Clinton Rossiter, ed. published by Harcourt, Brace & World, which included: *The Roots of American Communism* by Theodore Draper (1957); *The Communists and the Schools* by Robert W. Iversen (1959); *The Decline of American Communism* by David A. Shannon (1959); *American Communism and Soviet Russia* by Theodore Draper (1960); *Marxism: The View from America* by Clinton Rossiter (1960); *Communism and the Churches* by Ralph Lord Roy (1960); and *The Moulding of Communists* (1961) by Frank S. Meyer. Other sources were: Charles DeBenedetti and Charles Chatfield

(assisting author), *An American Ordeal: The Anti-War Movement of the Vietnam Era* (Syracuse, NY: Syracuse University Press, 1990); Richard Flacks, *Making History: The Radical Tradition in American Life* (New York: Columbia University Press, 1988); Lawrence Freedman, *The Evolution of Nuclear Strategy* (New York: St. Martin's Press, 1983); George F. Kennan, *The Cloud of Danger: Current Realities of American Foreign Policy* (Boston: Little, Brown and Company, 1977) and *The Nuclear Delusion* (New York: Pantheon Books, 1982); Donald Kagan and L. Pearce Williams, *The Cold War–Who Is To Blame?* (New York: Random House, 1967); and Alfred F. Young, ed. *Dissent: Explorations in the History of American Radicalism* (DeKalb, IL: Northern Illinois University Press, 1968).

Sources for background in education during this period were: Jerome Bruner, *The Process of Education* (New York: Vintage Books, rpts., 1963); "Education: Our Heritage and Our Future" (Special Diamond Jubilee Issue), *Phi Delta Kappan* 62 (January 1981); Diane Ravitch, *The Troubled Crusade: American Education, 1945–1980* (New York: Basic Books, 1983); and William Henry Schubert, *Curriculum Books: The First Eighty Years* (Washington, DC: University Press of America, 1980).

2. A representative sample of such writing was: James Becker, "What is Education for International Understanding?" *Social Education* 30 (January 1966): 30–31; A. S. Cevery, "Peace Education in the Family," *International Journal of Religious Education* 43 (February 1967): 20–21; H. Cleveland, "Building the Machinery of Peace," *International Journal of Religious Education* 40 (1964): 6–7; Stanley Elam, "International Threat to International Education," *Phi Delta Kappan* 49 (December 1967): 169; W. B. Elley, "Attitude Changes and Education for International Understanding," *Sociology of Education* 37 (Summer 1964): 318–325; and M. D. O'Shea, "Ecumenism and Education for Peace." *Religious Education Journal* 62 (March 1967): 169.

3. Michael Nagler, "Nonviolence," in Ernest Laszlo, ed. *World Encyclopedia of Peace, Vol. 2* (New York: Pergamon Press, 1986), 72–77. Also Louis Fischer, ed., *The Essential Gandhi*

(London: Allen and Unwin, 1963); Gene Sharp, *The Politics of Nonviolent Action* (Boston: Porter Sargent, 1973); and Malcolm Sibley, *The Quiet Battle: Writings on the Theory and Practice of Non-violent Resistance* (New York: Doubleday, 1963).

4. This definition was developed from several sources, including Lee Anderson, *Schooling and Citizenship in a Global Age: An Exploration of the Meaning and Significance of Global Education* (Bloomington, IN: Indiana University, Social Studies Development Center, 1979), 428; and James M. Becker, ed., *Schooling for a Global Society* (New York: McGraw-Hill, 1979), 233–234.

5. Leonard Kenworthy, "Studying Other Countries," *Social Education* 23 (4) (April 1959); "Teaching about the World: Secondary," *Educational Leadership* 21 (March 1964): 358–360; "Accepting the Selves of Others: People Around the World," *Childhood Education* 41 (March 1965): 333–338; and "International Dimension of Elementary Schools," *Phi Delta Kappan* 49 (December 1967): 203–207.

6. Saul H. Mendlovitz and Betty Reardon, "World Law and Models of World Order," National Council for the Social Studies, *Thirty-Eighth Yearbook* (Washington, DC: National Council for the Social Studies, 1968); Saul H. Mendlovitz, "Teaching War Prevention," *Social Education* 28 (October 1964): 328–330 and Betty Reardon, "World Law Fund: World Approach to International Education," *Teachers College Record* 68 (March 1967): 453–465.

7. Alan and Hanna Newcombe, *Peace Research Around the World,* (Oakville, Ontario: Canadian Peace Research Institute, 1969), 12–13. The Newcombes discussed Conflict Studies in America during the sixties, especially the work of Theodore F. Lentz at the St. Louis Peace Research Laboratory at Washington University and William Eckhardt at the Des Moines Peace Research Group.

8. A. Michael Washburn, "Peace Education Is Alive—But Unsure of Itself," *Social Science Record* 9 (Winter 1972): 65–66. Washburn, then director of the World Law Fund's University Program, discussed the conflict resolution approach in peace research and education that began in the fifties at several universities and continued throughout the sixties,

including interpersonal and international levels, as a potential core curriculum for future programs.

9. Merle Curti, "An Afterword-Peace Leaders and the American Heroic Tradition" in Charles DeBenedetti, ed., *Peace Heroes in Twentieth Century America* (Bloomington, IN: Indiana University Press, 1986), 256–270. Curti believed that violence was used to displace America's original natives and black slaves as a means to control labor and to maintain order in urban slums. Leaders of the civil rights and antiwar movements were considered peace heroes with "vision, courage, leadership and sacrifices" that resulted in deeds of "heroic significance."

10. Taylor Branch, *Parting the Waters: America in the King Years, 1954–1963* (New York: Simon and Schuster, 1988), 757.

11. Branch, 762.

12. Staughton Lynd, "The Freedom Schools: Concept and Organization" in Massimo Teodori, ed., *The New Left: A Documentary History* (Indianapolis, IN: Bobbs-Merrill, 1969), 102–11.

13. Leon Friedman, ed., *The Civil Rights Reader: Basic Documents of the Civil Rights Movement* (New York: Walker and Company, 1967), 70–79 with excerpts from Elizabeth Sutherland, ed., *Letters from Mississippi* (New York: McGraw-Hill, 1965).

14. Lynd, 104–105.

15. Friedman, 75.

16. Friedman, 77–78.

17. Friedman, 76. An intriguing chronicle of the development of Head Start programs for young black children in Mississippi, that started the year after Freedom Summer, has been written by Polly Greenberg in *The Devil Has Slippery Shoes: A Biased Biography of the Child Development Group of Mississippi* (London: Collier/Macmillan, 1969).

18. Doug McAdam, "The Biographical Consequences of Activism," *American Sociological Review*, 54 (October 1989), 744–760; *Freedom Summer* (New York: Oxford University Press, 1988); "Recruitment to High-Risk Activism: The Case of Freedom Summer," *American Journal of Sociology*, 92 (1986), 64–90; and "Gender as a Mediator of the Activist Experience: The Case of Freedom Summer," *American Journal of Sociology*, (March 1992), 1211–40.

19. Denise K. Magner, "Blacks and Whites on the Campuses: Behind Ugly Racist Incidents, Student Isolation and Insensitivity," *Chronicle of Higher Education,* 26 April 1989, 35; and William Damon, "Learning How to Deal with the New American Dilemma: We Must Teach Our Students About Morality and Racism," *Chronicle of Higher Education,* 3 May 1989, 35: B1–3.

20. Diane Ravitch, *The Troubled Crusade,* 190. Ravitch designed several working definitions for a discussion of liberal and radical elements in the antiwar movement. "Liberal" denoted those who believed that changes within the political system were possible, while "radicals" believed that the entire system needed to be replaced. "Activists" were politically active students, regardless of political orientation. The term "New Left" described students primarily associated with the group, Students for a Democratic Society.

21. U.S. News and World Report, *Communism and the New Left: What They're Up To Now* (Washington, DC: U.S. News and World Report, 1969), 30–31, 167. This investigative report attempted to link Communists with antiwar activists.

22. Wayne A. R. Leys and P. S. S. Rama Rao, *Gandhi and America's Educational Future* (Carbondale and Edwardsville, IL: Southern Illinois University Press, 1969), Foreword, n.p.

23. Gandhi's instructional method recommended for teaching children, rooted in nonviolence, was the subject of several research studies in America and abroad, such as M. S. Patel, The Educational Philosophy of Mohatma Gandhi (Ahmedadad, India: Navajivan Publishing House, 1952.

24. Bernard Sternsher, *Consensus, Conflict and American History* (Bloomington, IN: Indiana University Press, 1975), 229.

25. J. Ray Hays, ed., *Violence and the Violent Individual* (New York: SP Medical and Scientific Books, 1980), 422; and *Violence in America: Historical and Comparative Perspectives. A Report to the National Commission on the Causes and Prevention of Violence* (New York: Signet Books, 1969).

26. Barbara Habenstreit, *Men Against War* (Garden City, NY: Doubleday, 1973), 179–201.

27. Charles DeBenedetti, *The Peace Reform in American History,* (Bloomington, IN: Indiana University Press, 1980), 167–168 documented the efforts of the House Un-American Activities

Committee to identify "citizen peace seeking with Communist subversion." In 1981, the author was able to follow up his research with declassified documents, discussed in "A CIA Analysis of the Anti-Vietnam War Movement: October 1967," *Peace and Change: A Journal of Peace Research* 9 (Spring 1983): 36–39, published by COPRED-Consortium on Peace Research Education and Development. Michael Parenti, *The Anti-Communist Impulse* (New York: Random House, 1969), 72, also confirmed that "obsessive anti-communism" was used in the sixties whenever a "global enemy" menaced "the American Way of Life."

28. National Education Association, *Addresses and Proceedings,* Detroit Meeting, 30 June-5 July 1963 (Washington, DC.: NEA, 1963).

29. "W.C.O.T.P. and UNESCO: Close Consultation Planned," *Times Educational Supplement,* 2568 (August 7 1965), 200.

30. Robert Maheu, "UNESCO Is Your Organization," *National Education Association Journal* 54 (March 1965), 30.

31. *Landmarks in International Co-Operation* (New York: Office of Public Information, United Nations, 1965), ix.

32. *Landmarks,* 80.

33. *Landmarks,* 79–87.

34. *Landmarks,* 95–96.

35. *Landmarks,* 95–96.

36. *Peace and World Order Studies: A Curriculum Guide,* 1st ed. (New York: Transnational Academic Program, Institute for World Order, 1973).

37. Richard A. Falk and Saul H. Mendlovitz, *The Strategy of World Order* (New York: World Law Fund, 1966).

38. *Studies Toward Peace: A Compendium of Selected Undergraduate and Graduate Courses in "Peace and World Order,"* (New York: Student Forum on International Order and World Peace, 1969), ii.

39. *Studies Toward Peace,* ii.

40. *Studies Toward Peace,* iii.

41. Grenville Clark and Louis B. Sohn, *World Peace Through World Law: Two Alternative Plans* (Cambridge, MA: Harvard University Press, 1966) and "World Order: The Need for a Bold New Approach" *Social Education* 26 (November 1962), 397–401.

42. Richard A. Falk, "The Revolution in Peace Education," *Saturday Review of Literature* 49 (May 21, 1966): 59–61. See Note 6 for additional articles.
43. Betty Reardon, *Comprehensive Peace Education: Educating for Global Responsibility* (New York: Teachers College Press, 1988), 5.
44. "Fallout Shelters and the Schools," *National Education Association Journal* 51 (February 1962): 23; "Planning a School Fallout Shelter," *American School Board Journal* 143 (November 1961): 28; "Nuclear Bomb Shelter in Plans for New Schools at Federal Expense," *Nation's Schools* 68 (November 1961): 68–74.
45. Henry Cabot Lodge, "Atlantic Institute and the Future of the Free World," *National Association of Secondary School Principals' Bulletin* 47 (April 1963): 92–97; Christian Herter, "Common Market, the Trade Expansion Act and Atlantic Partnership," *National Association of Secondary School Principals' Bulletin* 47 (April 1963): 84–92; Lauris Norstad, "NATO Problem," *American Association of School Administrators Official Report* (1966) 15–62; Dean Rusk, "Education for Citizenship in the Modern World," *American Association of School Administrators Official Report* (1964), 30–40; "Our Concern for Peace in East Asia," *National Association of School Principals' Bulletin,* 52 (May 1968): 3–14; and William Westmoreland, Address to the American Association of School Administrators (Washington, DC.: American Association of School Administrators, 1969), 5–14.
46. The Danforth Foundation and the Ford Foundation, *The School and the Democratic Environment* (New York: Columbia University Press, 1960), 5.
47. John S. Gibson, *New Frontiers in the Social Studies: Goals for Students, Means for Teachers,* (Medford, MA: Tufts University, 1965).
48. Gibson, 5.
49. Gibson, 67.
50. Gibson, 67–68.
51. Gibson, 67–68.
52. Gibson, 68.
53. Gibson, 69.
54. Harold M. Long and Robert N. King, *Improving the Teaching*

of World Affairs: The Glens Falls Story (Washington, DC: National Council for the Social Studies, 1964).

55. Mailing to the membership of Association for Supervision and Curriculum Development (ASCD), 1 September 1964.

56. The Glens Falls Story (descriptive literature), (Washington, DC: Association for Supervision and Curriculum Development, 1964).

57. Long and King, 1.

58. Long and King, 16, 18.

59. Long and King, 20.

60. Long and King, 16.

61. Long and King, 18.

62. Other works published with some references to peace education during the sixties were: Russell D. Brackett, *Pathways to Peace* (Minneapolis: T. S. Denison, 1963) which reported on "people-to-peace in action" and various international educational exchanges, Peace Corps, and personal diplomacy projects and Arthur Larson, ed., *A Warless World* (New York: McGraw-Hill, 1963), 169–171, which called for the fields of education and public information to apply research in order to make a warless world possible. Other works published in peace research and history were: Peter Brock, *Pacifism in the United States: From the Colonial Era to the First World War* (Princeton: Princeton University Press, 1968); Blanche Wiesen Cook, ed., *Bibliography on Peace Research in History* (Santa Barbara, CA: ABC–CLIO, 1969); Merle Curti, *The American Peace Crusade, 1815–1860* (New York: Octagon Books, 1965) and *Bryan and World Peace* (New York: Octagon Books, 1969); Sondra R. Herman, *Eleven Against War: Studies in American Internationalist Thought, 1898–1921* (Stanford: Hoover Institute Press, 1969); and Lawrence S. Wittner, *Rebels Against the War: The American Peace Movement, 1941–1960* (New York: Columbia University Press, 1969).

63. Kenneth Boulding, *Stable Peace* (Austin, TX: University of Texas Press, 1978), 3.

7. GROWTH AND EXPANSION, 1971–1980

A FRAMEWORK AND A PROCESS

The decade of the sixties wound down with an extraordinary burst of violence in the spring of 1968.[1] The Vietnamese launched the devastating Tet offensive which resulted in increased American losses. President Lyndon Johnson had earlier promised that no escalation of the war (still undeclared) would occur yet the White House proposal for the 1968–69 budget included increased spending to continue the war. American hopes for a quick end to the conflict faded. Military analysts wrote frequently of the folly of continuing a war that had faint hope of a victory.

The war actually came closer to an end in 1968 when President Johnson consulted with the Council on Foreign Relations, a nongovernmental, advisory group (considered a semiofficial power elite by some political analysts) that consisted of former government officials such as Douglas Dillon, McGeorge Bundy, and Generals Omar Bradley and Matthew Ridgeway. After a seven-day review the men concluded that "the war was a military failure" that caused "divisiveness in the country." They advised Johnson to begin negotiations to end the struggle. On April 3rd, the first steps began with the announcement of diplomatic talks between American forces and North Vietnam. The initial peace talks failed and the war continued for five more years.

Martin Luther King Jr. was assassinated in Memphis in April 1968. New waves of violence were felt throughout America in over 75 cities. Americans living in urban areas remembered well the repercussions as fires and looting left areas burned out as if an aerial bombing had occurred. Remembered also were the real fears for the personal safety of families living in the affected area.

The campus rebellion at Columbia University, considered the largest national student strike in American history, also began in April, 1968. Students occupied campus buildings and demanded that they be permitted a voice in decision making. University officials responded with police arrest of 700 students and charges of police brutality. In other corners of the globe student uprisings also developed with massive protests in France, West Germany, Mexico, Czechoslovakia, and Poland.

In May Robert Kennedy was assassinated in a prelude to unprecedented violence during the week of the Democratic National Convention in Chicago. Reports from the Commission on the Causes and Prevention of Violence later determined that the mayhem was caused by a police riot.

The scenes of violence shifted repeatedly back to the college campus with riots and street fighting at the University of California at Berkeley, the University of Wisconsin at Madison, the University of Chicago, American University, and University of Tennessee, among others. Perhaps the most serious campus uprising occurred in the Spring of 1969 at Berkeley with 17 days of street fighting. A nonviolent march occurred with almost 30,000 people who protested the University's plans to turn a vacant campus lot into a shopping mall. Police shot at students and many were hospitalized. Scenes such as these were a prelude to the tragedy that occurred on college campuses in Ohio and Mississippi.

The deaths of four students at Kent State University in Ohio and two more at Jackson State University in Mississippi galvanized protest throughout the country with almost 500 campuses reporting unrest, strikes, or sit-ins in 1970.

The Vietnam War protests, especially after Nixon's reelection in 1972, included wider circles of Americans some of whom were not formally affiliated with an organization.[2]

However, peace movement groups expanded their ranks considerably. Veterans returned from combat in Vietnam and also joined in the dissent to protest the senseless killing of fellow Americans that was permitted to continue. Growing numbers of citizens expressed anger at a government seemingly insensitive to public opinion. Families reported that the Vietnam War era forced a wedge into their intimate circles with brother pitted against brother as had occurred during the Civil War. Parents became polarized by opposing forces when their children engaged in draft resistance and antiwar protest.

Americans slowly learned of the brutal treatment accorded to the enemy who were dehumanized as subhuman "gooks." News of the treatment of the Vietnamese civilian populations especially in the My Lai massacre (kept secret for a year), defoliation of the countryside, planned flooding of fields to cause starvation and other questionable tactics raised the consciousness of many Americans who finally became aware of what their government was doing in their names.

Information revealed by the secret Pentagon Papers proved equally as troubling. The bombing of Hanoi in the spring of 1974 was especially disastrous, with 15 American bombers shot down and sixty-two pilots killed. A few weeks later the United States signed a peace agreement that finally began the process for troop withdrawals.

The closing decade of the seventies brought a new political figure to center stage, a native Georgian named Jimmy Carter. His first executive order pardoned Vietnam draft evaders in an honest attempt to heal the deep scars in American society produced by the war. The antagonistic relationship with the Soviet Union that strained a period of détente was exacerbated by the Soviet invasion of Afghanistan in 1979.

Peace education in the sixties exhibited a tremendous growth in a period that could be considered as latent adolescence before attaining a stage of maturity in the eighties. Each of the basic components of peace education initiated in the sixties—global education, world order education, and conflict resolution—emerged from the sixties with a framework, rationale, philosophy, as well as practical skills, and strategies for success. New strands were added: human rights and development education and the feminist perspective.

Human rights and development education as new adjuncts to peace education were manifestations of increased advocacy of international organizations. These included the United Nations and peace organizations, such as IPRA (International Peace Research Association, founded in 1964) and its Peace Education Commission (founded in 1972) along with COPRED (Consortium on Peace Research Education and Development) as a North American affiliate of IPRA and its PEN (Peace Education Network). COPRED and its affiliated organizations were formed in the seventies.

Educational organizations exhibited strong leadership qualities. The Association for Supervision and Curriculum Development (ASCD) in 1973 proved to be a catalyst with a landmark publication titled *Education for Peace: Focus on Mankind.* A similar mission had advanced the cause with *Educating for Peace,* a project of the National Council for Teachers of English (1940).

Publication in America of Maria Montessori's work, *Education and Peace* in 1972 provided a philosophy and rationale for an emergent pedagogy in peace education. Elise Boulding, a pioneer sociologist, also shaped a complementary nonviolent philosophy and models. These provided a frame of reference regarding the socialization of the child.

In previous decades peace education appeared as "hidden history," gossamer threads of a chronicle held together sparsely by human efforts, limited written records, and rare examples of actual practices. By the seventies, however, peace education slowly attained recognition in a few areas of the educational community. Growing numbers of courses in peace studies and world order education proved that in some areas of the academic world education for peace was worthy of serious study.

As an outgrowth of the violence and dissent of the sixties, peace education developed a future core curriculum with conflict resolution becoming a viable method for teaching a new generation to live together in peace. In 1899 arbitration to resolve an international conflict was first used at the Hague Conference. This valuable strategy to resolve conflicts was known for almost a century. Failure to apply it, mediation, and similar forms of conflict resolution proved to be a backward misstep in history. As a result, peaceful resolution was shunted aside and violence and warfare adopted in its place. Curriculum and projects in nonviolent conflict resolution were initiated and developed in the seventies and further expanded into the eighties. Peace education gained a valuable addition with nonviolent conflict resolution as a basic paradigm.

PEACE EDUCATION: A LEGITIMATE AREA OF STUDY

Arising from the backdrop of violence and dissent in the sixties, peace education in the seventies became a legitimate, credible discipline. First, a Peace Education Commission became a part of the International Peace Research Association with members throughout the world who were involved in peace education. Meetings were held during conferences convened by international organizations. Researchers in North America eventually established the aforementioned COPRED, the affiliate of IPRA, which has made invaluable contributions to the development of a pedagogy. Its journal, *Peace and Change,* has served as a forum for dissemination of models and designs for peace education and other segments of peace research.

The Peace Education Network, an interest group of

COPRED, was organized originally as an information exchange. PEN has been described as a network of elementary and secondary teachers who shared their work with others interested in promoting peace education in the schools. The network bore similarities to the one conceived by the American School Peace League and American School Citizenship League in the early years of the century. PEN has concentrated on "introducing and developing nonviolent conflict resolution as a central concept of American peace education."

Betty Reardon, the pioneer peace educator, explained her involvement with PEN during the formative years of the seventies. The curriculums developed by PEN stressed new classroom methods such as participatory learning, inquiry, problem solving, and strategies often included values clarification, role playing simulation, and games as elements of the "new social studies."[3] In addition to concern about peace and justice issues, members of PEN were concerned about curriculum development and design that reflected the ethical dimension. Values education was described by Reardon as a target for criticism throughout the seventies. Teaching peace as a values issue continued to be an enigma for several decades.

The NEA in 1976 unveiled a bicentennial program that advanced global education. Titled "A Declaration of Interdependence" 20 projects were designed to enhance "education in an interdependent Global Community."[4]

Susan Carpenter designed a curricular framework and process for peace and education (1974) that included an array of peacemaking skills for the classroom. In addition, she believed that conflict resolution could be integrated throughout the curriculum. Carpenter underscored the problem that faced peace educators in the seventies as the need to articulate "general goals, purposes, approaches, and components of peace education." Her contributions evolved with a model that covered the basic components of peacemaking.

The peace transformation process envisioned by Carpenter included seven components:

Analysis: 1. Description of the peaceful and unpeaceful qualities in a relationship (of parties);
 2. Analysis of (the parties') attitudes, perceptions, values and goals . . .
Imaging: 3. Imaging more peaceful patterns . . .
Strategies: 4. Education of parties in the relationship to raise the levels of awareness;
 5. Confrontation by the less powerful party in order to acquire more power;
 6. Conflict resolution between the two conflicting parties through conciliation, and bargaining;
 7. Development of more harmonious, mutually beneficial patterns of relating.[5]

Carpenter's proposal provided a synthesis of two separate, distinct areas that characterized peace education in the seventies and later in the eighties. The first concentration involved the rational/cognitive realm with an emphasis on analysis and critical thinking skills. The second area concentrated on the creative/imaginative/affective domain with an emphasis on values, attitudes, and imagining alternative solutions as with conflict resolution of the global or world order perspectives. Analysis and critical thinking skills were also integrated into this second area, but with concern for the human feelings and emotions engendered, as a logical addition.[6]

Carpenter's dissertation can be considered as a landmark contribution to the emerging curriculum design and development of the process of peace education. A *Repertoire of Peacemaking Skills,* based on her dissertation, has been recommended as a work that is "well grounded theoretically . . . and also imminently practical."[7]

EXPANSION OF MAJOR COMPONENTS FROM THE SIXTIES:

During the sixties peace education goals were defined as components at various times of world affairs or international education, citizenship education, or education for international understanding. In the seventies peace education emerged from a camouflage of semantics in order to gain valid recognition as an educational discipline. This period was notable for its expanded study of, and insights into, the major components of peace education.

World Order Values

Beginning in 1970 the World Law Fund assumed an assertive role in the evolution of peace education. A. Michael Washburn, the director of the World Law Fund's University Program at that time defined the world order approach as:

> An international or global system of stable institutions
> designed to regulate large-scale violence and to achieve
> a just distribution of values.[8]

Washburn identified the obstacles faced by developers of peace studies in higher education as training for faculty, inadequate finances and budget arrangements, poor publicity, and lack of teaching materials.[9] At that time, he confirmed that World Law Fund materials were used in 300 peace-related courses.[10]

The World Law Fund, with almost two decades of experience, can be considered as a pioneer in the curriculum development of peace education. The Fund described its original mission as "the introduction of world order and peace into . . . all major educational systems of the world . . . graduate, undergraduate and secondary school levels."[11]

In the 1970s the World Law Fund changed its name to the Institute for World Order. Juergen Dedring, the noted peace researcher, recognized the Institute as "foremost in North America" with separate program sections for elementary, secondary, and postsecondary peace education.[12] Transnational cooperation was in evidence with the publication of a peace education volume, *Handbook on Peace Education* in collaboration with the German Society for Peace and Conflict Research, the German Institute for Educational Research, and the International Peace Research Association.[13]

Counterculture perspectives added another intellectual puzzle to the period. Diane Ravitch, at that time affiliated with Teachers College, Columbia University cited protests against university ties to military research, defense industries, and corporate interests.[14] A counterculture protest was sometimes typified in the public mind by the "hippie" and "drug culture." Counterculture perspectives revolved around the concept that a total transformation was needed in America to bring about peace, social justice, and the world order values. A gradual, incremental introduction of a perspective would not be sufficient. These added to the crosscurrents of intellectual thought that contributed to the evolution of world order education as a system and a peace education curriculum.[15]

An examination of other organizations and publications showed the influence of world order education. The International Conference on Expanding Dimensions of World Education, held in Ankara, Turkey (1976) accepted world order values as a key "to peace education" within the context of operating as an agent to relieve the problems of the oppressed.[16] In addition, UNESCO adopted a resolution that included "peace education for all of the member states of UNESCO."[17]

In 1978, an expanded mission for the Institute for World Order was revealed, along with a new funding source for the Institute, with the publication of the second edition of *Peace and World Order Studies: A Curriculum Guide.* The Institute's broader goals now included: a world order of peace, social justice, economic well-being, and ecological balance. The publication of the curriculum guide and a companion course manual also revealed that the Rockefeller Foundation had become a new financial underwriter of the Institute.[18] In subsequent years, Archibald Gillies, a former business associate of Nelson Rockefeller, would be named Executive Director of the Institute.

Global Perspective

Peace education with a global perspective was a theme that was expressed with many variations throughout the seventies. The interdependence of human beings and their needs, peacemaking skills, conflict resolution, and social justice were basic components.

A leading educational organization, the Association for Supervision and Curriculum Development (ASCD) provided an impetus for peace education curriculum development in 1973. In a landmark volume, *Education for Peace: Focus on Mankind,* peace education was given an expanded meaning, articulated by James Becker, who at that time was associated with the Foreign Policy Association. He believed that peace education was not so much an idealistic dream as:

> a need to reduce the militarization of our economy and our educational system to the point where problems like poverty and pollution can receive the attention needed to improve man's chances for survival.[19]

Becker proposed that the student learn that the world is a planet-wide society characterized by change, "conflict, ambiguity and increasing interdependence."[20]

In 1978, the ASCD once more provided a forum for peace education, but this time with the addition of a global perspective. A yearbook titled, *Improving the Human Condition: A Curricular Response to Critical Realities,* defined the new view as:

> An international or global perspective is not the development of a new course, but rather represents a new way of looking at all education for citizenship.[21]

The two volumes by ASCD involved the cooperative research of curriculum designers, psychologists, political scientists, and classroom teachers.

Lee Anderson, a colleague of Becker at Indiana University and later a professor at Northwestern University, also made a major contribution to the expansion of peace education with a global perspective in *Schooling and Citizenship in a Global Age*.[22] Anderson presented an overview of "the transformation of world history" which dramatized the transition of the world from "separate and isolated regional histories to an era in which world history has become . . . global history." The global perspective should be extended, Anderson stated, to history that would be "shared by all of the regions of the planet."[23] Expansion of the global perspective should include a planetary perspective as well, adding a new facet to peace education, though one expressed as early as 1968 by Kenneth Boulding.[24]

Anderson also clarified the semantic confusion of the term, "interdependence" providing as a definition: "The extent to which events occurring in any one part of the world system affect . . . events taking place in the other units of the system."[25] Anderson believed in the need for a new economic order in an effort to rectify the maldistribution of world income in recognition of the new area of human rights and development education. In addition, he outlined the new skills and citizen competencies that would be required for a global perspective, especially competent decision making and critical thinking, competencies not traditionally emphasized by the schools.

Becker, Anderson, and other educators during the seventies provided a design for peace education with a global perspective including the requisite skills that would reshape the thinking of many educators and students in the eighties.[26] The successful infusion of the global perspective into the curriculum of America's schools (in some states) offers one example of the success of a component that can be traced back to a peace education origin.

Other pioneers in global education, Patricia and Gerald Mische founded Global Education Associates as a nonprofit educational association (1973). This association links educators in 50 countries in a network that since 1973 has grown to encompass a wide variety of activities, conferences, workshops, and literature. The organization is currently trying to lay the foundation for world order structures which have a transcultural perspective. The organization expanded its horizons in the eighties, with books and curriculum materials, available for use in some parts of Africa, Asia, Europe, and North and South America. Institutes of educators and researchers have—and continue to—work cooperatively under the auspices of the Associates.[27]

Another organization, Global Perspectives in Education, also emerged as a key promoter of an international perspective in the seventies. Through its journal, *Intercom,* innovative teaching activities were developed and discussed and ideas for the integration of a global perspective in elementary and secondary schools were stressed. Steady growth and expansion would become further evident in the eighties, with the establishment of American Forum for Global Education (Global Perspectives in Education, Inc.), identified in that organization's literature as a "national resource center for global education."[28]

Expansion of Conflict Resolution

Throughout this period there was an outpouring of materials that were scholarly and pragmatic. These contributed to the formalization of peace education as a curriculum based on nonviolence and conflict resolution. These two basic strands became the foundations for peace education throughout the seventies. The influence continued into the eighties with a proliferation of curriculum and school-based action programs, such as school mediation, as alternatives to the growing violence in a rapidly changing, multicultural society.

Conflict resolution emerged in the seventies, along with

escalation of military action in Vietnam and with it increased citizen activism and feelings of powerlessness to change government policy. At the same time America faced growing military power in a great buildup of conventional and nuclear forces that continued to overshadow all, as in previous decades, with the danger of nuclear war. All of these factors contributed to the development of conflict resolution as a centerpiece for peace education in the seventies.

The experience in Vietnam brought about discernible changes in American attitudes and consciences. Especially on the college and university campus attention next shifted to an analysis of conflict studies and peace research.[29] Programs were reported at the University of Wisconsin, University of Washington, Stanford University, and Michigan State University. At that time A. Michael Washburn, Director of the World Law Fund program reported that scholars were "more concerned with research than with undergraduate teaching."[30] Yet, within a short period a methodology, language and "array of data banks" had emerged as a result of the concentration of research. By the eighties research-based courses and syllabi would be available at a large number of colleges and universities.

The research in conflict resolution in the seventies lighted the way for a tremendous growth spurt that followed in the eighties. The four basic areas of research into nonviolent conflict resolution generally included: (1) intrapersonal conflict, that is, internal conflicts within a person; (2) interpersonal conflict, such as conflicts of values or between family members; (3) intergroup conflicts, as among groups, communities or nations; and (4) conflicts concerning goals and objectives as the means or methods to resolve conflicts.

Reactions to conflict situations may involve avoidance of the issue, force or violence, nonviolence (reaching a consensus), or compromise. Conflict resolution as a major component in peace education involved alternatives to violent responses or aggression. Educators believed that children and young people could acquire the skills and strategies to settle problems

peacefully. Problem-solving skills, with opportunities to practice them, included analysis of scenarios or situations that
called for nonviolent strategies. These basic premises emerged
as the core of a curriculum for conflict resolution.[31]

A comprehensive study, *Conflict Resolution: Contributions of the Behavioral Sciences* (1971) was published during
this period.[32] The objectives of the study, which grew out of
a program on nonviolence at Notre Dame University,
included a "multidisciplinary approach . . . with an emphasis
on the operational, the feasible, by which a practitioner or
policy-maker can achieve some leverage."[33] A broad spectrum of viewpoints represented the fields of economics,
anthropology, government, communications, research, history, and foreign affairs.

A definitive study of nonviolence was published in the
seventies. Gene Sharp, Director of the Harvard University
Program on Nonviolent Sanctions, described nearly 200
methods of nonviolent social intervention (NVSI) or action
that had been used throughout history to effect social or
political change.[34]

By the eighties most of these methods, such as strikes,
marches and sit-ins, had been used with some degree of
success in Chile, Pakistan, and the Philippines.[35] The
far-reaching changes that would occur in Eastern Europe in
the period of 1989–1990 were viewed by many peace
researchers as a vindication of the force of nonviolence as
carried out by the people. Sharp stated that he perceived a
"major growth of non-violent struggle in the world" since the
mid-eighties.[36]

HUMAN RIGHTS EDUCATION AND DEVELOPMENT
EDUCATION

As an adjunct to the world order values, human rights
education came to the forefront from the international law of

human rights as codified in such documents as the Universal Declaration of Human Rights, the Charter of the United Nations, and the International Covenants on Human Rights.[37] In 1978, UNESCO organized a Congress on the Teaching of Human Rights (Vienna) which mandated that "equal emphasis should be placed on economic, social, cultural, civil and political rights" with "human rights education and teaching based on the principles" of the aforementioned international documents.

Objectives for human rights education were outlined as being: (1) to develop an awareness in students of the "universal yearning for human rights"; (2) to offer students basic knowledge concerning the protection of human rights; (3) to help students to experience "thinking critically about these issues" and especially discussion of specific cases of the denial of human rights; and (4) to develop a "concern or empathy" for those who have experienced denial of their rights.[38]

Implicit in teaching about human rights was the recognition that values would need to be identified as a "significant dimension of the life of learners" with a balance between the cognitive and affective methods of education.[39] This dimension of human rights education continued to be reshaped and redefined in the eighties, as a conceptual approach inherent in the peace education curriculum.

Development education has been defined as concern for the value of increasing material well-being.[40] Implicit in these studies was a concern for the unequal distribution of resources that limited human life as a form of subtle, indirect violence. The term "structural violence" has been used frequently in the literature of peace education to define this condition, which is usually imposed by economic institutions.[41] Critical thinking on the part of the learner was demanded in order to discern the inequities of conditions decreed for a large portion of humanity. Development education was further advanced as a goal that should be "part of lifelong learning," including the "ability to detect bias in the presentation of information."

The power of the multinational corporation had been cited frequently in the literature on development education as a principal actor in Third World nations. Corporate power had grown unhampered throughout the seventies and into the eighties with the imposition of oppressive working conditions and wage scales on laborers, especially upon women and child workers. With the growth of American corporate interests to include wider use of offshore industrial enterprises and licensing agreements, concerns about these and other conditions were first brought to light in the 1970s through tenets and teachings of development education.

A catalyst to the unfolding dialogue on development and human rights may have been the publication in the seventies of works by Paulo Freire, the noted Brazilian educator.[42] Through the process of peace education, he believed, learning needed to be linked to social action as in the pursuit of human rights or the enfolding of literacy to uneducated peasants. In other words, education must pass beyond the point where the teacher simply imparted a knowledge base as in the common metaphor described as "filling up an empty vessel." As an alternative, learners could reject the principles of the dominant elite and participate in bringing about social and political change. Such motivated learners could reject their inferior, illiterate states. This theory was embodied in Freire's theory of "conscientização" or "moral imagination" in a liberal translation from the Brazilian Portuguese.[43] Such ideas embodied in liberatory education created a spirit of ferment and motivated many to participate in grass-roots efforts to bring about social change in developing communities. Peace education in this case would be community development and would include literacy to bring about basic human needs as a necessary adjunct to human rights. Even in so-called developed nations, the ideal would be the involvement of "learners in local issues relevant to peace, development and human rights."[44]

FEMINIST PERSPECTIVE: LINKS BETWEEN SEXISM AND MILITARISM

Peace education gained a new strand in the seventies with efforts to promote equality between men and women and to consider the roots of militarism and sexism as necessary stages in any plans for an abolition of war.[45] A United Nations World Conference of the International Women's Year held in Mexico City in 1975 launched the efforts of women to gain greater participation in decision making for peace.[46]

By the eighties, definitive studies were completed by Betty Reardon, of Columbia University's Teachers College Peace Education Program and Brigit Brock-Utne, a Norwegian peace researcher, among others, which provided detailed and scholarly explorations of feminist perspectives.[47] One viewpoint concerned militarism as a dominant patriarchy that has existed over centuries. The second viewpoint was that imperialism, and especially capitalism and the corporation, were forms of "neocolonialism" and obstacles to global transformation.[48]

Efforts to delineate the parameters of the war system and sexism as discrimination against the efforts of women actually had its genesis in 1919. Women delegates from the Woman's Peace Party attempted to gain a place in the decision making at the Paris Peace Conference (see Chapter 3). An incident in the life of Emily Greene Balch, delegate with the Women's International League for Peace and Freedom (WILPF), who received the Nobel Peace Prize in 1946, shed considerable light on the perception that political and military decision making could be considered patriarchal. Director of the Nobel Institute, Gunnar Jahn stated:

> I want to say . . . that it would have been extremely wise if the proposal WILPF (and Balch) made . . . had been accepted by the Conference . . . few of the men listened to what the women had to say . . . In our patriarchal world suggestions which come from women are seldom taken seriously.[49]

Reardon has been especially vocal in her criticism of peace research as dominated by male decision making, especially in the academic world. Male researchers, she contends, have created a science, that she named "polemology, the study of war," that has excluded the community of feminine peace researchers. Support of peace research and world order studies have been withheld—attention as well as funding.[50] World order scholars in particular need to recognize that the values inherent in feminine socialization—care and concern for others and intuition as a valid thought process—need to be considered as a vital human viewpoint. Feminist studies, women's studies and world order research need to unite in a cooperative scholarship mode. Throughout the seventies Reardon reiterated the view in her writings that the human dimension has been lacking from peace research with emphasis instead on "weapons counting," arms control, and defense technicalities.[51]

*   *   *   *   *   *   *   *   *   *   *   *   *   *   *   *   *

Despite the accumulation of an expanded body of literature, a guide to information sources in the history of American education ignored the existence of peace education with no references to peace, global or world order education, nor to conflict resolution.[52] The *Education Index,* a major reference for researchers belatedly included a first reference to conflict resolution only in 1974 as an addition from the field of child psychology.[53]

PEACE EDUCATION AND THE CHILD

Throughout two decades, the sixties and the seventies, there was an extension of education to regress the history of minority oppression. Diane Ravitch outlined these central forces for social change as: affirmative action, sex equity in higher education, bilingual education, and the rights of handicapped children. Desegregation, busing, compensatory education, and mainstreaming were all added to the agenda for America's teachers.[54]

From the perspective of peace education, however, the original thrust of social welfare legislation in the seventies could be construed as methods to alleviate inequitable opportunity for the children of poverty. Translated into a care and concern for the basic rights of children, this philosophy had its heritage in the pedagogy of Rousseau, Froebel, Pestalozzi, and Dewey.

At various times in history, the rights of the child have been totally ignored. The persistence of child labor until the twenties was a case in point. Legislation prohibiting child labor occurred only after decades of lobbying for change by social reformers, many of whom were the same women involved in peace and suffrage issues. Little headway had occurred before then because child labor legislation encountered stiff resistance on the grounds that it was an insidious communist plot, one designed to "nationalize children."[55]

A new viewpoint concerning the child, however, emerged during the 1970s. The educational philosophy and pedagogy of Maria Montessori entered American education and became a significant influence. Montessori emphasized a concern for children as the touchstone for peace education. Written originally in the thirties, it was not until 1972 that her philosophy on peace education, as set forth in *Education and Peace,* was published in the United States and became more widely disseminated.[56]

Montessori as a peace educator and physician, based her rationale on concern for the survival of the child, with a bedrock of Christian theology providing the motive for peace. She was proposed as a candidate for the Nobel Peace Prize in 1949 and 1950, but did not receive the award. Her concern for the survival of children was expressed as:

> When we consider social questions, the child is ignored, as if he were not a member of society at all . . . If we

ponder the influence that education can have on the attainment of world peace, it becomes clear that we must make the child and his education our primary concern.[57]

Montessori worked with children in a multicultural setting in Italy and India. Her work helped form new perspectives for the potential and needs of children, considered as marginal in society—the poor, uneducated, and disabled. She foresaw the vital roles of both education and peace. Her work took her to India where nonviolent Gandhian philosophy added another dimension to her blueprint for the transformation of society.

Underlying her writings was the fundamental issue that peace was a moral issue that could not be ignored but was basic to all education. She declared that "education that represses and rejects the promptings of the moral self . . . erects obstacles and barriers." She believed, too, that "morality was . . . the very basis of social life."[58]

The philosophy of the inherent goodness of the child was articulated by Montessori: "We must have faith in the child as a messiah, as a savior capable of regenerating the human race and society."[59] Montessori also used theological metaphors: "The child's goal might be summed up in the word incarnation . . . a spiritual gestation." Education would be the force to insure that the fullest development of children would be possible, with education as the cornerstone of peace.

The evolution of her philosophy culminated in a political action plan:

> I would like to plant the first seeds of a social movement on behalf of the child . . . founding the Party of the Child . . . The protection of the child is a great new undertaking . . . The child can become the focus . . . a sphere of action that will enable mankind to work together.[60]

Concern for the child, especially the American minority child of poverty, was the incentive for compensatory legislation that was implemented by schools in the sixties and seventies, such as the Head Start program. The writings of educators and sociologists in addition to Montessori echoed similar concerns. Elise Boulding,[61] Judith Torney,[62] Howard Tolley Jr,[63] Vera L. Timm,[64] and Lillian Genser,[65] all underscored the effects of violence and rapid social change on the child. Their contributions in the seventies further enriched a growing pedagogy for peace education.

The issues of aggression and nonviolence were central to the formation of a socialization model. Elise Boulding proposed a model in 1974 that included internal and external factors that were involved in the early socialization process.[66] Boulding further delineated her model by proposing that the process of nonviolent social change provided "optimal opportunities" for the development of "emotional, cognitive, and intuitive capacities in home, school, and community."[67]

Boulding considered bonding responses, both social and spiritual as paramount. Altruism, as related to social bonding, coping, problem-solving play, and imagining an alternative future, were all considered as additional processes, depending on the child's developmental stage. These provided, Boulding believed, "a major resource for creative and peacemaking responses to be taken account of in the socialization process."[68]

Spiritual bonding was considered by Boulding to be the "development by the human of a relationship with the divine . . . reflected in the teachings concerning a divine-human covenant."[69] This bonding could be changed into a "transformation of the individual."

Boulding's model provided a philosophical and pedagogical rationale for a wide variety of curriculum projects in the seventies and later in the eighties that considered a core of spiritual and moral values as essential. Concern for the child's self-esteem as a valued member of the group included affirmation and assurance of love and concern. Strategies to resolve conflicts peacefully rounded out a nonviolent curricu-

lum. The philosophies of Montessori and Boulding contributed to peace education in a tangible manner that educators
could apply in the classroom.

A second area of concern involved the child's socialization
to war as a subtle, perhaps hidden dimension to education.
Howard Tolley Jr. stressed the importance of the relationship of socialization to war as a topic of great importance
during his experiences as a classroom teacher.[70] Tolley used
the questionnaire as a sampling instrument and surveyed
children on their attitudes toward the Vietnam War. Tolley
concluded that there was a general acceptance of war's
necessity among young children with "significant differences
in knowledge between children in each grade up to and
including seventh and eighth." Tolley did not concern his
study with attitudes toward nuclear war. His conclusion
offered proof of the "interdependence of war" with children
influenced by the opinions of their elders and reflecting
contemporary public opinion.[71] He emphasized the importance of changing children's attitudes toward war through
education.

PEACE EDUCATION CURRICULUM IN THE SEVENTIES

During the seventies, an awareness for peace education and
international understanding expanded into a formal methodology in the form of curriculum projects. The period between
1976 and 1979 was especially noteworthy. James Becker in
Schooling for a Global Society described many of these, the
result of an amendment (Title VI) to the National Defense
Education Act.[72] The adoption of peace education curriculum materials into a system, however, was another matter.
Susan Carpenter concluded that there were formidable
obstacles: "Elementary and secondary schools are subject to
more direct pressure from parents and the community." In
addition, many school personnel associated peace with

pacifism and believed peace education "might encourage students not to fight for their country," she stated.[73]

Curriculum for Spaceship Earth

David C. King used a spaceship to teach peace education. The world community existed in microcosm on the spaceship and technical terms for life on board were used frequently.[74] Terra II, another imaginative simulation, was designed for the middle grades by Peggy Mastrude. The setting was described:

> You and 100 others are on a huge spaceship called 'Terra II.' About ten months ago you looked out a porthole and saw Earth for the last time. It really looked small then—about the size of the moon . . . Terra II is a self-supporting small world in space.[75]

Introductory remarks explained that in the future humanity would be faced with a dilemma very similar to that of Terra II, especially the "need to use and sustain earth's resources . . . among all the earth's peoples."[76]

Students assumed roles according to the necessary functions on the spaceship. Science concepts were based on the various systems: food, air, and water. Science, mathematics, and language arts came alive during the lesson-simulation.

A social studies textbook for the elementary grades titled *Environments* embraced a global and planetary perspective. Written under the direction of David King and Global Perspectives in Education, the textbook also emphasized ecology and conservation.[77]

An examination of the student's world included units on "Living on Spaceship Earth" and "A Look at the Future":

> With new technology, people have world power. They can change all parts of the world's environment. With nuclear energy, people also have the terrible power to destroy life on the earth.[78]

The possibility of conflict resolution in settling differences was discussed: "Sometimes differences lead to war . . . The most powerful countries now have enough weapon power to destroy all life on earth." Learning to settle differences was considered important. Learning to work through the United Nations was also included as a theme.[79]

Peace Education Curriculum Guides

Four curriculum guides and handbooks for teachers were developed in the seventies, several the result of Quaker curriculum committees. They embodied principles for world order and nonviolence.

The first Quaker guide, *A Manual on Nonviolence and Children,* was published in 1977 with Stephanie Judson as editor and compiler. The realism of the classroom rang true with activities such as cooperative games and values-clarification exercises, with a core value of nonviolence.[80]

The second guide, *Friendly Classroom for a Small Planet,* was written by the staff of the Children's Creative Response To Conflict Program, under the auspices of the New York Yearly Meeting of the Society of Friends. Curriculum goals were similar to those developed by the first Quaker guide with confirmation that students needed activities to "deal constructively with conflict situations" within the classroom. Children learned skills to resolve conflicts and explored experiences to develop the themes of "cooperation, affirmation, and communication, and by providing a supportive environment." A portion of the book included experiences from workshops given by the program coordinators, with children and their teachers involved in games, skits, and creative scenarios used to develop alternative responses to conflict.[81]

Margaret Comstock developed a peace education curriculum for kindergarten titled *Building Blocks for Peace.* The primary objective was "to develop a child's ability to relate to

other children" with activities organized around the concept
of friendship. Children crafted friendship books with a short
description of each classmate. Comstock believed that
"peacekeeping requires empathy for others and the will to
settle disputes without force or violence . . . We can . . . train
a generation for peace."[82]

Two educators from the Dade County (Florida) Schools
published two curriculum guides, one for the elementary
grades and a second for the secondary. Both were the efforts
of the late Grace Contrino Abrams, then department
chairperson, Social Studies, at Fisher Junior High School in
Miami Beach and her sister Fran Contrino Schmidt, who was
curriculum chairperson at Fienberg Elementary School, also
in Miami Beach. Both were identified in the guides as
members of the Women's International League for Peace
and Freedom.[83]

Peace Is in Our Hands, a resource unit for kindergarten
through grade six, asked teachers to "re-examine the values
of our educational system and of our culture." They were
asked to help children: (a) to understand . . . feelings in a
constructive way; (b) handle feelings of aggression nonviolently; (c) build self-esteem; (d) cope with others' feelings
and actions with empathy; (e) understand that all people
have hopes and aspirations in common; and (f) to build world
citizenship. Other sections examined the causes of war and
"its effects on the human family and environment."[84] The
format was designed for practical classroom use with one
column for the teacher in which the concepts to be taught
were outlined, along with the materials and visual aids
needed. The second column had activities for the students
that were usually first-hand action-based projects. Teachers
also received detailed descriptions, lists of books, and other
media resources.

Learning Peace, the second of the guides, was a similar
resource unit for teachers in grades seven through twelve
with the goal of helping students to "develop an interest in
peace." Students investigated alternatives to war. The goal

of learning that conflicts could be resolved peacefully offered a viable choice. Extensive resources followed each unit.[85]

After the death of Grace Contrino Abrams, the memorial foundation in her honor continued to expand its activities with the design of additional curriculum materials throughout the seventies and eighties. In 1988, the Dade County Public School System adopted the Grace Contrino Abrams Peace Education Foundation program in conflict resolution with Fran Schmidt as coordinator of a pilot program to train student mediators (this will be discussed further in Chapter 9).

ANTICOMMUNIST ACTIVITIES IN THE SEVENTIES

Peace educators who were also involved in activism as antiwar protestors became the prime targets of investigations by the Federal Bureau of Investigation. Throughout the Vietnam War years, the FBI under the direction of J. Edgar Hoover engaged in illegal wiretapping and surveillance of peace movement leaders.[86] Because a broad spectrum of groups with differing ideologies were engaged in antiwar activism, with an expressed policy of nonexclusion in effect, it was plausible that Communist groups also joined in the protests.

The perception of America's political leaders in the seventies, particularly during the height of antiwar protests, was that all engaged in peace activities of any kind were lumped together as unpatriotic dupes of communist propaganda. A typical response that appeared in the eighties, ascribed to Dean Rusk, Secretary of State in the Kennedy and Johnson administrations, described the actions of antiwar activities as "foolish protests that made the peace movement an unwitting ally of the North Vietnamese."[87] To follow the dictates of conscience against moral principles, such as an unjust war, was still considered as disloyal as it had been for those who raised questions about America's entry into World War I.

The measures taken against antiwar protesters underscored the vital transformative force of public opinion. On October 15, 1969, the largest peace march attracted 500,000 people who demanded a moratorium on the war. In his memoirs Richard Nixon commented on the fact that this massive "protest for peace" destroyed whatever "small possibility may still have existed of ending the war in 1969." Earlier Nixon expressed his fear that Hanoi would "not believe him because of American public opinion." He further stated that the "only chance for my ultimatum to succeed . . (would be) to convince the Communists that I could depend on solid support at home if they decided to call my bluff."[88] Presumably, the idea that antiwar dissent could actually be based on ethical grounds was not well understood at that time by an officialdom which was dedicated to its own agenda.

Herbert Kelman and Lee Hamilton presented a strong case for the consideration of alternative perspectives to crisis situations that can have disastrous consequences:

> Such situations tend to be governed by means that strongly discourage dissent, treating it as an act of disloyalty that breaks national unity and resolve. This is precisely the context in which norms supportive of dissent as an obligation of loyal citizens must be asserted.[89]

The power of public opinion, and especially collective "people power," remained a cogent lesson learned from the seventies. At least one organization, the Institute for World Order, heeded the new revelation. In 1983 the Institute changed its name to the World Policy Institute and announced a more pragmatic approach. This was described as an "attempt to reach a broader range of audience, the policymakers, elected officials, the media, church groups, and grass-roots organizations."[90]

AFTERTHOUGHTS

The spirits of Concord and Walden Pond, Ralph Waldo Emerson and Henry Thoreau, may have been invisible benevolent specters amid antiwar protests as the moral crusade to end the war in Vietnam continued into the new decade of the seventies. Thoreau's model for civil disobedience in the face of injustice and Emerson's concern for the primacy of the individual conscience inspired growing numbers of Americans into activism. The idealism of youth merged with pragmatism. For many activists this decade changed the course of their lives. As a consequence, peace education and research were enriched as highly motivated individuals joined in efforts to learn more about the causes of conflict and to explore alternatives that would ameliorate change, or remove the circumstances that brought it about.

While the nuclear threat was an omnipresent factor in American life with schools actually planning fallout shelters, the major focus of peace education in the seventies was on conflict resolution. This was viewed as having practical value even beyond the period (Vietnam War) when the need to resolve conflicts was the greatest.

In colleges and universities peace studies courses usually included content, and perhaps case studies, in conflict resolution in course syllabi. Conflict resolution received the concerted efforts of other disciplines in the behavioral sciences. For elementary and secondary students, pioneering efforts in peace education, such as the Quaker curriculums and the Abrams Peace Education Foundation, provided students training in the basic skills on how to resolve family and classroom conflicts peacefully.

Perhaps the most vivid lesson of the seventies was that the Vietnam War was an injustice that ended because of the efforts of American citizens who brought about change. The younger generation especially could see that powerlessness and hopelessness could be overcome with action. In a previous century courageous abolitionists, convinced that slavery was morally wrong, changed history because of their convictions. Likewise, the younger generation of this era believed they could influence events in history because of their beliefs about the immorality of the Vietnam War.

The message of peace education was clearly one of hope. In spite of the power of nuclear weaponry to destroy all, humanity still had power to affect history. As the decade drew to a close, the potency of public opinion was recognized as a workable instrument for positive change.

With the vitality of the antiwar movement as a central force for peace in the sixties and seventies, peace education acquired a new dimension—activism as a basic component along with knowledge and skills. While theory and research still played an important role in education, the experiences and actions of those involved in constructive work for peace offered an enhanced viewpoint.

In past decades community projects or service to humanity were recognized as forms of peace education in action. By the close of the seventies, group activities symbolized peace as a positive, life-giving force to replace the narrower, negative context of peace as abolition or prohibition of war. The "action project" of an international nature grew out of an augmented global perspective from the seventies. The younger generation was encouraged to look beyond their immediate circle of family and friends to others in their community and then beyond America's borders.

This concept continued to mature from the seventies until a demarcation point in the eighties could be discerned, as a logical evolution. Action projects, such as International Workcamps for youth involved service in far corners of the globe. Within America's borders other volunteer projects for youth, including Habitat for Humanity, provided the chance to build homes for the elderly or homeless, renovate church halls, or restore community centers. Owing to the world order value of concern for the environment, projects to protect and maintain the delicate planetary ecology have grown in importance. For example, under the auspices of the

Nature Conservancy in the summer of 1989, young people in various parts of America cleaned oil-contaminated beaches, planted delicate seagrasses, or rescued endangered birds. Peace education with a global and planetary (ecological) perspective, infused with world order values, has thus shown its power to change young lives.

In the seventies and eighties, decision making and the belief that each individual had the right to be involved in resolving political issues became an important part of education for citizenship. Most important of all, the development of sound critical-thinking could act as an antidote to propaganda and biased messages. The power of the individual to bring about change remained as a lasting heritage for a new generation.

Concern for the child as articulated by Montessori and Boulding, who provided a model for nonviolent childrearing, called forth a timely message for the seventies. In a society often mired down in violence and personal domestic abuse against those too weak to defend themselves, the message of peace and nonviolence took on a new meaning.

The writings and action projects of the seventies echoed the view that concern for children should be the heart and core of peace education. The United Nations Declaration of Rights for the Child provided a historic perspective and one that spoke to the hearts of all educators—past, present, and future—not only in America, but in the undeveloped countries as well.

In our own country, warnings sounded that America had become an anti-child nation with the innocent and powerless often dehumanized and devalued. American political machinery was slow to respond to child labor and for almost a century permitted the deaths of youngsters in the mills of Lowell or mines of Mineral Point. The basic survival of the child as the future hope of our nation and humanity needed to receive renewed attention. With peace education, children's rights were recognized and instilled as an integral value. The cry that America needed to rededicate our society to children as a positive goal for peace education, was heard as a counterpoint during the seventies.

Notes

1. Background sources for this chapter were: Paul Boyer, *By the Bomb's Early Light: American Thought and Culture at the Dawn of the Atomic Age* (New York: Pantheon Books, 1985); McGeorge Bundy, *Danger and Survival: Choice about the Bomb in the First Fifty Years* (New York: Random House, 1988); Albert Carnesale and Richard N. Haasse, eds. *Superpower Arms Control: Setting the Record Straight* (Cambridge, MA: Ballinger Publishing Co., 1987); John Lewis Gaddis, *The Long Peace: Inquiries into the History of the Cold War* (New York: Oxford University Press, 1987); Mike Gravel, ed., *The Pentagon Papers: The Defense Department History of United States Decisionmaking on Vietnam* (Boston: Beacon Press, 1981); Tom Hayden, *Reunion: A Memoir* (New York: Random House, 1988); Richard Rhodes, *The Making of the Atomic Bomb* (New York: Simon and Schuster, 1986); and Thomas J. Schoenbaum, *Waging Peace & War: Dean Rusk in the Truman, Kennedy & Johnson Years* (New York: Simon and Schuster, 1988). Sources on education were: Charles E. Silberman, *Crisis in the Classroom: The Remaking of American Education* (New York: Random House, 1970); Gerald Weinstein and Mario Fantini, *Toward a Humanistic Education and Curriculum of Affect* (New York: Praeger, 1970).
2. Representative of the many books that appeared for the general public were Norma Sue Woodstone, *Up Against the War: A Personal Introduction to U.S. Soldiers and Civilians Fighting Against the War in Vietnam* (New York: Tower Publications, 1970). Others that offered different viewpoints on the Vietnam era were Allen Goodman, *The Lost Peace: America's Search for a Negotiated Settlement of the Vietnam War* (Stanford: Hoover Institute Press, 1978); Thomas Powers, *The War at Home* (New York: Grossman, 1973); and Nancy Zaroulis and Gerald Sullivan, *Who Spoke Up?: Ameri-*

can Protest Against the War in Vietnam, 1963–1975 (New York: Doubleday, 1984).

3. Betty Reardon, *Comprehensive Peace Education: Educating for Global Responsibility* (New York: Teachers College Press, 1988), 8.

4. Henry Steele Commager, "A Declaration of Interdependence," *Today's Education* (March–April 1976): 86.

5. Susan Lynn Carpenter, The Peace Transformation Process: Toward a Framework for Peace Education, Ph.D. diss., University of Massachusetts, 1975, 6, 81 and *A Repertoire of Peacemaking Skills,* (Fairfax, Virginia: Consortium on Peace Research Education and Development, George Mason University, 1974).

6. Carpenter, 82.

7. Betty Reardon, ed. *Educating for Global Responsibility: Teacher-Designed Curricula for Peace Education, K–12* (New York: Teachers College Press, 1988), 178.

8. A. Michael Washburn, "Peace Education Is Alive—But Unsure of Itself," *Social Science Record,* 9 (Winter 1972):61.

9. Washburn, 62.

10. Washburn, 61.

11. Washburn, 68.

12. Washburn, 62.

13. Christoph Wulf, ed. *Handbook on Peace Education* (Frankfurt am Main, Germany: International Peace Research Association, 1974).

14. Diane Ravitch, *The Troubled Crusade: American Education, 1945–1980* (New York: Basic Books, 1983), 198–199.

15. Sources for a general background on the world order education perspective were: William Boyer, "World Order Education: What Is It?" *Phi Delta Kappan* 56 (April 1975), 524–527, which discussed the fact that the National Council for the Social Studies recognized this perspective as a "legitimate part of the social studies program" and as an upgraded form of "political education and citizenship education and an instrument of social-cultural change"; and A. Michael Washburn, "The World Order Approach to Peace Education," Conference on Peace Research of the American Historical Association, August 26–27, 1972, ed., John Whiteclay Chambers II (Plattsburgh, NY: State University of New York).

16. *International Conference on Expanding Dimensions of World Education, Proceedings, Ankara, Turkey,* Nasrine Adibe and Frank A. Stone, eds., (Storrs, CT: University of Connecticut, World Education Project, 1976), 144.
17. *Proceedings,* 144.
18. *Peace and World Order Studies: A Curriculum Guide,* 2nd ed. (New York: Institute for World Order, 1978), Foreword and Acknowledgments, ii.
19. Association for Supervision and Curriculum Development (ASCD), *Education for Peace: Focus on Mankind* (Washington, DC: ASCD, 1973), 109. James Becker also wrote *Education for a Global Society* (Bloomington, IN: Phi Delta Kappa Educational Foundation, 1973). He included the role of the multinational corporation as a major component in global education issues and warned that leaving decisions about world resources solely to "the profit maximizing managers of multinational corporations" could result in "serious neglect of the social costs of their actions" and called for global regulatory agencies.
20. James M. Becker, ed. *Schooling for a Global Society* (New York: McGraw-Hill, 1979), 42–43.
21. Norman Abramowitz, Andrew J. Leighton and Stephen Viederman, "Global and International Perspectives," in *Improving the Human Condition: A Curricular Response to Critical Realities* (Washington, DC: ASCD, 1978), 162.
22. Lee Anderson, *Schooling and Citizenship in a Global Age: An Exploration of the Meaning and Significance of Global Education* (Bloomington, IN: Social Studies Development Center, Indiana University, 1979).
23. Anderson, 68.
24. Kenneth Boulding, "Education for Spaceship Earth" *Social Education* 32 (November 1968), 648–652.
25. Anderson, 428.
26. Representative publications in the seventies that included discussion of the global education perspective were: Council of Chief State School Officers, *Civic Literacy for Global Interdependence* (Washington, DC: Council of Chief State School Officers, Committee on International Education, 1976); Ward Morehouse, *A New Civic Literacy: American Education and Global Interdependence* (Princeton: Aspen Institute for Hu-

manistic Studies, 1975); and Edwin O. Reischauer, *Toward the 21st Century: Education for a Changing World* (New York: Knopf, 1973).

27. Gerald and Patricia Mische, *Toward a Human World Order* (New York: Paulist Press, 1977).

28. Global Perspectives in Education and American Forum for Global Education, Inc., descriptive literature.

29. Research undertaken by William Eckhardt concentrated on changes in the attitudes of students as well as on an acquisition of knowledge, discussed in his "Research and Education as Approaches to Peace and Justice," 3 *Peace and Change: A Journal of Peace and Research*, 1973: 44–60 and *Compassion: Toward a Science of Value* (Huntsville, Ontario: Canadian Peace Research Institute Press, 1972).

30. Washburn, "Peace Education Is Alive," 65.

31. Educators created a significant body of literature in the seventies, such as: Juergen Dedring, *Recent Advances in Peace and Conflict Research* (Beverly Hills: Sage Publications, 1976); Bernard Lafayette, Jr. Pedagogy for Peace and Nonviolence: A Critical Analysis of Peace and Nonviolence Studies Programs on College Campuses in the Northeastern U.S.A. diss., Harvard Univ., 1974; and Paul Wehr and A. Michael Washburn, *Peace and World Order Systems: Teaching and Research* (Beverly Hills: Sage Publications, 1976) which included a Conflict Intervention and Resolution Model.

32. *Conflict Resolution: Contributions of the Behavioral Sciences,* ed. Clagett G. Smith (Notre Dame, IN: University of Notre Dame Press, 1971).

33. *Conflict Resolution,* xv.

34. Gene Sharp, *The Politics of Nonviolent Action* (Boston: Porter Sargent, 1973).

35. "Notes and Comment" (Gene Sharp), Talk of the Town, *The New Yorker* (December 12, 1983): 43–44.

36. Gene Sharp quoted in Coughlin, Ellen K. "In Cold War's Waning, Peace Researchers See Vindication of Their Work," *Chronicle of Higher Education,* April 4, 1990, A6, A10.

37. Stephen Marks, "Peace, Development, Disarmament and Human Rights Education: The Dilemma Between the Status Quo and Curriculum Overload" *International Review of Education,* 29 (1983), 294.

38. Marks, 294.
39. Marks, 297.
40. Betty Reardon, *Comprehensive Peace Education,* 32.
41. Reardon, *Comprehensive Peace Education,* 7, 31.
42. Paulo Freire, *Pedagogy of the Oppressed* (New York: Seabury Press, 1970) and *Education for Critical Consciousness* (New York: Seabury Press, 1973).
43. Rivage-Seul, Marguerite K., "Peace Education: Imagination and the Pedagogy of the Oppressed." *Harvard Educational Review* 57 (May 1987), 153–169.
44. Marks, 299.
45. Betty Reardon, *Sexism and the War System* (New York: Teachers College Press, 1985), 2.
46. Birgit Brock-Utne, "The Development of Peace and Peace Education Concepts Through Three UN Women Decade Conferences" in Chadwick Alger and Michael Stohl, eds., *A Just Peace Through Transformation: Cultural, Economic, and Political Foundations for Change (Proceedings of the International Peace Research Association, Eleventh General Conference).* (Boulder, CO: Westview Press, 1988), 176.
47. Reardon, *Sexism and the War System* and Birgit Brock-Utne, *Educating for Peace: A Feminist Perspective* (New York: Pergamon Press, 1985).
48. Reardon, *Sexism,* 10–13.
49. Reardon, *Sexism,* 66–67.
50. Reardon, *Sexism,* 64.
51. Betty Reardon, "Transformations into Peace and Survival" in George Henderson, ed., *Education for Peace: Focus on Mankind,* 127–151 and *Militarization, Security, and Peace Education: A Guide for Concerned Citizens* (Valley Forge: United Ministries in Education, 1982).
52. F. Cordasco, ed. *The History of American Education: A Guide To Information Sources* (Detroit: Gale Research Company, 1979).
53. N. Bauer and J. Krivohlavy, "Cooperative Conflict Resolution in Internationalized Boy Dyads," *Journal of Child Psychology,* 15 (January 1974), 13–21.
54. Ravitch, 270.
55. Richard M. Fried, *Nightmare in Red: The McCarthy Era in Perspective* (New York: Oxford University Press, 1990), 43, 86.

56. Maria Montessori, *Education and Peace* (Chicago: Henry Regnery, 1972). Excerpts from the original 1932 Indian edition have been compiled by Aline D. Wolf, *Peaceful Children, Peaceful World: The Challenge of Maria Montessori* (Altoona, PA: Parent Child Press, 1989).
57. Montessori, *Education and Peace*, 55.
58. Montessori, xiv, xv.
59. Montessori, 14–15.
60. Montessori, 88–89.
61. Elise Boulding, "The Child and Non-Violent Social Change," *Handbook of Peace Education*, ed., Christoph Wulf, (Frankfurt am Main, Germany: International Peace Research Association, Education Committee, 1974):101–102.
62. Judith V. Torney, "Middle Childhood and International Education," *Intercom* (1971): 5–12.
63. Howard Tolley, Jr. *Children and War: Political Socialization To International Conflict* (New York: Teachers College Press, Columbia University, 1973).
64. Vera L. Timm, *Spare the Rod! Violence and Your Child* (Dayton, OH: Vera L. Timm, 1977).
65. Lillian Genser, ed. *Understanding and Responding to Violence in Young Children,* (Detroit: Center for Teaching About Peace and War, Wayne State University, 1976).
66. Boulding, 103.
67. Boulding, 103.
68. Boulding, 111.
69. Boulding, 111.
70. Tolley, viii.
71. Tolley, 136.
72. Becker, ed. *Schooling for a Global Society,* 196.
73. Carpenter, The Peace Transformation Process, 53.
74. David C. King, *International Education for Spaceship Earth* (New York: Thomas Y. Crowell, 1971).
75. Peggy Mastrude, "Terra II-A Spaceship Earth Simulation for the Middle Grades," *Intercom* (1971): 13–67, S–1.
76. Mastrude, 16.
77. David C. King, Jay L. Weisman, and Ronald Wheeler, *Environments* (New York: American Book Company, 1979).
78. King, Weisman and Wheeler, 313.
79. King, Weisman and Wheeler, 273.

80. Stephanie Judson, ed. *A Manual on Nonviolence and Children*. Philadelphia, Committee on Nonviolence and Children, Philadelphia Yearly Meeting, Religious Society of Friends. (Philadelphia: New Society Publishers, 1977).

81. *The Friendly Classroom for a Small Planet: A Handbook on Creative Approaches to Living and Problem Solving for Children* (Wayne, NJ: Avery Publishing Group, 1978),7.

82. Margaret Comstock, *Building Blocks for Peace* (Philadelphia: Jane Addams Peace Association, 1973), 3.

83. Grace C. Abrams and Fran C. Schmidt, *Peace Is In Our Hands* (Philadelphia: Jane Addams Peace Association, 1974). Preface, n.p.

84. Abrams and Fran C. Schmidt, *Peace Is In Our Hands,* Preface, 39–43.

85. Grace C. Abrams and Fran C. Schmidt, *Learning Peace* (Philadelphia: Jane Addams Peace Association, 1972), 31–34.

86. Tom Hayden, xvii–xviii (Introduction); Athan Theoharis, *Spying on Americans* (Philadelphia: Temple University Press, 1978); *Report on the Presidential Commission on Campus Unrest* (New York: Avon, 1971); *Staff Study of Campus Riots and Disorders,* October 1967, October 1968, May 1969 (Washington, DC: Government Printing Office, 1969); U.S. Senate Committee on Foreign Relations, *Impact of the Vietnam War,* Congressional Research Service, Foreign Affairs Division, June 30, 1971 and U.S. Senate Government Operations Committee, *Staff Study of Major Riots and Civil Disorders,* 1965–July 31, 1968 (Washington, DC: Government Printing Office, October 1968).

87. Thomas J. Schoenbaum, *Waging Peace & War: Dean Rusk in the Truman, Kennedy & Johnson Years,* 496.

88. McGeorge Bundy, *Danger and Survival: Choices About the Bomb in the First Fifty Years,* 539–540.

89. Herbert C. Kelman and V. Lee Hamilton, *Crimes of Obedience, Toward a Social Psychology of Authority and Responsibility.* (New Haven: Yale University Press, 1989), 330.

90. World Policy Forum (New York: World Policy Institute (newsletter, Spring 1983), 1.

8. MATURITY AND PROMISE, 1981–1990

Introduction

The eighties opened with a keen awareness of the nuclear war issues that faced America.[1] By the close of the decade changes in the structure of the Soviet empire of diverse, ethnic nationalities, credited to the liberal policies of Mikhail Gorbachev inaugurated a cycle of events that may have changed history. For those involved in peace education, research or activism, a sense of déjà vu was in order. Many of the principles that governed peace movements and political upheavals in past history which were taught in peace studies courses since the sixties—nonviolence, civil disobedience, personal empowerment, political participation of citizenry—became historic examples in Eastern Europe.

Nonviolent, bloodless revolutions in Poland, Hungary, Czechoslovakia, East Germany, and Bulgaria brought an end to four decades of Communist domination with dissidents forming new political coalitions and holding free elections. During the period of November–December of 1989 changes took place without Soviet intervention, as had occurred previously in Hungary and Czechoslovakia to suppress rebellion. Only the populace of Romania suffered the consequences of a violent revolution as a feared dictator was deposed and executed.[2] Lech Walesa, hero of the Solidarity movement in Poland, progressed from jailed dissident in 1981 to head of a new Polish government that literally eliminated the Communist Party. From 1981 to 1989 Walesa, a shipyard electrician, became the symbol of a successful nonviolent civil disobedience campaign. In a joint session of Congress, while visiting America he was awarded a medal as Congress pledged a million dollar aid plan for Poland and Hungary. In December, the unbelievable meeting of Gorbachev and Pope John Paul II highlighted an end to past ideological rivalry. The opening of diplomatic ties with the Vatican was announced. Gorbachev had revealed earlier in the year that he had been baptized as a child. Political, philosophical, and religious differences appeared to recede into the background as the will for liberty and democracy brought about widespread changes—without violence.

Those involved in peace activism in the eighties recognized that the tactics of nonviolent civil disobedience carried out successfully in Eastern Europe were already familiar ones from peace movements of past decades. Beginning with Gandhi's "Ahimsa", (Sanskrit for noninjury literally, "soul force," discussed in a previous chapter), nonviolence was used to bring about changes for the oppressed. In protest against the British Salt Tax, Gandhi organized a nonviolent march in 1931. Martin Luther King Jr. included Gandhi's tactics in his civil disobedience actions throughout the fifties and sixties in a civil rights movement that resulted in the first federal legislation for racial equality.

Peace activists continued to incorporate nonviolent civil disobedience in their protest agenda. Throughout the eighties they continued to refine the tactics of Gandhi and King in an antinuclear war movement that brought them to the corporate headquarters of defense contractors, the desert-testing grounds for nuclear weapons, and to the launches of the Trident submarine and Galileo satellite, a symbol of growing militarization of outer space. In the Philippines, a nonviolent revolution brought liberation and transformation in a "people's power" struggle that culminated in the election of Corazon Aquino (no longer in office by 1992). All of these events in world history undoubtedly will be a powerful influence in the nineties. Educators taught for decades that it was only through education and activism carried out with nonviolence that social and political change—a transformation for humanity—could take place.

Throughout the eighties, events in America produced compelling reasons for the growth of peace education and conflict resolution as a viable alternative for intergroup as well as international conflicts. Peace educators recognized that educating the general populace would be an essential first step.

In retrospect, events throughout the past decade revealed several cardinal principles that influenced the growth of peace education. These could be defined as (a) official government rejection of the use of negotiation or peaceful conflict resolution to settle international differences—with only a military response considered; (b) continued reliance on a state of nuclear terror that produced feelings of powerlessness in all, especially in the younger generation; (c) the importance of face-to-face dialogue as a tactic to diffuse fear of the "enemy" with people-to-people citizen diplomacy used as a vital force in reducing tensions. This latter tactic usually took the form of extra-governmental groups which coalesced around nonprofit-organizations, community or service groups, and professional societies, among others. Each one of these principles resulted in a thrust to include conflict resolution, nuclear war education, and personal transformation—as strategies to bring about changes in attitudes and feelings toward the "enemy."

More specific examples of events during the eighties were revealing. One showed a government that rejected most responses except military force. America officially denied the jurisdiction of the World Court (International Court of Justice) and rejected a decision concerning involvement in Nicaragua. The decade witnessed an incredible military build-up that continued unbridled during the administration of Ronald Reagan with national security in the hands of Caspar Weinberger, a former executive with the defense contractor, the Bechtel Corporation. The total sum of two trillion dollars included astronomical sums for nuclear weaponry that were often described as producing a "nuclear overkill". The Trident II submarine, for example was described as 38 times more lethal than the bomb dropped on Hiroshima. By 1986, Brent Scowcroft, national security advisor to Nixon and Ford, confounded the issue by assessing that the MX missile was a "twenty-five billion dollar turkey." At least 200 more of these missiles were needed, he stated, to be effective. Each year of the decade included announcements of gross mismanagement in military procurement with waste of taxpayers' money.

In addition to escalation of the arms race, an aggressive use of force was characterized by the invasion of Grenada, bombing of Lebanon, a bombing raid on Libya, and culminated in an invasion of Panama. As had happened in past decades, any criticism of official government policy was equated with unpatriotism and disloyalty.

Peace educators had recognized for decades the importance of dialogue with communication skills that could open avenues of understanding. Once the stage was set for the two superpowers to begin face-to-face meetings, an improvement was noted. Relations between the United States and the Soviet Union continued to improve with several meetings held first by Ronald Reagan in Geneva in 1985, and then in Washington and Moscow in 1987 as first steps toward establishing a mutual ground for negotiation on arms issues. In Geneva in 1985, Gorbachev expressed a desire to "stop the unprecedented arms race (that) has unfolded in the world (and) to prevent it from spreading into new spheres."

Before leaving office in 1988, Reagan achieved a political victory with Senate approval of a treaty eliminating medium- and shorter-range missiles based on land, a first major accord since the 1972 strategic arms limitation treaty. The much-hated Pershing 2 missiles installed by the United States in 1983 in Germany, amid massive protests, were removed in 1988. The Soviet Union ensured further progress by agreeing to summit meetings which were held in Geneva, Moscow, and Malta. Agreements reached at these meetings resulted in offers to ban chemical weapons. After George Bush succeeded Reagan in 1988, a definite turning point could be assessed. The first cuts in a Star Wars budget took place in November of 1989 as a symbolic milestone and reversal of the momentum that began in the Reagan years.

Throughout the decade, morality in government became a central issue with a procession of officials involved in nefarious dealings: the Iran-Contra affair, revealing that a secret foreign policy was being carried on for the purpose of circumventing Congressional controls (with convictions and repercussions continued into the 1990s); scandals in administration of the national public housing programs; and the involvement of Senatorial and Congressional leaders in the savings and loan frauds. Common Cause, a lobbying organization revealed that PACs (Political Action Committees) of the top ten defense contractors gave nearly three million dollars to congressional candidates in the election of 1988, especially to members of committees dealing with defense.

Revelations concerning several events also showed an effort to distort or hide the truth through false or misleading government disclosures and/or official secrecy. Distortion of the truth occurred in reporting the summit in 1986 at Reykjavik, Iceland, as a "glowing success" by President Reagan, but actually assessed as a failure and miscalculation of Gorbachev's proposals. The arms race escalation was expanded to include technological space weaponry, even after the feasibility of the Star Wars defense was criticized by scientists. Growing secrecy concerning the Star Wars project included funding for Zenith Star, a laser weapon project that would violate the 1972 ABM Treaty, described as a so-called "black" program with Congress not fully informed of either its funding or progress.

Throughout the decade there resurfaced concern about a conflict of interest especially in the close relationship between Department of Defense and major defense contractors, particularly the Bechtel Corporation whose executives became high-ranking officials in the departments of State and Defense. By the close of the eighties, several defense contractors were prosecuted after "unauthorized leaks" showed that they were in illegal possession of Pentagon documents that gave them inside information and an unfair advantage in bidding for defense contracts. Overcharges in the millions became standard operating procedures when dealing with the Pentagon. All of these events underscored the need for a new sense of morality in government as a component that would undergird the political sphere. Peace educators stressed that critical-thinking skills were essential for the citizen of the future, needed to question government action and policy.

Peace educators recalled past decades when ideologies had gripped America with fear. The so-called "evil empire" referred to frequently by Reagan appeared to fade away as Gorbachev himself announced that "the Cold War is dead." President Bush also announced the desire to "once and for all end the Cold War" and praised Gorbachev as the "dynamic architect of Soviet reform." His policies of glasnost and perestroika launched in 1987 began a policy of restructuring the Soviet political and economic spheres. The price of the Cold War, four decades of containment, détente and deterrence, had been assessed as: 58,000 Americans killed in Vietnam, 54,000 in Korea, and 15,000 Soviets killed in Afghanistan. The arms race for America was estimated at a cost of approximately 4.4 trillion dollars while for the Soviet nation, perhaps, the costs were even higher and resulted in a bankrupt economy where even the most basic needs for daily survival were lacking.

As the decade closed, disturbances in the Soviet Union were seen as previews of further unrest. Vignettes included a human chain of Baltic citizens in Lithuania, Latvia, and Estonia that linked one and a half million people who demanded freedom from the forced annexation that resulted from a secret Stalin-Hitler agreement in 1940. The Christmas of 1989 witnessed German citizenry of East and West Berlin united and chipping with hammers at the dreaded Berlin Wall, symbol of Communist oppression. After decades of

Communist repression and fear of nuclear attack, millions in East and West contemplated the consequences of a new era of peace and cooperation. The dreams of generations for a new world order—with peace, social justice, economic well-being, political participation, and ecological concern— could finally be considered as a distinct, though unlikely, possibility for the near future.

ELEMENTS IN THE DEVELOPMENT OF PEACE EDUCATION IN THE EIGHTIES

The building blocks of peace education that emerged in the eighties were: (1) peace education closely allied with global education and the world order perspective; (2) nuclear war or disarmament education; (3) conflict resolution or peace-making skills and the unique configuration of philosophy and process that evolved around it; (4) increased involvement of state- and community-mandated peace education programs in the schools; (5) aggressive roles for church and religious organizations in peace education; and (6) a growing emphasis on ecology at all levels, with an environmental ethic needed especially for global survival.

Several innovative elements also emerged without historical precedent from earlier decades: (1) the growing use of technology as an enhancement to global communications, used for peace education; (2) the founding of an institution dedicated to peace and conflict resolution, the United States Institute of Peace; (3) proliferation of grassroots, community-based programs for children and youth stressing U.S.-Soviet (and later post-Soviet) cultural, social, scientific, and educational exchanges.

Basically, any examination of curriculum and writings on peace education became a complicated undertaking. In the early eighties, few networks existed to enhance communications on a national level. It would be difficult for any one person or group to claim to have a comprehensive picture of organizations or individuals involved in curriculum design in the eighties.

However, one such network served as a model—the Peace Education Network of COPRED. Through this network those engaged in common projects such as the Teachers College Peace Education Program, Global Education Associates, Global Perspectives in Education, Educators for Social Responsibility, plus others who were organized only within a specific community or region, had access to a newsletter with current research projects and resources described, and were able to participate in broader interchanges at annual conferences. Those in the New York City area could share contacts with international groups through their access to the United Nations and other transnational contacts. Growing pains in the early days of organizations could also cause disruptions. Throughout the eighties, organizations began their activities and then ceased operations a short time later. Subscriptions to newsletters stopped mysteriously after two issues. By the close of the eighties, the Peace Education Program at Teachers College had in place a computer-based "Peace Education Curriculum Bank" that would be accessible on a national basis.[3]

In nearly every state, individuals, community-based groups or students rallied around a common interest in peace education or activities to promote greater understanding. Ian Harris reported on the growth of peace education in the Madison, Wisconsin area where a core group of 20 teachers designed a curriculum guide for elementary students, "Becoming Peacemakers," that received support within the schools.[4] The Minneapolis-St. Paul area had many organizations actively involved, with a Peace Child Festival organized for children, held on the grounds of the State Capitol. Boston became the hub of a New England network of peace education groups. In many states during the eighties, community groups, organizations, or institutions were engaged in a wide variety of peace education activities. The author, along with several colleagues began a series of community-wide seminars, Living Peacefully: Reducing Family Stress in a city in central Florida, where parents were invited to spend a Saturday learning conflict resolution skills while their children played with others in a cooperative, creative environment. As a result, a Florida Peace Network was organized with a Peace Education weekend workshop in 1990, and statewide Conferences held in 1991 and 1992.

EDUCATIONAL ELEMENTS IN THE FERMENTATION PROCESS

The growth of peace education in the 1980s should be placed in juxtaposition with the prevailing philosophy and pedagogy that dominated America's schools. John Goodlad, a critic of contemporary education, determined that an almost-uniform back-to-basics philosophy prevailed with students playing a passive rather than active role in their learning.[5] Minimum lip service was paid to the philosophy of educating the "whole child," or including elements other than the cognitive. The acquisition of content comprised the school curriculum along with a growth in testing, minimum performance standards, and basic competencies. These were changes mandated by state governments as school systems reacted to criticism and reform that dated from the seventies and early eighties.[6] Content that was testable and offered evaluation of student-faculty efforts dominated American education in the eighties from preschool through the secondary.[7] Teachers reported increased activities designed around "teaching for the test" to improve scores, which, if successful, were often publicized in community news headlines.

At the same time, the arts and aesthetics along with the affective domain—attitudes, feelings, emotions, moral and spiritual values—which for centuries had been deemed vital to the education of the whole child were relegated to minor roles or completely ignored.[8] Basic skills of reading and mathematics dominated the center stage in the 1980s.

External criticism of the schools meshed with other viewpoints, especially those of revisionist historians. The revisionists pointed out that the public schools still favored the social and economic status quo primarily for the benefit of the middle and upper-middle income groups of the community and to the growing disadvantage of minority groups.[9]

Psychological research, especially in the area of neuropsychology, articulated the theories of Alexander Luria and Lev Vygotsky that language and thought, as well as attitudes and emotions are closely allied with cognition particularly in the acquisition of knowledge and skills. Calls for a new paradigm of thinking and behavior reflected research on brain hemisphericity (right brain/left brain configurations) as related to learning styles and creative/critical thinking.[10]

Twin watchwords of transformation and empowerment emerged in the eighties and these were frequent buzzwords in educational writing.[11] Ernest Boyer, president of the Carnegie Foundation for the Advancement of Teaching, believed that the goals of education should be those inherited from Thomas Jefferson:

> Personal empowerment and civic engagement should be the primary ends of a high school education; empowerment to allow . . . our citizens to make analytical, critical, and creative decisions.[12]

In spite of frequent criticism, several areas of American education showed promise. Noteworthy have been improvements in the social studies curriculum. Developing an awareness of the necessity for multicultural/multiethnic classroom experiences has been in the forefront of that curriculum, with renewed emphasis on the college level.[13] The children who entered school in the late eighties will be the first high school graduates in the year 2000. By that time, demographic changes and shifts in population growth will be in evidence with combined minority groups—people of color—in the majority with the traditionally white, middle

class in the minority role.[14] The National Council for Social
Studies (NCSS) issued a Position Statement in 1988 that
underscored the essential skills needed for the children of the
21st Century—the communication skills in writing and
speaking, reading and research skills, as well as thinking and
interpersonal skills, such as dealing with conflict.

Recognition of these deep-rooted changes in American
society mandated a new way of thinking with overt teaching
of tolerance for the differences of others. These threads
became inherent in many nonviolent, peace education
programs especially with the introduction of conflict resolution skills-training in urban school systems, such as New
York, Newark, San Francisco, Milwaukee, and Miami.

Social studies educators and their professional organizations
have been in the forefront, calling for the restructuring of the
schools and the design of new paradigms for citizenship
education.[15] The survival of democracy in the next century
may depend on education of the citizenry with a global
perspective.[16] A merger of global education and multicultural
education has been proposed.[17] At least one comprehensive
school reform project included global education as a framework. Known as the American Forum in Global Education's
model schools network, the project was started in the fall of
1989. Its framework included four "domains of student
inquiry": human values; a study of systems; global issues and
problems, including peace and security, global environmental,
and human rights issues; and global history.[18]

The global perspective has been deemed "a moral creed
for scientific pedagogy . . . a perspective that can serve as a
framework for identifying problems," including the basic
problems of schooling in a democracy.[19] Curriculum developers have been equally vocal in proclaiming that a broader
definition of curriculum should be invoked. A classic definition of N. C. Kearney and W. W. Cook from 1958, defined:

> Curriculum . . . (as) all the experiences a learner has
> under the guidance of the school . . . not only was the

past to be reproduced, but the future was to be created as well.[20]

Innovations were called for—a futuristic outlook, pragmatic rather than theoretical practices. Back-to-basics, the old traditional science and discipline-oriented education of past generations was labeled as regression rather than progress for the future.[21]

Renewal of the curriculum with the aid of new technology was one solution proposed. Computers, interactive laser videodiscs, data bases, videotapes, distance learning, all augmented the social studies curriculum with creative applications.[22] A new blueprint of instruction for the twenty-first century was demanded for American education.

These building blocks for peace education in the eighties will be examined in greater detail in the remainder of this chapter as well as Chapter 9.

GLOBAL EDUCATION

Peace education, as global education, received further refinement by educators in the eighties. Several viewpoints set the stage for global education as an expression of pluralism, political socialization, and citizenship education.

Samuel Brodbelt, for example, believed that "global interdependence encourages youth on a world-wide basis to accept the responsibility to promote peace, cooperation and a sharing of knowledge and skills" as a form of citizenship education.[23] Roy Pellicano augmented Brodbelt's concept with concern for global education as "a type of citizenship education in a global environment . . . citizenship of an ecologically, socially, politically, and economically interdependent world."[24] Robert Hanvey and David King provided a delineation of the global perspective and a rationale for citizenship education with attention given to problems that "transcend the national, regional, or international."[25] Elements of these strands formed a foundation for global education, especially in the social studies curriculum of the eighties.

Global education was also perceived as an intercultural awareness and a central focus more in the sense of an international understanding. Mary McFarland believed that a study of Japan enabled students to assume "both national citizenship and a greater understanding of other citizens throughout the world."[26] In the early eighties, a model for introducing global perspectives into an existing curriculum was formulated by Anthony E. Conte and Lorraine A. Cavaliere. They suggested three strategies that involved process, content, and philosophy.[27]

Strategies for global education in 1979 reflected new curriculum guidelines outlined by The National Council for the Social Studies:

> The basic goal of social studies education is to prepare young people to be humane, rational, participating citizens in a world that is becoming increasingly interdependent.[28]

In 1988 a new Position Statement included the rationale and goals for the early childhood/elementary years and especially teaching skills for problem solving, decisionmaking, and "thoughtful value judgments." The ideal curriculum should include knowledge, skills, and attitudes, especially democratic norms and values such as justice and equality.[29] Most important, though, the Position Statement employed a sound research base on the developmental characteristics of children, stressing their need for direct experiences, hands-on activities, and experimentation. This contrasted sharply with the emphasis on passive learning, paper-and-pencil work, and abstract, symbolic activities which were common to the primary and elementary classrooms of the eighties.

Problems involving global education arose in the eighties as schools attempted to infuse the global perspective into the curriculum. Several basic perceptions were of special concern. First, the heavy reliance of schools on the textbook led to several studies of the content and attitudes that they presented. Cortes and Fleming assessed textbooks and found that since the 1950s children (and their textbooks) held hostile attitudes toward Cold War enemies. In addition, the "nationalistic bias is as persistent in today's schools (and textbooks) as in those used a generation ago."[30] This perhaps reflected concern for a hidden curriculum—the inculcation of patriotism and loyalty in American youth. Incidental global education was acquired from the informal curriculum, including television, which had a major influence on students' views about other nations and peoples.

Second, was the dilemma faced by educators who had no generally accepted definition for global education. One attempt at definition by David E. Vocke presented an overview of at least four approaches: (1) the traditional approach, (2) the world-centered approach, (3) the world order approach and (4) the single-issue approach.[31]

Vocke described the traditional approach as international education that included study of foreign policy and area studies assuming a "state-centric view of the world in which sovereign nations are the primary international actors." The second, or so-called world-centered approach stressed linkage between all the peoples and cultures of the world with an emphasis on "interdependence . . . the code word . . . with greater understanding and acceptance of diverse cultural practices." The third approach, world order studies, called for a "transformation of the current international political system . . . with an emphasis on alternative futures" and opened up study of drastic changes in the international system. Lastly, the single-issue approach drew attention to nuclear war, global poverty, world hunger, and population growth as basic issues that threaten the future of civilization.[32] Each approach, Vocke pointed out, called for a different stress on what should be included or excluded from the global education curriculum. During the 1980s, global education was refined, reexamined, implemented, and synthesized in a continually evolving process.

In addition to a lack of accepted definition, other inherent difficulties were identified by Mary Merryfield because global education "is controversial and even threatening to those interested in preserving the status quo."[33] Organizations involved in the development of global education programs have attempted to reach mainstream American education, but were wary of including "peace" or "peace education" in their efforts, according to Andrew F. Smither, executive director of Global Perspectives in Education:

> Peace and peace groups have been so tarred. If you mention the word peace, mainstream educational groups look at you as if you're from Mars.[34]

By 1990, Educators for Social Responsibility had indeed taken notice of this problem. Their literature referred to a "pedagogical emphasis on dialogue . . . critical thinking, cooperation, non-violent conflict resolution, decision-making, and social responsibility." Their curricula addressed "significant controversies in such areas as peace and war, security, and justice" but did not specifically refer to global education, peace education, nor to nuclear war education.[35]

By the late eighties, endorsement of global education by the National Governors' Association (1987) paved the way for a broader acceptance in the schools, with state boards of education in the forefront.

Betty Reardon, who was involved in the development of the World Order Models Project, the Peace Education Commission, Peace Education Network, and the Teachers College Peace Education Program from 1963 until the present, viewed global education as a curriculum antecedent of positive peace. Reardon described the term "global justice" as one being used also by teachers, but one "not as precise as the term "positive peace."[36]

In a definitive exploration of a contemporary viewpoint on peace education by one who has been in the forefront of curriculum development for several decades, Reardon's views carry the weight of authority. She delineated a primary difference from global education of previous decades (and a point of controversy):

> Some global education, however, in its earlier phases attempted to emulate one tradition of its parent discipline, social science. It sometimes claimed to be neutral and value-free . . . and ignored or rejected considerations of restructuring the international systems . . . Positive peace is an especially value-laden area, and current global education certainly is value-laden and emphasizes problems that involve many value questions.[37]

In the literature of organizations in the late eighties, inclusion of "human values" especially in the "model schools" project of the American Forum for Global Education, Inc., offered evidence that the debate has come full circle—values are an essential component of any global education curriculum.

Despite problems, David King (1987) had declared that global education had won wide acceptance with more than forty states passing course mandates for global or international education. New York State, for example, called for an "integration of global education concepts into most K-12 curriculum areas and required a global studies course in grade nine or ten."[38] This evidence of progress occurred in spite of sporadic opposition in several states from right-wing groups. The controversy spilled over frequently into the various journals of the national social studies organizations, where a forum was provided for ongoing debate.

Increased support for global education was also reported by the Wingspread Conference in 1984.[39] The support of national educational organizations for global education programs was noteworthy. Their campaign for global education had begun in the seventies. A wide range of groups were involved in several projects: The National Association of Secondary School Principals (NASSP) inaugurated a youth exchange program with mini-grants offered to principals by the National Association of Elementary School Principals (NAESP).[40] By the close of the eighties, institutions involved in teacher education had generally accepted inclusion of a global perspective as a condition of the National Council for Accreditation of Teacher Education (NCATE). Colleges of education included components of multicultural education as well as the global perspective in methods courses for future teachers.

CURRICULUM FOR GLOBAL EDUCATION

Examination of a comprehensive curriculum program, "Education in a World of Rapid Change" provided evidence that peace education with a global perspective, more narrowly defined as global education, could be translated into action in the classrooms of American schools.[41] The North Central Association of Schools and Colleges, as cosponsor, provided implementation of a program in global education.

Four publications under the direction of Jon Rye Kinghorn were developed and field-tested throughout America. The project, designed from 1977 to 1982, was carried out in cooperation with the Charles F. Kettering Foundation, a nonprofit, research-oriented organization established in 1927. Prime objectives were the integration of a global perspective into an existing social studies program. Four essential themes were adopted: (1) valuing diversity; (2) recognizing the interconnectedness of the modern world; (3) developing the capacity for effective working relationships; and (4) gaining knowledge of current world conditions, situations, and trends.[42] By the close of the eighties, educators generally agreed that the integration or infusion of peace education materials into an existing curriculum offered the greatest chances for success. Clearly, the North Central-Kettering program can be viewed as a milestone for curriculum design.

Delineated stages for development and implementation of the objectives were an integral part of the program. The four publications were a vehicle for the introduction of the global perspective, with students led to realize that "problems cannot be analyzed unless they are seen in a global context and cannot be managed without international cooperation."[43]

Throughout the eighties, State Boards of Education explored similar integration of global education into the curriculum. Michigan was one of 40 states that reported the initiation of global education course mandates.[44] In 1983, that state's guidelines for global education included: (a) definition, (b) rationale, (c) goals, (d) implementation, and (e) criteria for program development, including suggested classroom units of study and activities. The rationale reflected a variety of global education principles, including world order values, citizenship education, and disarmament education. According to the Michigan program, a global person would be one who would conscientiously . . . become involved in the peaceful resolution of conflict and the ultimate outlawing of war." Curriculum units included: intergroup conflict and control of violence, ecology, and language arts based on racial, cultural, and ethnic groups, and a study of families from a variety of cultures.[45]

Evaluation of the curriculum was considered an essential component of the instructional process. In the sensitive area of global education, appropriateness of materials was deemed a necessary first step. COPRED (Consortium for Peace Research Education and Development) formulated the criteria:

1. In describing other cultures . . . is as much attention paid to the Third World as to European nations? . . .

2. In discussing global poverty and development, does the examination of the causes of poverty include exploitation and . . . powerlessness of economically poor peoples? . . .
3. In discussing war, is the inevitability of violence and war rejected?[46]

Throughout the eighties, a myriad of materials that included a global perspective was designed for classroom use. Many reflected the philosophy of several leading organizations, such as Global Perspectives in Education, Global Education Associates, the Center for Teaching International Relations, and the Social Studies Development Center (Indiana University), among others. The pages of the Resource Directory (Appendix) bear witness to the many groups that were engaged in peace curriculum design. Through their efforts, America's children were introduced to the concept that they shared a common affinity with the human family along with the needs and concerns of others in all corners of Planet Earth. Perhaps students learned first in their classrooms that through an expanded knowledge of different cultures, they held the keys to communication and cooperation in our interdependent world.

WORLD ORDER APPROACH

The component of world order studies has been carried out by the World Policy Institute, (originally the Institute for World Order), mainly on the postsecondary level. The Institute had as its original goal since 1961 an educational mission to develop materials that taught world order values, such as peace, social justice, economic well-being, and ecological balance through research and education.

The educational agenda included publication of *Peace and World Order Studies: A Curriculum Guide* (from 1973 to 1984) and served as a model for the development of peace and social justice courses.[47] The newsletter of the Institute reported that the 1981 edition of the guide showed evidence of a "growth in the development . . . of courses . . . more narrowly defined as nuclear war education."

A fifth edition was published in 1989 under new auspices, The Five College Program in Peace and World Security Studies (PAWSS), edited by Donald C. Thomas and Michael T. Klare from Hampshire College. Former Hampshire College President Adele Simmons reflected on the proliferation of peace and world order courses since the earlier editions and especially that "peace studies has gained acceptance" in a field that "is both expanding and maturing" with a broad spectrum of multidisciplinary fields represented—arts, anthropology, psychology, philosophy, religious studies, literature, political science, and physics.[48] The editors reported that approximately 1,000 course syllabi were submitted with 93 chosen for inclusion in the guide.

A first policy shift in the Institute for World Order occurred with change of name in 1983. The rationale for the new label was to reflect a more pragmatic approach, and as previously noted, an "attempt to reach a broader range of audience." These targeted groups would include "policymakers, elected officials, the media, church groups, and grass-roots organizations."[49]

The voice of the Institute has been the quarterly journal, *World Policy,* which replaced *Macroscope.* The publication was described as "progressive internationalist in orientation" with the goal as an exploration of a "new alternative role for the United States with . . . new policy options." Envisioned was a new program to address two crucial issues: the arms race and deterioration of the world economy and the "links between them."[50] Finally, the Institute saw a new role for the United States on the world scene: that of "limiting United States' military power to strictly defensive purposes" as well as "providing constructive leadership . . . for peace, security, and a more productive and equitable world economy."[51]

Archibald L. Gillies, former president of the John Hay
Whitney Foundation and a "political and business associate
of Nelson A. Rockefeller from 1956 to 1968" has been
President of the Institute since 1982. Gillies also played an
active role in the political arena as a "co-founder of the
Citizens Party," a new national political party which nominated for President (1982), Barry Commoner, environ-
mental-issues activist.[52]

The original mission of the Institute for education and
research has been mobilized by the integration of economic
and political activism, replacing goals that were originally
peace education.[53] In contrast, the World Law Fund and the
Transnational Academic Program were vehicles for educational and research activities under the leadership of the
original organization.

The World Policy Institute, on the other hand, has designated the Security Project as its dominant blueprint in a
post-Reagan America with integrated political, economic, and
security policies.[54] Three perspectives proposed by the Security Project, prior to the breakup of Soviet Communism, were:
(1) economic forces are interconnected with the federal
deficits, unemployment, and Third World debt; (2) relations
with the Soviet Union needed to be stabilized, offering "both
sides immediate economic reward and new trade" and finally,
(3) the adoption of a noninterventionist policy toward Third
World countries. Arguing for "post-Cold War thinking" as a
way to increase our national security, economic issues were
identified as essentially "foreign policy issues," that overshadowed fear of the Soviet Union.[55]

By 1989 with the original mission of the Institute as an
educational organization (publication of *Peace and World
Order Studies*) now undertaken by others, public education
became a new priority.[56] This augmented goal was defined as
"promoting Institute materials and ideas to elected officials,
media and print journalists, membership organizations,
educators, and the public" with complimentary issues sent to
members of Congress.[57]

"THE DAY AFTER": CATALYST FOR NUCLEAR WAR EDUCATION?

Scholars have debated for several years the impact of a made-for-television movie, "The Day After," which was broadcast on November 20, 1983, and viewed by an estimated 75 to 100 million Americans. The TV show portrayed the vivid aftermath of a nuclear explosion on a city in Kansas, depicting the attempts of humans to survive in a devastated world. The video event was a mobilizing force for antinuclear activities as well as a forum for discussion by educators, clergy, scientists, and government decision makers.[58]

Editorials throughout the nation agreed that "a lot of people were left feeling empty and hopeless after seeing 'The Day After,' "[59] For those involved in peace activism, it was an experience that revealed the deep emotions harbored by many as evidence of the "psychic numbing" attributed to those facing the grim fact of their own deaths in a nuclear holocaust, an issue discussed by psychologists since the sixties. Students held a candlelight "peace vigil" attended by 1,500 at the University of Kansas, site of the fictitious movie. At the antinuclear teach-in at Columbia University, students were urged by Senator Alan Cranston to stimulate the "hardest, longest, best debate in American history" on nuclear-weapons policies and the prevention of nuclear war.[60]

Critics, however, proclaimed that the movie was "propaganda." Several studies confirmed that there were distinct changes in attitudes that took place as a result of "The Day After." From 1983 to 1988, changes in the policy agenda of President Reagan were apparent.[61] Did "The Day After" begin the important step toward activism for arms reduction? Did media-generated attitudes act as a catalyst in bringing American and Soviet foreign policy initiatives from stalemate to cooperation? The strong antinuclear movement that began in the early eighties and then lost momentum, gained new advocates. Finally, peace educators believed that "The

Day After" stimulated a marked increase in nuclear war education in American classrooms, and with it new respect for the potential of peace education.

Nuclear War or Disarmament Education

As they had done in the past, teachers from elementary to postsecondary were in the forefront in initiating discussion about nuclear war in their classrooms. In spite of the inherent dangers of bringing controversy to their personal or professional life, their school or community, teachers formed coalitions of interested educators. Teachers were responsible for the formation of a national organization, Educators for Social Responsibility (ESR) with the cardinal goal of teaching about nuclear war, including the fears and hopes for future solutions. However, since 1981 to the end of the decade, ESR also made a shift in emphasis as did the Institute for World Order, from "nuclear education" to "nuclear age education." Shelley Berman, president of ESR in 1988 emphasized that a broader agenda was now in place with an:

> understanding of social and ecological interdependence, conflict resolution skills, understanding the complexity of social issues, and helping young people feel they can make a difference.[62]

With publication of the 1990 Publications Catalog, as previously noted, a shift in emphasis included teaching conflict resolution skills and a broader agenda for teaching about the Soviet Union. Included also were units on Communism and Anticommunism and "Secrecy and Democracy" in an attempt to balance "individual freedom and national security."

In the early eighties, nuclear war education grew out of the questions raised by American children, reflecting on information that they gained from sources outside of their schools. Many teachers found they were unable to answer questions or supply accurate information. Some even expressed the opinion that these were ethical issues that belonged in the spheres of the family or the church.

Responsibility for teaching about nuclear war—the effects, fears, and hopes for the future—was central to the role of education, according to many educators. It was their concern for children that resulted in the design of innovative curriculum materials that brought a perceived "conspiracy of silence" on nuclear war to an end.

Peace education received reassurance from an official source in 1980, as the result of action by the United Nations. Disarmament education was designated as an "essential component of peace education." The rationale was defined as:

> Education or communication that would create an awareness of the factors underlying the production and acquisition of arms, of the social, political, economic, and cultural repercussions of the arms race and of the grave danger for the survival of humanity.[63]

Peace education, in this context, was to be confined to the areas of arms reduction, unilateral disarmament initiatives, general and complete disarmament under effective international control. However, there was an allusion to world order values as a discussion of a process aimed at transforming the system of armed nation-states. As further support for disarmament education, the United Nations Secretary General suggested that member nations allocate "one-tenth of one percent of military spending" for disarmament education.[64] Betty Reardon, of the Teachers College program, in a discussion of this UNESCO action expressed the hope that disarmament education could become a "global banner" as well as a major effort in education and research "to develop a new technology for peace,"[65] By 1988, Reardon predicted that an integration of nuclear age, disarmament, and global education should be considered by "integrating all of these (elements) into a comprehensive approach to peace education for global responsibility in a nuclear age."[66]

Between 1981 and 1983, several educational organizations assumed leadership positions, advocating education as preparation for peace. At the NEA convention in 1981, the executive director at that time, Terry Herndon, reported that 9,000 educators in attendance had resolved that:

> The methods of peace are superior to the methods of war and, in this nuclear age, may be basic to the survival of civilization.[67]

In March 1983 the ASCD, through its board of directors published a resolution supporting the nuclear freeze. They urged "open discussion in our schools of the nuclear freeze issue and other possible approaches to world peace."[68]

Stanley Elam, writing in a leading educational journal *Phi Delta Kappan* examined several approaches to peace education in various American schools and colleges. He concluded that educators were engaged in very little significant teaching on nuclear war. In addition, few "curricular materials on the nuclear threat have been developed by state departments of education."[69]

A second educational journal, *Teachers College Record,* devoted an entire issue to the theme of "Education for a Living World," exploring various aspects of peace education and teaching in a nuclear age. Douglas Sloan, editor, stated that: "Education for peace is not a peripheral matter but lies at the heart of the educational venture." The preparation of teachers was a target for criticism:

> Teacher education has been totally remiss in dealing with peace and disarmament education of any sort. As a result many teachers first encounter peace and disarmament education as something peripheral to that which they have themselves been taught are the proper concerns of education.[70]

The dilemma that faced educators was underscored by Alex Molnar, professor at the University of Wisconsin-Milwaukee in his column, "Contemporary Issues and the Schools." Molnar expressed the difficulty of teaching about nuclear war education from the vantage point of a citizen as well as an educator. "Nuclear policy may prove to be an exception because social issues are values issues," he wrote.[71]

A common belief of educators, especially in the public schools, was that social issues involving a judgment call in ethics belonged to outside agencies, the family and church, and had no place in the schools. The potential danger for indoctrination or propagandizing the younger generation was used as a persuasive argument. Yet, Molnar along with others, claimed that a clear judgment could not be made because secrecy was frequently invoked by a government that on occasion denied the truth to its citizenry and claimed national security would be threatened by full disclosure. The lies put forth by several administrations during the Vietnam War years remained in memory. The policy of secrecy was invoked several times throughout the eighties and into the nineties concerning the Iran-contra affair and visits to China by officials before and after the popular student rebellion was quelled. Because the government did not always adhere to standards of truth in informing its citizenry, educators in agreement with Molnar reasoned that alternative actions should be considered.

A second problem that the educator faced was the lack of suitable textbooks for teaching about nuclear war.[72] A survey of secondary history textbooks by Dan B. Fleming concluded that arms and disarmament received only "slight attention." He confirmed in a later study that an inordinate amount of space was given to the study of war. Textbook critics recognized that the value of militarism was being taught.

The controversy on teaching peace as a value became a heated one, when played out against the background of increased activism as an antinuclear movement developed a sense of urgency in the eighties. The famous clock on the cover of the *Bulletin of the Atomic Scientists,* symbolic of the minutes of survival ticking away for humanity, remained at three minutes to midnight in the early eighties (set back to seventeen minutes to midnight in 1992). A range of viewpoints proclaimed that nuclear warfare was the ultimate moral issue of all times and made irrelevant all past theories, such as the just war. Future victims were described as "nuclear hostages" by Bernard O'Keefe or in a state of "mutual bondage as superpawns" by Michael Novak.[73]

The first doubts of conscience about a nuclear holocaust appeared with greater frequency in educational literature of the early eighties. Educators especially related the dilemma of teaching about nuclear war to their central task: to prepare a new generation for life in a future society or to endow them with the skills to reconstruct a new one. Rethinking the implications of teaching peace as a value paled when placed alongside the grotesque danger of nuclear overkill.

Education received an additional ally, the church, which clarified the issue of nuclear war as a "moral issue of urgency." In 1984, the Catholic Bishops produced a pastoral letter, "The Challenge of Peace" which included a call for improved "social and cultural conditions all over the world," including the world order values and peace education.[74] By 1986, the Methodist Bishops blended their voices with their colleagues and claimed that "any moral case for deterrence . . . has been undermined by arms escalation." They, too called for a nuclear test ban and a freeze on production and deployment of weapons.[75]

Assessment of the issue of teaching values, critics believed, should also include an honest examination of the teaching of militarism as a value.[76] While criticism was aimed at peace educators who wished to teach alternatives to violence, with peace as a cherished value for citizenship, militarism was equated with patriotism and love of country. Dissent against militarism was usually interpreted as disloyalty, bordering on treason. Peace movements in past decades had been wholly ineffective in bringing the pressure of American citizenry to consider nonviolent solutions.

The thrust of educators to bring the vital issue of education about nuclear war into the classroom was a microcosm of events that surrounded the Nuclear Freeze movement.[77] Numbers of voters supported the Freeze in the 1982 elections. On June 12, 1982, for example, half a million people marched in New York City in support of a nuclear freeze. The potentiality of "people power" in bringing the Vietnam War to an end was a hopeful sign that the government would also one day recognize the serious need to reduce arms.

Scant agreement appeared however, concerning the content and the process for teaching nuclear war education. Usually included were discussions about technical data, firepower, scientific aspects of nuclear weaponry (and its effects, such as nuclear winter). Teaching about the Soviet Union and the origins of the Cold War included a common historical perspective. With the umbrella of an ecological ethic, concern for the fragile planet inhabited by all humanity was also taught as a viable bond that could unite many cultures and races. These became central to teaching nuclear age education. It appeared to be an impossibility to teach without concern for the affective—the values, attitudes, and emotions that would inevitably surface. Past prejudices, racial attitudes, fear of the enemy, were peripheral issues that needed to be brought to the center stage and confronted.

Peace education was given an eloquent benediction by the publication of Jonathan Schell's *The Fate of the Earth*. Similar to the Biblical prophets, Schell in poetic metaphors warned of mankind at an ecological crossroad where collective human intelligence was needed to seek out solutions:

> Our power has been in the verbal and mathematical models with which we describe the world and experiment with it . . . In so doing we have unleashed a force more powerful than we can use, captured a beast for

which we are unable to build a cage. In our hands, the
power that brought our world into existence has
become the power of destruction; alpha has become
omega.[78]

Peace educators could also take heart in the heritage of
writings on peace education of John Dewey that offered
confirmation for their work. His philosophy was deemed just
as timely in the eighties and was interpreted by one scholar
as:

The job of the educator was to teach the basic values
of peace and nonviolence as the correct and proper
method of social behavior . . . as a link between past
and present and the hope of the future.[79]

Conspiracy of Silence Comes to an End

By 1985, the perceived conspiracy of silence on teaching
about nuclear war was no longer an issue. Several leading
organizations and their journals appeared on the center stage
and offered resources that could be used in the classroom.
From 1985 into the 1990s, a proliferation of philosophical
and pedagogical arguments for teaching about peace or
nuclear war education appeared, disseminated in a multidisciplinary, interdisciplinary mode. Teachers in greater numbers contributed their own offerings based on design of
curriculum materials in several areas.

Using the format of special theme issues on Nuclear War
Education, a broad range of subject fields offered interest-
ing, introspective viewpoints. For the social studies educator,
Social Education took up the challenge of Alex Molnar with
a special issue, "Nuclear Weapons: Concepts, Issues, and
Controversies." Typical of the insights offered was that of
Shelley Berman of the Educators for Social Responsibility.
He shared that in social studies courses, educators would
need to consider several aspects: (1) a global awareness that

shifts our thinking away from the polarized us/them dichotomy; (2) limits on the use of military power in foreign policy; (3) a means to overcome deep prejudice toward an enemy; and (4) alternative systems of security other than weapons. A hopeful sign that peace education was developing a sense of awareness among students and teachers was reported with students in Brookline, Massachusetts, New York City, and Falmouth, Maine involved in the nuclear war curriculum designed by ESR.[80]

Physics Today, journal of the American Institute of Physics, produced a similar issue: "Nuclear Arms Education." Dietrich Schoeer, professor of physics at the University of North Carolina, Chapel Hill, revealed several discouraging aspects in undertaking arms-race educational efforts. He pointed out that "peer recognition for either research or teaching in the area is sparse" with little financial support. In addition, researchers in technical areas may face "disfavor within the government" as well as with influential foundations, such as the Ford Foundation and the National Science Foundation. Most important of all, though, was Schoeer's call for "a new generation of physicists interested in arms-race matters", with "an invisible college of independent arms-race scientists who are able to perform public-education functions . . . physicists . . . who are willing to learn as well as to educate." Schoeer also provided an impressive listing of resources, including several nongovernmental conferences and international societies functioning within the area of nuclear arms education.[81]

"Education and the Threat of Nuclear War" comprised an issue of the *Harvard Educational Review* in 1984. Of special interest were the perceptions of Eric Markusen and John B. Harris that "encouraging responses by educators" were emerging, especially by college and university faculty.[82] They were joined by John E. Mack, psychiatrist from Harvard, who reported on some of the psychological reasons why educators and parents may resist teaching about nuclear issues. Mack emphasized that discussions of nuclear weapons

and the arms race "are upsetting to children and adoles-
cents." However, he believed that the "deeper and truer
reason for the avoidance of this topic in school curricula is
fear of change and the challenge that education . . . is likely
to pose to prevailing assumptions embedded in the social
system."[83] Secondary school students, especially "undergo
the political socialization which will adapt them to the larger
society." Stimulation of questions about the basic assumptions of society are risks, according to Mack. Continued
acceptance of the status quo and the prevailing ideology may
be questioned.

Teaching about nuclear war was the focus also of a special
1985 issue of the *Phi Delta Kappan* with Paul Fleisher, a
teacher of the gifted in a Richmond, Virginia public school,
sharing his experiences. With limited treatment of the arms
race in available textbooks, Fleisher pointed out that "supplementary resources and units" would need to be provided
until textbooks changed. Of prime consideration was that
adults risked setting "a poor example of responsible adulthood" when they ignored or downplayed the nuclear arms
issue, an essential social issue of contemporary America.[84] In
an attempt to present a balanced viewpoint, *Phi Delta
Kappan* also included an opposing aspect by Ernest W.
Lefever, an advocate of deterrence and the peace-through-
strength philosophy. Lefever advanced the view that deterrence had "prevented war of any kind between the superpowers and between East and West in Europe."[85] Both
views, Fleisher's for a reduction of arms and lessening of the
arms race and Lefever's for a national security view,
represented the balanced treatment that was demanded from
peace education in the eighties.

Peace and Change, journal of COPRED (Consortium for
Peace Research Education and Development) explored
multiple philosophical, psychological, and pedagogical dimensions in a special issue, "Peace Education for the
Nuclear Age," in 1984. Barbara Stanford placed special
emphasis on the ecological aspect of peace education,

exploring "Thinking Beyond the Limits." The concept of limits to the present world order was present intuitively in the ideas of many young people, Stanford stated. However, this concept was "very rarely mentioned in most school curricula" and needed to be explored in education.[86] Visions of the future with a transformation of society, with new adaptations in human behavior called forth a futurist strand for peace education.[87] A systems-wide transformation would be needed to break out of the "old modes of thinking."

One of the most impressive efforts of the eighties was a multidisciplinary teaching guide, "Toward the Practice of Nuclear-Age Education," the efforts of the *Bulletin of Atomic Scientists* with Dick Ringler, University of Wisconsin as editor. An array of resources for postsecondary teachers illustrated how nuclear war education could include the physical, biological, ecological, and social sciences.[88]

Curriculum for Nuclear War Education

Educators involved in nuclear war education produced a proliferation of curriculum materials and inaugurated new programs. For example, the Coalition for a New Foreign and Military Policy, united approximately 50 national religious, labor, peace, research, and social action organizations working for a new peaceful, demilitarized United States foreign policy. Most groups provided curriculum materials or background information that could serve as resources for teachers or students.

The materials developed for a nuclear war curriculum by the NEA, the Union of Concerned Scientists, and Educators for Social Responsibility were noteworthy during this period. A curriculum guide was published as a cooperative effort of the three organizations and the Massachusetts Teachers Association. *Choices: A Unit on Conflict and Nuclear War* was written expressly for the junior high school student.[89] Basic principles of curriculum development were followed: a lesson capsule summary, objectives, materials, description of the lesson, activities (including keeping a journal, home-work, a short quiz), and worksheets. A separate teacher and study glossary were included and there was also an appendix of resources, organizations and periodicals. Conflict arose over the use of *Choices* in many of America's schools with the criticism mainly expressed that "it was skewed in favor of a nuclear freeze."[90]

Several school systems, such as Cambridge, Massachusetts continued to add peace studies to the curriculum. New York City developed tenth grade nuclear-issues discussions. Mil-waukee introduced "peace studies and the dilemma of the nuclear arms race into the curriculum. Ian Harris described two approaches to the infusion of nuclear war education into an existing curriculum: the "top-down" and the "from the bottom." The latter directly engaged teachers in the creation and implementation of the curriculum and succeeded in winning "broad support" within the Madison, Wisconsin schools.[91]

The organization, Educators for Social Responsibility expanded to a considerable degree after its establishment in 1981.[92] From a Boston-based group, it grew into a national organization with 100 chapters and 10,000 members in 36 states by 1988.[93]

The original goal of ESR has been the introduction of nuclear war education into elementary and secondary schools. Their concerns were curriculum development with pilot programs of "grade-appropriate materials that present different points of view on nuclear arms issues." Curriculum guides were designed for kindergarten through postsecond-ary, developed by and for educators and parents. Curriculum ideas and lessons were also created for a "National Day of Dialogue." This was held throughout America and provided an opportunity for parents and teachers "to listen to children's concerns and questions about nuclear war and to consider what should be taught." Anthony (Tony) Wagner, Executive Director and Roberta Snow, one of the original founders, presented the viewpoints of ESR frequently in educational journals.[94]

ESR designed *Dialogue: A Teaching Guide to Nuclear Issues* in 1983 to assist teachers and students in understanding the nuclear threat.[95] *Perspectives: A Teaching Guide to Concepts of Peace* contained separate chapters for kindergarten through grade twelve with a central focus of defining peace and encouraging cooperative behavior.[96] Peacemaking for students in a K-6 classroom included writing to pen pals in the Soviet Union.

Crossroads: Quality of Life in a Nuclear World was designed by the Jobs with Peace Education Task Force. Secondary English, social studies, and science curriculum handbooks were developed.[97] The Task Forces and handbooks set forth several common goals and areas of nuclear war education: to provide factual information about weaponry and to afford a conflict resolution component. To counteract possible feelings of powerlessness, students were encouraged instead (in an exercise named "Action Sheet") to write letters to state or federal officials on nuclear issues, design posters, write skits, craft bulletin boards, and become persistent writers of letters to the editor of their local newspapers.[98]

The Nuclear Age, prepared for the secondary school curriculum by Ground Zero contained technical information about nuclear weaponry, effects of a nuclear interchange and most important of all several action-oriented goals to prevent war. Learning activities included panel discussions, surveys and polls about nuclear weapons to ascertain people's attitudes, and a wide range of language arts activities, poetry, essays, art work, and song writing.[99]

John Zola, a junior high school teacher presented a wide range of viewpoints on nuclear war issues as well as practical classroom activities in *Teaching Peace*.[100] Key components should be "dialogue and active listening" according to Zola. Challenging students to listen and assess different viewpoints was considered a critical issue with a goal being to "complicate the thinking of students."

Nucleography: An Annotated Resource Guide for parents and educators on nuclear energy, war and peace was originally designed for use in the San Francisco Bay area.[101] Many organizations, local and national produced similar materials to assist in teaching about nuclear war issues. *Nucleography* was a comprehensive compilation of curriculum resources, children's books, visuals, and organizations, which was put together to meet the critical needs of teachers for materials that were not usually found in their textbooks.

These examples are only a few that are representative of an outpouring of instructional materials for nuclear education.[102] By 1990, resource directories were numerous with publishers exhibiting an encouraging response for materials on nuclear war issues.

The emphasis on communication skills—language arts on the elementary and secondary levels and communication education on the college level—brought a fresh insight into teaching nuclear war education. A call for a union of communication education and peace education was advanced as a method that could be centered on the humanities as well as on current social issues.[103] Of special interest was the centrality of student-teacher involvement that could be a positive outcome. Instead of Goodlad's passive classes of disinterested students, listening, persuasive speeches, formal debate about issues—all activities usually included in language arts and communication classes—were advanced as ones that could bring a renewed spirit of inquiry into the classroom. Peace education as a process was emphasized as a method of aiding students to take personal involvement in their education, to foster critical thinking, and to pose solutions to a basic problem for society. Especially on the secondary and postsecondary level, students could explore issues of war and peace in literature and the humanities— How did humanity in other historical periods respond to violence and conflict? This and similar questions could involve students in an independent or group process of exploring the past to help solve the problems of contemporary society. Clearly, educators in the eighties responded with concrete proposals to the nuclear war issues that demanded increasing degrees of social responsibility.

AFTERTHOUGHTS

History-making events throughout the eighties forced educators into leadership roles that may have been uncomfortable for some. Peace educators were usually branded as unpatriotic if criticism of government policy was involved. The decade began with a call from professional organizations and leading educators that curriculum developers recognize their responsibility to develop materials for teaching about the nuclear war issue. Textbooks had failed to include information or meaningful discussion of the use of nuclear weaponry to destroy civilization. Children and young people raised questions that could not be answered by their teachers. The classroom had ceased to have relevance when educators failed to address the most pressing moral issues of society.

The challenge was indeed met. In spite of continued controversy and criticism of peace education from conservative elements, most organizations showed unusual courage in putting their personal or professional concerns into the background and turned their attention to their first responsibility, the children and young people in their classrooms.

While beyond the scope of this study—which focuses on American peace education curriculum and writings— international peace education also showed growth and development in the eighties. Writings in other nations revealed an intriguing, indigenous flavor for peace education in various nations. Peace activism often joined with education as a form of consciousness-raising, whether peace education became "A-bomb education" in Japan or disarmament education in the Netherlands and several Eastern European countries. *Educación para la paz* in Latin American countries often revolved around the methods of Paulo

Freire, the Brazilian educator, who believed that literacy was central to social change. In Belgium, peace education bore a strong resemblance to moral or religious education while in France, *éducation pour la paix* was less developed, carried on by a small but active group. Each nation reacted to the unique configuration of needs for their own younger generation.[104]

Teachers who expressed interest in global education believed that international experiences would give them the background needed for in-depth teaching. Elise Boulding in *Building a Global Civic Culture* proposed a substitute for the traditional nation-states that have been involved in wars and conflict in past centuries. In a utopian wide-ranging discussion of transnational associations (also known as INGOs-International Nongovernmental Organizations) she emphasized the power that is possible when each individual or their family engaged in networking through membership in associations, service clubs, scouting groups, YWCAs, YMCAs, churches, or professional associations with common interests, across national borders.[105] Such transnational networks offered the educator a logical way to communicate and work together with others on an international level.

While the international flavor of peace education is not often in evidence, many professional organizations do indeed have links to others that facilitate the interchange of peace education ideas. For example, OMEP, the Organization Mondiale pour l'Education Préscolaire (International Organization for Early Childhood Education) met regularly at the annual and regional conferences of the National Association for the Education of Young Children. The author gave a presentation in peace education at the NAEYC annual conference in 1989 where educators from several nations participated in sharing events, concerns, and practices taking place in their countries. Articles in their journal confirmed a consciousness-raising under way in the eighties, one that brought the potentiality of peace education to early childhood educators.[106] The spadework of the eighties to offer transnational linkages has paved the way for a deeper understanding of global and peace education issues.

The pioneering endeavors of the World Council for Curriculum and Instruction were embodied in the words of the organization President, Estela C. Matriano: "I was one of the Filipino children who . . . lost my mother (and) became an orphan in the midst of this raging war." Matriano reflected the mission of many as the need to "build bridges for peaceful relations among peoples and nations."[107]

The eighties confirmed for many educators that a small, first step forward in the past can be the pathway to success in the future. The growth and maturity that resulted with the publication of numerous curriculum guides and insightful articles on various phases of peace education built on the efforts of those in the seventies and from previous decades.

Notes

1. Sources for historical background in this period were: Graham T. Allison et al. *Owls, Doves and Hawks: An Agenda for Avoiding Nuclear War* (New York: W. W. Norton, 1985); *Biographical Dictionary of Modern Peace Leaders,* ed. Harold Josephson (Westport, CT: Greenwood Press, 1985); *Biographical Dictionary of Internationalists,* ed. Warren F. Kuehl (Westport, CT: Greenwood Press, 1985); D. L. Davidson, *Nuclear Weapons and the American Churches: Positions on Modern Warfare* (Boulder, CO: Westview Press, 1983); Paul Johnson, *Modern Times: The World from the Twenties to the Eighties* (New York: Harper & Row, 1983); Paul R. Loeb, *Hope in Hard Times: America's Peace Movement and the Reagan Era* (Lexington, MA: Lexington Books, 1986); *Peace Archives: A Guide* (West Berkeley, CA: World Without War Council, Historians' Project, 1985); *Peace Heroes in Twentieth-Century America,* ed. Charles DeBenedetti (Bloomington, IN: Indiana University Press, 1986; *Swords into Plowshares: Nonviolent Direct Action for Disarmament,* ed. Arthur J. Laffin and Anne Montgomery (San Francisco: Harper & Row,

1987); and *World Encyclopedia of Peace, Vol. 2*, ed. Ervin Laszlo and J. Y. Yoo (Elmsford, NY: Pergamon Press, 1986).

Sources for background in education and psychology during this period were: Mortimer Adler, *The Paideia Proposal: An Educational Manifesto* (New York: Macmillan, 1982) and *The Paideia Program* (New York: Macmillan, 1984); Ernest L. Boyer, *High School: A Report on Secondary Education in America* (New York: Harper & Row, 1983); Robert Coles, *The Moral Life of Children* (Boston: The Atlantic Monthly Press, 1986) and *The Political Life of Children* (Boston: The Atlantic Monthly Press, 1986); *Ethics Teaching in Higher Education*, ed. Daniel Callahan and Sissela Bok (New York: Plenum Press, 1980); John I. Goodlad, *What Are Schools For?* (Bloomington, IN: Phi Delta Kappa Educational Foundation, 1979) and *A Place Called School: Prospects for the Future* (New York: McGraw-Hill, 1984); D. Bob Gowin, *Educating* (Ithaca, NY: Cornell University Press, 1981); *International Encyclopedia of Education*, eds. Torsten Husen and T. N. Postlethwaite, (Elmsford, NY: Pergamon Press, 1985); Matthew Lipman, et al. *Philosophy in the Classroom* (Philadelphia: Temple University Press, 1980); and Neil Postman, *The Disappearance of Childhood* (New York: Delacorte Press, 1982).

2. Background sources included: Lance Morrow, "Man of the Decade: Gorbachev, The Unlikely Patron of Change," *Time* (January 1, 1990), 42–45; Larry Martz, "Into a Brave New World," *Newsweek* (December 25, 1989), 40–44; Bruce W. Nelan, "Unfinished Revolution," *Time* (January 8, 1990), 28–34; and Fred Coleman, "Breaking from the Fold: Lithuanian Communists Say No To Moscow," *Newsweek* (January 1, 1990), 33.

3. Betty Reardon, ed., *Educating for Global Responsibility: Teacher-Designed Curricula for Peace Education, K–12* (New York: Teachers College Press, 1988), xvii.

4. Ian M. Harris, *Peace Education* (Jefferson, NC: McFarland & Co., Inc., 1988), 88. Harris discussed the pedagogy, philosophy, and classroom practices that are generally accepted for peace education programs with a realistic consideration of the controversy and issues facing the peace educator.

5. John I. Goodlad, "What Schools Should Be For," *Learning* (July/August 1980): 39–43.
6. Representative of Commission studies and calls for reform have been: National Commission on Excellence in Education, *A Nation at Risk: The Imperative for Educational Reform* (Washington, DC: United States Department of Education, 1983); *The Carnegie Study of American High Schools* (Washington, DC: Carnegie Foundation for the Advancement of Teaching, 1982); *Academic Preparation for College* (Washington, DC: The College Board, 1983).
7. Edward B. Fiske, "America's Test Mania," *New York Times* (Education Life), April 10, 1988, XII: 16 and Samuel J. Meisels, "Uses and Abuses of Developmental Screening and School Readiness Testing," *Young Children* 42 (January 1987): 4–9.
8. Elliot W. Eisner, *The Educational Imagination: On the Design and Evaluation of School Programs,* 2nd ed. (New York: Macmillan, 1985), 361. Discussion of the "Effective Schools Programs" was outlined in Carl D. Glickman, "Good and/or Effective Schools: What Do We Want?" *Phi Delta Kappan* 68 (April 1987): 622–624.
9 Jeannie Oakes discussed the tradition of tracking as it affects minority groups in "Keeping Track, Part 2: Curriculum Inequality and School Reform," *Phi Delta Kappan* 67 (October 1986): 150–151.
10. Lev S. Vygotsky, *Thought and Language,* edited and translated by E. Haveman and G. Vakos (Cambridge, MA: M.I.T. Press, 1962); Alexander R. Luria, *The Neuropsychology of Memory* (Washington, DC: V. H. Winston & Sons, 1976) and *The Working Brain: An Introduction to Neuropsychology* (London: The Penguin Press, 1973); Walter B. Essman, *Current Biochemical Approaches to Learning and Memory* (New York: Spectrum Publications, Inc., 1973); *Education and the Brain: The Seventy-Seventh Yearbook of the National Society for the Study of Education* (Chicago: The University of Chicago Press, 1978); Leslie A. Hart, *How the Brain Works* (New York: Basic Books, 1975); *The Brain and Human Learning* (White Plains, NY: Longman, 1983) and Charmaine Della Neve, Leslie A. Hart and Edgar C. Thomas, "Huge Learning Jumps Show Potency of Brain-Based Instructions,"

Phi Delta Kappan 68 (October 1986): 143–148; and Howard Gardner, *Frames of Mind: The Theory of Multiple Intelligences* (New York: Basic Books, Inc., 1983).

11. Research studies in the 1980s that have called for a transformation or rebuilding of the schools were: *A Nation Prepared: Teachers for the 21st Century* (New York: Carnegie Forum on Education and the Economy, 1986); Theodore Sizer, *Horace's Compromise* (Boston: Houghton Mifflin, 1984); and The William T. Grant Foundation on Youth, Washington, DC, "The Forgotten Half: Non-College Bound Youth in America," *Phi Delta Kappan*, 69 (February 1988): 409–418.

12. Ernest Boyer in Stephen M. Masiclat, "Teaching Ethics," *Phi Delta Kappan* 68 (December 1987): 276.

13. Carlos E. Cortes, *Multicultural Education and Global Education: Natural Partners for a Better World.* (Riverside, CA: University of California-Riverside, 1980).

14. I. McNett, *Demographic Imperatives: Implications for Educational Policy* (Washington, DC: American Council on Education, 1983).

15. David C. King, "Delay Persists in Social Studies Reform but Signs Point to Headway Just Ahead." ASCD Curriculum Update. (ERIC 287 272); Willard M. Kniep, "Social Studies within a Global Education," *Social Education* 50 (November/December 1986): 536; and Beverly T. Watkins, "Colleges Urged To Train Future Schoolteachers To Deal with Expected Influx of Immigrants." *Chronicle of Higher Education* (December 13, 1989) 36: A41–42.

16. Warren L. Hickman and Roy A. Price, "Global Awareness and Major Concepts," *The Social Studies* 71 (September/October 1980): 208–211.

17. Donna J. Cole, "Multicultural Education and Global Education: A Possible Merger," 33 *Theory into Practice* (September 1984): 151–154.

18. Willard M. Kniep, "Global Education as School Reform," *Educational Leadership* 46 (September 1989): 43.

19. Ulf P. Lundgren. "Curriculum from a Global Perspective," 121, in *1985 ASCD Yearbook: Current Thought on Curriculum.* (Alexandria, VA: Association for Supervision and Curriculum Development, 1985).

20. N. C. Kearney and W. W. Cook, "Curriculum," *Business Review* 36 (1958): 23–30, quoted in Lundgren, 131.
21. Lundgren, 133.
22. Charles S. White, "Teachers Using Technology," *Social Education* 51 (January 1987), 44–47; Royal Van Horn, "Laser Videodiscs in Education: Endless Possibilities," *Phi Delta Kappan* 68 (May 1987): 696–700; N. Estes, J. Herne, D. LeClercq, "Interactive Video through AppleWorks," Seventh International Conference on Technology and Education: New Pathways To Learning Through Educational Technology, *Proceedings, Volume 2,* Brussels, March 1990; "New Computerized World Information Service (NCWIS)," East/West/ North/South, For Dissemination and Exchange of Information on Global Problems (Disarmament-Development-Environment-Human Rights), Press Release #2, Geneva, 13 May 1989; and GEMNET, a Global Communications/Information Network, which matches schools, has an information service, and offers "Video Pals," communications exchange program between schools in Japan and the United States, a project devised by Global Education Motivators.
23. Samuel Brodbelt, "Global Interdependence: Increasing Student Awareness," *The Social Studies* 103 (May/June 1981): 103.
24. Roy R. Pellicano, "Global Education: A Definition and a Curriculum Proposal," *Orbit* (1981): 18.
25. Robert G. Hanvey, *An Attainable Global Perspective* (New York: Global Perspectives, Inc., 1987), 25 and David C. King, *Education for a World in Change: A Report* (New York: Global Perspectives in Education, Inc., 1980), 3.
26. Mary McFarland, "Japan as a Focus Culture for Global Education," *The Social Studies* 73 (July/August 1982): 165.
27. Anthony E. Conte and Lorraine A. Cavaliere, "Are Students Being Educated for the 21st Century?: An Infusion Model for Global Perspectives," *The Social Studies* 72 (March/April 1982): 74–79.
28. National Council for the Social Studies, "Revision of the NCSS Social Studies Curriculum Guidelines," *Social Education* 43 (April 1979): 261–268.
29. National Council for the Social Studies, "Social Studies for

Early Childhood and Elementary School Children Preparing for the 21st Century: A Report from NCSS Task Force on Early Childhood/Elementary Social Studies," *Social Education* 53 (January 1989): 14–23. See also Blythe S. Hinitz, *Teaching Social Studies to the Young Child: A Research and Resource Guide.* (New York: Garland Publishing, Inc., 1992).

30. Carlos E. Cortes and Dan B. Fleming, "Global Education and Textbooks," *Social Education* 50 (September 1986): 341–343.

31. David E. Vocke, "Those Varying Perspectives on Global Education," *The Social Studies* 79 (January/February 1988): 18.

32. Vocke, 18–20.

33. Mary Merryfield, "Evaluating Global Education Projects: A Case for Naturalistic Methodology," unpublished paper presented at the National Conference on Professional Priorities— Shaping the Future of Global Education. Easton, MD, May 1982, 8–9.

34. Phyllis La Farge, "Nuclear Education: Propaganda or Problem Solving," *Bulletin of the Atomic Scientists* (July/August 1988): 16 and sidebar, "Mainstreaming Global Education."

35. Educators for Social Responsibility (descriptive literature), 1990.

36. Betty Reardon, *Comprehensive Peace Education: Educating for Global Responsibility* (New York: Teachers College Press, 1988), 26.

37. Reardon, 29.

38. David King, ASCD Curriculum Update, 6.

39. "Shaping the Future of International Studies," Wingspread Conference. (New York: Global Perspectives in Education, Inc., 1984).

40. Wingspread Conference Report, 1–2.

41. Commission on Schools, North Central Association and the Charles F. Kettering Foundation, *Implementation Guide* (Dayton, OH: Charles F. Kettering Foundation, 1982).

42. Commission on Schools, North Central Association, 14.

43. Commission on Schools, North Central Association, *A Guide to Four Essential Themes—Global Realities,* 133.

44. *Guidelines for Global Education* (Lansing, MI: Michigan Department of Education, 1983), 1.

45. *Guidelines for Global Education,* 14.

46. COPRED, "10 Quick Ways To Evaluate Global Education Materials (leaflet) (Kent, Ohio: COPRED Peace Education Network, Kent State University, n.d.).

47. *Peace and World Order Studies: A Curriculum Guide,* 3rd ed. (New York: Transnational Academic Program, Institute for World Order, 1981).

48. *Peace and World Order Studies: A Curriculum Guide,* 5th ed. (Boulder, CO: Westview Press, 1989). Adele Simmons, Foreword xii-xiii.

49. *Peace and World Order Studies,* 5th ed. Preface and Acknowledgments, xvi.

50. *World Policy Forum* (newsletter) (New York: World Policy Institute, Spring, 1983), 1.

51. *World Policy Forum* (newsletter) (New York: World Policy Institute, Spring 1983), 1.

52. "Profile: New President of the World Policy Institute," *World Policy Forum* (Spring 1983), 9.

53. William Greider, "Does a Bear Sit in the Woods?", excerpt from *Rolling Stone* (January 17, 1985); *World Policy Forum* (Spring 1985), 3.

54. World Policy Institute (program description), (Summer 1988).

55. *World Policy Forum,* Spring 1984, 2.

56. *Peace and World Order Studies,* 5th ed., a project of PAWSS at Hampshire College. Publications, 1988–89 referred to the "former curriculum development program."

57. *World Policy Forum,* Spring 1983, 1.

58. Representative articles on "The Day After" are: "The Day After": Viewer's Guide (New York: Cultural Information Service, ABC Television Network, 1983); "TV's Nuclear Nightmare": Special Report, *Newsweek* (21 November 1983), 66; "The Day After Will Be Too Late" (advertisement) *USA Today* (21 November 1983), 9A; "All Noise on the Western Front" (editorial). *New York Times* (22 November 1983), 1, 24. George Bush, "Preserving Peace Through Deterrence," *New York Times* (21 November 1983), I, 23 19Ys, and "TV Atom War Spurs Vast Discussion," *New York Times* (22 November 1983), Y11.

59. "Battle of the Nuclear Stars," (editorial) *Chicago Tribune* (22 November 1983), 1, 10.

60. Malcolm B. Scully, "Telecast on Nuclear War Spurs Campus Activities," *Chronicle of Higher Education* (30 November 1983), 30: 3,

61. Studies reported were: Daniel B. Fleming, "Students and Parents' Views of 'The Day After' and the Place of Nuclear War Education in the Schools," *The Social Studies* (January/February 1985): 8–9; "Attitudes about Arms Control and Effects of 'The Day After,' " ED 257 699; " 'The Day After': Rhetorical Vision in an Ironic Frame," ED 251 872; "When Imagination Defies Television: 'The Day After' Effect," ED 257 764; " 'The Day After': Report of a Survey of Effects of Viewing and Beliefs about Nuclear War," ED 260 951; "Enhancing the Effects of 'The Day After' with an Educational Intervention," ED 261 950; " 'The Day After': Does the Media Really Have an Impact? Study I" (1984) and "What Difference Does It Make in Experienced Control? Study II and III," ED 260 953; and "Young Persons View 'The Day After'," ED 260 952.

62. Phyllis La Farge, "Nuclear Education," See Note 34.

63. United Nations Educational and Scientific Organization (Paris: World Congress on Disarmament Education, 1980), n.p.

64. UNESCO, n.p.

65. Betty Reardon, *Militarization, Security and Peace Education: A Guide for Concerned Citizens* (Valley Forge, PA: United Ministries in Education, 1982), 71–74.

66. Betty Reardon, *Comprehensive Peace Education*, 37. Reardon wisely predicted the problems ahead for disarmament education in the schools, because "the subjects are primarily political . . . The lack of consciousness about peace education and disarmament education as essentially political education . . . has served to impede the development of the field." Quoted in "The Status of and Recommendation for Disarmament Education," *Approaching Disarmament Education*, edited by Magnus Haavelsrud (Surrey, England: Westbury House, 1981), 115–116.

67. Terry Herndon, "A Teacher Speaks of Peace," *Phi Delta Kappan* 64 (April 1983): 530.

68. "ASCD Resolution on Nuclear Freeze," *Educational Leadership* (May 1983), 42.

69. Stanley Elam, "Educators and the Nuclear Threat," *Phi Delta Kappan* 64 (April 1983): 538.
70. Douglas Sloan, "Education for Peace and Disarmament," *Teachers College Record* (Fall 1982): 1.
71. Alex Molnar, "Nuclear Policy in a Democracy: Do Educators Have a Choice?" *Educational Leadership* (May 1983): 38.
72. Dan B. Fleming, "Nuclear War in High School History Textbooks," *Phi Delta Kappan* 64 (April 1983): 550–551, and "Nuclear War in Textbooks," *Peace and Change* (Summer 1984).
73. Bernard O'Keefe, *Nuclear Hostages* (Boston: Houghton Mifflin 1983) and Michael Novak, *The Spirit of Democratic Capitalism* (New York: Simon and Schuster, 1983).
74. Bishops' Pastoral Letter, Challenge of Peace. *Catholic Update.* (Cincinnati, OH: St. Anthony Messenger Press, 1983).
75. The United Methodist Council of Bishops, *In Defense of Creation: The Nuclear Crisis and a Just Peace, Foundation Document,* (Nashville, TN: Graded Press, 1986).
76. Books and articles that included opposing viewpoints concerning nuclear education and children's feelings about nuclear issues were: Daniel J. Christie and Linden Nelson, "Student Reactions To Nuclear Education, *Bulletin of the Atomic Scientists* (July/August 1988): 22–23; Robert Coles, *The Moral Life of Children* (Chapter VII: "Children and the Nuclear Bomb") (Boston: Atlantic Monthly Press, 1986); Paul R. Loeb, *Hope in Hard Times* (Part 1: Chapter 4 "Children and the Bomb," pps. 109–156) (Lexington, MA: Lexington Books, 1987) and Miranda Spencer, "What Are We Teaching Our Kids?: Nuclear-age Educators Say They Want Children To Think Critically. Conservative Critics See a Hidden Agenda" *Nuclear Times* (September/October 1988): 17–20. Annotated listings of several articles on the attitudes of children toward nuclear war and peace education appeared in Grant Burns, *The Atomic Papers: A Citizen's Guide To Selected Books and Articles On The Bomb, The Arms Race, Nuclear Power, The Peace Movement, and Related Issues* (Metuchen, NJ: The Scarecrow Press, 1984).
77. See Jerome Price, *The Antinuclear Movement* (Boston: Twayne Publishers, 1982).
78. Jonathan Schell, *The Fate of the Earth* (New York: Alfred A. Knopf, 1982), 513.

79. Charles F. Howlett, "The Pragmatist as Pacifist: John Dewey's Views on Peace Education, *Teachers College Record* 83 (Spring 1982): 448.

80. Shelley Berman, "A Break in the Silence: Raising Nuclear Issues in the Schools" *Social Education* 47 (November/December 1983): 501–502.

81. Dietrich Schoeer, "Teaching about the Arms Race." *Physics Today* 36 (March 1983): 52–53.

82. Eric Markusen and John B. Harris, "The Role of Education in Preventing Nuclear War," *Harvard Educational Review* 54 (August 1984): 302.

83. John R. Mack, "Resistances To Knowing in the Nuclear Age," *Harvard Educational Review* 54 (August 1984): 266.

84. Paul Fleisher, "Teaching Children about Nuclear War," *Phi Delta Kappan* 66 (November 1985): 215–216.

85. Ernest W. Lefever, "Teaching History and Politics in the Age of Nuclear Arms," *Phi Delta Kappan* 66 (November 1985): 217–218.

86. Barbara Stanford, "Thinking Beyond the Limits," *Peace and Change* (Summer, 1984), 5. An opposing viewpoint to the theory of limited growth and resources is Herbert I. London, *Why Are They Lying To Our Children?"* (New York: Stein and Day, 1984).

87. Stanford, 5–7.

88. Dick Ringler, "Toward the Practice of Nuclear-Age Education," *Bulletin of the Atomic Scientists* 37 (December 1984): 4s. Individual colleges and universities also assembled special publications on the nuclear war issue. Representative of such efforts were *Peace and War,* eds. Richard Butchko, Robert Cummings, Linda Hornback, Mario Mazzarella, and Harvey Williams. (Newport News, Va: Christopher Newport College, 1984); and "Vision of Peace Special Issue." Introduction by Vito Perrone. *North Dakota Quarterly Press,* University of North Dakota, 1988.

89. *Choices* (Washington, DC: National Education Association, 1983).

90. "Nuclear War Becomes Hot Topic in Schools, Stirs Up Controversy," *Wall Street Journal* (24 May 1983), 1. Other articles that discussed *Choices* were: Christie and Nelson,

"Student Reactions to Nuclear Education." See also Paul D. Werner and Paul J. Roy, "Measuring Activism Regarding the Nuclear Arms Race," *Journal of Personality Assessment* 49 (1985): 181–186.

91. Ian Harris, 88.
92. Educators for Social Responsibility, (descriptive literature), (Cambridge, MA: Educators for Social Responsibility, 1982, 1985 and 1988).
93. ESR, (descriptive literature), 1983.
94. Anthony Wagner, "Why Nuclear Education?" *Educational Leadership* 40 (May 1983): 40–41; Roberta Snow, *Decision-making in a Nuclear Age,* 2nd ed. (Cambridge, MA: Educators for Social Responsibility, 1983); and "A Decision-making Approach to Nuclear Education," *Harvard Educational Review* 54 (August 1984): 321.
95. *Dialogue: A Teaching Guide to Nuclear Issues* (Cambridge, MA: Educators for Social Responsibility, 1983).
96. *Perspectives: A Teaching Guide to Concepts of Peace* (Cambridge, MA: Educators for Social Responsibility, 1983), K–6 Guide, 67.
97. *Crossroads: Quality of Life in a Nuclear World, a High School English Curriculum* by Dan French, et al. (Boston: Jobs with Peace, 1983); *Crossroads: Quality of Life in a Nuclear World, a High School Social Studies Curriculum* by Dan French, et al. (Boston: Jobs with Peace, 1983); and *Crossroads: Quality of Life in a Nuclear World, a High School Science Curriculum* by Dan French and Connie Phillips (Boston: Jobs with Peace, 1983).
98. *Crossroads, High School Science Curriculum,* 10b.
99. *The Nuclear Age: A Curriculum Guide for Secondary Schools* (Washington, DC: Ground Zero, 1983).
100. John Zola, *Teaching about Peace and Nuclear War: A Balanced Approach* (Boulder, CO: Social Science Education Consortium, Inc., 1985), 13, and John Zola and Remy Sieck, *Teaching about Conflict, Nuclear War and the Future.* (Denver, CO: Center for Teaching International Relations, 1984).
101. *Nucleography: An Annotated Resource Guide for Parents and Educators on Nuclear Energy, War, and Peace,* edited by Jacqueline Barber et al. (Berkeley, CA: Nucleography, 1982).

102. Representative publications were: Pat Fellers, *Peace-ing it Together: Peace and Justice Activities for Youth* (New York: Harper & Row, 1984); Ruth Fletcher, *Teaching Peace Skills for Living in a Global Society* (New York: Harper & Row, 1986); and Robert A. Rubenstein and Mary L. Foster, eds. *Peace and War: Cross Cultural Perspectives,* (New Brunswick, NJ: Transaction Books, 1985).

103. Todd Fry, "Communication Education and Peace Education: A Beginning," *Communication Education* 35 (January 1986): 75–80.

104. International peace education programs were discussed in the following: "The Debate on Education for Peace" (Special Issue), *International Review of Education* 29 (1983); *A Just Peace Through Transformation: Cultural, Economic, and Political Foundations for Change, Proceedings of the International Peace Research Association, Eleventh General Conference,* edited by Chadwick Alger and Michael Stohl (Boulder, CO: Westview Press, 1988); David Hicks, ed., *Education for Peace: Issues, Principles, and Practice in the Classroom* (Great Britain) (London: Routledge, 1988); and Derek Heater, *Peace through Education: The Contribution of the Council for Education in World Citizenship* (London: Falmer Press, 1984).

105. Elise Boulding, *Building a Global Civic Culture: Education for an Interdependent World* (New York: Teachers College, 1988).

106. Peace education books and articles that related directly to early childhood education were: Joan Tephly, "Young Children's Understanding of War and Peace, *Early Child Development and Care* 20 (1985): 271–285; Margaret Weiser, "Childhood in a World of Tensions: 1985 World Council Meeting of OMEP" *OMEP Journal* (Organisation Mondiale pour l'Education Préscolaire—World Organization of Early Childhood Education (November/December 1985): 87–90, a meeting which discussed peace education programs in several countries; Nancy Carlsson-Paige and Diane E. Levin, *The War Play Dilemma: Balancing Needs and Values in the Early Childhood Classroom* (New York: Teachers College Press, 1987); and *Who's Calling the Shots?: How to Respond Effectively to Children's Fascination with War Play and War*

Toys. (Philadelphia: New Society Publishers, 1989); Louise Derman-Sparks, *Anti-Bias Curriculum: Tools for Empowering Young Children,* (Washington, DC: National Association for the Education of Young Children, 1989); Phyllis La Farge, *Strangelove Legacy* (New York: Harper & Row, 1987) and Kate Cloud, et al. *Watermelons, Not War* (Philadelphia: New Society Publishers, 1984).

107. Estela C. Matriano, quoted in *Peace Education and the Task for Educators,* edited by Terry Carson and Hendrik D. Gideonse (Bloomington, IN: World Council for Curriculum and Instruction, 1987), 1–2.

9.　BREAKTHROUGH AND INNOVATION, 1981–1990

A TIME OF PROGRESS

Breakthrough—making a distinct impact where previous resistance had occurred—became a reality for peace educators in the eighties. The impetus of the antinuclear movement in the early years of the decade with public demonstrations for arms reduction influenced the evolution of peace education that began in the seventies. In the post-Summit atmosphere of 1987–1989 especially, evidence of a true breakthrough with distinct innovations in program design and curriculum could be identified.

As stated previously in Chapter 8, outstanding progress was exhibited in several ways: with the establishment of the United States Institute of Peace, which exerted influence on conflict resolution and school mediation programs; assertive use of peace education by church groups; technology as an enhancement for the communication of peace education on a national and global scale; and grassroots programs for the development of American-Soviet friendship exchanges as peace education in action.

THE UNITED STATES INSTITUTE OF PEACE

Long advocated by peace educators, the United States Institute of Peace became a reality in 1985 after an advocacy campaign that spanned almost 14 years. Action was initiated with a citizen Ad Hoc Committee formed in 1975 with the

National Campaign under the leadership of Milton C. (Mike) Mapes, who had international experience with the Department of State and the Agency for International Development. Mapes died of leukemia a short while before the Institute was finally established.

The purpose of the academy, originally known as the National Academy of Peace and Conflict Resolution or the George Washington Academy of Peace was "to inquire into the empirical and historical nature of the process of peace . . . and to develop alternatives to conflict situations."[1]

The basic document proposed that the Academy would offer a two year postgraduate course of study offering a master's degree to include an internship that would emphasize "the skills necessary to achieve international cooperation . . . (and) the ability to resolve conflicts in a peaceful way."[2]

The members of the first commission included Senator Spark M. Matsunaga from Hawaii, John R. Dellenback, president of the Christian College Consortium, and Elise Boulding, sociologist and professor emerita from Dartmouth College, among others. Major persuasions for the establishment of the Peace Academy were presented in the final report:

> To benefit American international activities with a broad range of peacemaking skills . . . To activate the field of peace learning . . . To apply peacemaking knowledge and skills that will make the field of peace learning accessible . . . to scholars, analysts, policymakers, and decision-makers.[3]

Background was provided by the commission on previous efforts to establish an agency for peace. In the sixties, the establishment of the National Peace Agency and the Arms Control Research Institute were formed as two distinct organizations. These two entities merged to become the Arms Control and Disarmament Agency. Actually, the

National Peace Agency concept was not the first, but had been proposed as early as 1793.[4]

The final report revealed:

> In summary, the U.S. Academy of Peace is to be . . . a graduate educational institution . . . with a clear focus upon international concerns, including those related to military functions, nuclear proliferation, disarmament, world commerce, exploration, and use of space and the seas, technological sharing, human management, and cultural understandings.[5]

Officials from the state and education departments and the Arms Control and Disarmament Agency testified against the bill. Yet, the heads of those agencies as well as the Department of Defense and the commandant of the National Defense University were included in the final board of directors created by President Reagan. These actions set the stage for serious questions about the effectiveness of a future peace agenda.

Elise Boulding was a tireless advocate for the Institute of Peace, speaking and writing over the course of ten years in favor of its establishment. Boulding emphasized frequently that international institutions for peace were already operating successfully. The University for Peace in Costa Rica was approved by the United Nations in 1980. The United Nations University began operations in Tokyo in 1974. These research institutes addressed the basic problems of hunger, the use of natural resources, and human and social development, Boulding stated. Her final argument was that cost-effectiveness justified the establishment of these programs "because it's much cheaper to use the skills of conflict resolution than to use weaponry."[6]

The United States Institute of Peace was designed with three major functions: research, education and training, and information services. In 1983, legislation before the 97th Congress failed to pass before the end of the year.[7] In February 1983, Senators Matsunaga, Randolph, Hatfield, and Jepsen reintroduced the legislation in the 98th Congress. Over 150 congressional representatives became cosponsors of the bill. Final passage of Public Law 98-524 was achieved in 1984.

Between 1984 and 1988, a period of frustration and waiting ensued with operations delayed by political tactics. President Reagan took the entire year of 1985 to submit the names of nine nominees to the Board of Directors. The year of 1986 was occupied with a re-authorization of the Institute of Peace, as an amendment to the Senate Higher Education Bill. This passed in June 1986 with appropriations approved for $1.25 million. In 1987, a new director was appointed, Samuel W. Lewis, former Ambassador to Israel and five additional directors were confirmed. A total of $4.5 million in appropriations was approved for fiscal year 1988.[8]

In the few short years since its establishment, the primary activities carried on by the Institute can be considered as education and research, with grants available to nonprofit and public institutions, schools, colleges, public agencies, organizations and individuals.[9] Grant projects announced for the 1988 cycle were designated for research concerning: (1) the role of deterrence in avoiding war; (2) study of armed conflicts in the Third World; (3) teaching public understanding of the Geneva Conventions; (4) the relationship between different types of domestic regimes and the aggressive use of force internationally, and (5) the roles of religion, peace, and war.

The second goal obviously reflected a concern for long-range government policy. In 1990 after the Cold War was declared at an end, publication of a Pentagon document, titled "Military Operations in Low Intensity Conflict," confirmed that future military strategy would emphasize "an aggressive new role in the Third World" including training guerrilla forces to fight against "regimes unfriendly to the West."[10]

The United States Institute of Peace held a National Peace Essay Contest in 1987–88 for the first time for high school students, recalling the peace essay contests held by the American School Peace League from 1913 to 1915 that were used frequently to involve the younger generation. Winners were flown from their homes to Washington, DC for the awards.

The Institute was confirmed by peace scholars and researchers as primarily an educational venture. Its establishment was "considered a modest triumph for its supporters after so many years of effort."[11] One objection was expressed by Paul Kimmel, public policy fellow for the Society for the Psychological Study of Social Issues and the Association for the Advancement of Psychology, organizations that publicly supported the Peace Institute campaign for 16 years. Kimmel considered the prohibition against including grants of private money a serious flaw. Funding was repeatedly scaled down from an original $31 million in a first proposal to $4 million for 1985 and $5 million requested for 1989. The addition to the board of the Secretaries of Defense and State, the director of the Arms Control and Disarmament Agency, and the commandant of the National Defense University, underscored the need to "mobilize forces and nominate high-powered people to the board," Kimmel stated.[12]

Kenneth Boulding, who has been in the forefront of peace and conflict studies for past decades, believed that "one should not expect too much of it, (i.e., the Institute) and there will be some fear of its being corrupted." However, the existence of the Institute could have a "significant long-run effect," he believed, similar to the Council of Economic Advisors by way of creating "an official link between the peace and conflict research community and the government decision makers."[13]

NATIONAL PEACE INSTITUTE FOUNDATION

A second organization, operating independently of the Institute, the National Peace Institute Foundation (changed to the National Peace Foundation in 1990) was described as a "non-governmental volunteer organization concerned with the development of the United States Institute of Peace, peace education, conflict resolution and the United Nations."[14] The Foundation organized Regional Councils in 1986 with an agenda for long-range planning and workshops to develop educational programs in conflict resolution techniques.[15]

An additional goal for the Foundation was described as the coordination of "a national effort to push for a more balanced Board for the United States Institute of Peace." The final membership contained "no business leaders, no labor leaders, no women, no minorities and no professionals in the field of conflict resolution." It was further described as an "all white, all male Board." The situation was later remedied with the addition of women to the Board.[16] Foundation literature described Board members as primarily associated with the defense establishment, in foreign policy or diplomacy.

Educational projects of the National Peace Institute Foundation were described as being "on the leading edge of a new emphasis within the peace movement on peace education . . . fulfilling its goal of mainstreaming peace education."[17] One project slated for development in 1988 was described as an educational mass media effort: films for public broadcast and classroom use with classroom materials on conflict resolution for use in high schools. The developer of the program, Thatcher Drew, underscored that:

> The conflict resolution discipline is rarely reported. The lessons are not often taught in schools . . . the method has not yet penetrated beyond a relatively small circle.[18]

The films would be transmitted on Public Broadcast Stations with teacher guidelines available.

In sharp contrast to the initial, unbalanced composition of the Board of the U.S. Institute of Peace, the Foundation

Board of Directors and an Advisory Board could be considered as multiracial and nonsexist, with a well-rounded membership from the academic, research, religious, governmental, and business communities as well as peace activists. For example, Elise Boulding as well as her husband, Kenneth Boulding were included on the Advisory Board, along with Helen Caldicott, author of *Nuclear Madness,* and the founder of Women's Action for Nuclear Disarmament, and Bishop Raymond Hunthausen, activist archbishop of Seattle.[19]

CONFLICT RESOLUTION: ENTRANCE INTO AMERICAN CLASSROOMS

A renewed interest in conflict resolution as a revitalized area for peace education resulted from the aforementioned establishment of the United States Institute of Peace. The guidelines of Public Law 98-525, the United States Institute of Peace Act provided for grants or contracts:

> (1) to initiate, strengthen and support research on conflict resolution; (2) promote and advance the study of conflict resolution by educational, training, and research institutions; (and) (3) educate the Nation about and educate and train individuals in peace and conflict resolution theories, methods, techniques, programs, and systems.[20]

Grants awarded in 1987 showed programs that would ultimately affect future students from elementary through the college years. For example, an award was made to the American University for development of a multicourse Peace and Conflict Resolution concentration with the addition of a curriculum and peace information library.[21] A followup inquiry showed that the program did go into operation in January 1988 with an initial enrollment of 15, which increased to 32 enrollees by the Fall 1988 semester.[22]

A second grant was made to the Peace Education Program, Teachers College, Columbia University. With Betty Reardon as the Project's Director, this grant funded the development of model human rights courses that included peace education and curriculum guides for use in secondary and postsecondary schools.[23] Other grants were made to the Mississippi State University Center for International Security and Strategic Studies enabling Janos Radvanyi, the Project Director, to set up a trial workshop on the teaching of peace and conflict resolution education for secondary schools; and to the New Hampshire Council on World Affairs, allowing its Project Director, David Larson, of the University of New Hampshire, to establish a program intended to correlate the teaching of social studies and peace education.

Significant progress was made in the eighties in the integration of peace education and conflict resolution programs into public school systems. In 1983, the Milwaukee Board of School Directors passed a resolution on "Issues Related to Peace Education in the Milwaukee Public Schools." Recognition was given to the appropriateness of introducing "peace studies and the dilemma of the nuclear arms race" into school programs and curricula."[24]

In 1984, the School Board of Dade County, Florida accepted a resolution proposed by Congressman William Lehman to introduce peace education and nonviolent conflict resolution into the curriculum. Strategies were designed to help teachers "incorporate into their classrooms the use of negotiation, arbitration, conciliation and other non-violent means of peacefully resolving . . . conflicts."[25]

The Grace Contrino Abrams Peace Education Foundation, publishers of several curriculum guides in the 1970s (Chapter 7, pages 221–222) has been a consistent advocate for introducing conflict resolution into the schools of Miami, Florida. In 1988, the Dade County School Board approved funding for a pilot program on conflict resolution in 13 elementary and five junior high schools. Fran Schmidt,

Foundation cofounder acted as the coordinator in training teachers and students. By 1990, nonviolent conflict resolution and student mediation programs existed in a total of 14 schools from elementary through alternative high schools. In addition, the program titled "Dr. Martin Luther King, Jr. Fighting Fair (conflict resolution)" was provided for all 100 middle schools in Dade County. Dr. Charles Sukman, Peace Education Foundation Board member worked with the Metro Miami Action Plan for two years, "seeking ways to implement the goals of the School Discipline Act of 1984 . . . for the teaching of conflict resolution skills to students."[26]

Between 1986 and 1988, several large public school systems also introduced conflict resolution training for students and teachers. Public schools in San Francisco, Chicago, Colorado Springs, Asheville, North Carolina, New York City, Poughkeepsie, New York, and Greenfield, Massachusetts also initiated programs.[27] Model Peace Education programs, developed by Educators for Social Responsibility, have also been in place in several schools in New York City (Brooklyn and Manhattan).

Ambitious educational and advocacy efforts were promoted in New Jersey by a nonprofit organization, Global Learning, Inc., a group which had been in existence since 1974.[28] The group provided resources, curricular materials in global and nuclear war education, and linkages for teachers and students, from elementary through college. A Conflict Managers Program, based on the San Francisco Community Board Center program, was implemented in several schools in Newark, New Jersey with student teams trained in communication and conciliation to help others resolve their conflicts.[29]

On a nationwide scale in 1983, an organization for young people, Camp Fire, established a peace education project called "A Gift of Peace" for children in grades one through six.[30] Its activities were designed to encourage the "development of peacemaking skills among children, youth and

families for their homes, communities, nation, and world."
Camp Fire also emphasized the need for cooperation with
other groups interested in peace, such as the Educators for
Social Responsibility and the Minnesota Peace Child Project. Conflict-resolution skills were taught with the goal of
learning that "conflict cannot be eliminated but it can be
handled in positive, constructive ways."

Teaching children and young people how to handle anger
and conflict was also a way of improving the classroom and
school milieu. The primary method involved the use of
trained student facilitators or mediators in resolving conflict
between students, student groups on the school campus, or
with teachers or administrators. At Mount Diablo High
School in Antioch, California, facilitators were taught how to
solve their own problems by communicating their feelings
rather than using verbal barbs or openly fighting. The skills
of communication and decision making were applied, after
20 hours of training.[31]

Prevention of conflict and teaching students mediation
skills were also included in a program developed by the
University of New Mexico, Albuquerque in 1984.[32] The
trained peer mediators were shown that a "face-saving
opportunity for both parties" would bring about a solution
without a winner or loser. At Gilmore Middle School in
Racine, Wisconsin, an orientation period included acquaint-
ing teachers, students, parents, and the general public with
the program before training began.

The interpersonal skills that children and young people
were trained to use, helped them cope with conflict and
pressure. For this reason, conflict resolution programs
received renewed interest in the eighties. Educators expressed concern that only limited attention had been given to
the so-called human relations skills that would be needed
during an entire lifetime. Lasting patterns of social skills and
behavior were usually developed during the school years.
Based on research for his doctorate, Jeffrey L. Edleson,
State University of New York at Albany, developed a

paradigm that included group training for upper-elementary children. Several basic skills were taught, such as expressing feelings, suggesting solutions, role playing, identifying the problem situation, giving feedback, and brainstorming for alternatives. The three-stage program proposed by Edleson, was field-tested in the Madison, Wisconsin area.[33]

A catalyst for the development of conflict resolution programs in the classroom has been the National Association for Mediation in Education (NAME), affiliated with the Mediation Project at the University of Massachusetts at Amherst. Founded in the early eighties, NAME provided a central clearinghouse on mediation in education, sharing information about programs through a newsletter, national conference, and publication of instructional resources.[34] An *Annotated Bibliography for Teaching Conflict Resolution in the Schools* and a *Directory of Conflict Resolution Programs* were published in 1988. The annual conference that was held in Sante Fe, New Mexico in 1988 concentrated on cross-cultural issues and bias awareness, teaching conflict resolution in early childhood, elementary and secondary school programs, as well as funding, grantwriting and curricular developments.

Within the framework of peace education, varied activities for the classroom have been developed by the Traprock Peace Center in Deerfield, Massachusetts. A newsletter established a network of area teachers involved in some phase of peace and justice education and a Peace Education Library offered bibliographies and materials for the classroom. Curriculum packets were designed around topics such as "The Cooperative Classroom" or "Peace Heroes." A before-school workshop that was held for area teachers in August, 1988 included creative and critical-thinking skills, community-building strategies, and conflict resolution.[35]

A mediation project at Greenfield High School in Massachusetts was directed at resolving the problem of high school dropouts. The University of Massachusetts Mediation Project supervised the training for this program. Evaluation, however, revealed that "until students understand conflict itself and have developed their own negotiating skills, the process of mediation would be ineffective."[36]

CURRICULUM FOR CONFLICT RESOLUTION

Developed by the Grace Contrino Abrams Peace Education Foundation, Miami, a pioneer in the curriculum development of conflict-resolution materials, *Creative Conflict Solving for Kids* (grades four through nine) was first published in 1983.[37] Realistic treatment of anger was considered a first step so that solutions to the conflict problem could be worked out "creatively and fairly." Using worksheets with humorous drawings, the principles of conflict resolution were explored with specific steps for solving the problem: first, a "Plan of Action," then moving on to "Observing Conflict" and then to "Rules for Fighting Fair." The successful formula for the curriculum guides, which were written by Fran Schmidt and Alice Friedman, was based on their own firsthand experiences as classroom teachers.

A second curriculum guide (for grades four through nine), a variation of *Creative Conflict Solving*, titled *Fighting Fair: Dr. Martin Luther King Jr. for Kids* was published in 1986. Using the device of flashbacks that included the words of Dr. King, students read classroom worksheets and activity cards and viewed a videocassette as observers of a simulated conflict scenario on the basketball court.[38] The life work and principles of nonviolence that motivated the life of King were adapted to the lives of the young people in the process of solving their youthful conflicts. Identifying the problem, role playing, and even a "Conflict Resolution Rap," related appropriately to the age group of students. A third guide, *Peacemaking Skills for Little Kids* (Preschool-Kindergarten-grade one) appeared in 1988 with a hand puppet, poster, and audiocassette.[39] Developmentally appropriate activities that included nature study and care for the environment showed young children that they can be responsible for the world they live in. Books illustrate that conflicts could be solved without violence. *Fighting Fair for Families* (which included a poster) was completed in 1989 and incorporated many of the principles and strategies taught in the guides for the classroom.[40]

William J. Kreidler contributed more than 200 activities for "keeping peace in the classroom" with creative conflict resolution offered as a viable approach to classroom management.[41] The area of "power games" that commonly involved the teacher-student relationship was the focus for one chapter. Practical procedures for negotiating conflict with students and other problem-solving techniques were presented.

"Scriptotherapy: A Technique for Conflict Resolution" based on a dissertation by Roy E. Johnson, presented a different approach for teaching conflict resolution.[42] The parties involved in the conflict situation wrote their documents explaining their own personal points of view. The disputants then had a chance to set up a truce situation and review each other's points-of-view document.

Alternatives to Violence by Kathy Bickmore, with a *Teachers Guide* by John Looney, was a prime example of the influence a conflict resolution program could exert.[43] As originally conceived, the program was designed to teach conflict-resolution skills in a group setting. Workshops were offered in schools with Continuing Education Units for teachers and also in colleges.[44] In one Cleveland high school, a Mediation Service was established after the course was taught and reductions in fighting and discipline problems were reported. A noteworthy feature of the curriculum was presentation of conflict scenarios for role-playing. Conflicts commonly occurring in a school setting, such as between children, child-teacher, or at home were presented for problem solving.

Hopeful signs indicated that conflict-resolution programs were receiving acceptance. Mediation in schools was implemented in several school districts, as well as in juvenile correctional settings. It was integrated with law-related education programs, with mediation in special education situations, and training teachers to teach negotiation, truancy and drop-out prevention—a broad application of conflict-resolution skills for a variety of problems.[45]

Underlying the concept of teaching conflict-resolution or peacemaking skills to children and young people was the age-old belief that there could be an improvement in the minds and hearts of humanity as a transformation that was needed for society. The idea was promoted by Horace Mann and John Dewey especially at the turn of the century, where peace was viewed as logical progress for an enlightened humanity, as influenced by Darwin's theories. Throughout each decade, other peace educators expressed a similar hope in their writings.

Peace educators believed that peace was not only a content to be taught with facts and understandings (as in nuclear war education) but also a process, a way of life that should be lived for personal and societal fulfillment. Betty Reardon spoke of the "cycle of care, concern and commitment" as the "core of the peace learning process."[46] While peace educators did not overtly announce they were teaching moral and social values, there was tacit understanding that the Golden Rule virtues—love, truth, honesty, fairness, stewardship for Earth's resources, concern for others, and respect for living things—could be included in the classroom. Few believed that education could be entirely neutral or value free. Against the background of a society steeped in violence with militarism as a predominant value, peace educators used a pragmatic approach by moving nonviolent conflict resolution into the core of the peace education curriculum.

An example of a program that could make a significant difference in the classroom was designed in 1989. The Infusion Model of units (with separate grade levels) formulated as a "Model Project for Teaching Dr. King's Nonviolent Principles in Schools" was developed by the King Center

for Nonviolent Social Change. In Atlanta social studies and
the humanities—art, music, photography, creative drama,
writing—were integrated throughout as a practical consideration for the tight classroom schedule mandated by State
law. The units were: the life of Dr. King; the civil rights
movement; and the principles and application of "Kingian
Nonviolence." The Center expressed the goal of integrating
nonviolence and moral values because of the "disintegration
of the moral fiber of American youth." Thirty teachers
field-tested the model project. The Center reported that
these units were used in schools throughout the nation.[47]

PEACE EDUCATION PROGRAMS OF
CHURCHES/RELIGIOUS GROUPS

The world's religions have taught for centuries that personal
redemption, conversion, or change of heart can be a turning
point in a human life or even in human history. During the
eighties, religious leaders throughout the world engaged in
extraordinary efforts to unify their common beliefs. The
doctrinal differences of several leading denominations nar-
rowed during the decades as the result of serious study and
negotiations.

The theme was expressed often that any education for
peace would need to be a moral one and based on the
concept of a spiritual conversion or a turning away from a
slavish reliance on science and technology to solve all
problems of society. Also seriously questioned during the
eighties were the motives of a government actively planning
civilization's destruction while cloaked in the semantics of
"Nukespeak," a jargon based on euphemisms and disinfor-
mation.

Religious leaders turned their attention to an educational
campaign that taught the basic values of peace, nonviolence,
and social justice as essential for a heritage of hope. The
overwhelming need for world peace linked humans in a vast,

unseen network. A rich literature on the moral implications of the nuclear age invoked dialogue and may have had an impact on the spiritual and religious dimensions of American society. The stirrings of conscience in church leaders may have set them on paths that held the power to transform lives for generations to come. History can be changed by human actions, attitudes, and beliefs was the message from the literature of a wide range of religious denominations.

Several events in religion and church history were noteworthy. In 1984, the "Challenge of Peace, the Bishops' Pastoral letter" on the immorality of nuclear war offered a new insight that could lead to changes of attitudes for 50 million Catholics. In 1986, Pope John Paul II convened a historic gathering on the World Day of Prayer for Peace. Meeting in the shadow of the basilica of St. Francis in Assisi, 35 different religious denominations that represented 3.5 billion people pledged "to make peace a central aim of our prayer and action." The sentiment was expressed that we "either learn to walk together in peace or harmony, or we drift apart and ruin ourselves and others." Robert Muller of the United Nations expressed also the concept of the oneness of the human family and especially the precept "Thou shalt not kill not even in the name of a nation or religion." By the close of the decade, the unbelievable took place, of course, when Pope John Paul II and Mikhail Gorbachev met in a historic first meeting where rival ideologies were relegated to the background.

The contributions of religious educators in teaching about nuclear war issues, especially the formation of peace education programs for youth and adults, has been an extensive, positive force in the eighties. The materials and literature of religious organizations revealed a wide array of offerings with a spiritual dimension, based on Scriptural roots.

Educating for Peace and Justice comprised an extensive, four-volume curriculum guide with a dual purpose, appropriate for adoption in public or nonpublic schools. One volume, "Religious Dimensions" would be for church-based schools while the other three would be acceptable for nondenominational use. James and Kathleen McGinnis, the principal authors, were active in Catholic organizations for peace and social justice. The four volumes emphasized the world order values with a scriptural base and Christian theology. A balanced treatment of government defense policy was included. In their workshops and other writings, James and Kathleen McGinnis, as adoptive parents of a biracial child, also emphasized a multicultural strand. Their efforts also led to formation of a national network, Parenting for Peace, with chapters throughout America.[48]

Pax Christi, Catholic international peace organization, structured a Gospel-based concern for prayer, study, and action for a "Christian vision of disarmament, a just world order, primacy of conscience, education for peace and alternatives."[49] Peace education materials, primarily for adult education in Pax Christi community groups and for campus ministry programs, included study guides for making nonviolence a way of life, and supported special implementation of the "Bishops' Pastoral, The Challenge of Peace: God's Promise and Our Response."[50] Seasonal offerings were written by leading Catholic writers based on the principles of peace and nonviolence. Communities of Pax Christi members met regularly in major cities throughout America and have been an influence in campus ministry programs.

Curriculum materials were available from the National Catholic Education Association, including *Directions for Justice/Peace Education in the Catholic Elementary School* by Loretta Carey[51] and *Let Peace Begin with Me: Peace Book,* with *Teacher Guide,* written by Mary Kownacki, OSB.[52] Six study units guided children as they learned to express their feelings about peace by writing letters and other activities, including a closing prayer service with Scriptural readings.

The Jewish Peace Fellowship was founded in 1941 by Rabbi Abraham Cronbach, author of the *Jewish Peace Book*[53] (discussed in Chapter 4). The Fellowship encompassed all branches of Judaism with Jewish ideals and experiences that provided "inspiration for a nonviolent way of life" with a calling toward "peace, justice and compassion." Literature available included the guidelines for considering conscientious objection as related to Judaism, "Hassidism and the Love of Enemies," and literature on Arab-Jewish peacemaking in Israel. A representative peace education curriculum for Jewish religious education was included in Reardon's *Educating for Global Responsibility,* titled "The Rainbow Sign: A Jewish Curriculum for the Nuclear Age," grades 3–8, by Judith Axler and David Harbater. The themes of ecological concerns for the Earth were linked to Jewish traditions based on the Rainbow covenant, the Old Testament promise that God would never again destroy the world by flood. The Rainbow was a sign of Earth and Fulfillment.[54]

In 1987 delegates to the 200th General Assembly of the Presbyterian Church (U.S.A.) approved a policy statement titled "Christian Obedience in a Nuclear Age" that declared nuclear deterrence immoral. Efforts of the Presbyterian Church have been combined into the Presbyterian Peace Fellowship and Presbyterian Peacemaking Program.[55] The goals of the first group were "to discern, proclaim, educate and act for peace in, through and for the church; (and) to support the concerns of members who make commitments for peace and nonviolence."[56]

The Presbyterian Peacemaking Program developed educational resources for use in church-based programs for children and youth, such as "Peacemaking in the Family by Mister Rogers," who as Fred Rogers was an ordained Presbyterian minister. This was a curriculum design for teaching peacemaking skills within the family setting. *The Things That Make for Peace . . . Begin with the Children"* contained resources to develop skills to resolve conflict, "turn enemies into friends" and to be "stewards of God's earth." In the *Leader's Guide* for *The Things That Make for Peace* children were encouraged to watch a television show involving conflict of some type with their families and to discuss the conflict situation, how it was resolved, and to determine who were the peacemakers. The report "Peacemaking: The Believers' Calling" affirmed that peacemaking was "central to Christian faith" and that it was vital that children were helped to become caregivers and peacemakers."[57]

Shalom Congregations was designated as a peacemaking ministry of the Christian Church (Disciples of Christ).[58] Goals were "to discover/recover the gift and the vision of God's Shalom rooted in the Old Testament . . . through intentional experiences of worship, study and action." Begun in 1981 with ten congregations in ten different regions, involvement in the peacemaking ministry had expanded to 18 regions and 120 congregations by 1987.[59] A new church-wide priority was established by the General Assembly in 1987 that characterized Shalom Congregations as "communities dedicated to peace with justice." Special concern was given to "nurturing children and youth" with concepts that would offer "hope and opportunity in the midst of guilt and undue fear" and included counseling for young people concerning draft registration or military service.

The American Lutheran Church, the Lutheran Church in America, and the Association of Evangelical Lutheran Churches joined together in 1987 to form a new entity, the Evangelical Lutheran Church in America with a Department for Peace Education.[60] A quarterly, *Peace Petitions,* was first published in the Spring of 1988 and included resources for peacemaking programs. A second Lutheran program, the Office of Church in Society, provided "Action Ideas for Peacemaking" for use in Peace Bible Study groups and in children's programs.[61]

National Ministries—ABC was organized to provide resources for American Baptist churches for workshops and seminars on peacemaking. Materials for use in church study groups included a catalog listing of videos and films on peace and a special packet for Peace Sunday (May the first). The

Peace Program was established in 1980. An American Baptist Policy Statement on Peace was adopted in 1985 and urged members to become a witness of the church, with a "journey toward peace, justice and kingdom of God . . . to strengthen, sustain and encourage the gathered body."[62]

The United Methodist Church broke new ground with publication of *In Defense of Creation: The Nuclear Crisis and a Just Peace, a Pastoral Letter and Foundation Document* that concluded two years of study by the Council of Bishops.[63] A prominent feature was "Education for Peaceful Alternatives" which included: (1) cross-cultural study, especially with those called 'enemies': a capacity for conflict resolution including negotiations, mediation and conciliation; (3) comprehension of the causes of war, aggression, and violence; (4) knowledge of both armaments and disarmament strategies; (5) techniques of peaceable political action including nonviolent direct action; and (6) a "grasp of alternative perspectives on spirituality, ethics and lifestyle."

Other sections of the document on "The Peaceable Family" addressed the "nurture of spirituality . . . in the community of the family." A strong family life program was suggested with peacemaking as an opportunity. An additional proposal was for the establishment of "lay academies—centers for group study and reflection." Peace education was promoted actively as providing "peaceful alternatives for young children, youth and adults." Finally, "Churches at every level" were urged to "develop and provide adequate support for full-time ministries of peace education and action."[64]

The United Church of Christ, through the Office for Church in Society provided an eight-session curriculum for peace education appropriate for youth and adults. "Peace Futuring" explored the traditional Christian perspectives on war and peace by having participants write a peace scenario.[65] Emphasis was on the future perspective with hopeful outlooks projected and designed to enable those involved to reflect on their personal concepts and feelings.

Peace education continued to be a primary focus for the so-called traditional "Peace Churches," such as the Church of the Brethren and Mennonites, as its central mission for past generations.[66] Materials appropriate for peace education were available from the Brethren Peace Fellowship and emphasized pacificism and conscientious objection to military draft.

Curriculum and instructional resources provided by the Mennonite Central Committee included many projects for children that encouraged global linkages as they had done in decades past. Children could gather crayons to send overseas or engage in consciousness-raising activities that fostered the concept that water was precious.[67] A ten-session course on responding creatively to conflict was also designed by the Mennonite Conciliation Service and included a biblical perspective on conflict and decision making.[68]

Individual educators as members of the Society of Friends, continued to extend their influence through presentation of peace education and nonviolence. The leading role models for peace scholars have been Elise and Kenneth Boulding, as a sociologist and an economist, respectively, who have written extensively on peace issues, based on Quaker spirituality. Ian Harris, in a comprehensive study of peace education in theory and practice also considered his membership in a Quaker community as "strength and hope . . . (in) a nonviolent struggle for peace and justice."[69]

Of special interest was The Children's Creative Response to Conflict program established in 1972 by the New York Quaker Project on Community Conflict. Throughout the seventies and especially in the eighties the program expanded to include a wide range of curricular and supplementary materials and included workshops and courses for in-service, college, or graduate credit. *The Friendly Classroom for a Small Planet* was the handbook that has been generally accepted as a landmark publication for creating a peaceful classroom environment. A second edition was published in 1985 and incorporated several basic themes:

cooperation, communication, affirmation, and conflict resolution for children in kindergarten through grade 12.[70]

With the vision of a world at peace, religious groups
accepted the leadership roles demanded by the nuclear age.
Peace education in the eighties was endowed with the
sanction of church congregations as they entered a new phase
of community education with a spiritual dimension. By the
end of the eighties, congregations throughout America
arranged special exchange visits to the Soviet Union (and
later to independent Republics) and welcomed into their
homes and churches mothers, fathers, and children who just
a short decade ago were considered to be "the enemy."
Transformation or conversion in a spiritual dimension—in
the sense of a change in attitude that included a new vision of
humanity—may have been set in motion during the eighties
by the concerted efforts of church leaders who took up the
moral challenge of Scripture to "beat swords into plowshares."

TECHNOLOGY AND COMMUNICATIONS IN PEACE EDUCATION

In the twenties and thirties, peace educators had visions of
reaching out to foreign lands in gestures of world friendship
and good will. Their dreams became realities in the eighties
through computer technology and telecommunications.
These efforts created global linkages, previously unknown.

A joint venture of the University for Peace in Costa Rica
and the World Peace University, Eugene, Oregon, created a
Radio for Peace International as a unique experiment in
international communications.[71] James Latham, the Station
Manager and Maximilian Loeffler, as Program Director,
made an inaugural broadcast on September 10, 1987. A
shortwave radio station was first assembled in Oregon,
driven to California, shipped by truck to Miami, and flown to
Costa Rica. Air time was gradually increased from three

hours until broadcasting 24-hours a day became the standard broadcasting procedure.[72] In the first months of existence Radio for Peace International (RFPI) "was heard in all of the Americas, as far north as Canada, as well as in Europe, Africa, Australia and many Islands."[73]

Programs were broadcast exclusively on the issues of peace, food, social justice, and ecology. A broad array of programming was educational and cultural in nature and included courses from the two universities. Interviews, talk shows, an information exchange, news analysis, music, poetry, and plays comprised the agenda. The goal for the international short wave station was stated as one that would bring "the global human family into better understanding and communication with one another."[74] Sample presentations were: Global Peace Magazine, Common Ground (produced by The Stanley Foundation), American Lutheran Church, Peace Forum, United Nations, and Earthwatch.

Program supporters were invited to record a peace message on audiocassette for rebroadcast, sharing events related to peace education or social justice in their area. As an independent, nonprofit organization, the visionary design of RFPI harnessed the innovations of a new technology for peace education and created an unprecedented opportunity for the dissemination of viewpoints on peace issues. The invitation to all to become active participants in sharing opinions and events had the potential for opening up a new dimension of community education.

An additional breakthrough in telecommunications was provided by a satellite link up to RFPI that occurred in 1987. PEACESAT, a communication satellite, provided live coverage and instant communication throughout North and South America with a sole terminal at the University for Peace. PEACESAT was to be used for conferences and meetings with communications between the two universities. Richard Schneider, Director of World Peace University in

Oregon and Tapio Varis, Rector of the University for Peace, worked to complete arrangements. Schneider stated:

> The capacity to bridge the world with a positive message of the possible is an unparalled opportunity in an age of fear and pessimism. RFPI is a unique and serious opportunity for a voice of peace to be heard by humankind.[75]

The program of the World Peace University at Eugene was created in 1984 with first classes held in October 1985.[76] Workshops that were related to "inner peace, personal development and world peace" as the primary goals of the University emphasized "experiential learning" and created experiences that would produce "world citizen diplomats." Future plans included an International Research Library for Peace and the commission and publication of books.

The other half of the cooperative arrangement, the University for Peace in Costa Rica, was created by the United Nations in 1980 and implemented with formal activities in 1986. The first students entered in 1987. Education for peace and human rights was considered the central mission of the University for Peace. A Peace Education Symposium/Course on Family Life Education for Peace took place in July 1987 and was designed for students seeking knowledge, "attitudes and skills for their own marriages and parenting." By 1990, however, limited funding and political maneuvering appeared to severely handicap the academic programs at the University.[77]

The possibility of a Global "Electronic University" Consortium came closer to reality in 1986 with a series of multimedia peace teleconferences with interactive educational programs that used slow-scan television and computer conferencing.[78] Conferences and live lectures from three American universities were attended via satellite by students in Japan, China, California, Alaska, Hawaii, Fiji, and other

South Pacific locations.[79] Robert Muller, Chancellor of the University for Peace, was one of the instructors. The interactive communication included computer networking with modem, teleconferencing via slow-scan television, and facsimile transmission. A partnership with Global Education Associates has been proposed.

"Global Peace Awareness" was a project developed at the University of Oregon, Center for Advanced Technology in Education as an innovative social studies project for global education.[80] Telecommunications linked children in five countries to share "investigations into community history, cultural celebrations, and use of natural resources." The project will culminate with a newsmagazine that will include the experiences of the students. Certainly, the opportunity for developing cultural awareness on the personal, firsthand level offers exciting possibilities for the classroom of the nineties.

For the social studies educator, American computer technology brought simulations of global conflict scenarios into the classroom. "The Other Side: A Global Conflict Resolution Game" has been introduced as teaching the processes of cooperation and communication.[81] Students represented two independent nations and needed to develop strategies for maintaining a stable economy as well as national security. Students have learned to work "in a competitive or collaborative effort to build a bridge uniting the nations—a bridge of peace." Two computers could be connected with cables with other classrooms by computers or even with an international hookup. "Balance of Power" is another simulation that involved responding to world crisis without "provoking a nuclear conflict."[82] Students were provided with maps and a database for an accurate "portrayal of the world and relationships between countries." Telecommunications were also being used in many social studies classrooms to link students in different ethnic or cultural groups. A group of students from a suburban, middle class school, for example, could engage in electronic discussions with Navajo Indian students in their tribal school.

Peace education began with a simple form of communication in the villages of New England when Elihu Burritt distributed his "Olive Leaves for the Press" (1828). He used a broadside format delivered to newspapers and to communicate the Gospel message of peace. By the close of the eighties, the goals of peace education reached listeners in various parts of the globe by way of a communications satellite. These two events offered a unifying element in a record of human endeavors to communicate and educate for peace.

PEOPLE-TO-PEOPLE, AMERICAN-SOVIET (AND POST-SOVIET) PEACE EDUCATION IN ACTION

The dreams of peace educators, Jane Addams, Fannie Fern Andrews, and Lucia Ames Mead from the twenties and thirties, to have children and young people meet and share common dreams for peace were realized in the eighties. From various cities of America, young citizens ventured into foreign diplomacy as good will ambassadors abroad.

Several organizations were in the forefront by promoting American-Soviet educational, social, and cultural exchanges. In Minnesota, a nonprofit, nonpartisan organization named Connect/US-USSR, developed linkages and exchanges in order to build "mutually beneficial relationships between the people of the United States and the Soviet Union."[83] A sister city relationship was also developed between Minneapolis/St. Paul and the Soviet city of Novosibirsk with an emphasis on children and young people.[84] Ground Zero also had pairings of cities since the early eighties. Sister Cities International has grown to include several dozen pairings by 1989.

Especially important were the relationships being forged

by pairing a school in Minneapolis with a school in Moscow. The eleven-year-old students selected holidays and celebrations from America, sending information and materials to their Russian "counterparts for replicating an authentic celebration."[85]

The international language of art provided the initial impetus for exchange programs. Begun in 1984 the art exchange has continued each year with the selection of over 200 drawings from students in various corners of America who portrayed the life and culture of their regions.[86] The drawings chosen were then exchanged with an equal number of children's paintings from the former Soviet Union. The exhibits toured each country. In America as many as 30,000 people visited the exhibit in Boston. The Minnesota 4-H Clubs also produced a photo exhibit which was displayed at the Central Pioneer Palace in Moscow. Scenes from everyday life in America were the themes. Young people in the former Soviet Union also exchanged 100 photos and the joint exhibits from both countries were displayed during one month in each country.

The Samantha Smith Foundation, a nonprofit corporation carried on exchange programs to foster international understanding in the spirit of the ten-year-old child who was invited to visit the Soviet Union after writing a letter to Yuri Andropov, the Soviet Premier. Person-to-person projects were carried out with a summer exchange of teenagers from the former Soviet Union. Educational materials were also produced by the Foundation that was headed by Samantha's mother, Jane G. Smith, after the deaths of Samantha and her father in an airplane crash (1985).[87]

Parents and Teachers for Social Responsibility inaugurated several projects that involved children and young people. A musical, titled "The Heart of the Mountain" was performed by six children at the Second International Teachers for Peace Congress in Bonn, West Germany.[88] The exchange of short, simple songs recorded on cassette tape in American schools was developed for another activity, the

Earth Patch Project.[89] Tapes and pen pal letters were exchanged with children in several countries. Promoting global awareness as peace education in action was the major goal.

Peace Links, founded by Betty Bumpers in 1982, expanded its activities with a pen pal project to link families and children with former Soviet citizens in an "ice-melting, ground-breaking people-to-people exchange." Using citizen diplomacy at the grassroots level, women from the former Soviet Union visited America. A high school program, "Reach for Peace" was prepared which encourages young people to write to people in power and develop projects for global awareness. Peace Links will supply names and addresses of women and children from post-Soviet communities for a pen pal exchange.[90]

Skipping Stones, a magazine planned as an exchange between young people in America and other countries was designed to involve children and young people who could contribute stories and art works. A networking section would provide resources for teachers and parents. Peace, Justice, Social Issues, Energy, and Ecology were several of the themes planned. The project would be a joint one with the Aprovecho Institute in Cottage Grove, Oregon. The multilingual issues of 1989 included many drawings and sketches of children from around the world, using the universal language of art.[91]

Educators for Social Responsibility, designer of several curriculum guides for nuclear war education and conflict resolution, produced additional instructional materials that examined different viewpoints about the Soviet Union. "A Day at School in Moscow" included a videotape and study guide and depicted Soviet children and their schools.[92]

A historic first step also took place with formation of the American-Soviet Institute as a collaborative effort by Educators for Social Responsibility and the Soviet Ministry of Education at that time and Academy of Pedagogical Sciences. Jointly-produced projects planned would include videotapes, publication of articles on "nuclear age education and student and teacher exchanges." Twenty American and twenty Soviet educators met in August of 1988 to discuss ways to improve how each teaches about the other country. Preliminary work for *A Sourcebook for New Ways of Thinking in Education: A U.S.-Soviet Guide* was also proposed.[93]

Friendship exchanges between former enemies have been described as transnational citizen peacemaking (TCP) by Vincent C. Kavaloski. These contacts were defined as "communication between private citizens of two or more countries with a general intention of increasing mutual understanding and world peace." Furthermore, Kavaloski has proposed that such efforts are diametrically opposed to the adversarial nation-state concept of diplomacy and should be considered instead in the category of nonviolent social intervention (NVSI) as developed by Gene Sharp (discussed in Chapter 7, page 210.). This concept includes the idea that goals can be achieved by means of "social power."[94]

Children, parents, and teachers in the eighties worked together for a world without war with a positive plan for peace that was based on face-to-face contact as humans, rather than as Cold War enemies. While the examples cited were events in only a few cities, involving only small groups they offered evidence of hope that a new way of thinking about peace education had come about. This breakthrough considered peace education or a form of citizen peacemaking, as a natural correlate to direct political action programs. They were designed to promote a changed and more humane perspective of the people of the Soviet Union (and later of the new confederation) as families and friends. Many of these efforts began in the early eighties, far in advance of the announcement of the Cold War's demise (1989–1990) and preceded by several years the expressed wishes of the superpower leaders for increased interactions of American and Soviet people.

Afterthoughts

The entrance of nonviolent conflict resolution into America's classrooms proved to be serendipity. It may hold the key to preparing future generations for demographic changes of historic proportions. While not overtly stated as an exercise in social justice, conflict resolution has been promoted as basic for all young Americans. Teaching the skills of conflict resolution may ameliorate racial and ethnic tensions that have deteriorated to a considerable degree in recent years.

Peacemaking for understanding and communication may open up the minds of the younger generation to the thoughts and feelings of others who look or speak differently. Research has documented that racism and ethnocentrism can be deeply ingrained even in preschool-age children as a reflection of parental and other influences. With conflict resolution training, the young are taught to listen, empathize, and imagine what the other person is thinking or feeling with fair ground rules that apply to all. These usually involve learning to be truthful and refraining from name calling or "putdowns." In most training in peacemaking skills, the first step is learning to listen and perhaps to paraphrase what the other person has said to gain insight into the other's perception of the problem. True problem solving could involve a range of possibilities as the two opponents explore solutions: For example, by using an impartial referee or mediator, taking turns by sharing game equipment, toys, or materials, delaying any action or arriving at a solution by chance (tossing a coin). The final step could be to find "win/win" type solutions which are mutually beneficial to the parties.

Children today can relate to the "fairness" value which is often reflected in their journals of events and the actions of others in the school environment. Around them they see that life is NOT fair, that many come to school with advantages others may not have. They recognize early the growing differences that exist between the haves and the have nots. Their emerging concepts of justice, fairness, and the moral judgments that they make at different ages have been explored by Erik Ericson, Lawrence Kohlberg, and Robert Coles in classic studies. Teaching nonviolence, peacemaking, mediation, or negotiation will equip the younger generation with skills that they can use throughout their lifetimes.

To change the social interactions and group dynamics from a "win/lose" situation to the "win/win" solution in conflict resolution will take the persistent efforts of all in the classroom. Generations of social conditioning have taught us that competition and winning are the goals regardless of the negative effects on others. Competition has been a deeply ingrained value that has been equated with "excellence" in the classrooms of the eighties and nineties. Alfie Cohn has argued eloquently in *No Contest: The Case Against Competition,* that cooperative behavior should replace the overemphasis on competition and reliance on standardized tests, that is commonplace in the schools of the 1990s. Moreover, the infusion of cooperative learning in thousands of classrooms, based on the research of David and Roger Johnson, Robert Slavin, and others, is a positive innovation that holds much promise.[95]

Of the greatest importance, though, is the power of peacemaking skills to open minds to the overt, dangerous overtones of racism that have surfaced in American schools in the late eighties. Gerald J. Pine and Asa G. Hilliard III pleaded for an end to the "monocultural education and institutionalized racism" that has become prodominant in the public schools of America.[96] One of the areas that demands attention is the development of "psychological and social traits of character," described as "self-esteem, self discipline, vocational aspiration, idealism, moral judgment, and interpersonal expectations, including altruism, enlightened self-interest, and social justice." Only in such school communities that manifest such virtues can a true sense of democracy and a "celebration of diversity" take place, Pines and

Hilliard believe.[97] Such civic virtues have been advocated in our exploration of peace education literature dating as far back as the peace society journals and Horace Mann's *Lectures*. John Dewey's philosophy, and the writings of various authors in National Society for the Study of Education Yearbooks, such as *Character Education* (1932), gave prominence to these and similar civic virtues.

The formation of the National Association for Multicultural Education (NAME) in 1990 "to reduce racism and discrimination in society . . . (and) to promote the development of culturally responsible and responsive curricula" was a positive sign that others in education were as deeply concerned as those involved in peace and social justice activities.[98]

The goals of peacemaking—nonviolence and conflict resolution—have made only a limited impact in America's classrooms. The multicultural classroom of the nineties will need to change and open the door to alternatives. Peace education, for almost 200 years, has existed and yet has been rarely tried. Pines and Hilliard stated that change must come about for America's minority children. That change will be painful, but nonviolent conflict resolution needs to be a part of that change process, if the healing needed in our society is to actually occur. The Los Angeles riots in the spring of 1992 were a poignant remark of how much healing remains to be done.

Notes

1. U.S. Congress. House. Subcommittee on Education of the Committee on Labor and Public Welfare, *George Washington Peace Academy Act,* 1976, Hearing 94th Cong., 2nd sess. 13 May 1976, 3.
2. As regards the document proposing establishment of the United States Academy of Peace see: *Report of the Commission on Proposals for the National Academy of Peace and Conflict Resolution to the President of the United States and the*

Senate and House of Representatives of the United States Congress, (Washington, DC: U.S. Government Printing Office, 1981), 13.

3. *Report* (1981), 15–20.
4. *Report* (1981), 46. An early plan for a "Peace Office" appeared as "A Plan for a Peace Office for the United States . . . published in *Banneker's Almanac* for the year 1793" in Document 17. "II. Let a power be given to this Secretary to establish and maintain free schools in every city, village and township . . . to teach us not only to cultivate peace with all men, but to forgive . . . to love our very enemies . . . to inspire a veneration for human life . . . to introduce universal and perpetual peace in our country," in Silvio A. Bedini, *The Life of Benjamin Banneker* (New York: Charles Scribner's Sons, 1972), 319–320.
5. *Report* (1981), 221.
6. Elise Boulding, "Peace: An Active Skill," *Christian Science Monitor,* 30 December 1980.
7. Frank K. Kelly, *The United States Academy of Peace: A Long Step Toward Real Security,* (booklet), Washington, DC: National Peace Academy Foundation, 1983, 17.
8. United States Institute of Peace Update, May 1988, 7–13.
9. *Peace Institute Reporter,* National Peace Institute Foundation (later changed to the National Foundation), September 1986, 1.
10. David Wood, "Army To Branch Out in Third World Operations," *Times Picayune* (New Orleans), 12 January 1990. Discussed was a Pentagon document, "Military Operations in Low Intensity Conflict" approved by Army Chief of Staff, Gen. Carl E. Vuono.
11. Richard B. Gray, "United States Institute of Peace," in *World Encyclopedia of Peace,* eds. Ervin Laszlo and Jong Y. Yoo. (Elmsford, NY: Pergamon Press, 1986), 521.
12. Paul Kimmel in Colleen Cordes, "U.S. Peace Institute Created," *American Psychological Association Monitor* (November 1984): 7.
13. Kenneth Boulding, *Stable Peace* (Austin, Texas: University of Texas, Press, 1978) 142, 15. *Peace Institute Reporter,* April 1988, 2.
14. *Peace Institute Reporter,* April 1988, 1, 6.

15. *Peace Institute Reporter,* September 1986, 1, 3.
16. *Peace Institute Reporter,* December 1986, 8. An additional viewpoint on the "all white, all male" composition was expressed by Helen Thomas, "Reagan Has Nominated No Women To the U.S. Peace Institute," *St. Petersburg (Florida) Times,* January 25, 1986. By 1991, the Board included Elspeth Davies Rostow as chair, a professor at the University of Texas; and Mary Louise Smith, changes reported in the *United States Institute of Peace Journal* (August 1991), IV (4), 5.
17. *Peace Institute Reporter,* April 1988, 1.
18. *Peace Institute Reporter,* June 1988, 1 and 6.
19. National Peace Institute Foundation, descriptive literature, 1988.
20. Grant Awards, Appendix E, Budget Request, Fiscal Year, 1989, 79–90.
21. Grant Awards, 79–90.
22. Peace and Conflict Resolution Program, American University, Washington, DC: 8 August 1988.
23. Grant Awards, 79–90.
24. "Resolution on Issues Related to Peace Education in the Milwaukee Public Schools April 19, 1983." Original Resolution approved, ED 256 683.
25. *Peace Works,* (newsletter) Miami: Grace Contrino Abrams Peace Education Foundation, Winter 1987, 1.
26. *Peace Works,* Fall 1989, 1.
27. *Why Nuclear Education: Sourcebook,* ED 256 683, 8.
28. Global Learning, Inc., (descriptive literature), Montclair, NJ: Global Learning, Inc., 1988.
29. San Francisco Community Board Center for Policy and Training, School Initiatives Program, *Classroom Conflict Resolution Training for Elementary Schools* (San Francisco, 1987).
30. *A Gift of Peace,* (booklet), Kansas City, MO: Camp Fire, Inc., 1985.
31. Pietro P. Faconti and Allen Hagerstrand, "Conflict Management Program Helps Teens Help Teens," *National Association of Secondary School Principals' Bulletin* 71 (May 1987): 118–119.
32. Moses S. Koch and Suzanne Miller, "Resolving Student Conflicts with Student Mediators, *Principal* 66 (March 1987): 59–61.

33. Jeffrey L. Edleson, "Teaching Children To Resolve Conflict: A Group Approach," *Social Work* (November 1981): 488–492.

34. *The Fourth R* (newsletter), Amherst, MA: National Association for Mediation in Education, Promoting the Teaching of Conflict Resolution Skills in Schools, Fall 1987, 1–5.

35. *Traprock Report,* Deerfield, MA: Traprock Peace Center, July/August 1988, 4.

36. *Peace Lessons* (newsletter), Traprock Peace Center Education Program, April 1988, 2.

37. Fran Schmidt and Alice Friedman, *Creative Conflict Solving for Kids* (Miami: Grace Contrino Abrams Peace Education Foundation, 1983), 7.

38. Fran Schmidt and Alice Friedman, *Fighting Fair: Dr. Martin Luther King Jr. for Kids* (Miami: Grace Contrino Abrams Peace Education Foundation, 1986), S3, Lesson 2.

39. Fran Schmidt and Alice Friedman, *Peacemaking Skills for Little Kids* (Miami: Grace Contrino Abrams Peace Education Foundation, 1988).

40. Fran Schmidt and Alice Friedman, *Fighting Fair for Families* (Miami: Grace Contrino Abrams Peace Education Foundation, 1989).

41. William J. Kreidler, *Creating Conflict Resolution: More Than 200 Activities for Keeping Peace in the Classroom, K–6* (Glenview, IL: Scott, Foresman, 1984), 39–50.

42. Roy E. Johnson, "Scriptotherapy: A Technique for Conflict Resolution" (Ph.D. diss., Walden University), 1983, ED 244 205.

43. John Looney, *Alternatives to Violence,* (descriptive literature), Akron, Ohio: Peace Grows, 1988. Selections from the program appeared in Betty Reardon, *Educating for Global Responsibility,* 92–98.

44. *Alternatives to Violence,* ED 250 254.

45. Representative programs were: Edwin Fenton and Elsa R. Wasserman, *A Leader's Guide to Improving School Climate through Implementing the Fairness Committee: A Manual for Students and Teachers* (Cambridge, MA: Moral Education Resource Fund, Harvard Graduate School for Education, 1985); and Larry Ray, et al., *Mediation in the Schools: A Report, Directory and Bibliography* (Washington, DC: American Bar Association, 1985).

46. Betty Reardon, *Comprehensive Peace Education: Educating for Global Responsibility*, 22.
47. King Center (Martin Luther King Jr. Center for Nonviolent Social Change (Atlanta: King Center, 1989), descriptive literature.
48. James McGinnis and Kathleen McGinnis, et al., *Educating for Peace and Justice, Vols. I, II, III, and IV* (St. Louis, MO: Institute for Peace and Justice, 1981 and 1985); *Parenting for Peace and Justice* (Maryknoll, New York: Orbis Books, 1981); *Peace Puppets and Global Family Puppets* (videotapes with guidebook) (St. Louis: Institute for Peace and Justice, 1987); and James B. McGinnis, *Bread and Justice: Toward a New International Economic Order* (New York: Paulist Press, 1979).
49. *Pax Christi, USA* (Journal) (Spring 1988): 2.
50. Challenge of Peace, *Catholic Update* (Cincinnati, OH: Saint Anthony Messenger Press, 1983).
51. Sister Loretta Carey, *Directions for Justice/Peace Education in the Catholic Elementary School* (Washington, DC.: National Catholic Education Association, 1984).
52. Sister Mary Lou Kownacki, OSB, *Let Peace Begin with Me: Peace Book* and *Teacher Guide* (Erie, PA: Pax Center, 1983).
53. Jewish Peace Fellowship, descriptive literature, pamphlets, articles and books, Nyack, NY: Jewish Peace Fellowship, 1988.
54. Betty Reardon, *Educating for Global Responsibility*, 52–60, included resources for Jewish peace education.
55. Presbyterian Peace Fellowship, (descriptive literature), 1987.
56. Presbyterian Peacemaking Program, Peacemaking Resource List, Presbyterian Church (USA), Louisville, KY: Peacemaking Program, 1988.
57. *The Things That Make for Peace . . . Begin with the Children,* New York: Presbyterian Church (USA) Distribution Service, 1985.
58. Shalom Partners, DHM/Regional Agreement, Indianapolis, IN: Shalom Congregations, Division of Homeland Ministries, 1986.
59. Shalom Partners, Suggestions for Implementation, Indianapolis, IN: Shalom Congregations, 1988.
60. Department for Peace Education, (descriptive literature) Chicago: Evangelical Lutheran Church in America, 1988.

61. *Action Ideas for Peacemaking*, Minneapolis, MN, Office of Church in Society, American Lutheran Church, 1988.
62. "Breaking Down the Walls," (descriptive literature), Valley Forge, PA: National Ministries, American Baptist Churches/ USA, 1987.
63. *In Defense of Creation: The Nuclear Crisis and Just Peace, Foundation Document,* The United Methodist Council of Bishops (Nashville, TN: Graded Press, 1986), 79–81.
64. *In Defense of Creation,* 85–88.
65. *Peace Futuring,* (New York: Office for Church in Society, United Church of Christ, 1982).
66. Brethren Peace Fellowship, (descriptive literature). New Windsor, MD: 1987.
67. Resource Catalog, 1987–1988, Akron, PA: Mennonite Central Committee, 1987.
68. *Conciliation Quarterly Newsletter.* Akron, PA: Mennonite Central Committee U.S. Peace Section, Fall 1989.
69. Elise Boulding, *One Small Plot of Heaven: Reflections on Family Life by a Quaker Sociologist.* (Wallingford, PA: Pendle Hill Publications, 1989) and Ian Harris, *Peace Education* (Jefferson, NC: McFarland & Co., Inc., 1988), Preface, xi.
70. The Children's Creative Response to Conflict program (descriptive literature), Nyack, NY: Children's Creative Response to Conflict, Fellowship of Reconciliation, 1988.
71. Newsletter of RFPI: Radio Wave of Global Communications, Eugene, OR: Radio for Peace International, July/August 1988.
72. General Information, Radio for Peace International, 1.
73. Program Schedule for July/August 1988, Eugene, Oregon: RFPI.
74. "New Short Wave Radio Station at the University for Peace," *Dialogue* (newspaper), San Jose, Costa Rica: University for Peace, July 1987.
75. Natural Resources and the Promotion of Peace (descriptive literature), San Jose, Costa Rica: University for Peace, 1988.
76. General Information, Eugene, OR: World Peace University, 1988.
77. "University for Peace Recent Activities," *Dialogue,* San Jose, Costa Rica, July 1987 and Joyce Hackel, "U.N.–Created University for Peace, Its Funds Short, Languishes in the

Mountains of Costa Rica, *Chronicle of Higher Education* 37 (17 October 1990), A45–47.

78. Takeshi Utsumi, "Establishing a Global 'Electronic University,' " *Breakthrough* (Global Education Associates) (Fall 1987/Spring 1988): 27–28.

79. Takeshi Utsumi, 28.

80. "Global Peace Awareness" as "A Model Curriculum Using Global Telecommunications" was presented by Leslie Conery and Lynne Schrum at the Second International Conference on Technology and Education, March 1990, Brussels, described in the *Conference Proceedings,* 451–453, an accomplishment that established "a cooperative international group." See also World Information Clearing Centre, "Press Release #2: New Computerized World Information Service (NCWIS), East/West/North/South," (Geneva: NCWIS, 13 May 1989), 1, for dissemination of information on global problems of disarmament, development, environment, and human rights; and GEMNET, global communications network, a component of Global Education Motivators, including a sister-school partnership and "Video Pals," between schools in Japan and the U.S., descriptive literature, (Chestnut Hill, PA: Chestnut Hill College, 1990). PeaceNet Online Community, computer-based information system, by the early 1990s included 3,000 organizations and activists, described as an "International Communications Network for Peace and Human Rights." Institute for Global Communications, 18 DeBoom St., San Francisco, CA 94107.

81. Educational Software Catalog, (Cambridge, MA: Tom Snyder Productions, 1988), 20.

82. Software Catalog, (Northbrook, IL: Mindscape Educational Division, 1989), 44.

83. Connect/USA-USSR (descriptive literature), Minneapolis, MN: Connect/USA-USSR, 1988.

84. "Erecting a Cultural Bridge from Moscow to Minnesota," *Minneapolis Star Tribune,* 6 December 1987, 41A.

85. Connect/USA-USSR, (descriptive literature) and Announcing the 1988 US-USSR Art Exchange, Minneapolis, MN: Connect/USA-USSR, 1988.

86. Connections Newsletter, Winter/Spring 1988, 1, 3.

87. Samantha Smith Foundation, (descriptive literature), Hallowell, ME: Samantha Smith Foundation, 1988.

88. Parents and Teachers for Social Responsibility (descriptive literature), Moretown, VT: Parents and Teachers for Social Responsibility, 1988.

89. *Yopp!* (newsletter), Moretown, VT: Parents and Teachers for Social Responsibility, Summer 1988, 6–7.

90. Peace Links, (descriptive literature). Washington, DC: Peace Links, 1990.

91. *Skipping Stones,* (Cottage Grove, OR: Aprovecho Institute, 1989).

92. "Educating for New Ways of Thinking: An American-Soviet Institute," Hampshire College, (descriptive literature) Amherst, MA, 7–21 August 1988.

93. ESR, descriptive literature, 1989.

94. Vincent C. Kavaloski, "Transnational Citizen Peacemaking as Nonviolent Action," *Peace & Change* 15 (April 1990); 174, 176, 192–193.

95. Alfie Kohn, *No Contest: the Case Against Competition* (Boston: Houghton Mifflin, 1986) and *The Brighter Side of Human Nature: Altruism and Empathy in Everyday Life* (New York: Basic Books, 1990). The successful infusion of cooperative learning as an accepted practice in America's classrooms in the 1990s, is largely attributed to the research of David and Roger Johnson, *Creative Conflict,* (Edina, MN: Interaction Book Company, 1987) and *Circles of Learning* (Alexandria, VA: Association for Supervision and Curriculum Development, 1984); and Robert E. Slavin, *Cooperative Learning* (New York: Longman, 1983, 1991), and *Using Student Team Learning,* 3rd ed. (Baltimore, MD: Center for Research on Elementary and Middle Schools, The Johns Hopkins University).

96. Gerald J. Pine and Asa G. Hilliard III, "Rx for Racism: Imperatives for America's Schools," *Phi Delta Kappan* 71 (April 1990): 593–600.

97. Pine and Hilliard, 599.

98. National Association for Multicultural Education, "Founding Statement and Goals." NAME, P.O. Box 9657, Arlington, VA 22219.

10. WHERE HAVE WE BEEN? WHERE ARE WE GOING?

A BLUEPRINT FOR THE FUTURE

The chronicle of peace education for almost two hundred years has been a fragile one held together by gossamer webs. At times, peace education was disguised by semantics, masquerading as international friendship or world citizenship, as a precursor of citizenship education. A clear blueprint for the future, however, has been left to us as our heritage.

Several areas appear to be written in a bold hand and beckon us to concentrate on several strands from the past as a guide to the future: (1) ecology and preservation of the planet; (2) nonviolence and conflict resolution; (3) change of attitude or transformation of the individual; (4) an expanded criteria for citizenship and patriotism; and (5) enhanced roles for women in peace negotiations and political decision making.

ECOLOGY AND PRESERVATION OF THE PLANET

The peace education curriculum in the eighties contained a common element that unified a broad range of topics and viewpoints, that of ecology and preservation of the global environment. Since astronauts projected a new image of our planet as a huge, blue ball spinning in space, educators have taken up the challenge to prepare new generations for global citizenry. By the close of the eighties, most curriculum design for the classroom included a component of environmental studies or ecology. Some programs were more extensive than others in stressing personal responsibility and a moral commitment for sharing the earth's resources. The seeds for nurturance of an environmental ethic were planted.

Foreshadowing of an ecological concern was shown as early as the twenties by Lucia Ames Mead who believed that true patriotism was shown by "saving forests and water-power" and "creating beauty, happiness and health for multitudes." In the sixties, concern for world problems first involved the children in America's classrooms. Through the NEA (Committee on International Relations) and especially its advocacy of UNICEF, children collected funds to help alleviate problems of hunger and poverty among the world's children. Many individual communities in America still carry on that tradition.

In the nineties, children and young people in increasing numbers have developed an environmental ethic. Student Pugwash is typical of many organizations with an ecological mission. Student Pugwash has been in operation since 1955, with chapters established at colleges and universities throughout the world. Developing greater public awareness of environmental damage and the impact of science and technology on human lives, are a few of the issues that have involved young people.

Since the seventies the preparation of a new generation for an interdependent, interrelated world has been an objective for global education. Multicultural education and the global perspective had been established as logical components for the curriculum in a majority of the states by the close of the eighties. The pioneering work of Leonard Kenworthy, James Becker, and Lee Anderson, (Chapter 7), among others, included the strong leadership of professional educational organizations. Their journals provided a forum for the interchange of ideas and solutions that directly influenced decision makers for inclusion of the global perspective in the curriculum. Almost three decades were required for this transformation.

The global education curriculum of the seventies reinforced ecological concern as a valid component of peace education. The shock waves generated by the Club of Rome's treatise, *Limits To Growth* (1972), the research of Anne and Paul Ehrlich (*The Population Bomb*), and others, forced America (and the world) to heed the warning: environmental policies in the past may result in the collapse of social, economic, and ecological systems if changes were not made. Concern for the environment has been a central core value for peace education in the eighties and a guide for the future. It has been presented as: stewardship of the earth's resources; conservation of natural resources; and commitment to a personal lifestyle based on ecological concern.

Betty Reardon's definitive compilation of teacher-designed curriculums for peace education, *Educating for Global Responsibility* (1988) included "commitment to life . . . with environmental and ecological education" as an integral component for positive peace.[1] Reardon's dedication to an ecological base for peace education actually spanned almost three decades. Her involvement began in 1963 with the World Order Models Project (World Policy Institute) that included the world order values of concern for the environment, economic welfare, prevention of war, political participation, and social justice.

Many concepts for environmental preservation were already included in the science curriculums of the elementary and secondary schools. The perspective of a Science-Technology-Society (STS) curricular strand has included the impact of science and technology on the problems of contemporary society with concentration on air and water pollution, conservation of natural resources, and toxic waste management, among many separate issues. With the infusion method (integration of a topic in various areas instead of introducing a new curriculum) care and concern for the environment can be included at each grade level in science or social studies.

In addition, the language arts can enhance the communication skills needed for responsible citizenship. Classroom experiences can be designed to show how letter writing to decision makers, listening to different viewpoints (resource speakers), journal writing, poster making, speech writing, and small group discussions can clarify issues as students share their ideas on ways to solve environmental problems.

Educators reassessed experiential learning as related to direct involvement of our younger generation in community-based problems. The National Society for Internships and Experiential Education, founded in 1972 has as its mission "the effective use of experience as an integral part of education, in order to empower learners and promote the common good."[2] Through community service-learning students can experience "cross-cultural awareness and personal growth."

Experiential learning has an enhancement value as well, in providing the means to influence larger groups of the general population. Community development was used interchangeably with the term "experiential learning" and described as an "umbrella concept" that included ways for groups of humans to "improve their living conditions and ways of life."[3] In community-based organizations throughout America, as seen in the wide range of activities in the eighties, groups of citizenry educated others in the concepts of peace education and activism, became role models, and shared concrete strategies for bringing about change.

A renewed focus on experiential learning for American education in the nineties was complementary to the philosophy of John Dewey, especially as articulated in his *Experience and Education* (1938). Dewey's learning-by-doing concept has since been enhanced by several decades of research, including Jean Piaget's and Maria Montessori's, on how children and young people learn best. Jane Addams and her associates at Hull House practiced a form of experiential learning that influenced generations of young people for the helping professions.

Peace education with an ecological component proved to be a method for direct, active involvement of children and young people. By participation in community projects, students could feel that they shared responsibility for environmental problems and could be involved in problem-solving activities that involved recycling, pollution control, or waste management. The most pressing problems of their community could usually be matched with an identical concern of others in distant corners of the globe. Students could be encouraged to develop an awareness of the ecological systems that were experienced by all as they shared our planet.

Peace education that stressed development of an environmental ethic made a strong case for inclusion in the traditional curriculum. Teaching skills to reduce violence and conflict have proved of benefit to the entire school culture. By helping a new generation to assume responsibility for the problems humanity has imposed upon the Earth, educators can encourage inquiry into solutions. The cooperation of the United States and the Soviet Union on environmental issues appeared as a hopeful sign. Groups of Soviet environmental officials visited several areas of America and announced cooperative projects, including an exchange of information.[4]

Finally, the author as participant and observer can attest to the enthusiasm of groups of middle school students involved in an experiential learning project in environmental studies. They cleaned the Gulf sands as part of a national project known as BeachSweep, working in groups that included Houmas Indians, Vietnamese refugees, and the children of shrimp fishermen and oil rig workers. They realized a sense of ownership in their local community. Obviously, many experienced a sense of wonder and delight when an unexpected treasure, such as a bird's nest or delicate wildflower, was discovered among the dunes. Direct involvement can nurture an awareness for ecological problems as well as the beauty of the natural world. After picking up dozens of styrofoam cups, one student commented that she would never again toss one away. Marking blanks on a worksheet could never compare to the impact of an environmental lesson on the effects of waste and pollution, studied firsthand on the beach under sunny skies. Through infusion of an ecological component in the curriculum, a new generation can experience personal involvement in efforts to save our fragile planet's resources.

NONVIOLENCE AND CONFLICT RESOLUTION

Kenneth Boulding shaped the metaphor of "islands of stable peace" in the "middle of an ocean of unstable peace" as a guide to a learning process that he believed held great promise. Boulding painted a picture of a "turning point" where the islands grow and merge into lakes in the midst of a "continent of stable peace." The dream of peace and nonviolence can be achieved, according to Boulding, because inevitably an "imperceptible shift in the nature of the system" will carry us "over a kind of watershed into a very different social landscape."[5] Peace educators can relate this metaphor to the development of nonviolent conflict resolution in the classrooms of America's schools during the eighties.

Violence in America has become a pervasive, insidious factor in contemporary society with elements that invade life from childhood (violent electronic games and war toys) through an entire lifespan (victimization of the elderly). Violence has been linked with increased rates of crime, homicide, proliferation of guns, and drug abuse as negative forces that impact on life in present-day society.

Peace educators, on the other hand, have pointed out repeatedly in recent years that violence should be viewed as a malaise in society that could lead to a complete breakdown in the civilized behavior needed for harmonious living in a multicultural society. Projected demographic changes in the approaching millennium carry the seeds of a revolution. The predominantly white majority will be unseated by a coalition of minority people of color. The riots in Newark, Chicago, and Detroit in the sixties are still memories easily recalled by many Americans.

Violence should be viewed as a problem that deserves the concerted, united efforts of all in education. Teaching children to live in harmony with others, to respect the differences of others, to use interpersonal skills to resolve conflicts with others—called attention to a prime responsibility for all in education. Children and young peopled need a safe, secure world in which to grow and mature.

The addition of the field of Peace Psychology, a division of the American Psychological Association, augurs well for peace education in the nineties. Several voices from the profession expressed the hope that there would be strengthened ties with those working for peace and justice issues. As an enhancement of the psychological aspects of peace, psychologists in the pages of the Division newsletter emphasized a "multidisciplinary, multidivisional, multinational and cultural context of peace psychology." One contribution by Helen M. Mehr outlined the many ways that this mission could be addressed. In addition, the suggestion was made that interest groups be established for conflict resolution, peace education, and environmental issues.[6]

The first seeds of peace education in the 1800s planted by the writers of the peace society journals, recognized violence as a destructive force in personal or communal life and an impediment to progress. Peace was celebrated as the sign of a civilized society. Horace Mann proclaimed in his orations and reports that violence was a scourge on humanity. As America poised on the edge of a new millennium—the twentieth century—an outpouring of writings proclaimed that humans had the means to overcome and root out violence. With intelligence and reason, human action could bring about the peaceful world that Darwin envisioned in his theories of evolution and progress. The beacon to illuminate the darkness was an antecedent of conflict resolution. The first use in history of arbitration was at the Hague Conference in 1899. The tools to settle international differences have existed since that time, enhanced by a rich knowledge base of international conciliation and conflict resolution, but ignored, relegated to dusty law treatises, or rejected in place of military force as the primary response.

Nonviolence has validity on the international level. Conflict resolution theory and practice began in the fifties, with a variety of formats designed for educational use throughout the seventies and eighties in a variety of settings and in a multidisciplinary mode. Certainly, children in the future can be taught the lessons of recent historical events, where nonviolence was the primary strategy for the citizenry of Eastern Europe to overthrow Communist domination.

A new generation is now being trained in our colleges and universities in an array of peace and conflict studies programs. Students are learning the tools developed by social and political scientists to improve intergroup and international relations. Moreover, a consortium has been formed, the Five College Program in Peace and World Security Studies (PAWSS). This group has addressed a much-needed component in peace education, future career paths for those trained in the peace field.[7] Our college-trained young people have the potential for bringing about significant changes on a national or international level. The monograph on careers developed by PAWSS included an extensive listing of practical information for the student considering peace and conflict studies.

Classroom teachers can confirm that children come to school with problems from home and community that directly affect their classroom roles and learning. Once the family and church could be counted on to inculcate principles of harmonious, ethical behavior or bolster the moral virtues required for healthy interactions with others. Changed attitudes toward the family and mores of society have placed an added burden on all in education. Peace educators believe that it is possible to teach that violence is not the only response and that there are alternatives for conflict situations. We can teach our younger generation the skills to resolve conflicts and live in peace with each other. The outpouring of curriculum guides and practical programs for student mediation in the seventies and eighties were a testimony to the far-sightedness and genuine concern of America's teachers. Conflict resolution has credibility for interpersonal relations and in group dynamics. The leitmotiv of nonviolence and conflict resolution, along with the development of an environmental ethic, offered concrete evidence that the efforts of peace educators deserved greater attention.

From an "ocean of unstable peace," a small but courageous group of educators had the vision to see a "turning point" where violence in the schools could be lessened. The "islands of stable peace" could influence and shape an improved school environment.

CHANGE OF ATTITUDE OR TRANSFORMATION OF THE INDIVIDUAL

Peace educators kept alive a concern for values as a force for the transformation of the individual and society for almost two hundred years. Examination of the earliest documents in peace education, the peace society journals in the mid-nineteenth century, revealed that the teacher and clergy were united in a mission to teach morals and ethics in the common schools. This goal was also reflected by many of the early pioneers in the curriculum field, such as Johann Friedrich Herbart and Charles A. McMurry, and cited often in the early yearbooks of the National Herbart Society. Ethical principles were considered an essential factor in education for citizenship and for the inculcation of patriotism.

Educators viewed the dawning of the new century in the year 1900 with a missionary zeal. They sincerely believed that a more peaceable society was possible through the moral and ethical education of America's children. Values, morals, and ethics, thus, have formed a solid foundation for peace education for almost two centuries.

As a corollary to teaching morals and ethics, the concept that education could bring about a change or transformation in the individual and in society was expressed often. John Dewey, Horace Mann, and Jane Addams, among many others, believed that beneficial changes could come about by peaceful, gradual, and nonviolent means. Horace Mann, in particular, viewed the common schools as the agent for transforming human society in America.

The mission of transformation expressed by the early school pioneers evolved through many decades, muted at times, but expressed as a recurrent theme. The emphasis on international friendship and goodwill, world citizenship, and renewed international cooperation at various times was another expression that the attitudes of society toward those in other parts of the world could be shaped by positive concern and respect for their differences. Moreover, peace education emerged in the seventies as a major process for transformation of the individual within the educational process. Susan Carpenter formulated a framework for a curriculum of peacemaking skills needed for changing the attitudes of present and future generations.

In the eighties, a serious treatise by Sissela Bok, daughter of the pioneer sociologist Gunnar Myrdal and peace researcher, Alva Myrdal, proposed renewed attention to the "fundamental human values" as a framework for bringing about a world without nuclear war.[8] Bok argued eloquently for a framework of four principles of conduct that are "basic to a great many moral, religious, and political traditions" to serve as a "strategy for peace."[9] These principles were nonviolence, veracity, fidelity, and publicity. These could act as an ethical antidote for the opposite, negative principles of violence, deceit, betrayal, and excessive secrecy.

Underlying Bok's treatise was the principle that "you have more power to change yourself than to affect others." Bok believed that tangible links existed between the action of an individual and a community or nation. A strategy of peace would ideally begin with "home, family and friends, (and) in community service" with the "personal and the piecemeal." As a result of such seemingly humble origins a potentiality existed for expanding the "reach of these spaces or territories of peace."[10] Boulding's metaphor of "islands of peace" in a "continent of unstable peace" could be considered a related concept. Change of attitude or transformation of the individual can begin on the most basic level—in the human heart and mind.

In a postscript to the book, Erik Erikson, whose theories of childhood development form a generally accepted theory for educators, commented on Bok's "fresh scrutiny" of a strategy of peace as one of great importance to all. Bok included "trust and hope as the first lifelong 'virtues' necessary for a potentially sound morality."[11] Erikson's theory recognized "basic trust" as necessary in the very first stage of life, a universal human need and vital to the development of a child's conscience.

Douglas Sloan of Teachers College reached a conclusion similar to Bok's by calling for inclusion of the whole spectrum of human experiences—the personal, social, moral, and aesthetic. Sloan considered this necessary as a balance to the "mis-education, non-education" of contemporary America as grounded in a narrow, limited theory of cognition. Sloan was critical of the emphasis on "verbal and logical mathematical skills" because "technical reason has taken root in the heart of modern education."

Instead, Sloan called for an education of imagination which he believed would bring "a love of truth and feeling for beauty, a sense of meaning and fresh wonder" in order to deepen human insight and transform our way of thinking.[12] The education that Bok and Sloan envisioned was one that encompassed the social, intellectual, and spiritual capacities of human life as a concept that would harmonize the whole person, rather than focus only on cognition. Consideration of the importance of the moral and aesthetic found deep roots in the peace education chronicle over the course of two centuries of American education. Sloan, Bok, and others who were seriously concerned about contemporary education confirmed that a new way must be found to engage future generations with the moral, spiritual, and aesthetic— the roots of education for the entire human lifespan.

Attitude change and social influence were the heart of a study of the basic question of how people change. Phillip Zimbardo and Michael Leippe outlined new research on the psychology of social influence, especially as related to pressing issues of society, such as "raising environmental consciousness . . . censorship . . . promotion of healthful lifestyles." The authors concluded that the interplay of attitude systems (behaviors, cognitions, and feelings) can be influenced by outside agents and "influenced internally by each other."[13] These new developments and the addition of Peace Psychology, point to the potential for a future multidisciplinary approach for all who share similar goals for a peaceful world.

Hannes Adomeit, Director of Soviet and Central European Studies at Tufts University pointed out it was in the "world of ideas" that change came to Eastern Europe in the era of November and December of 1989. Millions witnessed the end of an ideology that had held the masses of several nations under oppressive control for four decades. Adomeit believed that "their ideologies failed to explain developments in the real world . . . with elites . . . forced to abandon their monopolistic grip on power."[14] Scholars and researchers will be engaged in future assessment of the causes and forces that brought about such deep-seated changes in attitudes and collective human minds. Peace education for future generations will require a change in attitude — a new mindset—that will recognize that true education cannot be a narrowly conceived training of mental faculties, but must embrace the aesthetic, affective, and ethical as well.

EXPANDED CRITERIA FOR CITIZENSHIP AND PATRIOTISM

Peace education in America has been presented as a viewpoint that was basically utopian and futuristic with the vision of an ideal world of peace. This concept also embodied a philosophy of hope in the future. Throughout American history, men and women have searched for new ways to live and work together. Brook Farm and the Fruitlands communities in New England, the Shakers, the Amana colony—all recalled experiments designed to elicit new ways of thinking about society.

The doctrine of hope in the future with education as an instrument for change has been underscored throughout the pages of the chronicle of peace education. Peace educators have been a part of the visionary, utopian strand in American history and involved in efforts for reform that addressed serious issues, such as child labor, the right to vote for women, and safe working conditions for industrial workers. Peace educators have been involved in antislavery, the socialist-labor, and the suffrage movements. Such radical ventures eventually came into the mainstream of American society with legislation to ameliorate conditions.

With one exception, pacifism, as practiced by several leading peace educators, never came into the American mainstream. The campaign against peace educators in the twenties and thirties resulted in their being branded as part of the "socialist-Pacifist plot." Any activism against the prevailing war mentality of that time was viewed as unpatriotic and un-American. The Alien and Sedition Act suppressed unpopular opinions of the war with anti-German and anti-foreigner persecution. From this historic date on through subsequent decades, peace education and activism were equated with socialism and communism. Examination of primary sources, however, suggested that the reform efforts were pioneering ventures that included industrial unionism and reactions against the dominance of the trusts. Peace education or any strain of pacifism—however ideal, patriotic, or praiseworthy—was never considered as an enhanced variant of good citizenship nor given a fair chance for evaluation in American education.

The concepts of patriotism and Americanism were usurped instead by investigative bodies as revealed by the National Security League (1917) and the Lusk Commission (1920) reports. Documents revealed an early version of our present-day military-industrial complex, the Wall Street financial interests and armament makers. These were confirmed by further studies in the postwar years (Nye Committee) and reinforced until the present day by a documentation of excessive profits for defense contractors. Wars have been a profitable venture for a vested, small interest group.

Peace education and the pacifism advocated by many, such as Jane Addams, were never integrated in any way into the American political mainstream, as were other efforts for reform. However, persistent voices have been raised to protest the militarization of the schools for the past fifty years. Researchers such as Judith Torney, Howard Tolley, and Robert Coles, among others, over the course of several decades turned their attention to a subtle force in American education, the political socialization of children and young people. This is a cross-current that has shaped their ideas and actions as they matured into adults. The first entrance of the military into the schools (National Defense Act of 1920) was the occasion for criticism by John Dewey and other members of the academic community. Throughout several decades, educators have occasionally questioned the military's use of the secondary and postsecondary schools with inclusion of a military curriculum. The removal of military training, especially secondary school units, to a neutral location would ameliorate an unfair balance in favor of the political socialization of the younger generation.

A new, expanded view of patriotism and love of country is vital to an intelligent, objective appraisal of education's future. Betty Reardon, for example, has argued that the American social order has fostered "competition, alienation, and various anti-community forces."[15] A scholarly assessment of the historical and philosophical perspectives of the American Peace Movement by Sandra J. Rafter called for America's educators to question how they can encourage traits such as "cooperativeness, understanding, sharing, empathy" which are needed for "effective and reflective educational leadership."[16]

Peace educators have also underscored that serious problems still exist from the Vietnam War years. Attention has been drawn to a common trait found in many of America's young people. This has been described as a blind obedience to authority. The research of psychologist, Stanley Milgram in the seventies and Herbert Kelman and V. Lee Hamilton in the eighties has grave implications for the American social conscience and especially the political socialization of our younger generation.[17] Milgram's conclusions were that ordinary people when asked to carry out actions incompatible with "standards of morality" do not have the resources needed to resist authority. Examples throughout the seventies have occurred with the case of Richard Nixon and his associates in the Watergate scandal, involvement of American troops at the My Lai massacre during the Vietnam War, the financial scandals in several Wall Street firms, and the Iran-Contra affair.

The virtues of loyalty and patriotism have been highly cherished values. Peace educators believe that a new form of patriotism is one that engages in inquiry and asks questions, that does not blindly accept, but assesses several viewpoints before coming to a conclusion. An unquestioning, uncritical obedience would not be in the best interests of the schools or the individual. For the new century, our children need to learn to reason and think independently. Perhaps we have placed a misdirected valence on compliant children at the expense of the creative, independent thinkers that the society of the future will demand. A balance will need to be developed.

Peace educators have believed that love of country involved a critical appraisal and examination of motives behind government actions, based on ethics and morality. Peace educators have suffered vilification, persecution, and imprisonment for motives that were in the best interests of developing an enlightened, intelligent form of citizenship.

Recent historical viewpoints have shed new light on the vehemence of attacks against peace educators. Since the early days of American political history, Wilbur Zelinsky has argued that Americanism has been celebrated as a civil religion with "a set of beliefs and rituals, which are understood in some transcendental fashion."[18] Glorification of American nationalism has been considered as a substitute theology that involved "the intellect, imagination, and the emotions." Persons who dared to question were branded with charges of "blasphemy and sacrilege" as if they had committed "heinous crimes."[19] The chronicle of peace education confirmed that during the nineteenth century, the millennial quest for world peace took on the trappings of a religious mission for humanity. The pages of textbooks such as *Beacon Lights of Patriotism* (1894), equated Americans as the chosen people with a Protestant Christianity enshrined as the Holy Grail for America's citizenry. By the close of the nineteenth century, the moral forces of the community were engaged in serious attempts to eliminate war from civilization with the "brotherhood of man" as their ideal.

An enhanced, enlightened concept of patriotism is needed to include those who accept the failings and inconsistencies, the positive and the negative, along with the victories, but who believe healthy dissent and questioning will make a stronger citizenry. The peace educator cannot stand by and witness decline or disintegration but believes love of country demands a new, more critical patriotism. For future generations, conflicting views about love of country, patriotism, and criteria for American citizenship must undergo a reassessment and be brought into the critical light of serious inquiry. Patriotism and good citizenship can no longer be equated solely with military support or battlefield heroics.

ENHANCED ROLES FOR WOMEN IN PEACE NEGOTIATIONS AND POLITICAL DECISION MAKING

One hundred years ago, an impressive event took place, the Columbian Exposition held in Chicago in 1893. An assembly of women from two continents produced a volume of their addresses that permitted us access to the ideas of women on the "social, business and political affairs of humankind" along with their concern for a "greater future for the human race."[20] These women faced the coming of a new millennium as does our contemporary society with a renewed sense of hope for the future. Foremost among the problems discussed by the women and articulated by their editor, Mary Eagle, was that of the "relations of men and women in the work of the world and division of its profits and its honors."[21] Interspersed throughout the volume were reflective yearnings for freedom and independence in financial, economic, political (voting), and other social areas where their freedom was controlled by others.

Topics ranged from a discourse on "Woman's Place in Letters" by a young Annie Nathan Meyer, founder of Barnard College, who at twenty-six displayed a philosophical and literary approach to woman's place in world literature. "Woman is still in her first age. She is slowly awakening from a long sleep, and is just beginning to look about her and see the world around," she stated.[22] An address on peace by a lawyer, Mary Elizabeth Lease from Wichita, Kansas, boldly challenged the "horrible inconsistency between religious belief and action."[23] Lease echoed many themes of the same period by calling for the establishment of the Golden Rule "in human affairs" and also to govern the world. Lease boldly called for a central mission for women—to take their rightful place along with men:

> The mothers of this nation, the mothers of the world, shall no longer rear their sons to be slain . . . If men can not get along without the shedding of blood . . . let them no longer set themselves up as guides and rules, but confess their self-evident inefficiency and turn the management of affairs over to the mothers, who will temper their justice with love and enthrone mercy.

The prophecy of the French novelist, Victor Hugo was invoked: "In the twentieth century war will be dead, famine will be dead, royalty will be dead, but the people will live."[24]

Lofty sentiments for enhanced, responsible roles for women have echoed throughout the almost two hundred years of the chronicle of peace education. Women have taken advocacy roles for women's rights, prison reform, temperance, and the antislavery movement, along with participation in peace and benevolent societies. These noble undertakings involved the ancestors and descendents of these women writing in the nineteenth century. All of these efforts were carried out in addition to full-time responsibilities as wives, mothers, and community members. Only a minority were members of the professions. Margaret Fuller, editor of *The Dial,* a literary magazine that appeared in Concord during the 1840s, spoke of the "magnetic or electric influence" of women as a moral force in society. She was also one of the earliest to recognize the inherent nature of women to oppose war.

The role of the female school teacher as a source of intellectual power and patriotism was extolled during the early nineteenth century with woman deemed the molder of character and chief educator of humanity. Separate peace societies for women urged them to consolidate their energies in order to change "public opinion by forming themselves into a society" or exerting pressure with male family members.

Clearly, for the past one hundred years, women have raised voices in vain for a greater voice in peace and political decision making. During this time, generations of women have been trained in all of the skills of diplomacy, political and social science—the same array of skills that men involved in national affairs and international relations possess. Women in generations past have enriched our intellectual, political, spiritual or cultural lives. Several women have been awarded the Nobel Prize, including the most recent (1992)—to Rigoberto Menchu, Guatemalan Indian rights activist. Decades of networking and coalition building have prepared women for the group dynamics needed to survive at the diplomatic table, when negotiation skills must be finely honed.

Yet, in actuality, women have been shunted aside, first in the negotiations following World War I when it was reported that "few of the men listened to what the women had to say . . . In our patriarchal world suggestions which come from women are seldom taken seriously." Yet, even proposals of the Woman's Peace Party were presented to President Woodrow Wilson long before the peace negotiations. In fact his own Fourteen Points bore a strong resemblance to the women's proposals. At the Malta Summit in 1989, an international women's peace group was treated with the same disdain experienced seventy years ago. They were refused contact or a meeting that they requested with the summit leaders.[25]

The feminist perspective in contemporary peace education in the eighties has been represented by Betty Reardon, Birgit Brock-Utne, and others. In her definitive study, *Sexism and the War System,* Reardon applied the microscope of discernment to various areas with unsettling results. The present world order, she stated is "authoritarian and growing more so through the process of militarization . . . the inevitable consequence of the national security state." Reardon believed these are "cultural problems" and cannot be addressed from an exclusively psychological approach. In the final analysis, it will be an advocacy for the "equal value and dignity of all persons" as a task for education, and peace education in particular.[26] Women have been persistently excluded from political power or political decision making (with rare exceptions). This is in sharp contrast to the fact that the sociologist and peace activist Alva Myrdal served as cabinet minister for disarmament in Sweden during the 1960s. One of the special assistants in the U.S. Arms Control and Disarmament Agency at that time was Betty Lall, who wrote that women were likewise excluded from the SALT treaty negotiations.[27] Through the human capacity to change attitudes and beliefs and even a dominant ideology as seen in Eastern Europe, the transformation and empowerment of the individual can be possible. Through a "convergence of positive masculine and feminine values" Reardon believed that a cultural transformation, demanded of a truly human society, can finally emerge.[28]

A viewpoint on the involvement of women in peace activities was studied by Ruth Roach Pierson. She concluded that there "has not been a consistent women's response to war and revolution."[29] On the other hand, Christiana Dugan studied the political socialization of five women involved in peace education at the college or university levels. All were deeply affected by war, determined to "work for peace," and were sustained by a great deal of contact with spirituality during childhood.[30] The political socialization of women, from childhood through adulthood, shaped a strong sense of social responsibility. Thus, socialization can be considered the driving force that motivated peace educators and social reformers for past decades. The power of education is a forceful message.

Other women, however, in past history have taken up arms and are presently doing so with greater degrees of responsibility in military and naval affairs. Women were in command positions during the operations in Panama (1989). Furthermore, women in the armed forces came close to equality and served with distinction in sensitive battle positions during the Gulf War (1991) though several were subjected to assault and sexual harassment. The neglected history of women in the armed forces, along with their achievements is slowly being addressed. The unresolved dilemma, however, concerned the approximately 17,000 children who were left behind with friends or relatives when a single parent or both parents were assigned to the Persian Gulf War.

A more cooperative effort among peace researchers, governmental organizations, and activists was fostered by Birgit Brock-Utne, who along with Elise Boulding, studied the field of peace research and agreed that "there had been too much preoccupation with the technicalities of the arms race and too little research on the alternative conflict solutions and on the human and social aspects of the arms race."[31] Both called for a greater inclusion of the research of women.

Women working with peace issues at the close of the eighties, have long existed on hopes and promises with a belief that one day there would be a more harmonious, egalitarian balance. Elise Boulding emphasized that women have the power to "interact with men's culture and men's skills and produce a more listening and peaceable world civic culture." Her scholarly treatise on a global civic culture was one based on a future that included women using the networking potentials of the nongovernmental organization (NGO) and the international nongovernment organization (INGO), the service, and professional organizations to enhance the development of the world civic culture.[32]

* * * * * * * * * * * * * * * *

At this endpoint of the chronicle of peace education, there is one common dream that could unite all—concern for children. This is the one unique thread that binds all through these past decades we have studied. Children and young people should be the heart and core of peace education. All need to be provided with a safe and stable environment for their optimal development. All other goals should take a secondary role in human lives with the welfare of children as a primary goal. The U.N. Declaration of Rights for the Child has provided a document and guidelines for America's and the world's children. The basic survival of the child should be the future hope of our nation and others.

As decades of an arms race have finally ended, two superpowers have become bankrupt and mired in debt. In a note of irony, a mere footnote in history, the image of the child—under the guise of infant mortality statistics—did make a final impression. Eduard Shevardnadze, the last Foreign Minister of the Soviet Union, named as head of his native Georgia, recalled a meeting with American Ambassador Thomas J. Watson, who said:

> Signs of a falling standard of living have begun to appear . . . We have suddenly found that infant mortality is rising in the United States . . . few in our country are aware that this is a consequence of the arms race.

Shevardnadze nodded in agreement, "Both of us have lost the arms race."[33] Each year, the Children's Defense Fund has calculated the mounting debts for the world's military expenditures and the dismal record for social expenditures. These statistics have been widely disseminated.[34] At this historical crossroad, the basic survival of all of our children should call us back to the central task of strengthening American families, rebuilding American communities and schools, and working tirelessly for a safe world of peace.

The goodness of the child as recognized by Rousseau, Pestalozzi, Froebel, and Montessori has never been recognized as an integral truth by a society that has largely abandoned natural law and absolutes like truth, goodness, love, and beauty. Perhaps, one day, even Montessori's dream of The Party of the Child will be realized. She argued eloquently that a world of peace for all children is their rightful inheritance. As a nation founded on hope, a peaceful world for all of our children could be a dream and a cord that binds all humanity. America, in this last decade of the century, can be an example to the rest of the world. Priorities for children can easily be understood and translated into the universal language that all know—a peaceful world, love, care, and concern for all children. Such dreams—and peacemaking—would no longer be an opaque puzzle or hidden history, but a clear path for action.

Notes

1. Betty Reardon, *Educating for Global Responsibility,* 47.
2. National Society for Internships and Experiential Education, (descriptive literature), (Raleigh, North Carolina, 1989).
3. Paul S. Denise and Ian M. Harris, eds., *Experiential Education for Community Development* (Westport, CT: Greenwood Press, 1989), 7.
4. "U.S. and Soviets Cooperating On Environmental Issues." *Times-Picayune* (New Orleans), 13 January 1990.
5. Kenneth Boulding, *Stable Peace* (Austin, Texas: University of Texas Press, 1978), 66.
6. Helen M. Mehr, "What Can I Do for Peace & Social Justice as a Psychologist?" *Division 48 Newsletter,* The Division of Peace Psychology of the American Psychological Association 1 (2) (April 1991), 11.
7. *Peace and World Order Studies: A Curriculum Guide,* 5th ed., (Boulder, CO: Westview Press, 1989) and Daniel C. Thomas, *Guide To Careers and Graduate Education in Peace Studies,* 1st ed. (Amherst, MA: Five College Program in Peace and World Security Studies, 1987).
8. Sissela Bok, *A Strategy of Peace: Human Values and the Threat of War* (New York: Pantheon Books, 1989).
9. Bok, 152.
10. Bok, 152.
11. Erik Erikson, "A Postscript," in Bok, 153–155.

12. Douglas Sloan, *Insight-Imagination: The Emancipation of Thought and the Modern World* (Westport, CT: Greenwood Press, 1983), 191–246.
13. Philip G. Zimbardo and Michael R. Leippe, *The Psychology of Attitude Change and Social Influence.* (Philadelphia: Temple University Press, 1991), Foreword, xv; Preface, xvii-xviii.
14. Hannes Adomeit, "Scholars Have Played a Key Role in Initiating and Interpreting the Changes Sweeping Europe," *Chronicle of Higher Education,* 13 December 1989 (Point of View), 36: A64.
15. Betty Reardon, "Peace As an Educational End and Process" in *Peace and World Order Studies: A Curriculum Guide,* ed. Burns J. Weston et al. (New Brunswick, NJ: Transaction Books, 1978), 32.
16. Sandra J. Rafter, An Historical/Philosophical Examination of the American Peace Movement and Its Implications for Education, Ph.D. diss., Graduate College of the University of Iowa, Iowa City, Iowa, 1985, 131.
17. Stanley Milgram, *Obedience to Authority: An Experimental View* (New York: Harper & Row, 1974).
18. Wilbur Zelinsky, *Nation Into State: The Shifting Symbolic Foundations of American Nationalism.* (Chapel Hill: University of North Carolina Press, 1988), 233.
19. Zelinsky, 233.
20. *The Congress of Women,* Mary Kavanaugh Oldham Eagle, ed. (Original edition, 1894) Reprint Edition (New York: Arno Press, 1974).
21. *The Congress of Women,* Publishers' Preface, n.p.
22. Annie Nathan Meyer, "Woman's Place in Letters," in *The Congress of Women,* 135–137.
23. Mary Elizabeth Lease, "Synopsis of 'Peace'," in *The Congress of Women,* 412–413.
24. Lease, 413.
25. Reardon, 326 and "Activists Sidelined by Storm," *Times-Picayune* (New Orleans), 3 December 1989. A women's peace network, led by Margaret Papandreou of Greece, attempted to meet with George Bush and Mikhail Gorbachev at the Malta Summit, having sent "representatives to all summit meetings," but were unsuccessful.

26. Betty Reardon, *Sexism and the War System* (New York: Teachers College Press, 1985), 32 and 326.

27. Elise Boulding, "Perspectives of Women Researchers on Disarmament, National Security and World Order." In *Approaching Disarmament Education,* edited by Magnus Haavelsrud (Surrey, England: Westbury House, 1981), 16

28. Reardon, 326.

29. Ruth Roach Pierson, "Women in War, Peace and Revolution," in *Images of Women in Peace and War: Cross-Cultural and Historical Perspectives,* Sharon Macdonald, et al., eds. (Madison: University of Wisconsin Press, 1987), 225.

30. Christiana Dugan, The Political Socialization of Five Women Who Teach Peace Studies, Abstract, Ph.D. diss., Graduate School of Drew University, Madison, New Jersey, July 1991, 1.

31. Birgit Brock-Utne, "The Development of Peace and Peace Concepts Through Three UN Women Decade Conferences," *A Just Peace Through Transformation: Cultural, Economic, and Political Foundations for Change* (Proceedings of the International Peace Research Association, Eleventh General Conference), Chadwick Alger and Michael Stohl, eds. (Boulder, Colorado: Westview Press, 1988).

32. Elise Boulding, *Building a Global Civic Culture: Education for an Interdependent World* (New York: Teachers College Press, 1988).

33. Shevardnadze, Eduard. *The Future Belongs to Freedom,* Translated by Catherine A. Fitzpatrick. (New York: The Free Press, Div. of Macmillan, 1991), 82–83.

34. Children's Defense Fund. *A Report Card, Briefing Book, and Action Primer.* (Washington, DC: Children's Defense Fund, 1990) and Ruth Leger Sivard, *World Military and Social Expenditures* (Leesburg, VA: World Priorities, Inc., 1974–1990).

BIBLIOGRAPHY

Aberdeen, Countess of. "The Coming Triennial Meeting of the Council of Women of the United States at Washington," *The Arena*, 23 (February 1895), 340.

Abramowitz, Norman, Andrew J. Leighton, and Stephen Viederman. "Global and International Perspectives." In *Improving the Human Condition: A Curricular Response to Critical Realities*. Washington, DC: Association for Supervision and Curriculum Development, 1978.

Abrams, Grace C., and Fran C. Schmidt. *Learning Peace*. Philadelphia: Jane Addams Peace Association, 1972.

———. *Peace Is in Our Hands*. Philadelphia: Jane Addams Peace Association, 1974.

Abrams, Grace Contrino Peace Education Foundation. *Peace Works*. Newsletters (1988–1990). Miami: Abrams Peace Education Foundation.

"Activists Sidelined by Storm." *Times-Picayune*, 3 December 1989.

Addams, Jane. "Disarmament and Life." In *Jane Addams on Peace, War and International Understanding*, edited by Allen F. Davis. New York: Garland Press, 1976, 173–178.

———. Memorabilia and Student Publications, Rockford Female Seminary. Rockford, IL: Archives, Rockford College.

———. *Memorials to Anna P. Sill, 1840–1889*. Rockford, IL: Daily Register Electric Print, 1889.

————. *My Friend, Julia Lathrop*. New York: Macmillan, 1935.

————. *Newer Ideals of Peace*. New York: Macmillan, 1906.

————. *Peace and Bread in Time of War*. New York: Macmillan, 1917.

Adibe, Nasrine, and Frank A. Stone, eds. *International Conference on Expanding Dimensions of World Education Proceedings,* Ankara, Turkey. Storrs, CT: University of Connecticut, World Education Project, 1976.

Adler, Mortimer J. *How To Think about War and Peace*. New York: Simon and Schuster, 1944.

Adomeit, Hannes. "Scholars Have Played a Key Role in Initiating and Interpreting the Changes Sweeping Europe," *Chronicle of Higher Education,* 13 December 1989, 36: A64.

Advocate of Peace (1828–1831). New York: American Peace Society. New York: Clearwater Publishing, 1978. Micro-opaque.

Alger, Chadwick, and Michael Stohl, eds. *A Just Peace Through Transformation: Cultural, Economic, and Political Foundations for Change (Proceedings of the International Peace Research Association, Eleventh General Conference),* Boulder, CO: Westview Press, 1988.

"All Noise on the Western Front." *New York Times,* 22 November 1983, 1, 24.

Alonso, Harriet Hyman. *The Women's Peace Union and the Outlawry of War, 1921–1942*. Knoxville, TN: University of Tennessee Press, 1989.

American Advocate of Peace (1834–1836). Hartford, CT: Connecticut Peace Society. New York: Clearwater Publishing, 1978. Micro-opaque.

American Association for International Conciliation. *Towards an Enduring Peace: Symposium of Peace Proposals and Programs, 1914–1916.* New York: American Association for International Conciliation, 1916.

American Association of School Administrators. *Morale for a Free World: America and Not America Only. Twenty-Second Yearbook.* Washington, DC: American Association of School Administrators, A Department of the National Education Association of the United States, formerly the Department of Superintendence, February, 1944.

———. *Schools for a New World. Twenty-Fifth Yearbook.* Washington, DC: American Association of School Administrators, A Department of the National Education Association of the United States, February, 1947.

American Baptist Church. "Breaking Down the Walls." Descriptive Literature. Valley Forge, PA: National Ministries, American Baptist Churches/USA, 1987.

American Forum for Global Education (Global Perspectives in Education). Descriptive Literature. New York: American Forum for Global Education, 1989–1990.

American Lutheran Church. *Action Ideas for Peacemaking.* Minneapolis, MN: Office of the Church in Society, 1988.

American School Citizenship League. *American School Citizenship League: An Eleven Year Survey of the Activities of the American School Peace League from 1908–1919.* Boston, 1919.

American School Peace League. *Proceedings, 1913–1914.* Boston: American School Peace League, 1914.

———. *Proceedings, 1915.* Boston: American School Peace League, 1915.

————. *Report of the History Committee*. Brookline, MA: American School Peace League, 1913–1914.

————. *Yearbook, 1913–1914*. Boston: American School Peace League, 1913.

American University. Peace and Conflict Resolution Program. Washington, DC: American University, August 1988.

Anderson, Lee. *Schooling and Citizenship in a Global Age: An Exploration of the Meaning and Significance of Global Education*. Bloomington, IN: Indiana University, 1979.

Andrews, Fannie Fern. "The American School Peace League and the European War." *Proceedings, The American School Peace League, 1914–1915*. Boston: The American School Peace League, 1915: 9–10.

————. "Charms of Kidney Pond." *New England Magazine* 38 (April 1908): 222–228.

————. "Course of Study in Good-Will." *Religious Education* 6 (February 3, 1912): 570–573.

————. *The Freedom of the Seas: The Immunity of Private Property at Sea in Time of War*. The Hague, Netherlands: M. Nijhoff, 1917.

————. The Mandatory System After the World War. Master's degree thesis, Radcliffe College, 1923.

————. *The Holy Land under Mandate*. Boston: Houghton Mifflin, 1931.

————. *Memory Pages of My Life*. Boston: Talisman Press, 1948.

————. "Parents' Associations and the Public Schools." *Charities* 17 (November 24, 1906): 335–343.

———. "Relation of Teachers to International Peace." *Journal of Education* 68 (December 17, 1908).

———. "The Relation of Teachers to the Peace Movement." *Education* 28 (January 1908):279–289.

Andrews, Fannie Fern, and Ella Lyman Cabot. *A Course in Citizenship*. Boston: Houghton Mifflin, 1914.

Association for Supervision and Curriculum Development. *Education for Peace: Focus on Mankind*. Edited by G. Henderson. Washington, DC: Association for Supervision and Curriculum Development, 1973.

———. "ASCD Resolution on Nuclear Freeze." *Educational Leadership* 40 (May 1983):42.

———. *Improving the Human Condition: A Curricular Response to Critical Realities*. Washington, DC: Association for Supervision and Curriculum Development, 1978.

———. Letter to membership, 1 September 1964 (concerning Glens Falls project). Washington, DC: Association for Supervision and Curriculum Development.

"Attitudes about Arms Control and Effects of 'The Day After,' " ERIC document ED 257 699.

Bandura, Albert, and R. H. Walters. *Social Learning and Personality Development*. New York: Holt, Rinehart and Winston, 1963.

Barber, Jacqueline, ed. *Nucleography: An Annotated Resource Guide for Parents and Educators on Nuclear Energy, War, and Peace*. Berkeley, CA: Nucleography, 1982.

Barnet, Richard J. *Roots of War*. New York: Atheneum, 1972.

Bartlett, Ruhl J. *The League to Enforce Peace*. Chapel Hill: University of North Carolina, 1944.

"Battle of the Nuclear Stars." *Chicago Tribune,* 22 November
   1983:1, 10.

Bauer, N., and J. Krivohlavy, "Cooperative Conflict Resolution
   In Institutionalized Boy Dyads," *Journal of Child Psychology*
   15 (January 1974):13–21.

Beacon Lights of Patriotism. Edited by Henry B. Carrington. New
   York: Silver and Burdett, 1894.

Beals, Charles, ed. *Second National Peace Congress. Proceedings.*
   Boston: American Peace Society, 1909.

Beard, Charles E., drafter. *Report of the Commission on Social
   Studies, Part I. Charter for the Social Sciences in the Schools.*
   New York: Charles Scribner's Sons, 1932.

Becker, James M. *Education for a Global Society.* Bloomington,
   IN: Phi Delta Kappa Educational Foundation, 1973.

————, ed. *Schooling for a Global Society.* New York: McGraw-
   Hill, 1979.

————. "What Is Education for International Understanding?"
   Social Education 30 (January 1966):30–31.

Beckwith, George C. *Peace Manual of War and Its Remedies.*
   Boston: American Peace Society, 1847.

Bedini, Silvio A. *The Life of Benjamin Banneker.* New York:
   Charles Scribner's Sons, 1972.

Berman, Shelley. "A Break in the Silence: Raising Nuclear Issues
   in the Schools." *Social Education* 47 (November/December
   1983):501–502.

"Bibliography on Peace and War." *Arena* 23 (February 1895):138–
   144.

Bibliography on Peace Research in History. Edited by Blanche Wiesen Cook. Santa Barbara, CA: ABC-CLIO, 1969.

Bickmore, Kathy. *Alternatives to Violence, A Manual.* Akron, OH: Peace Grows, Inc., 1987.

Biographical Dictionary of Modern Peace Leaders. Edited by Harold Josephson. Westport, CT: Greenwood Press, 1983.

Bishops' Pastoral Letter, Challenge of Peace. *Catholic Update.* Cincinnati, OH: St. Anthony Messenger Press, 1983.

Blair, Frank. "Social Function of History." National Herbart Society for the Scientific Study of Teaching, *Fourth Yearbook,* (Washington Meeting, 1898), edited by Charles A. McMurry (Chicago: University of Chicago Press, 1898), 44–56.

Blake, Katherine D. (Devereaux). "Peace Heroes." *The Kindergarten-Primary Magazine* 24 (March 1912):179.

Bohlen, Charles. *Witness to History: 1929–1969.* New York: W. W. Norton & Co., 1973.

Bok, Sissela. *A Strategy for Peace: Human Values and the Threat of War.* New York: Pantheon Books, 1989.

Bonser, Frederick G. *The Elementary School Curriculum.* New York: Macmillan, 1921.

Boorstin, Daniel J. *Hidden History: Exploring Our Secret Past.* New York: Harper & Row, 1987.

Boulding, Elise. "The Child and Non-Violent Social Change." In *Handbook of Peace Education.* Frankfurt am Main, Germany: International Peace Research Association, Education Committee, 1974.

———. "Peace: An Active Skill." *Christian Science Monitor,* 30 December 1980.

———. "Perspectives of Women Researchers on Disarmament, National Security and World Order." In *Approaching Disarmament Education,* edited by Magnus Haavelsrud (Surrey, England: Westbury House, 1981), 16.

———. *Building a Global Civic Culture: Education for an Interdependent World.* New York: Teachers College Press, 1988.

———. *One Small Plot of Heaven: Reflections on Family Life by a Quaker Sociologist.* Wallingford, PA: Pendle Hill Publications, 1989.

Boulding, Kenneth. "Education for Spaceship Earth." *Social Education* 32 (November 1968):648–652.

———. *Stable Peace.* Austin, TX: University of Texas Press, 1978.

Bourne, Randolph S., compiler. *Towards an Enduring Peace: Symposium of Peace Proposals and Programs, 1914–1916* (New York: American Association for International Conciliation, 1916).

Boyer, Ernest. In Stephen M. Masiclat, "Teaching Ethics." *Phi Delta Kappan* 68 (December 1987):276.

Boyer, William. "World Order Education: What Is It?" *Phi Delta Kappan* 56 (April 1975):524–527.

Brackett, Russell D. *Pathways to Peace.* Minneapolis, MN: T. S. Denison, 1963.

Branch, Taylor. *Parting the Waters: America in the King Years, 1954–1963.* New York: Simon and Schuster, 1988.

Brethren Peace Fellowship. Descriptive Literature. New Windsor: MD, 1987.

Brinton, Howard H. *Quaker Education.* Wallingford, PA: Pendle Hill, 1949.

Brock, Peter. "The Peace Testimony in 'A Garden Enclosed.' " *Quaker History* (Autumn 1965):72–74.

———. *Pacifism in the United States: From the Colonial Era to the First World War*. Princeton: Princeton University Press, 1968.

Brock-Utne, Birgit. "The Development of Peace and Peace Education Concepts through Three UN Women Decade Conferences." In *A Just Peace through Transformation: Cultural, Economic, and Political Foundations for Change*, edited by Chadwick Alger and Michael Stohl. (Proceedings of the International Peace Research Association, Eleventh General Conference). Boulder, CO: Westview Press, 1988.

———. *Educating for Peace: A Feminist Perspective*. New York: Pergamon Press, 1985.

Brodbelt, Samuel. "Global Interdependence: Increasing Student Awareness." *The Social Studies* 103 (May/June 1981):103.

Brooks, Annie Sills. *Adventuring in Peace and Goodwill*. Boston: Pilgrim Press, 1930.

Brooks, Van Wyck. *Literature in New England: The Flowering of New England, 1815–1865*. Garden City, NY: Garden City Publishing, 1944.

Brumbaugh, M. G. "Method of the Social Function of History." National Herbart Society for the Scientific Study of Teaching, *Fourth Yearbook* (Washington Meeting, 1898), edited by Charles A. McMurry (Chicago: University of Chicago Press, 1898), 31–43.

Buell, Lawrence. *Literary Transcendentalism: Style and Vision in the American Renaissance* (Ithaca, NY: Cornell University Press, 1973).

Bundy, McGeorge. *Danger and Survival: Choices about the Bomb in the First Fifty Years*. New York: Random House, 1988.

Burns, Grant. *The Atomic Papers: A Citizen's Guide To Selected Books and Articles On the Bomb, The Arms Race, Nuclear Power, The Peace Movement, and Related Issues.* Metuchen, NJ: The Scarecrow Press, 1984.

Burritt, Elihu. "Letter to George Bancroft, 'An Early Document in the Peace Movement, 21 April 1840.' " In Letters to *The Outlook* by M. A. DeWolfe Howe. *The Outlook* (21 September 1907):134–136.

Bush, George. "Preserving Peace through Deterrence." *New York Times,* 21 November 1983, I, 23.

Butterfield, Fox. "Why Asians Are Going To the Head of the Class." *New York Times Education Life Supplement,* 3 August 1986, XII, 18.

Cabot, Ella Lyman, Fannie Fern Andrews, and others. *A Course in Citizenship and Patriotism.* Boston: Houghton Mifflin, 1914.

Calumet (1831–1835). New York: American Peace Society. New York: Clearwater Publishing, 1978. Micro-opaque.

Camp Fire, Inc. *A Gift of Peace.* Kansas City, MO: Camp Fire, Inc., 1985.

Carey, Sister Loretta. *Directions for Justice/Peace Education in the Catholic Elementary School.* Washington, DC: National Catholic Education Association, 1984.

Carlsson-Paige, Nancy, and Diane E. Levin. *The War Play Dilemma: Balancing Needs and Values in the Early Childhood Classroom.* New York: Teachers College Press, 1987.

————. *Who's Calling the Shots?: How To Respond Effectively To Children's Fascination with War Play and War Toys.* Philadelphia: New Society Publishers, 1989.

Carnegie Forum. *A Nation Prepared: Teachers for the 21st Century*. New York: Carnegie Forum on Education and the Economy, 1986.

Carnegie Foundation for the Advancement of Teaching. *Carnegie Study of American High Schools*. Washington, DC: Carnegie Foundation for the Advancement of Teaching, 1982.

Carpenter, Susan Lynn. The Peace Transformation Process: Toward a Framework for Peace Education. Ph.D. diss., University of Massachusetts, 1976.

――――. *A Repertoire of Peacemaking Skills*. Fairfax, VA: Consortium on Peace Research Education and Development, George Mason University, 1974.

Carpozi, George, Jr. *Red Spies in Washington*. New York: Trident Press, 1968.

Carr, William G. *Education for World-Citizenship*. Stanford, CA: Stanford University Press, 1928.

Carrington, Henry B., ed. *Beacon Lights of Patriotism or Incentives to Virtue and Good Citizenship. In Prose and Verse with Notes, Dedicated to American Youth*. New York: Silver and Burdett, 1894.

Carson, Terrance R., and Hendrik D. Gideonse. *Peace Education and the Task for Peace Educators*. Bloomington, IN: World Council for Curriculum and Instruction, 1987.

"Center in Geneva Builds an Unusual Library on Higher Education but Funds Are Limited," *Chronicle of Higher Education* 35 (25 January 1989), A38.

Cevery, A. S. "Peace Education in the Family," *International Journal of Religious Education* 43 (February 1967):20–21.

Challenge of Peace, Bishops' Pastoral Letter. *Catholic Update*. Cincinnati, OH: Saint Anthony Messenger Press, 1983.

Chambers, John Whiteclay II, ed. *The Eagle and the Dove: The American Peace Movement and U.S. Foreign Policy, 1900–1922.* New York: Garland Publishing, Inc., 1976.

Chambers, Whittaker. *Witness.* New York: Random House, 1952.

Chatfield, Charles, ed. *Peace Movements in America.* New York: Schocken Books, 1973.

Children's Creative Response To Conflict. Descriptive Literature. Nyack, New York: Children's Creative Response to Conflict, Fellowship of Reconciliation, 1988.

Children's Defense Fund. *Children 1990: A Report Card, Briefing Books and Action Primer.* Washington, DC: Children's Defense Fund, 1990.

Choices. Washington, DC: National Education Association, 1983.

Christie, Daniel J., and Linden Nelson. "Student Reactions To Nuclear Education." *Bulletin of the Atomic Scientists* 44 (July/August 1988):22–23.

Clark, Grenville, and Louis B. Sohn. "World Order: The Need for a Bold New Approach." *Social Education* 26 (November 1962):397–401.

———. *World Peace Through World Law: Two Alternative Plans.* Cambridge, MA: Harvard University Press, 1966.

Cleveland, H. "Building the Machinery of Peace." *International Journal of Religious Education* 40 (1964):6–7.

Cloud, Kate, et al. *Watermelons, Not War.* Philadelphia: New Society Publishers, 1984.

Cole, Donna J. "Multicultural Education and Global Education: A Possible Merger." *Theory into Practice* 33 (September 1984):151–154.

Coles, Robert. *The Moral Life of Children.* Boston: Atlantic Monthly Press, 1986.

———. *The Political Life of Children.* Boston: Atlantic Monthly Press, 1986.

College Board. *Academic Preparation for College.* Washington, DC: The College Board, 1983.

Commager, Henry Steele. "A Declaration of Interdependence," *Today's Education* (March-April 1976):86.

Commission on Small Books of the John Dewey Society. *Teaching World Affairs in American Schools: A Case Book.* New York: Harper & Brothers, 1956.

Comstock, Margaret E. *Building Blocks for Peace.* Philadelphia: Jane Addams Peace Association, 1973.

Conery, Leslie, and Lynne Schrum. "A Model Curriculum Using Global Telecommunications" (Global Peace Awareness Project, University of Oregon). Paper presented at the Second International Conference on Technology and Education, Brussels. *Conference Proceedings* (March 1990):451–453.

Conflict Resolution: Contributions of the Behavioral Sciences. Edited by Clagett G. Smith. Notre Dame, IN: University of Notre Dame Press, 1971.

The Congress of Women. Edited by Mary K. Eagle. Chicago: American Publishing House, 1894. Reprint. New York: Arno Press, 1974.

Connect/USA-USSR. Descriptive Literature. Minneapolis, MN, 1988.

———. Announcing the 1988 US-USSR Art Exchange. Minneapolis, MN: Connect/USA-USSR, 1987.

————. Connections Newsletter. Minneapolis, MN: Connect/ USA-USSR, Winter/Spring 1988: 1–3.

Consortium on Peace Research Education and Development. "10 Quick Ways to Evaluate Global Education Materials." Kent, OH: COPRED-Peace Education Network, Kent State University, n.d.

Conte, Anthony E., and Lorraine A. Cavaliere, "Are Students Being Educated for the 21st Century?: An Infusion Model for Global Perspectives," *The Social Studies* 73 (March/April 1982):74–79.

Cook, Blanche Wiesen, ed. *Bibliography on Peace Research in History*. Santa Barbara, CA: ABC-CLIO, 1969.

Cordasco, Francesco, ed. *History of American Education: A Guide to Information Sources*. Detroit: Gale Research Company, 1979.

Cordes, Colleen. "U.S. Peace Institute Created." *American Psychological Association Monitor* (November 1984):7.

Cortes, Carlos E. *Multicultural Education and Global Education: Natural Partners for a Better World*. Riverside, CA: University of California-Riverside, 1980.

Cortes, Carlos E., and Dan B. Fleming. "Global Education and Textbooks." *Social Education* 50 (September 1986):376 + .

Cott, Nancy. *Decades of Discontent: The Women's Movement, 1920–1949*. Westport, CT: Greenwood Press, 1983.

————. *The Grounding of American Feminism*. New Haven: Yale University Press, 1987.

Coughlin, Ellen K. "In Cold War's Waning, Peace Researchers See Vindication of Their Work." *Chronicle of Higher Education,* 4 April 1990, 46:A6 + .

Council of Chief State School Officers. *Civic Literacy for Global Interdependence.* Washington, DC: Council of Chief State School Officers, Committee on International Education, 1976.

Course with Type Studies, Books 1, 2, 3, and 4. An American Citizenship Course in United States History. Published for the American School Citizenship League. New York: Charles Scribner's Sons, 1921.

Craig, John M. *Lucia Ames Mead (1856–1936) and the American Peace Movement.* Lewiston, NY: Edwin Mellen Press, 1990.

Creel, George. *How We Advertised America.* New York: Harper & Brothers, 1920.

Cronbach, Abraham. *The Jewish Peace Book for Home and School.* Cincinnati: Union of American Hebrew Congregations, 1932.

———. *The Quest for Peace.* Cincinnati: Sinai Press, 1937.

Curti, Merle. "An Afterword-Peace Leaders and the American Heroic Tradition." In *Peace Heroes in Twentieth Century America,* edited by Charles DeBenedetti. Bloomington, IN: Indiana University Press, 1988.

———. *The American Peace Crusade, 1815–1860.* New York: Octagon Books, 1965.

———. *Bryan and World Peace.* New York: Octagon Books, 1969.

Damon, William. "Learning How To Deal with the New American Dilemma: We Must Teach Our Students about Morality and Racism." *Chronicle of Higher Education,* 3 May 1989, 35:B1–3.

Danforth Foundation and the Ford Foundation. *The School and the Democratic Environment.* New York: Columbia University Press, 1960.

Davis, Allen, F., ed. *Jane Addams on Peace, War and International Understanding.* New York: Garland Press, 1976.

Dawley, Alan. *Struggles for Justice, Social Responsibility and the Liberal State.* Cambridge, MA: Belknap Press of Harvard University Press, 1991.

" 'Day After': Does the Media Really Have an Impact?" Study I (April 1984) and "What Difference Does It Make in Experienced Control?" Study II and III (1984). ERIC document 260 953.

" 'Day After': Report of a Survey of Effects of Viewing and Beliefs about Nuclear War." ERIC document 260 951.

" 'Day After': Rhetorical Vision in an Ironic Frame." ERIC document 251 872.

" 'Day After' Viewer's Guide." New York: ABC Television Network, Cultural Information Service, 1983.

" 'Day After' Will Be Too Late." Advertisement. *USA Today,* 21 November 1983: A9.

Debate on Education for Peace (Special Issues). *International Review of Education* 29 (1983).

DeBenedetti, Charles. *The Peace Reform in American History.* Bloomington, IN: Indiana University Press, 1980.

———. "A CIA Analysis of the Anti-Vietnam War Movement: October 1967." *Peace and Change: A Journal of Peace Research* 9 (Spring 1983):36–39.

———, ed. *Peace Heroes in Twentieth Century America.* Bloomington, IN: Indiana University Press, 1986.

Dedring, Juergen. *Recent Advances in Peace and Conflict Research.* Beverly Hills: Sage Publications, Inc., 1976.

DeHuszar, George, ed. *New Perspectives on Peace.* Chicago: University of Chicago Press, 1944.

Denise, Paul S., and Ian M. Harris, eds. *Experiential Education for Community Development.* Westport, CT: Greenwood Press, 1989.

Derman-Sparks, Louise. *Anti-Bias Curriculum: Tools for Empowering Young Children.* Washington, DC: National Association for the Education of Young Children, 1989.

Deutschland Erwacht (Germany Awakened). Siemenstadt, Germany: Bilderdienst Alton-Bienfeld, 1933.

Dewey, John. *Human Nature and Conduct.* New York: Henry Holt & Co., 1922.

———. *Impressions of Soviet Russia and the Revolutionary World.* New York: New Republic, 1929.

———. *Schools of Tomorrow.* New York: E. P. Dutton & Company, 1915.

Dialogue: A Teaching Guide To Nuclear Issues. Cambridge, MA: Educators for Social Responsibility, 1983.

Dilling, Elizabeth. *The Red Network: A "Who's Who" and Handbook of Radicalism for Patriots.* Kenilworth, IL, Published by the author, 1934.

Disciples of Christ. Shalom Partners, DHM Regional Agreement. Indianapolis, IN: Shalom Congregations, Division of Homeland Ministries, 1986.

———. Suggestions for Implementation. Indianapolis, IN: Shalom Congregations, 1988.

Division 48 Newsletter: The Division of Peace Psychology 1 (2) (April 1991):5.

Draper, Theodore. *American Communism and Soviet Russia*. New York: Harcourt, Brace and World, 1960.

————. *The Roots of American Communism*. New York: Harcourt, Brace and World, 1957.

Dugan, Christiana. The Political Socialization of Five Women Who Teach Peace Studies. Ph.D. diss. Graduate School of Drew University, Madison, New Jersey, July 1991.

Dunne, Michael. *The United States and the World Court, 1920–1935*. New York: St. Martin's Press, 1988.

Eagan, Eileen. *Class, Culture and the Classroom: The Student Peace Movement of the 1930s*. Philadelphia: Temple University Press, 1981.

Eagle, Mary Kavanaugh Oldham, ed. *The Congress of Women*. Original edition, 1894. Reprint Edition. New York: Arno Press, 1974.

Eagleton, Clyde. *Analysis of the Problem of War*. New York: Ronald Press Company, 1937.

Eckhardt, William. *Compassion: Toward a Science of Value*. Huntsville, Ontario: Canadian Peace Research Institute Press, 1972.

————. "Research and Education as Approaches to Peace and Justice," 3 *Peace and Change: A Journal of Peace and Research* (1973):44–60.

Edleson, Jeffrey L. "Teaching Children To Resolve Conflict: A Group Approach," *Social Work* (November 1981): 488–492.

Educational Policies Commission. *American Education and International Tensions*. Washington, DC: National Education Association, 1949.

Educators for Social Responsibility. Descriptive Literature. 1982, 1983, 1985, 1988, 1989, and 1990. Cambridge, MA: Educators for Social Responsibility.

Einstein, Albert. "Education and World Peace: A Message to the Progressive Education Association," *Progressive Education* II (December 1934):440.

Eisner, Elliot W. *The Educational Imagination: On the Design and Evaluation of School Programs,* 2nd ed. New York: Macmillan, 1985.

Elam, Stanley M. "Educators and the Nuclear Threat." *Phi Delta Kappan* 64 (April 1983):533–538.

————. "International Threat to International Education." *Phi Delta Kappan* 49 (December 1967):169.

Ellerd, Arthur A., Jr. "Winning the Peace: The Second World Renaissance," *School and Society* 61 (January 6, 1945):1–3.

Elley, W. B. "Attitude Change and Education for International Understanding." *Sociology of Education* 37 (Summer 1964):318–325.

Ellul, Jacques. *Propaganda.* New York: Vintage Books, 1973.

"Elm." "Christianity and Patriotism." *Southern Literary Messenger* 8 (September 1842):600–606.

"Enhancing the Effects of 'The Day After' with an Educational Intervention." ERIC document 261 950.

"Erecting a Cultural Bridge From Moscow to Minnesota," *Minneapolis Star Tribune,* 6 December 1987, 41A.

Erikson, Erik H. "A Postscript" in Sissela Bok, *A Strategy of Peace.* New York: Pantheon Books, 1989.

Escalona, Sybille, and John Mack. "Children and the Threat of Nuclear War." In *Behavioral Science and Human Survival,* edited by M. Schwebel. Palo Alto: Science and Behavior Books, 1965.

Essman, Walter B. *Current Biochemical Approaches to Learning and Memory.* New York: Spectrum Publications, Inc., 1973.

Estes, N., J. Herne, and D. LeClercq. "Interactive Video through AppleWorks," Seventh International Conference on Technology and Education: New Pathways To Learning Through Educational Technology, *Proceedings, Volume 2,* Brussels, March 1990.

Evangelical Lutheran Church in America. Descriptive Literature. Department for Peace Education, 1988.

Faconti, Pietro P., and Allen Hagerstrand. "Conflict Management Program Helps Teens Help Teens." *National Association of Secondary School Principals' Bulletin* 71 (May 1987):118–119.

Fairchild, Edward T. President's Address. National Education Association *Bulletin,* September 1913. Washington, DC: National Education Association, 1913.

Falk, Richard A. "The Revolution in Peace Education." *Saturday Review of Literature,* 49 (21 May 1966):59–61 + .

———. *Explorations at the Edge of Time: The Prospects for World Order* (Philadelphia: Temple University Press, 1992).

Falk, Richard A., and Samuel S. Kim. *An Approach To World Order Studies and the World System.* New York: Institute for World Order, 1982.

Falk, Richard A., and Saul H. Mendlovitz. *The Strategy of World Order.* New York: World Law Fund, 1966.

"Fallout Shelters and the Schools." *National Education Association Journal* 51 (February 1962):23.

Fellers, Pat. *Peace-ing It Together: Peace and Justice Activities for Youth.* New York: Harper & Row, 1984.

Fenton, Edwin, and Elsa R. Wasserman. *A Leader's Guide to Improving School Climate through Implementing the Fairness Committee: A Manual for Students and Teachers.* Cambridge, MA: Harvard Graduate School for Education, Moral Education Resource Fund, 1985.

Finch, J. G., "Interactive Video Through AppleWorks," Seventh International Conference on Technology and Education: New Pathways To Learning Through Educational Technology, *Proceedings, Volume 1,* Brussels, March 1990, 199–200.

Fink, Clinton F. "Fannie Fern Andrews." *Biographical Dictionary of Internationalists.* Edited by Warren F. Kuehl. Westport, CT: Greenwood Press, 1983.

Fischer, Louis, ed. *The Essential Gandhi.* London: Allen and Unwin, 1963.

Fiske, Edward B., "America's Test Mania." *New York Times,* Education Life, 10 April 1988, XII: 16.

Fiske, John. *American Political Ideas Viewed from the Standpoint of Universal History.* New York: Harper & Brothers, 1885.

Flacks, Richard. *Making History: The Radical Tradition in American Life.* New York: Columbia University Press, 1988.

Fleisher, Paul. "Teaching Children about Nuclear War." *Phi Delta Kappan* 66 (November 1985):215–216.

Fleming, Dan B. "Nuclear War in High School History Textbooks." *Phi Delta Kappan* 64 (April 1983):550–551.

———. "Nuclear War in Textbooks," *Peace and Change* X (Summer 1984):71–78.

————. "Students and Parents: Views of 'The Day After' and the Place of Nuclear War Education in the Schools," *The Social Studies* 75 (January/February 1985):8–9.

Fletcher, Ruth. *Teaching Peace Skills for Living in a Global Society*. New York: Harper & Row, 1986.

Forbes, J. Malcolm, Mrs. (Rose Dabney Forbes). *The Peace Movement and Some Misconceptions*, n.p., n.d. In Lofland, John. *Peace Movement Organizations and Activists in the U.S.: An Analytic Bibliography*. Binghamton, NY: Haworth Press, 1991.

Ford Foundation, and the Danforth Foundation. *The School and the Democratic Environment*. New York: Columbia University Press, 1960, 5.

Foster, Catherine. *Women for All Seasons: The Story of the Women's International League for Peace and Freedom*. Athens, GA: University of Georgia Press, 1989.

Fowler, Robert Booth. *Carrie Catt: Feminist Politician*. Boston: Northeastern University Press, 1986.

Frank, Glenn. "The Approaching Renaissance of Western Civilization." Third Lecturers' Conference on Public Opinion and World Peace. Washington, DC: International Lyceum and Chautauqua Association, 1922.

Freire, Paulo. *Pedagogy of the Oppressed*. New York: Seabury Press, 1973.

————. *Education for Critical Consciousness*. New York: Seabury Press, 1973.

French, Dan, et al. *Crossroads: Quality of Life in a Nuclear World, a High School Curriculum. An English Curriculum. A Social Studies Curriculum. A Science Curriculum*. Boston: Jobs with Peace, 1983.

Fried, Richard M. *Nightmare in Red: The McCarthy Era in Perspective.* New York: Oxford University Press, 1990.

Friedman, Leon, ed. *The Civil Rights Reader: Basic Documents of the Civil Rights Movement.* New York: Walker and Company, 1967.

Friendly Classroom for a Small Planet: A Handbook on Creative Approaches To Living and Problem Solving for Children. (Joint authorship by Priscilla Prutzman, et al.) Wayne, NJ: Avery Publishing Group, 1978.

Fry, Todd. "Communication Education and Peace Education: A Beginning." *Communication Education* 35 (January 1986):75–80.

Fuller, Margaret. *Woman in the Nineteenth Century and Kindred Papers Relating to the Sphere, Conditions, and Duties of Woman.* Boston: John P. Jewett & Company, 1888.

Gaddis, John Lewis. *The Long Peace: Inquiries into the History of the Cold War.* New York: Oxford University Press, 1987.

Garbarino, James, Kathleen Kostelny, and Nancy Dubrow. *No Place To Be a Child: Growing Up in a War Zone.* New York: Lexington Books, 1991.

Gardner, Howard. *Frames of Mind: The Theory of Multiple Intelligences.* New York: Basic Books, Inc., 1983.

———. *The Unschooled Mind: How Children Think and How Schools Should Teach.* New York: Basic Books, 1991.

Genser, Lillian, ed. *Understanding and Responding to Violence in Young Children.* Detroit: Wayne State University, Center About Peace and War, 1976.

Gibson, John S. *New Frontiers in the Social Studies: Goals for Students, Means for Teachers,* Medford, MA: Lincoln Filene

Center for Citizenship and Public Affairs, Tufts University, 1965.

Glens Falls Story. Descriptive Literature. Washington, DC: Association for Supervision and Curriculum Development, 1964.

Glickman, Carl D. "Good and/Effective Schools: What Do We Want?" *Phi Delta Kappan* 68 (April 1987):622–624.

Global Education Motivators. Descriptive Literature. Chestnut Hill, PA: Chestnut Hill College, 1990.

Global Learning, Inc. Descriptive Literature. Montclair, NJ: Global Learning, Inc., 1988.

Global Perspectives in Education, Inc. "Shaping the Future of International Studies." Wingspread Conference. New York: Global Perspectives in Education, Inc., 1984.

Goodlad, John I. "What Schools Should Be For?" *Learning* (July/August 1980):39–43.

Grant Foundation Commission on Youth. "The Forgotten Half: Non-College Bound Youth in America." *Phi Delta Kappan* 69 (February 1988):409–418.

Gray, Richard B. "United States Institute of Peace." In *World Encyclopedia of Peace,* edited by Ervin Laszlo and Jong Y. Yoo. Elmsford, NY: Pergamon Press, 1986.

Greenberg, Polly. *The Devil Has Slippery Shoes: A Biased Biography of the Child Development Group of Mississippi.* London: Collier-Macmillan, 1969.

Greider, William. "Does a Bear Sit in the Woods?" Excerpt from *Rolling Stone* (January 17, 1985). In *World Policy Forum* (Spring 1985):3.

Guidelines for Global Education. Lansing, MI: State of Michigan, Department of Education, 1983.

Haavelsrud, Magnus, ed. *Approaching Disarmament Education.* Surrey, England: Westbury House, 1981.

Habenstreit, Barbara. *Men Against War.* Garden City, NY: Doubleday, 1973.

Haberton, John. "The Ideal Citizen." In *Beacon Lights of Patriotism,* edited by Henry B. Carrington. New York: Silver and Burdett, 1894.

Hackel, Joyce. "U.N.-Created University for Peace, Its Funds Short, Languishes in the Mountains of Costa Rica." *Chronicle of Higher Education* (17 October 1990), 37:A45–47.

Hampshire College. "Educating for New Ways of Thinking: An American-Soviet Institute." Amherst, MA, 7–21 August 1988.

Handbook of Peace Education. Edited by Christoph Wulf. Frankfurt am Main, Germany: International Peace Research Association, 1974.

Hanvey, Robert G. *An Attainable Global Perspective.* New York: Global Perspectives in Education, Inc., 1987.

Hapgood, Norman. *Professional Patriots: An Exposure of the Personalities, Methods and Objectives Involved in the Organized Effort to Exploit Patriotic Impulses in These United States During and After the Late War.* New York: Albert and Charles Boni, 1927.

Harbinger of Peace (1828–1831). New York: American Peace Society. New York: Clearwater Publishing, 1978. Microopaque.

Harper, Ida Husted, ed. *The History of Woman Suffrage,* Vol. V, n.p.: National American Woman Suffrage Association, 1922.

Harris, Ian. *Peace Education.* Jefferson, NC: McFarland & Co., Inc., 1988.

Harrison, Benjamin. "The Critical Conditions of Labor." In *Beacon Lights of Patriotism,* edited by Henry B. Carrington. New York: Silver and Burdett, 1894.

Hart, Leslie A. *How the Brain Works.* New York: Basic Books, 1975.

————. *The Brain and Human Learning.* White Plains, NY: Longman, 1983.

Harvard Encyclopedia of American Ethnic Groups. Edited by Stephen Thernstrom. Cambridge: Harvard University Press, 1980.

Havighurst, Robert. "An Educational Problem." In *New Perspectives on Peace,* edited by George de Huszar. Chicago: University of Chicago Press, 1944.

Hayden, Thomas. *Reunion: A Memoir.* New York: Random House, 1988.

Hays, J. Ray, ed. *Violence and the Violent Individual.* New York: SP Medical and Scientific Books, 1980.

Heater, Derek. *Peace Through Education: The Contribution of the Council for Education in World Citizenship.* London: Falmer Press, 1984.

Heckscher, August. *Woodrow Wilson.* New York: Charles Scribner's Sons, 1991.

Henderson, George, ed. *Education for Peace: Focus on Mankind.* Washington, DC: Association for Supervision and Curriculum Development, 1973.

Herbart Society for the Scientific Study of Teaching. *First Yearbook.* Denver Meeting of the National Education

Association, 1895. 2nd ed. Edited by Charles A. McMurry. Chicago: University of Chicago Press, 1907.

————. (National) Herbart Society for the Scientific Study of Teaching. *Fourth Yearbook.* Washington Meeting of the National Education Association. Edited by Charles A. McMurry. Chicago: University of Chicago Press, 1898.

Herman, Sondra. *Eleven Against War: Studies in American Internationalist Thought, 1898–1921.* Stanford: Hoover Institute Press, 1969.

Herndon, Terry. "A Teacher Speaks of Peace." *Phi Delta Kappan* 64 (April 1983):530.

Herter, Christian. "Common Market, the Trade Expansion Act and Atlantic Partnership." *National Association for Secondary School Principals Bulletin* 47 (April 1963):84–92.

Hickman, Warren L. and Roy A. Price. "Global Awareness and Major Concepts." *The Social Studies* 71 (September/October 1980):211.

Hicks, David, ed. *Education for Peace: Issues, Principles, and Practice in the Classroom.* London: Routledge, 1988.

Hinitz, Blythe F. *Teaching Social Studies To the Young Child, A Research and Resource Guide.* New York: Garland Publishing, Inc., 1992.

History of Woman Suffrage, Vol. V. Edited by Ida Husted Harper. n.p.: National American Woman Suffrage Association, 1922.

Hostetler, Lana. "From Our President, Scuds, Sorties, and Yellow Ribbons: The Costs of War for Children." *Young Children* 46 (3) (March 1991): 2.

Howlett, Charles F. *Troubled Philosopher: John Dewey and the Struggle for World Peace*. Port Washington, NY: Kennikat Press, 1977.

————. "The Pragmatist as Pacifist: John Dewey's Views on Peace Education." *Teachers College Record* 83 (Spring 1982):448.

Impact of the Vietnam War. Senate Committee on Foreign Relations, Congressional Research Service, Foreign Affairs Division, June 30, 1971.

Inglis, Fred. *The Cruel Peace, Everyday Life in the Cold War*. New York: Basic Books, 1991.

International Conference on Expanding Dimensions of World Education Proceedings, Ankara, Turkey. Edited by Nasrine Adibe and Frank A. Stone. Storrs, CT: University of Connecticut, World Education Project, 1976.

Irving, David. *Göring: A Biography*. New York: William Morrow and Company, Inc., 1989.

Iversen, Robert W. *The Communists and the Schools*. New York: Harcourt, Brace and World, 1959.

Jacobs, Ida T., and John J. DeBoer, eds. *Educating for Peace: A Report of the Committee on International Relations of the National Council of Teachers of English*. New York: D. Appleton-Century Company, 1940.

Jacobson, Harold, ed. *Biographical Dictionary of Modern Peace Leaders*. Westport, CT: Greenwood Press, 1983.

Jacobson, Robert L. "Center in Geneva Builds an Unusual Library on Higher Education but Funds Are Limited." *Chronicle of Higher Education*, 25 January 1989, 35:A38.

Jaffe, Louis. " 'American Education and International Tensions (1949)'." *Harvard Educational Review* 20 (Winter 1950):1–10.

Jewish Peace Fellowship. Descriptive Literature. Nyack, NY: Jewish Peace Fellowship, 1988.

———. Literature on Pamphlets, Articles and Books. Nyack, NY: Jewish Peace Fellowship, 1988.

John Dewey Society. *Education for a World Society: Promising Practices Today. Eleventh Yearbook.* New York: Harper & Brothers, 1951.

———. *The Public Schools and Spiritual Values. Seventh Yearbook.* New York: Harper & Brothers, 1944.

———. Commission on Small Books. *Teaching World Affairs in American Schools: A Case Book.* New York: Harper & Brothers, 1956.

Johnson, David W., and Roger T Johnson. *Creative Conflict.* Edina, MN: Interaction Book Company, 1987.

Johnson, David W., and Roger T. Johnson, et al. *Circles of Learning.* Alexandria, VA: Association for Supervision and Curriculum Development, 1984.

Johnson, Roy E. "Scriptotherapy: A Technique for Conflict Resolution," Ph.D. diss., Walden University, 1983, ERIC document 244 205.

Johnston, Bertha. "To Exercise the Heroic Impulses: A Substitute for Military Drill." *The Kindergarten-Primary Magazine* 24 (April 1912):220–222.

Jordan, David Starr. "Our Blighted Race." *Journal of Education* 82 (9 September 1915):213.

———. *Towards an Enduring Peace: Symposium of Peace Proposals and Programs, 1914–1916.* New York: American Association for International Conciliation, 1916.

————. *Ways to Lasting Peace.* Indianapolis: Bobbs-Merrill, 1916.

Jordan, Elizabeth, *War's End: In Time of War, Prepare for Peace.* Greensburg, PA: King-Murphy, 1940.

Josephson, Harold, ed. *Biographical Dictionary of Modern Peace Leaders.* Westport, CT: Greenwood Press, 1983.

Judson, Stephanie, ed. *A Manual on Nonviolence and Children.* Philadelphia: Committee on Nonviolence and Children, Philadelphia Yearly Meeting, Religious Society of Friends. Philadelphia: New Society Publishers, 1977.

Kaestle, Carl. The Evolution of an Urban System: New York City, 1750–1850. Ph.D. diss., Harvard University, 1970.

Katz, Michael. *Class, Bureaucracy and Schools: The Illusion of Change in America.* New York: Praeger, 1971.

Kavaloski, Vincent C. "Transnational Citizen Peacemaking as Nonviolent Action." *Peace and Change* 15 (April 1990):173–193.

Kearney, N. C., and W. W. Cook. "Curriculum." *Business Review* 36 (1958):23–30 in *1985 ASCD Yearbook: Current Thought on Curriculum.* Alexandria, VA: Association for Supervision and Curriculum Development, 1985.

Keen, Sam. *Faces of the Enemy: Reflections of the Hostile Imagination.* New York: Harper & Row, 1986.

Kelly, Frank K. *The United States Academy of Peace: A Long Step Toward Real Security.* Washington, DC: National Peace Academy Foundation, 1983.

Kelman, Herbert C. and V. Lee Hamilton. *Crimes of Obedience: Toward A Social Psychology of Authority and Responsibility.* New Haven: Yale University Press, 1989.

Kenworthy, Leonard. "Accepting the Selves of Others: People Around the World." *Childhood Education* 41 (March 1965):333–338.

———. In *Education for a World Society: Promising Practices Today. Eleventh Yearbook.* The John Dewey Society. New York: Harper & Brothers, 1951.

———. "International Dimensions of Elementary Schools." *Phi Delta Kappan* 49 (December 1967):203–207.

———. *Introducing Children to the World in the Elementary and Junior High Schools.* New York: Harper & Brothers, 1956.

———. "Studying Other Countries." *Social Education* 23 (April 1959).

———. "Teaching about the World: Secondary." *Educational Leadership* 21 (March 1964):358–360.

———. *Twelve Trailblazers of World Community.* Kennett Square, PA: The Friendly Press, 1988.

Kimmel, Paul. In Cordes, Colleen, "U.S. Peace Institute Created." *American Psychological Association Monitor* (November 1984):7.

King Center (Martin Luther King Jr. Center for Nonviolent Social Change). Descriptive Literature. Atlanta: King Center, 1989.

King, David C. "Delay Persists in Social Studies Reform but Signs Point to Headway Just Ahead." *ASCD Curriculum Update.* Alexandria, VA, August 1987. ERIC document 287 272.

———. *Education for a World in Change: A Report.* New York: Global Perspectives in Education, Inc., 1980.

———. *International Education for Spaceship Earth.* New York: Thomas Y. Crowell, 1971.

King, David C., Jay L. Weisman, and Ronald Wheeler. *Environments*. New York: American Book Company, 1979.

Kinghorn, Jon Rye, ed. *Clinical Workshop for School Improvement*. Dayton, OH: Commission on Schools, North Central Association of Schools and Colleges and the Charles F. Kettering Foundation, 1982.

————. *Guide to Four Essential Themes—Global Realities*. Dayton, OH: Commission on Schools, North Central Association and the Charles F. Kettering Foundation, 1982.

————. *Implementation Guide*. Dayton, OH: Commission on Schools, North Central Association and the Charles F. Kettering Foundation, 1982.

Kniep, Willard M. "Social Studies within a Global Education." *Social Education* 50 (November/December 1986):536–542.

————. "Global Education as School Reform." *Educational Leadership* 46 (September 1989):43–45.

Koch, Moses S. and Suzanne Miller. "Resolving Student Conflicts with Student Mediators." *Principal* 66 (March 1987):59–61.

Kohn, Alfie. *No Contest: The Case Against Competition*. Boston: Houghton Mifflin, 1986.

————. *The Brighter Side of Human Nature: Altruism and Empathy in Everyday Life*. New York: Basic Books, 1990.

Kownacki, Sister Mary Lou. *Let Peace Begin with Me: Peace Book and Teacher Guide*. Erie, PA: Pax Center, 1983.

Kreidler, William J. *Creative Conflict Resolution: More Than 200 Activities for Keeping Peace in the Classroom, K-6*. Glenview, IL: Scott Foresman, 1984.

La Farge, Phyllis. "Nuclear Education: Propaganda or Problem Solving." *Bulletin of the Atomic Scientists* 44 (July/August 1988):16.

————. *Strangelove Legacy*. New York: Harper & Row, 1987.

Lafayette, Bernard, Jr. Pedagogy for Peace and Nonviolence: A Critical Analysis of Peace and Nonviolence Studies Programs on College Compuses in the Northeastern U.S.A. Ph.D. diss., Harvard University, 1974.

LaFeber, Walter. *The American Age: United States Foreign Policy at Home and Abroad Since 1750*. New York: W. W. Norton & Company, 1989.

Lake Mohonk Conferences on International Arbitration, 1895–1916. Edited by Lawrence M. Haughton. New York: Lake Mohonk Conferences. New York: Clearwater Publishing, 1976. Micro-opaque.

Landmarks in International Co-Operation. New York: United Nations, Office of Public Information, 1965.

Larson, Arthur, ed. *A Warless World*. New York: McGraw-Hill, 1963.

Laszlo, Ervin, and Jong Y. Yoo, eds. *World Encyclopedia of Peace*. Vols. 1 and 2. New York: Pergamon Press.

Latham, E. V. "The Use of Current Events in the Study of Historical Geography." *Proceedings of the High School Conference,* University of Illinois. Urbana, IL: University of Illinois, 1914.

Lawson, David C. Swords into Plowshares, Spears into Pruning-hooks: The Intellectual Foundations of the First American Peace Movement, 1815–1865. Ph.D. diss., Albuquerque, New Mexico, University of New Mexico, 1975.

Lease, Mary Elizabeth. "Synopsis of 'Peace'." In *The Congress of Women,* edited by Mary Kavanaugh Oldham Eagle. Chicago: American Publishing House, 1894. Reprint. New York: Arno Press, 1974.

Lefever, Ernest W. "Teaching History and Politics in the Age of Nuclear Arms." *Phi Delta Kappan* 66 (November 1985):217–218.

Lentz, Theodore F. *Towards a Science of Peace: Turning Point in Human Destiny.* New York: Bookman Associates, Inc., 1955.

Lewin, Kurt. *Resolving Social Conflicts: Selected Papers on Group Dynamics.* New York: Harper & Row, 1948.

Leys, Wayne A. R., and P. S. S. Rama Rao. *Gandhi and America's Educational Future.* Carbondale and Edwardsville, IL: Southern Illinois University Press, 1969.

Lifton, Robert J. "Beyond Psychic Numbing: A Call to Awareness." *American Journal of Orthopsychiatry* 52 (1982):619–629.

———. *Home from the War.* New York: Simon and Schuster, 1973.

Lingo, W. R. "World Peace Through Education with Text of Plan." *Education Review* 70 (October 1925):128–133.

Lobingier, Elizabeth M., and John L. Lobingier. *Educating for Peace.* Boston: Pilgrim Press, 1930.

Lodge, Henry Cabot. "Atlantic Institute and the Future of the Free World." *National Association of Secondary School Principals Bulletin* 47 (April 1963):92–97.

Loeb, Paul R. *Hope in Hard Times.* Lexington, MA: Lexington Books, 1987.

Lofland, John, Victoria L. Johnson, and Pamela Kato. *Peace Movement Organizations and Activities in the U.S.: An Analytic Bibliography.* Binghamton, NY: Haworth Press, 1991.

London, Herbert I. *Why Are They Lying To Our Children?* New York: Stein and Day, 1984.

Long, Harold M., and Robert N. King. *Improving the Teaching of World Affairs: The Glens Falls Story.* Washington, DC: National Council for the Social Studies, 1964.

Looney, John. *Alternatives to Violence.* Descriptive literature. Akron, OH: Peace Grows, 1988.

Lowe, Boutelle Ellswood. *International Education for Peace.* Brooklyn, NY: F. Weidner Publishing, 1929.

Lundgren, Ulf. P. "Curriculum from a Global Perspective." In *1985 ASCD Yearbook: Current Thought on Curriculum.* Alexandria, VA: Association for Supervision and Curriculum Development, 1985.

Luria, Alexander R. *The Neuropsychology of Memory.* Washington, DC: V. H. Winston & Sons, 1976.

———. *The Working Brain: An Introduction to Neuropsychology.* London: Penguin Press, 1973.

Lusk Commission. *Revolutionary Radicalism: Its History, Purpose and Tactics with an Exposition and Discussion of the Steps Being Taken and Required to Curb It Being the Report of the Joint Legislative Committee (of New York State) Investigating Seditious Activities.* Albany, NY: J. B. Lyon, 1920.

Lynd, Staughton. "The Freedom Schools: Concept and Organization." In *The New Left: A Documentary History,* edited by Massimo Teodori. Indianapolis, IN: Bobbs-Merrill, 1969:102–111.

McAdam, Doug. "The Biographical Consequences of Activism," *American Sociological Review* 54 (October 1989):744–760.

———. *Freedom Summer*. New York: Oxford University Press, 1988.

———. "Gender as a Mediator of the Activist Experience: The Case of Freedom Summer." *American Journal of Sociology* 97 (March 1992), 1211–40.

———. Recruitment to High-Risk Activism: The Case of Freedom Summer," *American Journal of Sociology* 92 (1986), 64–90.

McCulloch, Catherine Waugh. Illinois Friends of Woman Suffrage. Notebook. Evanston, IL: Northwestern University Woman's Library, 1943.

Macdonald, Sharon, et al., eds. *Images of Women in Peace and War: Cross-Cultural and Historical Perspectives*. Madison: University of Wisconsin Press, 1987.

McFarland, Mary. "Japan as a Focus Culture for Global Education." *The Social Studies* 73 (July/August 1982):165.

McGinnis, James B. *Bread and Justice: Toward a New International Economic Order*. New York: Paulist Press, 1979.

McGinnis, James and Kathleen McGinnis, et al. *Educating for Peace and Justice*. Vol. I, II, III, and IV. St. Louis, MO: Institute for Peace and Justice, 1981 and 1985.

———. *Parenting for Peace and Justice*. Maryknoll, NY: Orbis Books, 1981.

———. *Peace Puppets and Global Family Puppets*. Videotapes with Guidebook. St. Louis, MO: Institute for Peace and Justice, 1987.

McGinnis, Kathleen, and Barbara Oehlberg. *Starting Out Right: Nurturing Young Children as Peacemakers*. Oak Park, IL: Meyer & Stone Books, 1988.

Mack, John E. "Psychosocial Effect of the Nuclear Arms Race." *Bulletin of the Atomic Scientists* 37 (1981):18–23.

———. "Resistances To Knowing in the Nuclear Age." *Harvard Education Review* 54 (August 1984):266.

Mack, John E., and Sybille Escalona, "Children and the Threat of Nuclear War." In *Behavioral Science and Human Survival,* edited by M. Schwebel. Palo Alto, CA: Science and Behavior Books, 1965.

MacLeish, Kenneth. Letter. Private printing, 1919 by Archibald MacLeish. Rockford, IL: Archives, Rockford College.

McMurry, Charles A. *Pioneer History Stories.* Winona, MN: Jones & Kroeger, 1891.

———. Primary source materials collection. DeKalb, IL: Archives, Northern Illinois University.

———. *Special Method for History and Literature in the Common Schools.* Bloomington, IL: Public School Publishing, 1893.

McNett, I. *Demographic Imperatives: Implications for Educational Policy.* Washington, DC: American Council on Education, 1983.

Magner, Denise K. "Blacks and Whites on the Campuses: Behind Ugly Racist Incidents, Student Isolation and Insensitivity." *Chronicle of Higher Education,* 26 April 1989:35.

Magruder, Frank Abbott. *National Governments and International Relations.* Boston: Allyn and Bacon, Inc., 1943.

Maheu, Robert. "UNESCO Is Your Organization." *National Education Association Journal* 54 (March 1965):30.

Mann, Horace. *Lectures on Education.* Boston: Ide & Dutton, 1855.

Marchand, C. Roland. *The American Peace Movement and Social Reform, 1898–1918.* Princeton: Princeton University Press, 1972.

Marks, Stephen. "Peace, Development, Disarmament and Human Rights Education: The Dilemma Between the Status Quo and Curriculum Overload." *International Review of Education* 28 (1983):289–310.

Markusen, Eric, and John B. Harris. "The Role of Education in Preventing Nuclear War." *Harvard Educational Review* 54 (August 1984):302.

Masiclat, Stephen M. "Teaching Ethics," *Phi Delta Kappan* 68 (December 1987):276.

Mastrude, Peggy. "Terra II: A Spaceship Earth Simulation for the Middle Grades." *Intercom* (1971):13–67.

Matriano, Estela C. In *Peace Education and the Task for Educators,* edited by Terry Carson and Hendrik D. Gideonse. Bloomington, IN: World Council for Curriculum and Instruction, 1987, 1–2.

May, Mark. *A Social Psychology of War and Peace.* New Haven: Yale University Press, 1943.

Mead, Edwin, "Heroes of Peace." *The Outlook* (14 November 1908):577–582.

———. "The Teaching of Peace." *The Outook* 83 (16 June 1906):355–357.

Mead, Lucia Ames. *Law or War.* Garden City, NY: Doubleday, Doran & Co., 1928.

———. *Great Thoughts for Little Thinkers.* New York: G. P. Putnam's Sons, 1889.

————. "How Schools Should Instill Patriotism." *Journal of Education* 80 (July 9, 1914).

————. *Memoirs of a Millionaire.* Boston: Houghton Mifflin, 1889.

————. *Milton's England.* Boston: L. C. Page & Co., 1903.

————. *Patriotism and the New Internationalism.* Boston: Ginn & Co., 1906.

————. "Practical Suggestions for Peace Day." *Journal of Education* (May 7, 1914).

————. *Primer of the Peace Movement.* Boston: American Peace Society, 1904.

————. *Swords or Plowshares.* New York: G. P. Putnam's Sons, 1912.

————. *To Whom Much Is Given.* New York: Thomas Y. Crowell, 1899.

Mehr, Helen M. "What Can I Do for Peace & Social Justice as a Psychologist?" *Division 48 Newsletter,* the Division of Peace Psychology of the American Psychological Association 1 (2) (April 1991):11.

Meikeljohn, Alexander. *Education Between Two Worlds.* New York: Harper & Brothers, 1942.

Meisels, Samuel J. "Uses and Abuses of Developmental Screening and School Readiness Testing," *Young Children* 42 (January 1987):4–9.

Mendes, H. Pereira. "The Solution of War." *North American Review* 161 (August 1895):161–169.

Mendlovitz, Saul H. "Teaching War Prevention" *Bulletin of the Atomic Scientists* (February 1964), and *Social Education* 28 (October 1964):328–330.

Mendlovitz, Saul H., and Betty Reardon. "World Law and Models of World Order." National Council for the Social Studies. *Thirty-Eighth Yearbook.* Washington, DC: National Council for the Social Studies, 1968:160–170.

———. "World Law Fund: World Approach to International Education." *Teachers College Record* 68 (May 1967):453–465.

Mennonite Central Committee. Resource Catalog, 1987–1988. Akron, PA: Mennonite Central Committee, 1987.

Mennonite Conciliation Service. *Conciliation Quarterly Newsletter.* Akron, PA: Mennonite Central Committee, 1989.

Merryfield, Mary. "Evaluating Global Education Projects: A Case for Naturalistic Methodology." National Conference on Professional Priorities—Shaping the Future of Global Education, Easton, MD, May 1982.

Meyer, Annie Nathan. "Woman's Place in Letters." In *The Congress of Women,* edited by Mary Kavanaugh Oldham Eagle. Chicago: American Publishing House, 1894. Reprint. New York: Arno Press, 1974.

Meyer, Frank. *Moulding of Communists.* New York: Harcourt, Brace, and World, 1961.

Michigan Department of Education. *Guidelines for Global Education.* Lansing, MI: Michigan Department of Education, 1983.

Milgram, Stanley. *Obedience to Authority: An Experimental View.* New York: Harper & Row, 1974.

Milwaukee Public Schools. "Resolution on Issues Related to Peace Education, 19 April 1983." ERIC document 256 683.

Mindscape Corporation. Software Catalog. Northbrook, IL: Mindscape Educational Division, 1989.

Mische, Gerald and Patricia. *Toward a Human World Order.* New York: Paulist Press, 1977.

Molnar, Alex. "Nuclear Policy in a Democracy: Do Educators Have a Choice?" *Educational Leadership* 40 (May 1983):38.

Montessori, Maria. *Education and Peace.* Chicago: Henry Regnery, 1972.

Moore, Eoline W. "Are We Educating for Peace?" *School and Society* 70 (24 December 1949):425–426.

Morehouse, Ward. *A New Civic Literacy: American Education and Global Interdependence.* Princeton: Aspen Institute for Humanistic Studies, 1975.

Morison, Samuel E., and Henry Steele Commager. *The Growth of the American Republic.* New York: Oxford University Press, 1950.

Murray, Mary. *History of the United States of America. Written in Accordance with the Principles of Peace.* Boston: Benjamin B. Mussey & Co., Inc., 1852.

Murray, Robert K. "Communism and the Great Steel Strike of 1919." *Mississippi Valley Historical Review* 38 (1951):445–466.

Nagler, Michael. "Nonviolence." In *World Encyclopedia of Peace, Vol. 2,* edited by Ernest Lazlo. New York: Pergamon Press, 1986:72–77.

National Association for Mediation in Education. *The Fourth R* (Newsletter). Amherst, MA: National Association for Mediation in Education, Fall 1987.

National Association for Multicultural Education. "Founding Statement, Goals, and Objectives." Baton Rouge, LA: National Association for Multicultural Education, 1990.

National Commission on Excellence in Education. *A Nation at Risk: The Imperative for Educational Reform.* Washington, DC: United States Department of Education, 1983.

―――. "Revision of the NCSS Social Studies Curriculum Guidelines." *Social Education* 43 (April 1979):261–278.

――― "Social Studies for Early Childhood and Elementary School Children Preparing for the 21st Century: A Report from NCSS Task Force on Early Childhood/Elementary Social Studies." *Social Education* 53 (January 1989):14–23.

National Council of Teachers of English. *Educating for Peace.* Edited by Ida T. Jacobs and John J. DeBoer. New York: D. Appleton-Century Company, 1940.

National Education Association. *Addresses and Proceedings, Detroit Meeting, 30 June–5 July 1963.* Washington, DC: National Education Association, 1963.

National Education Association. Department of Superintendence. *Character Education. Tenth Yearbook.* Washington, DC: National Education Association, 1932.

―――. Department of Superintendence. *Bulletin.* Cincinnati Meetings, 24–26 February 1915. Washington, DC: National Education Association, 1915.

―――. *Social Change and Education. Thirteenth Yearbook.* Washington, DC: National Education Association, 1935.

―――. National Elementary Principal. *Spiritual Values in the Elementary School. Twenty-Sixth Yearbook.* Washington, DC: Department of Elementary School Principals, National Education Association, 1947.

(National) Herbart Society. *First Yearbook*. Denver Meeting, 1895. Edited by Charles A. McMurry. Chicago: University of Chicago Press, 1907.

National Herbart Society for the Scientific Study of Teaching, *Fourth Yearbook*. *Washington Meeting, 1898*. Edited by Charles A. McMurry. Chicago: University of Chicago Press, 1898.

National Peace Institute Foundation. (Now the National Peace Foundation). Descriptive literature. Washington, DC.: National Peace Institute Foundation, 1989.

National Security League. *Proceedings of the Congress of Constructive Patriotism*. Washington, DC: National Security League, 1917.

National Society for Internships and Experiential Education. Descriptive Literature. Raleigh, NC: National Society for Internships and Experiential Education, 1989.

National Society for the Scientific Study of Education. *The First Yearbook*. Including "Some Principles in the Teaching of History" by Lucy Maynard Salmon. Edited by Charles A. McMurry. Chicago Meeting, 27 February 1902. Chicago: University of Chicago Press, 1902.

———. *Fourth Yearbook*. Washington Meeting of the National Education Association. Chicago: University of Chicago Press, 1902.

———. *Course of Study in the Common School. Part I. Second Yearbook*. Cincinnati Meeting, 25 February 1903. Chicago: University of Chicago Press, 1903.

National Society for the Study of Education. *Second Report of the Society's Committee on New Materials of Instruction. Twentieth Yearbook*. Atlantic City Meeting, 26 February 1921. Bloomington, IL: Public School Publishing Company, 1921.

————. *The Social Studies in the Elementary and Secondary School. Part II. Twenty-Second Yearbook.* Cleveland Meeting, 27 February 1923. Bloomington, IL: Public School Publishing Company, 1923.

————. *Extra-Curricular Activities. Twenty-Fifth Yearbook. Part II.* Bloomington, IL: Public School Publishing Company, 1926.

————. *International Understanding Through the Public-School Curriculum. Part I and Part II. Thirty-Sixth Yearbook.* Bloomington, IL: Public School Publishing Company, 1937.

————. *Education and the Brain. Seventy-Seventh Yearbook.* Chicago: University of Chicago Press, 1978.

Neve, Charmaine D., Leslie A. Hart, and Edgar C. Thomas. "Huge Learning Jumps Show Potency of Brain-Based Instruction." *Phi Delta Kappan* 68 (October 1986):143–148.

Newcombe, Alan and Hannah. *Peace Research Around the World.* Oakville, Ontario: Canadian Peace Research Institute, 1969.

"New Computerized World Information Service (NCWIS)," Geneva, Switzerland: Press Release #2, NCWIS, 13 May 1989.

Nordholt, Jan. *Woodrow Wilson: A Life for Peace.* Berkeley, CA: University of California Press, 1991.

Norstad, Lauris. "NATO Problem." *American Association of School Administrators' Official Report* (1966). Washington, DC: American Association of School Administrators, 1966.

North Central Association and the Charles F. Kettering Foundation Commission on Schools. *Implementation Guide.* Dayton, OH: Charles F. Kettering Foundation, 1982.

————. *A Guide to Four Essential Themes—Global Realities.* Dayton, OH: Charles F. Kettering Foundation, 1982.

Novak, Michael. *The Spirit of Democratic Capitalism.* New York: Simon and Schuster, 1983 and Lanham, MD: University Press of America, 1991.

Nuclear Age: A Curriculum Guide for Secondary Schools. Washington, DC: Ground Zero, 1983.

"Nuclear Bomb Shelter in Plans for New Schools at Federal Expense." *Nation's Schools* 68 (November 1961):68–74.

"Nuclear War Becomes Hot Topic in Schools, Stirs Up Controversy." *Wall Street Journal,* 24 May 1983.

Nye, Gerald P. "Educating for War or Peace?" *Progressive Education* (May 1935):309–314.

Oakes, Jeannie. "Keeping Track, Part 2: Curriculum Inequality and School Reform." *Phi Delta Kappan* 67 (October 1986):150–151.

O'Keefe, Bernard. *Nuclear Hostages.* Boston: Houghton Mifflin, 1983.

Oneal, James, and G. A. Werner. *American Communism: A Critical Analysis of Its Origins, Development and Prophecies.* New York: E. P. Dutton, 1947.

O'Shea, M. D. "Ecumenism and Education for Peace." *Religious Education Journal* 62 (March 1967):169.

Parenti, Michael. *The Anti-Communist Impulse.* New York: Random House, 1969.

Parents and Teachers for Social Responsibility. Descriptive Literature. Moretown, VT: Parents and Teachers for Social Responsibility, 1988.

———. *Yopp!* Newsletter. Moretown, VT: Parents and Teachers for Social Responsibility, 1988.

Paringer, John. *John Dewey and the Paradox of Liberal Reform.* Albany, NY: State University of New York Press, 1990.

Parkinson, Henry J. *The Imperfect Panacea: American Faith in Education, 1765–1965.* New York: Random House, 1968.

Parkinson, W. D. "Public School and Military Drill." *Journal of Education* 82 (11 November 1915):451–453.

Parrington, Vernon L. *Main Currents in American Thought: An Interpretation of American Literature from the Beginnings to 1920, Vol. Three: 1860–1920: Beginnings of Critical Realism in America.* New York: Harcourt, Brace, 1958, 31.

Passy, Frederic. "The Advance of the Peace Movement Throughout the World." *Review of Reviews* 17 (February 1898):183–188.

Patel, M. S. *The Educational Philosophy of Mahatma Gandhi.* Ahmedabad, India: Navajivan Publishing House, 1952.

Patterson, D. S. *Toward a Warless World: The Travail of the American Peace Movement, 1887–1914.* Bloomington, IN: Indiana University Press, 1980.

———. "Nicholas Murray Butler." In *Biographical Dictionary of Internationalists,* edited by Warren F. Kuehl. Westport, CT: Greenwood Press, 1983:495–496.

Pax Christi USA. Erie, PA: Pax Christi USA, Spring 1988.

Peace and War, edited by Richard Butchko, Robert Cummings, Linda Hornback, Mario Mazzarella, and Harvey Williams. Newport News, VA: Christopher Newport College, 1984.

Peace and World Order Studies: A Curriculum Guide, 1st ed. New York: Transnational Academic Program, Institute for World Order, 1973.

————. 2nd ed. New York: Institute for World Order, 1978.

————. 3rd ed. New York: Institute for World Order, 1981.

————. 4th ed. New York: Institute for World Order, 1985.

————. 5th ed. Boulder, CO: Westview Press, 1989. (Publication of the Five College Program in Peace and World Security Studies—PAWSS).

Peace Commission of Friends World Committee for Consultation. *Peace Study Outline: Problems of Applied Pacifism.* Philadelphia: Peace Commission of the Friends World Committee for Consultation, 1941.

Peace Institute Reporter. (Washington, DC: National Peace (Institute) Foundation, 1986–1990).

Peace Links. Descriptive Literature. Washington, DC: Peace Links, 1990.

PeaceNet Online Community. Descriptive Literature for an International Communications Network for Peace and Human Rights. San Francisco, CA: Institute for Global Communications Network, 1992.

Pellicano, Roy R. "Global Education: A Definition and a Curriculum Proposal." *Orbit* (1981):18.

Perrone, Vito. Introduction to "Vision of Peace Special Issue," *North Dakota Quarterly Press* (1988).

Perspectives: A Teaching Guide To Concepts of Peace. Cambridge, MA: Educators for Social Responsibility, 1983.

Peterson, Patti McGill. "Student Organizations and the Anti-War Movement in America, 1900–1960." In *Peace Movements in America,* edited by Charles Chatfield. New York: Schocken Books, 1973:122–123.

Pierce, Bessie L. *Civic Attitudes in American School Textbooks.* Chicago: University of Chicago Press, 1930.

————. *Citizens' Organizations and the Civic Training of Youth: Report on the Commission on the Social Studies, Part III.* New York: Charles Scribner's Sons, 1933.

Pierson, Ruth Roach. "Women in War, Peace and Revolution." In *Images of Women in Peace and War: Cross-Cultural and Historical Perspectives,* edited by Sharon Macdonald and others. Madison: University of Wisconsin Press, 1987.

Pine, Gerald J., and Asa G. Hilliard III. "Rx for Racism: Imperatives for America's Schools." *Phi Delta Kappan* 71 (April 1990):593–600.

"Planning a School Fallout Shelter." *American School Board Journal* 143 (November 1961):28.

Poling, Paul N. *Let Us Live for God and the Nations.* Philadelphia: Presbyterian Church in the United States, Board of Christian Education, 1951.

Presbyterian Church (USA). *The Things That Make For Peace . . . Begin with the Children.* New York: Presbyterian Church, Distribution Service, 1985.

Presbyterian Peace Fellowship. Descriptive Literature. New York: Presbyterian Peace Fellowship, 1987.

Presbyterian Peacemaking Program. Peacemaking Resource List. Louisville, KY: Presbyterian Peacemaking Program, 1988.

Price, Jerome. *The Antinuclear Movement.* Boston: Twayne Publishers, 1982.

Project for Global Education. *Organizing for Peace and World Order Studies: A Guide for Strategies and Methods.* New York: Institute for World Order, n.d.

Prutzman, Priscilla, and others. *The Friendly Classroom for a Small Planet: A Handbook on Creative Approaches To Living and Problem Solving for Children.* Wayne, NJ: Avery Publishing Group, 1978.

Radio for Peace International. Newsletter of RFPI. Eugene, OR: RFPI (July/August 1988).

————. General Information. Eugene, OR: RFPI, 1988.

————. Program Schedule for July/August. Eugene, OR: RFPI, 1988.

Rafter, Sandra J. An Historical/Philosophical Examination of the American Peace Movement and Its Implications for Education. Ph.D. diss., University of Iowa, Iowa City, Iowa, 1985.

Ravitch, Diane. *The Troubled Crusade: American Education, 1945–1980.* New York: Basic Books, 1983.

Ray, Larry and others. *Mediation in the Schools: A Report, Directory and Bibliography.* Washington, DC: American Bar Association, 1985.

Reardon, Betty. *Militarization, Security and Peace Education: A Guide for Concerned Citizens.* Valley Forge, PA: United Ministries in Education, 1982.

————. "World Law Fund: World Approach to International Education." *Teachers College Record* 68 (March 1967):453–465.

————. *Comprehensive Peace Education: Educating for Global Responsibility.* New York: Teachers College Press, 1988.

————. *Educating for Global Responsibility: Teacher-Designed Curricula for Peace Education, K–12.* New York: Teachers College Press, 1988.

——. "Peace as an Educational End and Process." In *Peace and World Order Studies: A Curriculum Guide,* edited by Burns J. Weston and others. New Brunswick, NJ: Transaction Books, 1978.

——. *Sexism and the War System.* New York: Teachers College Press, 1985.

——. "Transformations into Peace and Survival." In *Education for Peace: Focus on Mankind,* edited by George Henderson. Washington, DC: ASCD, 1973.

Reardon, Betty, and Willard Kneip, "Defining Global Education by Its Content." *Social Education* 50 (1986):437–446.

Reischauer, Edwin O. *Toward the 21st Century: Education for a Changing World.* New York: Knopf, 1973.

Report of the Commission on Proposals for the National Academy of Peace and Conflict Resolution to the President of the United States and the Senate and the House of Representatives of the United States Congress. Washington, DC: U.S. Government Printing Office, 1981.

Report of the Commission on Social Studies, Part I. A Charter for the Social Sciences in the Schools. Drafted by Charles E. Beard. New York: Charles Scribner's Sons, 1932.

Report on the Presidential Commission on Campus Unrest. New York: Avon, 1971.

Report on the Zurich Congress of the Women's International League for Peace and Freedom (1919). Reprint. Edited by John Whiteclay Chambers II, *The Eagle and the Dove.* New York: Garland Publishing, Inc., 1976.

Revoldt, Darryl. "Edwin Ginn." In *Biographical Dictionary of Internationalists,* edited by Warren F. Kuehl. Westport, CT: Greenwood Press, 1983.

————. "Lucia True Ames Mead." In *Biographical Dictionary of Internationalists,* edited by Warren F. Kuehl. Westport, CT: Greenwood Press, 1983.

————. "Edwin D. Mead." In *Biographical Dictionary of Internationalists,* edited by Warren F. Kuehl. Westport, CT: Greenwood Press, 1983.

Revolutionary Radicalism: Its History, Purpose and Tactics with an Exposition and Discussion of the Steps Being Taken and Required to Curb It Being the Report of the Joint Legislative Committee Investigating Seditious Activities. Albany, NY: J. B. Lyon, 1920.

Rhodes, Richard. *The Making of the Atomic Bomb.* New York: Simon and Schuster, 1986.

Ringler, Dick. "Towards the Practice of Nuclear-Age Education." *Bulletin of the Atomic Scientists* 37 (December 1984):4s.

Rippa, S. Alexander. *Education in a Free Society: An American History.* 4th ed. New York: Longman, 1980.

Rivage-Seul, Marguerite K. "Peace Education: Imagination and the Pedagogy of the Oppressed." *Harvard Educational Review* 57 (May 1987):153–169.

Rockford Seminary Magazine. Rockford, IL: Rockford Female Seminary (Rockford College), 1873–1881.

Rogers, Fred, and Hedda B Sharapan. "Helping Parents, Teachers, and Caregivers Deal with Children's Concerns About War." *Young Children* 46 (3) (March 1991):12–13.

Rogers, Lester B., Fay Adams, and Walker Brown. *The Story of Nations.* New York: Henry Holt and Company, 1934.

Rossiter, Clinton. *The View from America.* New York: Harcourt, Brace and World, 1960.

Roy, Ralph Lord. *Communism and the Churches.* New York: Harcourt, Brace and World, 1960.

Rubenstein, Robert A., and Mary L. Foster, eds. *Peace and War: Cross Cultural Perspectives.* New Brunswick, NJ: Transaction Books, 1985.

Rugg, Harold O. "Do the Social Studies Prepare Pupils Adequately for Life Activities?" In National Society for the Study of Education. *The Social Studies in the Elementary and Secondary School. Part II. Twenty-Second Yearbook.* Bloomington, IL: Public School Publishing, 1923.

Rusk, Dean. "Education for Citizenship in the Modern World." *American Association of School Administrators' Official Report.* Washington, DC, 1964:30–40.

———. "Our Concern for Peace in East Asia." *National Association of School Principals' Bulletin,* 52 (May 1968):3–13.

Salmon, Lucy Maynard. "Some Principles in the Teaching of History." *The First Yearbook,* edited by Charles A. McMurry. National Society for the Scientific Study of Education. Chicago: University of Chicago Press, 1902.

Samantha Smith Foundation. Descriptive Literature. Hallowell, Maine; Samantha Smith Foundation, 1988.

San Francisco Community Board Center for Policy and Training. *Classroom Conflict Resolution Training for Elementary Schools.* San Francisco: School Initiatives Program, San Francisco Community Board Center for Policy and Training, 1987.

———. *Conflict Resolution: A Secondary School Curriculum.* San Francisco: School Initiatives Program, 1987.

Scanlon, David G. "Pioneers of International Education, 1817–1914." *Teachers College Record,* 62 (January 1959):202–219.

Schell, Jonathan. *The Fate of the Earth.* New York: Alfred A. Knopf, 1982.

Schmidt, Fran and Alice Friedman. *Creative Conflict Solving for Kids.* Miami: Grace Contrino Abrams Peace Education Foundation, 1983.

———. *Fighting Fair: Dr. Martin Luther King, Jr. for Kids.* Miami: Grace Contrino Abrams Peace Education Foundation, 1986.

———. *Fighting Fair for Families.* Miami: Grace Contrino Abrams Peace Education Foundation, 1989.

———. *Peacemaking Skills for Little Kids.* Miami: Grace Contrino Abrams Peace Education Foundation, 1988.

Schoeer, Dietrich. "Teaching about the Arms Race." *Physics Today* 36 (March 1983):52–53.

Schoenbaum, Thomas J. *Waging Peace & War: Dean Rusk in the Truman, Kennedy & Johnson Years.* New York: Simon and Schuster, 1988.

Schwebel, M., ed. *Behavioral Science and Human Survival.* Palo Alto: Science and Behavior Books, 1965.

Scully, Malcolm B. "Telecast on Nuclear War Spurs Campus Activities." *Chronicle of Higher Education,* 30 November 1983:30, 3.

Second National Peace Congress. *Proceedings,* edited by Charles E. Beals. Boston: American Peace Society, 1909.

Shaler, N. S. "The Last Gift of the Century." *North American Review* 161 (December 1895):674–684.

Shalom Partners. DHM/Regional Agreement. Indianapolis, IN: Shalom Congregations, Division of Homeland Ministries, 1986.

————. Suggestions for Implementation. Indianapolis, IN: Shalom Congregations, 1988.

Shannon, David A. *Decline of American Communism*. New York: Harcourt, Brace, and World, 1959.

Sharp, Gene. *The Politics of Nonviolent Action*. Boston: Porter Sargent, 1973.

————. "Notes and Comment" (Gene Sharp). Talk of the Town, *New Yorker* (December 12, 1983):43–44.

————. In Ellen K. Coughlin, "In Cold War's Waning, Peace Researchers See Vindication of Their Work." *Chronicle of Higher Education*, 4 April 1990, 36:A6 + .

Shevardnadze, Eduard. *The Future Belongs to Freedom,* trans. by Catherine A. Fitzpatrick. New York: The Free Press (Macmillan), 1991.

Sibley, Malcolm. *The Quiet Battle: Writings on the Theory and Practice of Non-violent Resistance*. New York: Doubleday, 1963.

Sivard, Ruth Leger. *World Military and Social Expenditures*. Leesburg, VA: World Priorities, Inc., 1974–1990.

Sizer, Theodore. *Horace's Compromise*. Boston: Houghton Mifflin, 1984.

Skipping Stones. Cottage Grove, OR: Aprovecho Institute, 1989.

Slavin, Robert E. *Student Team Learning: An Overview and Practical Guide*. Washington, DC: National Education Association, 1983.

————. *Using Student Team Learning*. 3rd ed. Baltimore, MD: Center for Research on Elementary and Middle Schools, The Johns Hopkins University, 1986.

———. *Cooperative Learning.* New York: Longman, 1991.

Sloan, Douglas. "Education for Peace and Disarmament." *Teachers College Record* (Fall 1982):1.

———. *Insight-Imagination: The Emancipation of Thought and the Modern World.* Westport, CT: Greenwood Press, 1983.

———. "Toward an Education for a Living World." *Teachers College Record* 84 (Fall 1982):1–14.

Slye, Ronald C., and Saul H. Mendlovitz. "World Order." In *World Encyclopedia of Peace, Vol. 2,* edited by Ervin Laszlo. New York: Pergamon Press, 1986.

Smith, Clagett G., ed. *Conflict Resolution: Contributions of the Behavioral Sciences.* Notre Dame, IN: University of Notre Dame Press, 1971.

Smith, Franklin. "Peace as a Factor in Social and Political Reform." *Popular Science* 53 (June 1898):225–240.

Smith, Henry L. "Education for World Friendship and Understanding-Abstract." *Proceedings, Atlanta Meeting, 8 June–4 July 1929.* Washington, DC: National Education Association, 1929:231–237.

Smith, Henry L., and Sherman C. Crayton. *Tentative Program for Teaching World Friendship and Understanding in Teacher Training Institutions and in Public Schools for Children Who Range from Six to Fourteen Years of Age.* Bloomington, IN: Indiana University, Bureau of Cooperative Research, 1929.

Smith, Samantha Foundation. Descriptive Literature. Hallowell, ME: Samantha Smith Foundation, 1988.

Snow, Roberta. *Decisionmaking in a Nuclear Age.* 2nd ed. Cambridge, MA: Educators for Social Responsibility, 1983.

————. "A Decisionmaking Approach To Nuclear Education." *Harvard Educational Review* 54 (August 1984):321.

Social-Democratic Party. *Milwaukee Municipal Campaign Book, 1912.* Milwaukee: County Central Committee of the Social-Democratic Party, 1912.

Spencer, Miranda. "What Are We Teaching Our Kids?: Nuclear-age Educators Say They Want Children To Think Critically." *Nuclear Times* (September/October 1988):17–20.

Staff Study of Campus Riots and Disorders, October 1967, October 1968, May 1969 (U.S. Senate Government Operations Committee). Washington, DC: U.S. Government Printing Office, 1969.

Staff Study of Major Riots and Civil Disorders, 1965–July 31, 1968 (U.S. Senate Government Operations Committee). Washington, DC: U.S. Government Printing Office, October 1968.

Stanford, Barbara. *Peacemaking: A Guide to Conflict Resolution for Individuals, Groups and Nations.* New York: Bantam Books, 1976.

————. "Thinking Beyond the Limits." *Peace and Change* (Summer 1984):5.

Stave, Bruce M. *Socialism and the Cities.* Port Washington, NY: Kennikat Press, 1975.

Stead, W. T. "Internationalism as an Ideal for the Youth of America," *The Chautauquan,* LIV (May 1909):333–337. Reprint. In *The Eagle and the Dove,* edited by John Whiteclay Chambers II. New York: Garland Publishing, 1976.

Sterling, Dorothy. *Ahead of Her Time: Abby Kelley and the Politics of Antislavery.* New York: W. W. Norton & Co., 1991.

Sternsher, Bernard. *Consensus, Conflict and American History.* Bloomington, IN: Indiana University Press, 1975.

Stewart, Grace Hull and C. C. Hanna. *Adventures in Citizenship: Literature for Character.* Boston: Ginn and Company, 1928.

Student Forum on International Order and World Peace. *Studies Toward Peace: A Compendium of Selected Undergraduate and Graduate Courses in "Peace and World Order."* New York: Student Forum on International Order and World Peace, 1969.

Studies Toward Peace: A Compendium of Selected Undergraduate and Graduate Courses in "Peace and World Order." New York: Student Forum on International Order and World Peace, 1969.

Sumner, Charles. "The True Grandeur of Nations." In *Beacon Lights of Patriotism,* edited by Henry B. Carrington. New York: Silver and Burdett, 1894.

Sutherland, Elizabeth, ed. Letters from Mississippi. New York: McGraw-Hill, 1965.

Süttner, Bertha von. "Universal Peace--From a Woman's Standpoint." *North American Review* 169 (July 1899):50–61.

Talbott, Guy. *Essential Conditions of Peace.* Gardene, CA: Institute Press, 1938.

Teaching World Affairs in American Schools: A Case Book, edited by Samuel Everett. New York: Harper & Brothers, 1956.

Teodori, Massimo, ed. *The New Left: A Documentary History.* Indianapolis: Bobbs-Merrill, 1969.

Tephly, Joan. "Young Children's Understanding of War and Peace." *Early Child Development and Care* 20 (1985):272–285.

Theoharis, Athan. *Spying on Americans*. Philadephia: Temple University Press, 1978.

Thernstrom, Stephen, ed. *Harvard Encyclopedia of American Ethnic Groups*. Cambridge, MA: Harvard University Press, 1980.

Thomas, Daniel C. *Guide to Careers and Graduate Education in Peace Studies*. 1st ed. Amherst, MA: Five College Program in Peace and World Security Studies, 1987.

Thomas, Helen. "Reagan Has Nominated No Women To the U.S. Peace Institute." *St. Petersburg Times,* 25 January 1986.

Tiegs, Ernest W. and Fay Adams. *Teaching the Social Studies: A Guide To Better Citizenship*. New York: Ginn & Company, 1959.

Timm, Vera L. *Spare the Rod! Violence and Your Child*. Dayton, OH: author, 1977.

To Establish the United States Academy of Peace: Report of the Commission on Proposals for the National Academy of Peace and Conflict Resolution to the President of the United States and the Senate and House of Representatives of the United States Congress. Washington, DC: U.S. Government Printing Office, 1981.

Tolley, Howard, Jr. *Children and War: Political Socialization to International Conflict*. New York: Teachers College Press, 1973.

Tom Snyder Productions. Education Software Catalog. Cambridge: Tom Snyder Productions, 1988, 1990.

Torney, Judith V. "Middle Childhood and International Education." *Intercom* (1971):5–12.

Towards an Enduring Peace: A Symposium of Peace Proposals and Programs, 1914–1916. New York: American Association for International Conciliation, 1916.

Townsend, Lucy F. *The Best Helpers of One Another: Anna Peck Sill and the Struggle for Woman's Education.* Chicago: Educational Studies Press, 1988.

Traprock Peace Center. Descriptive Literature. Deerfield, MA: Traprock Peace Center, 1988.

————. *Peace Lessons* newsletter (April and July/August 1988). Deerfield, MA: Traprock Peace Center Education Program.

"TV's Atom War Spurs Vast Discussion." *New York Times,* 22 November 1983:Y11.

"TV's Nuclear Nightmare: Special Report." *Newsweek* (21 November 1983):66.

Tyack, David B. *The One Best System: A History of American Urban Education.* Cambridge, MA: Harvard University Press, 1974.

Tyler, Ralph. *Basic Principles of Curriculum and Instruction.* Chicago: University of Chicago Press, 1949.

United Church of Christ. *Peace Futuring.* New York: Office for Church in Society, United Church of Christ, 1982.

United Methodist Council of Bishops. *In Defense of Creation: The Nuclear Crisis and Just Peace, Foundation Document.* Nashville, TN: Graded Press, 1986.

United Nations Education and Scientific Organization. "World Congress on Disarmament Education," 9–13 June 1980. Paris: World Congress on Disarmament Education, 1980.

"U.S. and Soviets Cooperating on Environmental Issues." *Times-Picayune* (New Orleans), 13 January 1990.

U.S. Bureau of Education. *Peace Day Bulletin.* Washington, DC: U.S. Bureau of Education, 1912.

U.S. Congress. House. Subcommittee on Education of the Committee on Labor and Public Welfare. *George Washington Peace Academy Act, 1976.* Hearing, 94th Cong., 2nd sess., 13 May 1976. Washington, DC: U.S. Government Printing Office, 1976.

U.S. Congress. House. *Colonization of America's Basic Industries by the Communist Party of the U.S.A.,* 83rd Cong. 2nd sess., September 3, 1954.

———. *Communist Activities Among Aliens and National Groups, Hearings, Part I,* 81st Cong., 1st sess., 1950.

———. *Communist Activities Among Professional Groups in the Los Angeles Area, Hearings, Part I,* 82nd Cong., 2nd sess., 1952.

———. *The Communist Conspiracy: Strategy and Tactics of World Communism: Part I, Communism Outside the United States, Section E; The Comintern and the CPUSA (Communist Party of the United States of America). House Report No. 2244,* 84th Cong., 2nd sess., May 29, 1956.

———. *Investigation of Un-American Activities in the United States, Hearings, Vol. 7,* 76th Cong., 1st sess., 1939.

———. *Organized Communism in the United States. House Report No. 625,* 83rd Cong., 2nd sess., August 19, 1953.

———. *Special Committee To Investigate Communist Activities in the United States, Investigation of Communist Propaganda. Report No. 2290,* 71st Cong., 3rd sess., January 17, 1931.

———. Committee on Un-American Activities. *World Communist Movement: Selective Chronology, 1918–1957.* Published in three volumes, prepared by the Legislative Reference Service of the Library of Congress. Volume II: 1946–1950.

U.S. Congress. Senate. Committee on Foreign Relations. *Impact of the Vietnam War.* Congressional Research Service, Foreign Affairs Division, June 30, 1971.

U.S. News and World Report. "Communism and the New Left: What They're Up To Now." Washington, DC: *U.S. News and World Report,* 1969:30–31, 167.

United States Institute of Peace. Budget Request, Fiscal Year, 1989. Washington, DC: United States Institute of Peace, 1988.

———. Face-to-Face: Conversations on U.S.-Soviet Summitry. Descriptive Literature. Washington, DC: United States Institute of Peace, 1988.

———. Solicited Grants, 1988. Descriptive Literature. Washington, DC: United States Institute of Peace, 1988.

———. Update. Washington, DC: United States Institute of Peace, May 1988.

United States Institute of Peace. *Journal.* Vols. I, II, III, IV, and V (1988–1992). Washington, DC: United States Institute of Peace.

University for Peace. *Dialogue.* Newspaper. San Jose, Costa Rica: University for Peace, July 1987.

———. "University for Peace Recent Activities." *Dialogue.* San Jose, Costa Rica, July 1987, 7.

———. Natural Resources and the Promotion of Peace. Descriptive Literature. San Jose, Costa Rica: University for Peace, 1988.

———. "New Short Wave Radio Station at the University for Peace." *Dialogue,* San Jose, Costa Rica: University for Peace, July 1987, 7.

Utsumi, Takeshi. "Establishing a Global 'Electronic University,'" *Breakthrough* (Global Education Associates). Fall 1987/Spring 1988, 27–28.

Van Horn, Royal. "Laser Videodiscs in Education: Endless Possibilities." *Phi Delta Kappan* 68 (May 1987):696–700.

Van Voris, Jacqueline. *Carrie Chapman Catt: A Public Life.* New York: The Feminist Press at City University of New York, 1987.

Violence and the Violent Individual, edited by J. Ray Hays. New York: SP Medical and Scientific Books, 1980.

Violence in America: Historical and Comparative Perspectives. A Report to the National Commission on the Causes and Prevention of Violence. New York: Signet Books, 1969.

"Vision of Peace Special Issue," Introduction by Vito Perrone. *North Dakota Quarterly Press,* University of North Dakota, (1988).

Vocke, David E. "Those Varying Perspectives on Global Education," *The Social Studies* 79 (January/February 1988):18.

Vrooman, Harry C. "Ethics of Peace." *Arena* 11 (December 1894):118–127.

————. "The Abolition of War: A Symposium." *Arena* 23 (February 1895):138–144.

Vygotsky, Lev S. *Thought and Language.* Edited and translated by E. Haveman and G. Vakos. Cambridge, MA: M.I.T. Press, 1962.

Wagner, Anthony. "Why Nuclear Education?" *Educational Leadership* 40 (May 1983):40–41.

Warren, Austin. *The New England Conscience.* Ann Arbor, MI: University of Michigan Press, 1966.

Washburn, A. Michael. "Peace Education Is Alive: But Unsure of Itself." *Social Science Record* 9 (Winter 1972):61–68.

————. "The World Order Approach to Peace Education," Conference on Peace Research of the American Historical Association, August 26–27, 1972, edited by John Whiteclay Chambers II. Plattsburgh, NY: American Historical Association.

Watkins, Arthur. *America Stands for Pacific Means: A Book for Boys and Girls on the Principles and Practice of Social Cooperation.* Washington, DC: National Capitol Press, 1937.

Watkins, Beverly T. "Colleges Urged To Train Teachers To Deal with Expected Influx of Immigrants," *Chronicle of Higher Education,* 13 December 1989, 36:A41–42.

Watson, Goodwin. "Does World-Mindedness Depend upon Good-Will or Information? Upon Character or Intelligence?" *Religious Education* 21 (1926):188–194.

"W.C.O.T.P. and UNESCO: Close Consultation Planned." *Times Educational Supplement,* 2568 (7 August 1965):200.

"W.C.O.T.P. and UNESCO Is Your Organization." *National Education Association Journal,* 54 (March 1965):30.

Wehr, Paul and A. Michael Washburn. *Peace and World Order Systems:* Teaching and Research. Beverly Hills: Sage Publications, 1976.

Weinstein, James. *Ambiguous Legacy: The Left in American Politics.* New York: New Viewpoints, 1975.

Weiser, Margaret. "Childhood in a World of Tensions: 1985 World Council Meeting of OMEP." *OMEP Journal* (Organisation Mondiale pour l'Education Préscolaire) (November/ December 1985):87–90.

Werner, Paul D. and Paul J. Roy. "Measuring Activism Regarding the Nuclear Arms Race." *Journal of Personality Assessment* 49 (1985):181–186.

Westmoreland, William. "Address to the American Association of School Administrators." Washington, DC: American Association of School Administrators, 1969.

"When Imagination Defies Television: 'The Day After' Effect." ERIC document ED 257 764.

White, Charles S. "Teachers Using Technology." *Social Education* 51 (January 1987):44–47.

"Why Nuclear Education: Sourcebook." ERIC document ED 256 683.

Widom, Cathy. "The Cycle of Violence." *Science* 244 (April 1989):160–165.

Will, Thomas E. "The Abolition of War." *Arena* 23 (February 1895):127–137.

William T. Grant Foundation Commission on Youth. "The Forgotten Half: Non-College Bound Youth in America." *Phi Delta Kappan* 69 (February 1988):409–418.

Wingspread Conference. "Shaping the Future of International Studies." New York: Global Perspectives in Education, Inc., 1984.

Winkler, Karen. J. "Sociologists, Psychologists Urge Study of Questions Concerning Nuclear War." *Chronicle of Higher Education,* 11 September 1985, 31:7 and 12.

Winter, Carl. "A Unit on Peace." *Social Education* 3 (January 1939):33–36.

Wittner, Lawrence S. *Rebels Against the War: The American Peace Movement, 1941–1960.* New York: Columbia University Press, 1969.

Wolf, Aline D. *Peaceful Children, Peaceful World: The Challenge of Maria Montessori.* Altoona, PA: Parent Child Press, 1989.

Woman's Peace Party. *Addresses at the Organizing Conference, 10 January 1915.* Chicago: Woman's Peace Party, 1915.

Women's International League for Peace and Freedom. "Towards Peace and Freedom," *Report on the Zurich Congress of the Women's International League for Peace and Freedom (1919).* Reprint in *The Eagle and the Dove,* edited by John Whiteclay Chambers II. New York: Garland Publishing, Inc., 1976.

Wood, David. "Army To Branch Out in Third World Operations." *Times-Picayune,* 12 January 1990.

"Words of Fire: Hiroshima Survivor Interview." *Los Angeles Catholic Worker (Catholic Agitator),* August 1983:1–2.

World Information Clearing Centre. "Press Release #2: New Computerized World Information Service (NCWIS), East/West/North/South." Geneva: New Computerized World Information Service (NCWIS), 13 May 1989.

World Peace University. General Information. Eugene, OR: World Peace University, 1988.

World Policy Forum. New York: World Policy Institute, 1983 and 1988.

World Policy Institute. Program Description. New York: World Policy Institute, 1988.

Wulf, Christoph, ed. *Handbook on Peace Education.* Frankfurt am Main, Germany: International Peace Research Association, 1974.

"Young Persons View 'The Day After.' " ERIC document ED 260 952.

Zelinsky, Wilbur. *Nation Into State: The Shifting Symbolic Foundations of American Nationalism.* Chapel Hill: University of North Carolina Press, 1988.

Zimbardo, Phillip G., and Leippe, Michael R. *The Psychology of Attitude Change and Social Influence.* Philadelphia: Temple University Press, 1991.

Zola, John. *Teaching about Peace and Nuclear War: A Balanced Approach.* Boulder, CO: Social Science Education Consortium, Inc., 1985.

Zola, John, and Remy Sieck. *Teaching about Conflict, Nuclear War and the Future.* Denver: Center for Teaching International Relations, 1984.

APPENDIX: RESOURCE DIRECTORY

This Resource Directory is subdivided topically into seven parts as follows:

    I. Curriculum Guides: Instructional Materials or Resources

    II. Conflict Resolution: Student Mediation or School Programs

    III. Children/Youth/Parents: Organizations, Activities, or Resources

    IV. Development Education/Human Rights Education

    V. Global Education

    VI. Religious Organizations and Resources

    VII. Post-Soviet/American Friendship and Exchange Programs

I. CURRICULUM GUIDES: INSTRUCTIONAL MATERIALS OR RESOURCES

Abrams, Grace Contrino Peace Education Foundation, Inc. 2627 Biscayne Blvd., Miami, FL 33137 (*Peace Works* and *Peace Pages* newsletters).

Addams, Jane Peace Association, 1213 Race St., Philadelphia, PA 19107.

American Bar Association, Special Committee on Youth Education for Citizenship, 1155 E. 60th St., Chicago, IL 60637.

American Friends Service Committee, 1501 Cherry St., Philadelphia, PA 19102, (Peace Education Resource Catalog).

Brown, William C., P.O. Box 539, Dubuque, IA 52001 (*Cooperative Learnings, Cooperative Lives,* Grs. 1–8).

Camp Fire, Inc. Product Services Division, 4601 Madison Ave. Kansas City, MO 64112 (A Gift of Peace, Grs. 1–6 and In Pursuit of Peace, Grs. 7–12).

Center for Citizenship Education, 1100 17th St. NW, Suite 1000, Washington, DC 20036.

Center for New National Security (Norie Huddle), 2405 Nemeth Court, Alexandria, VA 22306.

Center for Nonviolence and Voluntary Service, P.O. Box 1315, Santa Ana, CA 92702 (*Seven Steps to Global Change,* booklet).

Center for Social Studies Education, 115 Mayfair Dr., Pittsburgh, PA 15228 (*Lessons of the Vietnam War*).

Center for Teaching International Relations, University of Denver, Denver, CO 80210 (Catalog).

Children's Book Council, 350 Scotland Rd., Orange, NJ 07050 (Posters for Peace and annotated listing of peace books).

Citizen Education for Peace Project, University of California-Irvine, P.O. Box 6021, Irvine, CA 92716–6021 (Quest for Peace Broadcast Series)

Concerned Educators Allied for a Safe Environment (CEASE), 17 Gerry St., Cambridge, MA 02138.

COPRED (Consortium on Peace Research Education and Development), Center for Analysis & Resolution of Conflict,

George Mason University, 4400 University Dr., Fairfax, VA 22030. (*Peace and Change,* journal of a national organization for peace research).

Council on Interracial Books for Children, 1841 Broadway, New York, NY 10023 (Catalog "Resources to Counter Racism, Sexism and Other Forms of Prejudice").

Educational Film & Video Project, 5332 College Ave., Suite 101, Oakland, CA 94618 (Catalog).

Educators for Social Responsibility, 12 Garden St., Cambridge, MA 02138 (Curriculum Guides).

ERIC Clearinghouse for Social Studies/Social Science Education, 855 Broadway, Boulder, CO 80302.

Federation of American Scientists, 307 Massachusetts Ave., NE, Washington, DC 20002 (Nuclear War Education materials).

Finish Point, The, 1509 S. Neil, Champaign, IL 61820 (Video for social studies, "Students Want Peace," Grs. 10–12).

Florida Coalition for Peace and Justice (Coalition of sixty ecumenical groups), P.O. Box 2486, Orlando, FL 32802 (*Just Peace* newsletter).

Foreign Policy Association, 205 Lexington Ave., New York, NY 10016.

Foundation for P.E.A.C.E., P.O. Box 244, Arlington, VA 22210 (Newsletter with references for teachers).

Friends Peace Committee, 1501 Cherry St., Philadelphia, PA 19102.

Fund for Peace, Joel Brooke Memorial, 345 E. 46th St., Suite 810B, New York, NY 10017 (Resource Guide).

Garland Publishing, 1000A Sherman Ave., Hamden, CT 06514. *Teaching Social Studies to the Young Child* (1992), by Blythe Hinitz, including peace and global education resources.

Ground Zero, 806-15th St. NW #421, Washington, DC 10005.

Ground Zero Pairing Project, P.O. Box 19329, Portland, OR 97219 (*Nuclear Age,* Grs. 9–12).

Hampshire College, (PAWSS Project), Amherst, MA 01002 (*Guide to Careers and Graduate Education in Peace Studies*).

High Falls Publications, 4408 E. Groveland Rd., Geneseo, NY 14454 (*Peacebuilding,* textbook).

I. N. Thut World Education Center, University of Connecticut, School of Education, Storrs, CT 06268.

Indiana University Press, Tenth and Morton Streets, Bloomington, IN 47405 (*Peace Heroes in Twentieth-Century America*).

Institute for Peace and Justice, 4144 Lindell, #400, St. Louis, MO 63108 (Curriculum Guides and other books).

Institute for Security and Cooperation in Outer Space, 8 Logan Circle, NW, Washington, DC 20005-3737 (International non-weapons development of outer space).

Intercommunity Center for Justice and Peace, 20 Washington Square North, New York, NY 10011 (*Corporate Responsibility,* Grs. 1–adult).

International Association for the Study of Cooperation in Education (ASCE), (Ted and Nancy Graves), 136 Liberty St., Santa Cruz, CA 95060.

International Peace Academy, Inc., 777 United Nations Plaza, New York, NY 10017 (Training seminars, publications, and teaching materials).

Jobs with Peace, 76 Summer St., Room 300, Boston, MA 02110 (*Crossroads* and other guides).

Kimbo Education, 10 No. Third Ave., Long Branch, NJ 07740 ("Teaching Peace" and "Hug the Earth," song cassettes).

Lawyers' Committee on Nuclear Policy, 500 Fifth Ave., New York, NY 10110-0296 (Statement on the Illegality of Nuclear Warfare; Bibliography).

League of Women Voters Education Fund, 1730 M. Street, NW, Washington, DC 20036.

Librarians for Nuclear Arms Control, 100 B 60552, Pasadena, CA 91106 (Newsletter).

Media Network, 121 Fulton St., 5th Fl., New York, NY 10038 (Guides to media on disarmament, global, multicultural, and environmental issues).

Michigan Media, University of Michigan Media Resources Center, 400 Fourth St., Ann Arbor, MI 41803 (Audiovisual materials on nuclear issues).

Milwaukee Peace Education Center, 2437 N. Grant Blvd., Milwaukee, WI 53210 (Guides).

Muste, A. J. Memorial Institute, 339 Lafayette St. New York, NY (Materials on nonviolence and peace leaders).

National Catholic Educational Association, Suite 100, 1077 30th St. NW, Washington, DC 20007 (*Everyday Issues Related to Justice,* Grs. 1–8).

National Center for Appropriate Technology, P.O. Box 3838, Butte, MT 59702 ("Connections"-ecological concerns, Grs. 5–6).

National Council for the Social Studies, Publications Sales Dept., 2030 M. St. NW, Washington, DC 20036.

National Education Association, 1210 Sixteen St., NW, Washington, DC 20036.

National Science Teachers Association, 1742 Connecticut Avenue NW, Washington, DC 20009 (*Nuclear Education,* special issue of *Journal of College Science Teaching*).

Nuclear Age Peace Foundation, 1187 Coast Village Rd., Suite 123, Santa Barbara, CA 93108 (Swackhamer Prize Essay contest and *Waging Peace* series).

Nuclear Free America, 325 E. 25th St., Baltimore, MD 21218 (Maps of Nuclear-Free Zones).

Nuclear Information and Resource Service, 1346 Connecticut Ave., NW, Washington, DC 20036.

Ohio Commission on Dispute Resolution and Conflict Management, 77 South High St., Columbus, OH 43266-0124.

Ohio Peacemaking Education Network (OPEN), Governor's Communications Office (Lynne Harbert), Columbus, OH 43266.

Oregon Peace Institute, 921 SW Morrison, Portland, OR, 97205. (*Elementary Curriculum Guide,* including books, audiovisual and other sources.)

Peace Channel, 921 SW Morrison, Portland, OR 97205. (Loans free peace and justice videotapes to cable access centers throughout America.)

Peace Development Fund, 44 North Prospect St., P.O. Box 270, Amherst, MA 01004 (Teaching Peace grants to groups and organizations).

Peace Education Program in Louisville (Judy Schroeder), 318 W. Kentucky St., Louisville, KY 40203.

Peace Education Program of the Waianae Coast, 87-766 A Lahaina St., Waianae, HI 96762 (*Our Experiences in Peace Education,* Grs. 3–12).

Peace Education Resource Center, Philadelphia Yearly Meeting of Friends, 1515 Cherry St., Philadelphia, PA 19102.

Peace Grows, Inc. 475 West Market S., Akron, OH 44303 (*Alternatives to Violence Manual,* workbooks with *Teacher's Guide*).

Peace Links (Woman Against Nuclear War), 723 1/2 8th St., SE, Washington, DC 20003 (Peace Panel Packet).

Peace Museum, 430 W. Erie St., Chicago, IL 60610 (Traveling exhibits of photographs and visual arts).

Peace Resource Center, 331 N. Milpas #F, Santa Barbara, CA 93103 (*Guide to Non-Military Jobs for Scientists*).

Penichet Publishing Co., 2514 S. Grand Ave., Los Angeles, CA 90007 (*Peace Catalog: A Guidebook*).

Pittsburgh Peace Institute, 1139 Wightman St., Pittsburgh, PA 15217 (*Simpleton Story,* Grs. 9–Adult).

Promoting Enduring Peace, Inc., P.O. Box 5103, Woodmont, CT 06460 (Free reprints of articles on peace issues).

Public Education for Peace Society, 4340 Carson St., Burnaby, BC V5J 2X9 (Canada) (*Conflict and Changes,* Grs. 7–10).

Radio for Peace International, P.O. Box 10869 (World Peace University), Eugene, OR 09774 or Apartado 88, Santa Ana, Costa Rica (Global education and Sister School project).

Social Science Education Consortium, Inc., 855 Broadway, Boulder, CO 80302 (*Teaching about Peace and Nuclear War*).

Stanford Program on International and Cross-Cultural Education (SPICE), 200 Lou Henry Hoover Bldg., Stanford Univ., Palo Alto, CA 94305–6012 (*Bibliography of Nuclear Age Educational Resources and Choices in International Conflict,* Grs. 7–College).

Teachers College Press, Columbia University, New York, NY 10027 (*Educating for Global Responsibility* by Betty Reardon and other books).

Theatre Peace (Marghi Dutton), 6350 Bell Springs Rd., Garberville, CA 95440 (Peace through improvisations and creative drama).

Traprock Peace Center, Woolman Kill Keets Rd., Deerfield, MA 01342 (*Perspectives at Work*).

UNESCO, 2 United Nations Plaza, Room 900, New York, NY 10017.

UNICEF, 866 United Nations Plaza, New York, NY 10017.

Union of Concerned Scientists, 26 Church St., Cambridge, MA 02238 (Videos on space weapons, Gr. 7–adult).

United States Institute of Peace, 1550 M St., NW, Suite 700, Washington, DC 20005 (Grants for individuals and groups).

University for Peace, P.O. Box 199-1250, Escazu, Costa Rica, C. A. (Peace education and human rights mission).

War Resisters League, 339 Lafayette St., New York, NY 10012.

Westview Press, 5500 Central Ave., Boulder, CO 80301 (Catalog, Peace Studies and International Relations).

Wilmington College Peace Resource Center, Pyle Center, Box 1183, Wilmington, OH 45177 (Hiroshima collection and peace resource center newsletter).

Women's International League for Peace and Freedom, 1213 Race St., Philadelphia, PA 19107 (Peace education resources).

World College West, 101 S. San Antonio Rd., Petaluma, CA 94952 (Multicultural curriculum).

World Council on Curriculum and Instruction, School of Education, Indiana University, Bloomington, IN 47450.

World Peace University, P.O. Box 10869, Eugene, OR 97440.

World Policy Institute, 777 United Nations Plaza, New York, NY 10017 (World order values literature and resources).

World Without War Council, 1730 Martin Luther King Jr. Way, Berkeley, CA 94709 (Guide to Peace Archives).

YMCA of the U.S.A., National Board, World Relations Department, 726 Broadway, New York, NY 10003 (Peace Sites for peace resources and group facilitation).

II. CONFLICT RESOLUTION: STUDENT MEDIATION OR SCHOOL PROGRAMS

Abrams, Grace Contrino Peace Education Foundation, Inc. (Fran Schmidt, Educational Specialist), 2627 Biscayne Blvd., Miami, FL 33137 (Dade County, Florida "Fighting Fair Conflict Management Program" and guides *Creative Conflict Solving for Kids* and *Fighting Fair: Martin Luther King Jr. for Kids,* Grs. 4–7).

American Bar Association, Special Committee on Dispute Resolution, School Mediation Clearinghouse, 1800 M St., Suite 200 South, Washington, DC 20036 (Directory and Bibliography).

Arkansas International Center, UALR, 1802 S. University Ave., Little Rock, AR 72204. Conflict Management Educators, interdisciplinary program for teacher education.

Center for Global and Peace Education, School of Education/ Miller Hall 324C, Western Washington University, Bellingham, WA 98225 (Network for teacher education materials).

Center for Peace and Conflict Studies, Wayne State University, 3049 Faculty Administration Bldg., Detroit, MI 48202 (Model of conflict resolution in the school environment; training of students and staff.)

Center for Teaching Peace (Colman McCarthy), 4501 Van Ness St., NW, Washington, DC 20016 (Course in conflict resolution).

Children's Creative Response to Conflict Program, Box 271, Nyack, NY 10960. (Program started in 1972, including bias awareness; trains teachers and students.)

Commission on the Study of Peace, c/o Dr. Robert A. Rubenstein, Northwestern Univ., Dept. of Anthropology, Evanston, IL 60201. (Publishes *Directory of Anthropologists Working on Topics of Peace, Conflict Resolution, and International Security* and quarterly, *Human Peace.*)

Committee for National Security, 1601 Connecticut Ave., NW, Suite 301, Washington, DC 10009.

Community Board Center for Policy and Training, School Initiatives Program, 149 9th St., San Francisco, CA 94103 (Conflict Manager training for elementary, middle, and secondary).

Cornerstone: A Center for Justice and Peace, 940 Emerson St., Denver, CO 80218 (Conflict management).

Educators for Social Responsibility, 23 Garden St., Cambridge, MA 02138 (*Perspectives* and *Elementary Perspectives: Teaching Concepts of Peace and Conflict*).

ESR (Educators for Social Responsibility) Metro (New York) Model Peace Education Program, 490 Riverside Dr., Rm. 27,

New York, NY 10027. (Resolving Conflict Creatively Program (RCCP)).

Global Learning, Inc., 40 So. Fullerton Ave., Montclair, NJ 07042 (Conflict Manager program for New Jersey schools).

Harvard Graduate School for Education, Moral Education Resource Fund, Larson Hall, 12 Appian Way, Cambridge, MA 02138 (*Fairness Committee Manual*).

Iowa Peace Institute, 917 Tenth Ave., P.O. Box 480, Grinnell, IA 50112. (*Mediation Process—Why It Works: A Model Developed by Students* and other publications).

King Center (Martin Luther King, Jr. Center for Nonviolent Social Change, Inc.) 449 Auburn Ave. NE, Atlanta, GA 30312–1590 (Teaching Guide and model project for infusion of nonviolence into the curriculum).

Martin Luther King, Jr. Commission, 1100 Raymond Blvd., Newark, NJ 07102 (Teaching guide and materials).

Mediation Training Institute, Teacher Mediation Training Project, 112 Burr Mountain Rd., Torrington, CT 06790 (Teacher-student mediation training).

National Association for Mediation in Education (NAME), 425 Amity St., Amherst, MA 01002 (*Annotated Bibliography, Directory of Student Mediation Programs,* and *The Fourth R,* newsletter).

National Conference on Peacemaking and Conflict Resolution and Network for Community Justice and Conflict Resolution (NCPCR), George Mason University, 4400 University Dr., Fairfax, VA 22030.

National Peace Foundation, 1835 K St., NW, Suite 610, Washington, DC 20006. (Programs and materials in conflict education and peace education. Special issue, Fall-Winter 1991, *Peace Reporter*.).

New York City Board of Education, division of High Schools, 131 Livingston St., Brooklyn, NY 11201 (*Nuclear Issues: Health Education and Conflict Resolution*).

North Carolina Center for Peace Education/North Carolina Educators for Social Responsibiliy, 118A E. Main St. Carrboro, NC 27510.

Ohio Commission on Dispute Resolution and Conflict Management, 77 S. High St., Columbus, OH 43266–0124. (Brochure).

Ohio School Conflict Management Demonstration Project, 77 South High St., Columbus, OH 43266-0124. (Student mediation programs).

Outcomes Associates, P.O. Box 7285, Princeton, NJ 08543-7285 ("Getting Along" Curriculum)

Parenting Press, Inc., (Elizabeth Crary), Suite B, P.O. Box 15163, Seattle, WA 98115 (Children's Problem-Solving series, ages 3–8).

Peace Grows, Inc. 475 West Market St., Akron, OH 44303 (*Alternatives to Violence: A Manual for Teaching Peacemaking in Youth and Adults*).

Public Education for Peace Society, 4340 Carson St., Burnaby, BC V5J 2X9, Canada (*Peer Conflict Resolution Through Creative Negotiation*, Grs. 4–6).

School Mediation Associates (Richard Cohen), 702 Green St., #8, Cambridge, MA 02139.

School Mediator's Alternative Resolution Team (SMART), New York City Board of Education/Youth Bureau, 50 Court St., 8th Floor, Brooklyn, NY 11201.

Scott, Foresman and Co., 1900 E. Lake Ave., Glenview, IL 60025 (*Creative Conflict Resolution* by William J. Kreidler).

Speech Communication Association, 5105 Backlick Rd., Bldg. E, Annandale, VA 22003 (*Mediation,* Grs. 12–adult).

University of New Mexico, Program for Assistance in Equity (Norma Milanovich), College of Education, Albuquerque, NM 87131 (*Frustration Is . . . Conflict in the Classroom*).

West Publishing Co., 164 W. Hillcrest Dr. #200, Thousand Oaks, CA 91360 (*Conflict Resolution*).

Westchester Mediation Center CLUSTER, Inc., 201 Palisade Ave., Box 281, Yonkers, NY 10703. (School Mediation Program with Student Mediators).

Western New York Peace Center, 472 Emslie, Buffalo, NY 14212 (Friendly Creature Features, puppet shows, and conflict resolution workshops, Grs. K–2, guides and videos).

III. CHILDREN YOUTH/PARENTS: ORGANIZATIONS ACTIVITIES, OR RESOURCES

Abrams, Grace Contrino Peace Education Foundation, Inc., 2627 Biscayne Blvd., Miami, FL 33137 (*Fighting Fair for Families* and *Peacemaking Skills for Little Kids,* Preschool–Gr. 2).

Animal Town Game Company, P.O. Box 2002, Santa Barbara, CA 93120 (Cooperative games, puzzles).

Association for Childhood Education International, 3615 Wisconsin Ave., NW., Washington, DC 20016 (Literature).

Boise Peace Quilt Project, P.O. Box 6469, Boise ID 83707 (Quilt stitched by former Soviet and American mothers based on children's drawings—note cards, information).

Box Project, (Nancy A. Normen), P.O. Box 435, Plainville, CT 06062 (Families share a box of material goods directly with a family in poverty; also publishes a newsletter).

Center for Psychological Studies in the Nuclear Age. 1493 Cambridge St., Cambridge, MA 02139 (Books and resources available for parents on psychological concerns, including children's fears of war).

Center on War & the Child, P.O. Box 487, 35 Benton St., Eureka Springs, AR 72632 (Militarization of children and their victimization by war; war toys).

Children as the Peacemakers Foundation, 950 Battery St., 2nd Fl., San Francisco, CA 94111.

Children as Teachers of Peace, 999 Green St., San Francisco, CA 94133.

Children for Old Growth, P.O. Box 1090, Redway, CA 95560 (Environmental issues, newsletter with children's writings, Adopt A Tree, and tape exchange).

Children's Book Council, Inc., 350 Scotland Rd. Orange, NJ 07050 (Posters and annotated listing of Peace Books).

Children's Campaign for Nuclear Disarmament, Box 550, RD#1, Plainfield, VT 05667.

Children's Defense Fund (Marian Wright Edelman), 122 C St., NW, Washington, DC 20001 (Annual costs of defense versus benefits to children).

Children's Music Network (Sarah Pirtle), 54 Thayer Rd., Greenfield, MA 01301 (Newsletter on music/peace values).

Children's Peace Statue, Kids' Committee, P.O. Box 12888, Albuquerque, NM 87195-2888. (Camy Condon). (Project to help build a Children's Peace Statue in Los Alamos similar to one in Hiroshima. Newsletter, *The Crane* and Pen-Pals Project).

Concerned Educators Allied for a Safe Environment (CEASE), (Peggy Schirmer), 17 Gerry St., Cambridge, MA 02138.

(Network of parents and children, peace education materials, and *CEASE News*).

Family Pastimes, R.R. 4, Perth, Ontario, Canada, K7H 3C6 (Nonviolent games).

Friendly Creature Features, Western New York Peace Center, 472 Emslie, Buffalo, NY 14212 (Puppet Shows and Conflict Resolution Workshops).

Grandmothers for Peace International, 909-12th St., Suite 118, Sacramento, CA 95814.

Holistic Education Review, 39 Pearl St., Brandon, VT 05733. (Journal for parents and educators, including global education and cooperative learning).

Hope Publishing House, P.O. Box 60008, Pasadena, CA 91006 (Children and Nonviolence–families).

Institute for Peace and Justice, 4144 Lindell, St. Louis, MI 63108 (*Starting Out Right,* preschool).

International Friendship League, 55 Mount Vernon St., Boston, MA 02108 (Pen pals in English-speaking nations, ages 7–70).

International Language Villages, Concordia College, Moorhead, MN 56560.

It's Our World Too, P.O. Box 326, Winterport, ME (Young people's clubs and activities).

Jalmar Press, 45 Hitching Post Dr., Rolling Hills, CA 90274 (*He Hit Me Back First* and *Learning the Skills of Peacemaking*).

"Kids Meeting Kids," Box 8H, 380 Riverside Dr., New York, NY 10025 (Pen pals, ages 8–18).

Laser, 15 Walnut St., Northampton, MA 01060 (Newsletter, ages 9 and up).

430   **Peace Education in America**

Legacy: International Youth Program, 1141 No. Grebe Rd., Arlington, VA 22201 (Camp for global understanding, ages 9–18).

Little Friends for Peace, (Mary Jo Park), 4405 29th St., Mount Rainier, MD 20712 (Peace Camp Curriculum and *Peacemaking for Little Friends,* ages 4–12).

Los Angeles Alliance for Survival, 13 Sunset Ave., Los Angeles, CA 90291 (Exchange a Dakin toy teddy bear for a war toy).

Lotus Light, Inc., P.O. Box 2, Wilmot, WI 53192 (*Peace Trek Family Coloring Book*).

Marquis Project, 107 7th St., Brandon, MB R7A 3S5, Canada (*Choices: Family Global Action Handbook*).

Middle Tennessee State University, Dept. of Home Economics, (Joyce Maar), Box 86, Murfreesboro, TN 37132. (Video, "Teaching Young Children Peacemaking Attitudes.")

Milwaukee Peace Education Center, 2437 N. Grant Blvd., Milwaukee, WI 53210 (Peacemaking activities, books for children and parents).

Namchi United Enterprises, P.O. Box 33852 Station D, Vancouver, B.C., Canada V6J 4L6 (*We Can Do It! Peace Book for Kids of All Ages*).

National Association for the Education of Young Children, 1834 Connecticut Ave., NW., Washington, DC. 20009–5786 (*Helping Young Children Understand Peace, War and the Nuclear Threat* and *The Anti-Bias Curriculum*).

National Student Campaign Against Hunger, 29 Temple Pl., Boston, MA 023111 (College students).

New Society Publishers, 4722 Baltimore Ave., Philadelphia, PA 19143 (Books, cooperative games)

Nuclear Age Peace Foundation, 1187 Coast Village Rd., Suite 123, Santa Barbara, CA 93108 (Annual Swackhamer Prize for student essays on war/peace problems).

OMEP–USNC (Organization Mondiale pour l'Education Présco-laire)–World Organization for Early Childhood Education, U.S. National Committee (Journal and World Assemblies). c/o Perry Koulouras, Treasurer, OMEP–USNC, 24000 Lahser Rd., Southfield, MI 48034.

Pantheon Books, 201 E. 50th St., New York, NY 10001 (*Peace in the Family*).

Parenting for Peace & Justice, 4144 Lindell Blvd., St. Louis, MO 63108 (Books, videotapes, national network).

Parenting for Peaceful Families (Barbara Oehlberg), Family Life Education, 1332 W. 28th St., Cleveland, OH 44113.

Parenting Press, Inc., Suite B, P.O. Box 15163, Seattle, WA 98115 (Catalog; *Kids Can Cooperate,* and Children's problem solving Series).

Parents and Teachers for Social Responsibility, Inc., P.O. Box 517, Moreton, VT 05660 (Newsletter *"Yopp!"*).

Peace Child (musical play), 2345 King Pl, NW, Washington, DC 20007.

Peace Child Festival, Minneapolis/St. Paul. See Twin Cities Metropolitan Church Commission.

Peace Child Foundation, 3977 Chainbridge Rd., Fairfax, VA 22030.

Peace Links, 747 8th St., SE, Washington, D.C. 20003 (Peace Pal Bunny; resource for parents).

Peace Resource Center, 4211 Grand Avenue, Des Moines, IO 50312.

Peacemaking for Children, 2437 N. Grant Blvd., Milwaukee, WI 53210 (Magazine on peace themes and activities, ages 5–18).

Playmill of Maine, RFD #3, Box 89, Dover-Foxcroft, ME 04426 (Peace Train, puzzles, and other toys).

Provident Book Stores, 616 Walnut Ave., Scottdale, PA 15688–1999 (Catalog of books, games, and music).

St. Luke UCC Peace Fellowship, 1400 South St., Burlington, IA 52601 (*Bibliography of Peace Books*).

Skipping Stones, c/o Aprovecho Institute, 80574 Hazelton Rd., Cottage Grove, OR 97424 (Multicultural journal for children's writing and sharing).

Smilin' Atcha Music, P.O. Box 446, Chester, NY 10918 (Teaching Peace music cassettes, ages 3–10).

"Stop War Toys Campaign," War Resisters League, Box 1093, Norwich, CT 06360.

Student Pugwash USA, 1638 R St., NW, 32, Washington, DC 20009 (Environmental/Science/Technology/Science issues with chapters at colleges throughout the world).

Toys for Peace, 205 E. Leeland Hgts. Blvd., Lehigh Acres, FL 33936 (List of "Toys for Peace").

Twin Cities Metropolitan Church Commission, 122 W. Franklin, Rm. 218, Minneapolis, MN 55404 (Peace Child Doll and resource for Peace Child Festival).

Ungame Corp., Au-Vid Corp., 1440 S. State St. College Blvd., #20 Anaheim, CA 92806 (Cooperative board games).

United Campuses to Prevent Nuclear War, 309 Pennsylvania Ave., SE., Washington, D.C. 20003 (College students).

United Nations Children's Fund, United States Committee for UNICEF, 331 E. 38th St., New York, NY 10016 (Traveling exhibit of Chidren's Art).

United States Institute of Peace, P.O. Box 27720 Central Station, Washington, D.C. 20038 (Essay contest for high school: National Peace Essay Contest).

Women Against Military Madness, 3255 Hennepin Ave., S., Suite 125-B, Minneapolis, MN 55408.

Women's Action for Nuclear Disarmament (WAND), P.O. Box B, Arlington, MA 02174.

World Pen Pals: University of Minnesota, Minneapolis, MN 55455 (12 years and up).

Youthlink, 4835 Penn Ave., S., Minneapolis, MN 55409 (Newsletter and pen pal exchanges).

IV. DEVELOPMENT EDUCATION/HUMAN RIGHTS EDUCATION

Akwesasne Notes, Mohawk Nation, Rooseveltown, NY 13683 (Native American struggle for human rights).

American Civil Liberties Union, 156 Fifth Ave., New York, NY 10017.

Amnesty International, 332 Eighth Ave., 10th Fl., New York, NY 10001. Educators' Network (Brochure of curriculum guides included in a booklet, "Educators for Human Rights").

Amnesty International USA Educators Network, 655 Sutter St., San Francisco, CA 94102 (*Human Rights Education: The Fourth R*).

Brown, William C. Co., P.O. Box 539, Dubuque, IA 52001 (*Rich World, Poor World,* Grs. 7–10 and other books).

Church World Service, P.O. Box 968, Elkhart, IN 46516-0968 (*World Food Day Curriculum* for three groups: K–Gr. 3; Grs. 4–7; and Grs. 8–12).

Consultative Group on Early Childhood Care and Development, UNICEF House-H2F, 3 United Nations Plaza, New York, NY 10017 (Human rights issues for young children in the Third World, especially children in war regions. Journal, *Coordinators' Notebook* for educators).

Data Center, 464 19th St., Oakland, CA 94612–2297. (Information services on human rights abuses, guides to resources on Third World, computerized information services. Brochure).

Defense for Children International–USA (Kay Castelle), 210 Forsyth St., New York, NY 10002 (Convention on the Rights of the Child).

Food First (Institute for Food and Development Policy), 1885 Mission St., San Francisco, CA 94103 (Curriculum, Grs 4–8).

Global Learning, Inc., 1018 Stuyvesant Ave., Union, NJ 07083. (Curriculum Guide, *Wants, Needs and Rights: An Introduction to Human Rights).*

Grassroots Leadership, 2300 E. 7th St., P.O. Box 9586, Charlotte, NC 28299 (Social justice community activism in the South).

Heifer Project International, P.O. Box 808, Little Rock, AR 72203. (Grass-roots projects in Third World countries, with farm animals and livestock donated to fight hunger. Newsletter, *Sharing Life).*

Highlander Research and Education Center, Route 3, Box 370, New Market, TN 37820 (Books and resources for social change in Appalachia and the South).

International League for Human Rights, 777 United Nations Plaza, NY 10017 (Newsletter).

International Nursing Services Association, Development Education Project, P.O. Box 15086, Atlanta, GA 30333 (Third World health improvement projects).

National Congress of American Indians, 1346 Connecticut Ave., Washington, DC 20036.

Nuclear Pie, 2316 Cherokee Dr., NW, Calgary, Alberta T2L OX7 (*Nuclear Pie: 14 Fables*–nuclear war and development issues).

Oxfam-America, Educational Resources, 115 Broadway, Boston, MA 02116.

Peace Brigades International, Box 1233, Harvard Square, Cambridge, MA 02238. (Support for human rights and social justice as part of unarmed peace teams of volunteers).

Peace Corps. 806 Connecticut Ave., NW, Washington, DC 20525.

Pueblo To People, 1616 Montrose #3600, Houston, TX 77006.

Roosevelt Center for American Policy Studies, 316 Pennsylvania Ave., SE, Suite 500, Washington, DC 20003 (*Dealing with Interdependence: U.S. and Third World,* Grs. 11–adult).

United States Committee for UNICEF, Det. 1008C, 331 E. 38th St., New York, NY 10016 (Catalog and "Reaching the Children: A Development Education Kit").

Video Project, 5332 College Ave., Suite 101, Oakland, CA 94618 (Videos on human rights).

Wayne State University, Center for Peace and Conflict Studies, 5229 Cass Ave., Detroit, MI 48201 ("Declaration of the Rights of the Child and the Child's Declaration of Rights and Responsibilities").

V. GLOBAL EDUCATION

American Forum for Global Education (Global Perspectives in Education, Inc.), 45 John St., Suite 1200, New York, NY 10038 (Model Schools project–Global Education and publications).

Americans for Middle East Understanding, Inc., 475 Riverside Dr., Rm. 771, New York, NY 10115 (Video on Mideast issues, Gr. 7–adult).

Arkansas International Center, University of Arkansas at Little Rock (Barbara Stanford) 2801 South University, Little Rock, AR 72204 *Costa Rica,* Grs. 9–12. Catalog.

Cambridgeport Press, 14 Chalk St., Cambridge, MA 02139 (*The Vietnam War*–textbook, Grs. 11–adult).

Center for Global Education, Augsburg College, 731-21st Ave. So., Minneapolis, MN 55454.

Center for Science in the Public Interest, 1775 S St., NW, Washington, DC 20009.

Central America Resource Center, 1701 University Ave., SE, Minneapolis, MN 55414 (*Directory of Central America Classroom Resources*).

Council on International Education Exchange, 205 E. 42nd St., New York, NY 10017 (Exchange of U.S. high schools with secondary schools in other countries).

Council on Learning, 271 North Ave., New Rochelle, NY 10801 (Global Education series for college level).

Countdown 2001, 110 North Payne St., Alexandria, VA 22314 (*Educator's Guide* and newsletter).

David M. Kennedy Center for International Studies, Brigham Young University, 280 Herald R. Clark Bldg., Provo, UT 84602 (Catalog of Publications, including *Culturgram* series).

Edumate Educational Materials, 3746 Sixth Ave., San Diego, CA 92103 (Global Education games, books, and posters).

Experiment in International Living, Brattleboro, VT 05301 (International education exchange program).

ExPro, c/o Department of Sociology, Boston College, Chestnut Hill, MA 02167 (Citizens' Peace Treaty).

Facts on File, Inc. 460 Park Ave. South, New York, NY 10016 (*Global Guide to International Education* and *World Education Encyclopedia*).

Foreign Policy Association, Publications Dept. 727 7th Ave., New York, NY 10019 ("Great Decisions", Grs. 11–adult; and *Teacher's Resource Guide: Lessons on Current U.S. Foreign Policy Issues,* Grs. 9–12 Social Studies).

Global Education Associates, 475 Riverside Dr., Suite 456, New York, NY 10115 (*Breakthrough/Whole Earth Papers*).

Global Education Motivators, Inc. Montgomery County Intermediate Unit Bldg., Montgomery Ave., Paper Mill Rd., Erdenheim, PA 19118.

Global Learning, Inc. (Jeffrey L. Brown), 40 South Fullerton Ave., Montclair, NJ 07042. (Network for New Jersey's teachers/students for international linkages—New Jersey and the world—model program and conflict management).

Global Perspectives in Education, Inc., 45 John St., Suite 1200, New York, NY 10038 (Reports from Wingspread Conferences and *Intercom* reprints).

Global Tomorrow Coalition, 1325 G Street, NW, Suite 915, Washington, DC 20005 (Global Issues Education Packets).

International Christian Youth Exchange, 134 W. 26th St., New York, NY 10001 (Ages 16–24).

International Exchange, Youth for Understanding, 3501 Newark St., NW, Washington, DC 20016.

Mershon Center, Citizenship Development and Global Education Program, Ohio State University, 199 W. 10th Ave., Columbus, OH 43201 ("Your Community in the World" materials).

Odyssey of the Mind Association, P.O. Box 27, Glassboro, NJ 08028 (International problem solving competition, K–12).

One Thousand (1000) Crane Club, Hiroshima International School, 3-49-1, Kurakake, Asakitu-ku, Hiroshima-shim, Hiroshima-ken, Japan (739-19) (Children make and send origami cranes here and they are taken to the Sadako Monument; *Sadako and the Thousand Cranes,* children's peace book).

Planetary Citizens, 777 United Nations Plaza, New York, NY 10017.

Population Reference Bureau, Inc., 1337 Connecticut Ave., NW, Washington DC 20036.

SCOLA, 2500 California St., Omaha, NE 68178. (Brings foreign TV news programs to schools and colleges, available to cable systems or individuals via satellite).

Social Science Education Consortium, Inc. 855 Broadway, Boulder, CO 80302. (Catalog of materials).

Social Studies Development Center, Indiana University, Bloomington, IN 47405 (Global/Multicultural education).

Social Studies School Service, 10,000 Culver Blvd., Dept. Y3, Culver City, CA 90230 (Global Education Catalog, books, classroom units).

Stanley Foundation, 420 E. Third St., Muscatine, IA 52761 (Literature, classroom materials).

UNESCO Unipub, 345 Park Ave. So. New York, NY 10010 (*UNESCO Courier* magazine, International School Project).

United Nations, UNA-USA, Publications Department, 485 Fifth Ave., New York, NY 10017–6104 (Model United Nations Conferences for student participation).

United Nations High Commissioner for Refugees (UNHCR), Grand Central P.O. 10, New York, NY 10017 (Free loan films).

Upper Midwest Women's History Center for Teachers, 6300 Walker St., St. Louis Park, MN 55416 (Global Education unit on Third World Through Women's Perspective, Grs. 8–12).

U.S. Committee for UNICEF, 331 E. 38th St., New York, NY 10016 (Classroom materials).

World Affairs Materials, P.O. Box 726, Kennett Square, PA 19348 (Studying the World and the United Nations System).

World Council for Curriculum and Instruction, School of Education, Indiana University, Bloomington, IN 47405 (Membership information).

World Eagle, 64 Washburn Ave., Wellesley MA 02121 (Monthly social studies resource).

World Future Society (Edward Cornish), 4916 St. Elmo Ave., Bethesda, MD 20814–5089 (Futurist strand, global education).

World Press in Review, 230 Park Ave., New York, NY 10169 ("News and Views" from the Foreign Press).

Worldwide Learning Resources (Barbara Stanford), 12406 Colleen Dr., Little Rock, AR 72212 (Sister school exchange programs between American and Central American schools).

VI. Religious Organizations and Resources

AGAPE, Greenwich Rd., Ware, MA 01082 (Slides and audiocassettes on nonviolence, Grs. 6–college).

Alba House Communications, P.O. Box 595, Canfield, OH 44406-0595 (Way of the Covenant, adult audio cassettes).

American Baptist Churches/USA, Peace Program, National Ministries, P.O. Box 851, Valley Forge, PA 19482-0851 (Peacemaking resources).

American Bible Society, 1865 Broadway, New York, NY 10023 (Poster, "Love One Another: The Global Rule").

Augsburg Publishing House, 426 S. 5th St., Minneapolis, MN 55415 (*Justice in an Unjust World*).

Bahai Community of the United States, Wilmette, IL 60091 (Literature on global peace and spiritual change).

Baptist Peace Fellowship, 499 Patterson St., Memphis, TN 38111 (Resource Guides).

Bread for the World, 32 Union Square East, New York, NY 10003.

Brethren Press, 1451 Dundee Ave., Elgin, IL 60120 (*Young Peacemakers Project Book,* preschool–Gr. 6).

Brown, William C., P.O. Box 539, Dubuque, IA 52001 (*Achieving Social Justice,* Grs. 11–12; *Leaven,* adult education).

Buddhist Peace Fellowship, P.O. Box 4640, Berkeley, CA 94704. (Quarterly, *Buddhist Peace Fellowship*).

Campaign for Human Development, 1312 Massachusetts Ave., NW, Washington, DC 20005.

Catholic Peace Fellowship, 339 Lafayette St., New York, NY 10012.

Catholic Worker (newspaper) 36 E. First St., New York, NY 10003.

Center for the Study and Practice of Christian Nonviolence, 918 No. Main St., Brockton, MA 02401.

Christian Church (Disciples of Christ), 222 S. Downey Ave., P.O. Box 1986, Indianapolis, IN 46206 (Shalom Congregations).

Christian Family Movement, P.O. Box 272, Ames, IA 50010 ("Peaceworks").

Church World Service, P.O. Box 968, Elkhart, IN 46515–0968 (Catalog of free-loan films, posters, and booklets).

Church World Service, Office on Global Education, 2115 N. Charles St., Baltimore, MD 21218-5755. *Resources for Learning and Teaching about Global Issues* (hunger, World Food Day).

Clergy and Laity Concerned, 198 Broadway, New York, NY 10014.

Commission on Peace and Social Concerns, Brethren in Christ Church, Box 27, Mount Joy, PA 17552.

Credence Cassettes, P.O. Box 41491, Kansas City, MO 64141 (Audiocassettes on peace/justice themes).

Disciples Peace Fellowship (Disciples of Christ), P.O. Box 1986, Indianapolis, IN 46406. (Newsletter, *DPF News Notes*).

Evangelicals for Social Action, 5107 Newhall St., Philadelphia, PA 19144.

Faith and Life Press, Box 347, Newton, KS 67114.

Fellowship of Reconciliation, Box 271, Nyack, NY 10960.

Friends Journal, 1501 Cherry St., Philadelphia, PA 19102.

Friends World Committee for Consultation, Sect. of the Americas, 1506 Race St., Philadelphia, PA 19102. (*Friends of the World,* books and audiovisual materials available).

Heifer Project International, P.O. Box 808, Little Rock, AR 72203. (*Church School Curriculum.* Fund-raising for donation of farm animals to Third World nations).

Herald Press, 616 Walnut Ave., Scottdale, PA 15683–1999 (Mennonite Church peace issues).

Hi-Time Publishing, P.O. Box 13337, Milwaukee, WI 53213 (*Beatitudes: Challenging Us to Justice and Peace,* Grs. 7–8).

Institute for Peace and Justice, 4144 Lindell, St. Louis, MO 63108 (*Education for Peace and Justice, Vol. I, II and III,* 1985).

Interfaith Foundation, 110 Maryland Ave., NE, Suite 509, Washington, DC 20002 (*Global Debt Crisis: Question of Justice*).

Jewish Peace Fellowship, Box 271, Nyack, NY 10969.

Leadership Conference of Women Religious, 1330 Massachusetts Ave., NW, Washington, DC 20005.

Lutheran Peace Fellowship, 2481 Como Ave. West, St. Paul, MN 55108 (Congregational peace groups, Packet for Peacemakers).

Mennonite Central Committee, U.S. Peace Section, 21 So. 12th St., Akron, PA 17501 (*Conciliation Quarterly Newsletter*).

Mennonite Publishing House, 616 Walnut Ave., Scottdale, PA 15683. (Catalog).

National Catholic Educational Association, Suite 100, 1077 30th St. NW, Washington, DC 20007–3852 (*Directions for Justice/ Peace Education in the Catholic Elementary School*).

National Catholic Rural Life Conference, 4625 N.W. Beaver Dr., Des Moines, IO, 50322.

National Council of Churches of Christ in the USA, 475 Riverside Dr., New York, NY, 10015.

Network (Catholic Social Justice Lobby), 806 Rhode Island Ave., NE, Washington, DC 20018.

North American Board for East-Wast Dialogue, c/o Sr. Katherine Howard, OSB, St. Benedict's Convent, 104 Chapel Lane, St. Joseph, MN 56374–0277 (Endorsements for adoption of a Universal Declaration on Non-Violence, adopted by members of the Board and the Dalai Lama).

Oblate Media and Communication Corp. 5901 West Main St., Suite A, Belleville, IL 62223–4409.

Orbis Books, Maryknoll, NY 10545 (Catalog on peace/justice).

Parallax Press, P.O. Box 7355, Berkeley, CA 94707 (*Being Peace,* Buddhist practices for peaceful behavior).

Paulist Press, 997 Macarthur Blvd., Mahwah, NJ 07430 (*Peace Reader, Just Demands of the Poor,* and others).

Pax Christi USA, 345 E. Ninth St., Erie, PA 16503 (*Way of Peace: A Guide to Nonviolence,* Grs. 7–adult; *Spark of Light . . . Center of Love;* and *A New Moment: An Invitation to Nonviolence,* Grs. 11–adult).

Peace Works, 932 North Kostner, Chicago, IL 60651 (Musical drama on Bishops' Peace Pastoral).

Plough Publishing House (Hutterite Brethren), Route 213, Rifton, NY 12471 (Catalog).

St. Mary's Press, Winona, MN 55987 (*Christian Call to Justice and Peace with Manual,* Grs. 7–12).

Salt (Claretian Publications), 221 W. Madison, Chicago, IL 60606.

Shalom Catholic Worker House, 2100 N. 13th St. Kansas City, KS 66104 (Olive Branch, classroom activities, elementary or secondary).

Sheed and Ward, P.O. Box 419281, Kansas City, MO 64141 (*Catechism of Catholic Social Teaching,* Grs. 9–adult).

Sojourners Peace Ministry, (Jim Wallis), 1309 L St., NE, Washington, DC 20005 (Monthly magazine).

Twenty-Third Publications, P.O. Box 180, Mystic, CT 06355 (*On the Path to Peace, Peacemakers in the Nuclear Age,* leaflets and other books).

United Methodist Office for the United Nations, Department of Peace and World Order, 777 United Nations Plaza, New York, NY 10017–3535 (Peace with Justice unit).

United Ministries Peacemaking in Education Program, Box 171, Teachers College, Columbia University, New York, NY 10027.

U.S. Catholic Conference Office of International Justice and Peace, 1312 Massachusetts Ave., NW, Washington, DC 20005.

World Council of Churches, 475 Riverside Dr., New York, NY 10015.

VII. AMERICAN FRIENDSHIP AND EXCHANGE PROGRAMS WITH PEOPLE OF THE FORMER SOVIET UNION

Ark Communication Institute, 250 Lafayette Circle, Lafayette, CA 94549 (*Global Partners,* book on exchanges with people of the former Soviet Union).

Beyond War Distribution, 222 High St., Palo Alto, CA 94301–
1097 (*Breakthrough,* book and video).

Center for International Understanding, Box 183, Quichee, VT
05059 (Summer camps with former Soviets).

Center for Psychological Studies on the Nuclear Age, 1493
Cambridge St., Cambridge, MA 02139 (*Differences: USA/
USSR,* Grs. 10–college).

Center for Soviet-American Dialogue, 14426 NE 16th Pl., Bel-
levue, WA 98007.

Chidren's Art Exchange, P.O. Box 503, Middlebury, VT 05753.

Connect US-USSR (Paula DeCosse), 4835 Penn Ave. So.,
Minneapolis, MN 55409 (children's art exchange and sister
city projects with children from the former Soviet Union).

Continuum, 370 Lexington Ave., New York, NY 10017
(*Citizen Diplomats,* book on relations with the former Soviet
Union).

Council on International Education Exchange, 205 E. 42nd St.,
New York, NY 10017.

Earthstewards Network, Holyearth Foundation, P.O. Box 10697,
Bainbridge Island, WA 98110 (Citizen diplomacy).

Educators for Social Responsibility, 23 Garden St., Cambridge,
MA 02138 (Resource materials and videotapes for increased
understanding of the people of the former Soviet Union).

Ground Zero Pairing Project, P.O. Box 19329, Portland, OR
97219 (Secondary School Education Package on the former
Soviet Union, Grs. 9–12).

Institute for Soviet-American Relations, 1608 New Hampshire
Ave., NW, Washington, DC 20009 (Peace pal letters with
former Soviet children, families, and schools).

International Peace Walk, Box 53412, Washington, DC 20009 (Citizen diplomacy).

International Workcamps, (Volunteers for Peace, Inc.) 43 Tiffany Rd., Belmont, VT 05730 (*International Workcamp Directory*).

Kids Meeting Kids, Box 8H, 380 Riverside Dr., New York, NY 10025 (Pen pals exchange visits with children in the former Soviet Union).

Pax Christi USA, 348 E. 10th St., Erie, PA 16503 (Sent with *Good News: Scripture Journal* of the former Soviet Union).

Peace Child Youth Exchange (Norma Johnson), 1977 Chain Bridge Rd., Fairfax, VA 22030.

Peace Links, 747 8th St. SE, Washington, DC 20003 (Pen pals with people in the former Soviet Union, *Pen Pals for Peace Newsletter.* "Reach for Peace" for high schools).

South Carolina ETV Network, P.O. Drawer L, Columbia, SC 29250 (*Face to Face: Conversations on U.S.-Soviet Summitry*, instructional package of videos, postsecondary).

University of Kentucky (Lance W. Brunner, Associate Professor of Music), Lexington, KY 40506 (Database of U.S.-former Soviet Union joint projects).

Youthlink, 4835 Penn Ave., S., Minneapolis, MN 55409 (Pen pal letters between American students and those from the former Soviet Union).

NAME INDEX

Abrams, Grace Contrino, 221–222
Abrams, Grace Contrino Peace Education Foundation, 222, 291–292, 295–296
Adams, Fay, 153
Addams, Jane, 39–40–41, 51–55, 56, 62, 68–70, 101, 326, 336
Adler, Mortimer, 137, 140
Alcott, Bronson, 52
American Advocate, The, 4, 16
American Association of School Administrators, 142
American Baptist Church, National Ministries, 302–303
American Forum in Global Education, 244, 249
American Heritage Foundation, 184
American Institute of Physics, 263
American Peace Society, 4, 16, 18, 20
American School Citizenship League, 38, 39, 64 ,74, 76, 78–79, 82, 100, 102, 117
American School Peace League, 5, 38, 40–43, 49, 59, 62, 64, 74–77, 79, 110
American Socialist Party, 64–65
American-Soviet Institute, 311
American Union Against Militarism, 70
American University, 198, 290
Anderson, Lee, 167, 207, 324
Andrews, Fannie Fern, 5, 32, 39, 41–47, 83–85, 179
Aprovecho Institute, 311
Aquino, Corazon, 235
Arms Control and Disarmament Agency, 285–286, 288
Arms Control Research Institute, 285
Arndt, Christian O., 149
Association for Supervision and Curriculum Development (ASCD), 7, 185, 200, 206–207
Axler, Judith, 301

447

Carey, Loretta, 300
Carnegie, Andrew, 50
Carnegie Endowment for World Peace, 104
  later the Carnegie Endowment for International Peace, 156,
  185–186
Carpenter, Susan, 202, 218–219, 332
Carr, William G., 81, 107
Carrington, Henry B., 27–28
Carter, Jr. James Earl (Jimmy Carter), 199
Catt, Carrie Chapman, 60, 100–103
Cavaliere, Lorraine A., 246
Center for Research on Conflict Resolution (University of Michigan), 188
Center for Teaching International Relations (CTIR), 252
Chadsey, Charles E., 78
Chambers, Whittaker, 156
Channing, William Ellery, 30
Chicago, University of, 27, 198
Children's Creative Response to Conflict Program, 220, 304
Childs, John, 119
Christian Church (Disciples of Christ), 302
Christian Citizen, The, 17
Church Peace Union, 116
Civil Liberties Bureau, 70
Civil Rights Act of 1964, 175
Civil Rights Bill of 1966, 175
Clark, Grenville, 168, 181
Claxton, Philander P., 78
Clinton, William, 187
Coffin, William Sloane, 170
Columbia University, 40, 98, 255
Commission on Social Studies, 106
Commission on the Causes and Prevention of Violence, 198
Committee on Nonviolence and Children, 177
Commoner, Barry, 254
Communist Party, 118, 155–156, 234
Communist Party of America, 63, 155–156
Comstock, Margaret, 220
Conferences on the Cause and Cure of War, 101–103
Congress of Constructive Patriotism, 70

World Peaceways, 116
World Policy Institute, 7, 223, 253–254

Yalta Conference, 141
Yeltsin, Boris, 141
Young People's Socialist League, 121
Young Workers Communist League of America, 121

Zelinsky, Wilbur, 338
Zola, John, 267

SUBJECT INDEX

Anticommunism
  and antiwar investigations
    by FBI, 222
  and excesses of McCarthy-
    ism, 158, 161
  and loyalty oaths required,
    159
  as national policy, 154–157
  and opposition to peace ed-
    ucation, 38, 44, 56, 69,
    71, 118, 124
  and problems with teaching
    ideologies, 142, 147, 184
Arbitration, first use of, 30, 44
Atomic age, 133–135
  and atomic bomb or fall-out
    shelters in schools, 182
  and atomic energy accep-
    tance, 135, 182
  and atomic power, 134–135
  and moral issues, 134
  as a positive force, 135, 182

"Brotherhood of man," 23,
    31, 105, 143
  classroom activities on, 144
  ideal of, 54, 100, 105
  reinterpretation of, 120, 140

Children
  and child labor laws, 123,
    215, 226
  and the children's fund
    (UNICEF), 180
  and Montessori influence,
    200, 214–218
  and the Party of the Child,
    216
  and philosophy of inherent
    goodness, 216
  poems of, 174
  poverty of, 216–217
  prayers of, 110, 150
  socialization of, 218
Citizenship education
  and community projects,
    74–75
  curriculum program on,
    115, 117, 183, 185
  as direct link to peace edu-
    cation, 73, 79, 81, 153,
    185
  and expanded view, 73, 132,
    137, 245
  Good Citizenship Test, 106
  and literature integrated,
    79–81
  and nineteenth-century ori-
    gins, 22, 30–31, 44, 73,
    78, 86
  and Progressive Education
    reforms, 74–75, 115
  and public education for
    peace, 78, 137–138

ABOUT THE AUTHOR

ALINE M. STOMFAY-STITZ is an Associate Professor of Education at Christopher Newport University, Newport News, Virginia. She earned her B.A. degree in English from Barnard College, her Master's in Education from Case Western Reserve University, and her doctorate in Curriculum and Instruction from Northern Illinois University. She has given workshops and presentations on teaching children conflict-resolution skills at national and international educational conferences. She has written articles on peace education for an international peace research association journal and other articles in professional publications.